Step by Step

MICROSOFT®
ASP.NET
STEP BY STEP

G. Andrew Duthie

PUBLISHED BY
Microsoft Press
A Division of Microsoft Corporation
One Microsoft Way
Redmond, Washington 98052-6399

Library of Congress Cataloging-in-Publication Data
Duthie, G. Andrew, 1967-
    Microsoft ASP.NET Step by Step / G. Andrew Duthie.
       p. cm.
    Includes index.
    ISBN 0-7356-1287-0
    1. Internet programming.   2. Active server pages.   3. Web servers.   I. Title.

   QA76.625 .D88   2001
   005.2'76--dc21   2001051311

Printed and bound in the United States of America.

1 2 3 4 5 6 7 8 9   QWT   7 6 5 4 3 2

Distributed in Canada by Penguin Books Canada Limited.

A CIP catalogue record for this book is available from the British Library.

Microsoft Press books are available through booksellers and distributors worldwide. For further information about international editions, contact your local Microsoft Corporation office or contact Microsoft Press International directly at fax (425) 936-7329. Visit our Web site at www.microsoft.com/mspress. Send comments to *mspinput@microsoft.com*.

Acquisitions Editor: David Clark
Project Editor: Barbara Moreland

Body Part No. X08-06093

Contents

Acknowledgments vii

Finding Your Best Starting Point ix
  Corrections, Comments, and Help x • Visit the Microsoft Press
  World Wide Web Site xi

Installing the Sample Files xiii
  System Requirements xiii • Install the Sample Files on Your
  Computer xiv

Conventions Used in this Book xvii

Part I   Getting Started with ASP.NET   1

Chapter 1 ASP.NET Overview 3
  Understanding Microsoft .NET 3 • ASP.NET Architecture 14 •
  Conclusion 16

Chapter 2 Using ASP.NET Development Tools 17
  Notepad ".NET" 18 • Visual Studio .NET 22 • Chapter 2 Quick
  Reference 28

Part II   ASP.NET Web Development Fundamentals   29

Chapter 3 ASP.NET Development Overview 31
  ASP.NET Project Types 31 • ASP.NET File Types 34 • Languages
  Used in this Book 35 • Working with Multiple Languages 36 •
  Visual Studio .NET Features 37 • Chapter 3 Quick Reference 49

Chapter 4 Understanding Programming Basics 51
  Expressions, Variables, and Constants 52 • Procedures 61 • Flow
  Control 64 • Error Handling 70 • Understanding Object-Oriented
  Programming Basics 73 • Chapter 4 Quick Reference 77

Part III   ASP.NET Web Applications   79

Chapter 5   Creating an ASP.NET Web Application 81

Creating a Web Application with Visual Studio .NET 81 • Creating
a Web Application with the .NET SDK 82 • Chapter 5 Quick
Reference 95

Chapter 6   Managing Application State 97

Using Application State 98 • Using Session State 102 • State and
Scalability 107 • Configuring Session State Storage 108 • Using
Client-Side Cookies for State Storage 113 • ASP.NET Server
Control State 114 • Chapter 6 Quick Reference 115

Chapter 7   Configuring an ASP.NET Application 117

Understanding ASP.NET Configuration 117 • ASP.NET
Configuration Elements 123 • Setting and Retrieving Custom
Application Settings 165 • Chapter 7 Quick Reference 166

Chapter 8   Security in ASP.NET..167

The Importance of Security 168 • Security Basics 169 • Enabling
Authentication 191 • Using Authorization 199 • Using
Impersonation 203 • Understanding Code Access Security 204 •
Security Resources 204 • Chapter 8 Quick Reference 205

Part IV   ASP.NET Web Forms   207

Chapter 9   Creating Web Forms 209

Anatomy of an ASP.NET Web Form 209 • Event Handling 240 •
Page Runtime Structure 245 • Using Code-Behind in Web
Forms 247 • Chapter 9 Quick Reference 250

Chapter 10   Using Server Controls 251

Types of Controls 251 • Chapter 10 Quick Reference 296

Chapter 11   Accessing and Binding Data 297

Understanding ADO.NET 298 • Creating and Opening
Connections 301 • Reading and Updating Data with
Commands 308 • Using Datasets 317 • Reading Data with
Datareaders 330 • Data-Binding 331 • Chapter 11 Quick
Reference 350

Chapter 12   Creating Custom Server Controls 351

Creating Your First Control 352 • Adding Functionality 363 •
Creating Custom Controls Through Composition 383 • Creating
Templated Controls 384 • Extending Existing Controls 390 •
Chapter 12 Quick Reference 394

Part V   ASP.NET Web Services   395

Chapter 13   Creating and Using Web Services 397

Understanding XML-Based Web Services 398 • Creating a Web
Service 400 • Using a Web Service 415 • Chapter 13 Quick
Reference 425

Chapter 14   Using Caching to Improve Performance 427

Understanding Caching 428 • Using Output Caching 428 •
Caching Arbitrary Data 437 • Chapter 14 Quick Reference 444

Chapter 15   Deploying an ASP.NET Application 445

Understanding the Structure of ASP.NET Applications 446 •
Deploying a Web Application Manually 451 • Deployment
Options in Visual Studio .NET 455 • Chapter 15 Quick
Reference 459

Chapter 16   Tracing and Debugging ASP.NET Applications 461

Tracing 462 • Debugging 468 • Chapter 16 Quick
Reference 476

Appendix A   Migrating from ASP to ASP.NET......................................**477**

Migration Overview 477

Appendix B   Additional Code Listings **489**

Chapter 4 489 • Chapter 11 490 • Chapter 12 493

Afterword **497**

Index..**499**

About the Author..**521**

Acknowledgments

The list of people to whom I am grateful for their assistance and support in the production of this book is long, and I hope that I don't leave anyone out. If I missed anyone, please know that your contributions are appreciated.

First I would like to thank my mother for her unceasing support and encouragement. During the process of writing this book, I made the transition from working as a consultant for someone else to starting and running my own company, something that my mother assured me I would eventually have to do. Once again, Mom, you were right.

Several members of the ASP.NET development team provided invaluable support along the way. My thanks to Scott Guthrie and Susan Warren, for their willingness to take time out of their schedules early and often to share information about this exciting new technology with authors and helping us to share it with readers. Thanks also to Erik Olson for his assistance in reviewing this book and helping me make it better, and especially to Rob Howard, for cheerfully making himself available to answer my many questions and for his hard work in making sure that authors and developers alike have the best possible information. To the extent that this book is successful in helping you learn ASP.NET, they deserve a good deal of credit. Any shortcomings of the book are mine alone.

I appreciate the support and assistance provided by my acquisitions editor, David Clark, and the team at Microsoft Press. Writing about beta software is never easy, but David and the folks at Microsoft Press did everything in their power to make it easier, making sure that I always had the latest versions of the software and whatever other resources I needed.

I'd also like to thank Rob Caron for his assistance and his hard work on documenting these technologies. Rob and I worked at the same company while I was writing my first book, and I'm glad that even though he's now 3,000 miles away, we still manage to keep in touch from time to time.

My thanks go to my production team and editors at TIPS Technical Publishing, especially Bob and Lynanne. Your efforts and patience did not go unnoticed.

Finally, I must express my deep and eternal gratitude for the continued support and love of my wife, Jennifer. She is a blessing to me in the best possible sense of the word, and by being there for me day in and day out in countless ways, she makes it possible for me to bring these words to you. My wish for the world is that everyone might be blessed with such a partner and friend!

G. Andrew Duthie

November, 2001

Finding Your Best Starting Point

ASP.NET Step By Step is designed to provide a comprehensive introduction and overview of developing Web applications with ASP.NET. The goal of this book is to help you become competent at the basic skills necessary for creating and using ASP.NET applications. To help you get there as quickly and easily as possible, this book has been divided into six parts, each composed of one or more chapters related to a specific topic. Over the course of these parts and chapters, you'll learn about the new .NET development platform and the part ASP.NET plays in it. You'll also learn the skills necessary to take advantage of ASP.NET Web Forms, Server Controls, and XML-based Web services.

Depending on the skills and experience you bring to this book, you may wish to start with a particular part that is of interest to you or skip over certain parts entirely. The following table can help you decide where to start in this book.

If you are	Follow these steps
New to programming	1 Install the sample files as described in "Installing the Sample Files" on page xiii.
	2 Learn about the background of the .NET Framework and ASP.NET by reading Chapters 1–4. Then either work through Part III if you want to know more about the technologies underlying ASP.NET, or work through Part IV if you want to get straight into the coding.
	3 Work through the rest of the parts and chapters based on your interest in their topics.

If you are	Follow these steps
Switching from classic ASP or similar technologies	**1** Install the sample files as described in "Installing the Sample Files" on page xiii. **2** Read or scan Parts I and II if you're interested in the background of .NET and ASP.NET. **3** Work through Parts III, IV, and V for basic Web Forms and Web Services skills and custom Server Control development skills. **4** Work through Part VI for additional ASP.NET application skills.
Referencing this book after working through the chapters	**1** Use the index to locate information about specific topics, and use the table of contents to locate information about general topics. **2** Read the Quick Reference at the end of each chapter for a brief review of the major tasks in each chapter.

Corrections, Comments, and Help

Every effort has been made to ensure the accuracy of this book and the contents of the sample files on the CD-ROM. Microsoft Press provides corrections and additional content for its books through the World Wide Web at the following Web site:

> *http://mspress.microsoft.com/support/*

If you have problems, comments, or ideas regarding this book or the sample files on the CD-ROM, please send them to Microsoft Press.

Send e-mail to:

> mspinput@microsoft.com

Or send postal mail to:

> Microsoft Press
>
> Attn: Developer Step by Step Series Editor
>
> One Microsoft Way
>
> Redmond, WA 98052-6399

Please note that product support is not offered through the above addresses. For help with ASP.NET, you can connect to Microsoft Technical Support on the Web at *support.microsoft.com/directory*, or for additional developer information about ASP.NET, go to *www.microsoft.com/net* and search on ASPNET.

Visit the Microsoft Press World Wide Web Site

You are also invited to visit the Microsoft Press World Wide Web site at the following location:

http://mspress.microsoft.com/

You'll find descriptions for the complete line of Microsoft Press books (including others by G. Andrew Duthie), information about ordering titles, notice of special features and events, additional content for Microsoft Press books, and much more.

Installing the Sample Files

The CD-ROM inside the back cover of this book contains sample files that you can use as you work through the exercises in the book. All of the code necessary to work through the exercises is included in the text of the exercise. You may also use the sample files to reduce the amount of typing you need to do, or to verify your code against the completed sample. With the files and the step-by-step instructions in the chapters, you'll learn by doing, which is an easy and effective way to acquire and remember new skills.

System Requirements

Before you break the seal on the ASP.NET Step by Step CD-ROM package, be sure that you have the correct version of the .NET Framework installed and that your operating system meets the minimum requirements for running ASP.NET applications.

This book was written to work with the Beta 2 or later release of ASP.NET and the .NET Framework. If you are using the Beta 1 or earlier release, you will need to upgrade in order to make effective use of the examples in the book. The sample files require approximately 500 Kb of hard disk space.

ASP.NET applications can be run only on Windows 2000 or later with Internet Information Services installed. The examples in this book were written and tested on Windows 2000, but they should work without modification on Windows XP Professional or Windows .NET Server.

Install the Sample Files on Your Computer

Use the following steps to install the sample files on your computer's hard disk so that you can use them with the exercises in this book:

1   Ensure that Internet Information Services is installed and running. You can check this by opening the Services applet in Control Panel and looking for the IIS Admin and World Wide Web Publishing services, both of which should have a status of Started. If these services are installed and started, skip to step 3.

2   If Internet Information Services has not been installed, install it using the Add/ Remove Windows Components portion of the Add/Remove Programs Control Panel applet. If one or both of the services described in step 1 has not been started, you can start them by right-clicking the service and selecting Start. You can set these services to start automatically by right-clicking the service, and selecting Properties, then changing the start-up type to Automatic.

important

The default installation of Internet Information Services is not configured for secure Internet use. If you are installing Internet Information Services for the first time, you should review the information in Chapter 8 and take the recommended steps to secure your server *before* connecting it to the Internet. Failure to follow this recommendation may result in your server being attacked or compromised.

3   Remove the CD-ROM from the back of the book and insert it into your CD-ROM drive. If you have autorun enabled, the starting menu will launch automatically. Otherwise, browse to your CD-ROM drive, and find the file StartCDF.exe in the root folder andnd double-click it.

4   The starting menu will provide you with several options. Choose Install Sample Files.

5   Follow the instructions for installing the sample files.

6   After you finish working through the exercises in this book, you can uninstall the sample files to free up hard disk space. To uninstall the sample files, select Microsoft ASP.NET SBS Files from Add/Remove Programs in the Control Panel.

In addition to installing the sample files by using the set-up program, you can also browse the files directly. The files are organized by chapter number for easy reference.

note

Some of the sample files need to be compiled using the command-line compilers for Visual Basic .NET or C#. Batch files have been included on the CD to simplify the compilation process, but in order to use these batch files you need to add the path to the folder containing the command-line compilers to your PATH environment variable. By default, the compilers are located in the %windir%\ Microsoft.NET\Framework\%version% folder, where %windir% is the Windows directory, and %version% is the version number of the .NET Framework. To find the actual values for your system, locate the Microsoft.NET directory under the Windows directory in Windows Explorer, and expand the Microsoft.NET node and its Framework child node. The version number should be the name of the folder underneath Framework.

The procedure for adding the path to this folder in Windows 2000 is as follows.

1   Right-click the My Computer icon on the desktop and select Properties.

2   Select the Advanced tab, then click the Environment Variables button.

3   In the Environment Variables dialog, scroll down in the System Variables listbox, and locate and select the Path variable. Click the Edit button.

4   Add the path to the folder containing the vbc.exe and csc.exe to the end of the string in the Variable Value textbox, preceded by a semicolon.

5   Click OK, then click OK again to close the Environment Variables dialog, and then click OK to close the Properties dialog.

Note, too, that for other command-line tools, such as wsdl.exe, you may also need to add other paths to the PATH environment variable. If you have problems running any of the command-line tools, you can use the Search facility of Windows 2000 (found by selecting Start, Search, For Files or Folders...) to search for the location of these tools. Then add the path to their location to the PATH environment variable.

Conventions Used in this Book

Countless time can be saved when using this book if you take the time to understand how instructions, keys, notes, and so on are used *before* you start the first chapter. Please take a moment to read the following list, which shows the conventions for these and other elements.

- Hands-on exercises for you to follow are given in numbered lists of steps (1, 2, and so on).

- A plus sign between two key names means that you must press those keys at the same time. For example, Press Alt+Tab means that you hold down the Alt key while pressing the Tab key.

- Notes labeled NOTE provide additional information or tips about a topic.

- Notes labeled IMPORTANT alert you to essential information that you should check before continuing the chapter.

PART I

Getting Started with ASP.NET

ASP.NET Overview

In this chapter, you will learn about

✓ *The structure and architecture of Microsoft's .NET platform initiative*

✓ *Which products and languages make up the .NET platform*

✓ *Where ASP.NET fits into the .NET initiative*

✓ *What makes ASP.NET different from earlier versions*

ASP.NET is not just an upgrade—not by a long shot. ASP.NET provides the most advanced Web development platform created to date. What's more, ASP.NET has been rebuilt from the ground up to create an entirely new and more flexible infrastructure for Web development.

What makes ASP.NET so revolutionary is that it's based on Microsoft's new .NET platform, or more accurately the .NET Framework. In order to understand clearly where and when to use ASP.NET, let's take some time to go over the Microsoft .NET platform, the products that it comprises, and where ASP.NET fits within Microsoft .NET.

Understanding Microsoft .NET

Microsoft .NET is an umbrella term that describes a number of recently released technologies from Microsoft. Taken together, these technologies are the most substantial changes to the Microsoft development platform since the transition from 16-bit to 32-bit development.

Microsoft .NET includes the following technology areas:

- .NET Framework
- .NET Enterprise Servers
- .NET languages and language tools

In the next section, you'll learn about these technologies and how you can use them to speed up your development of robust, high-performance Web- or Forms-based applications on the Microsoft Windows platform.

.NET Framework

The .NET Framework is an essential technology for ASP.NET development. It provides the basic system services that support ASP.NET, as well as Windows Forms development, the new rich client development technology provided by .NET. Much like the Windows NT 4.0 Option Pack, which was an add-on to Windows NT 4.0 that added Internet Information Server 4.0 and Active Server Pages technologies to NT 4.0, the .NET Framework is an add-on to Windows 2000, Windows NT 4.0, and Windows 98/ME that adds the basic supporting system services for .NET technologies. The framework will also be built into newer releases of the Windows server operating system line, including the Windows .NET Server line.

important

While Visual Studio .NET will be supported on the Windows 9x, Windows NT, Windows 2000, and Windows XP platforms, the full framework won't be available on all platforms. Most importantly, while other platforms can be used as ASP.NET clients, ASP.NET applications will run on only Windows 2000 and later.

The .NET Framework consists of two main parts:

- common language runtime
- .NET Framework class library

Common Language Runtime

The common language runtime (runtime) provides a runtime environment for the execution of code written in .NET languages. The runtime manages the execution of .NET code, including memory and object lifetime management. In addition to these management services, the runtime makes it possible for developers to perform debugging, exception handling, and inheritance across multiple languages.

Performing these tasks requires that the language compilers follow the Common Language Specification (CLS), which describes a subset of the data types supported by the runtime that are common to all of the languages used in .NET.

The individual language compilers compile the code written by developers into an intermediate language called Microsoft Intermediate Language (IL or MSIL). This IL is then either compiled to native code by the runtime at install time or compiled Just-In-Time (JIT) at first execution.

Code that is compiled to IL and managed by the runtime is referred to as *managed code*. It's called this because the runtime takes responsibility for managing the execution of the code, including the instantiation of objects, allocation of memory, and garbage collection of objects and memory.

Components written in managed code and executed by the runtime are referred to as *.NET managed assemblies*, or just *assemblies* for short. Assemblies are the basic unit of deployment in the .NET world and are quite similar to COM components. The difference is that, whereas a COM component contains or has an associated type library to describe how clients should interact with it, an assembly contains a *manifest*, which is the set of metadata that describes the contents of the assembly. Among other advantages, the self-describing nature of .NET components means that they don't need to be registered on a computer in order to work!

This metadata also describes the dependencies and version information associated with an assembly. Not only does this make it much easier to ensure that all necessary dependencies of an assembly are fulfilled, but it also means that multiple versions of the same assembly can be run side by side on the same computer without conflict. This is a major step in resolving "DLL Hell," the bane of many developers' existence. Just ask any Web developer who's worked with more than one version of ActiveX Data Objects (ADO), and you're sure to get an earful about applications being broken by a new version of ADO. With .NET, this should be a thing of the past. As long as the consuming application knows which version of an assembly it's designed to use, it can locate the correct version among multiple versions of the same assembly by querying the assembly's metadata.

There's a great deal more to the runtime, and you'll learn about it in future chapters. If you need information on the runtime, do a search on "common language runtime" in either the .NET Framework SDK documentation or the MSDN Library documentation for Visual Studio .NET.

.NET Framework Class Library

The .NET Framework class library is designed to support the efforts of developers by providing base classes from which developers can inherit. This a hierarchical set of .NET classes that developers can use in their own applications. These classes, which are organized by containers referred to as *namespaces,* provide both basic and advanced functionality that developers can easily reuse. They include classes that support basic common datatypes; classes that provide access to data; and classes that support such system services as drawing (which is good news for anyone who's had to use a third-party component for dynamically creating graphics in an ASP application), network functionality (including DNS and reverse DNS lookups), and many others.

The library also contains the classes that form the basis of ASP.NET, including the *Page* class (a part of the *System.Web.UI* namespace) from which all ASP.NET pages are derived, as well as many other classes in the System.Web namespace and its children. Future chapters will discuss several of these classes.

note

The ASP.NET QuickStart Tutorial (installed with the .NET Framework SDK samples) contains a useful Class Browser sample application that can be used to view the various classes of the .NET Framework class library.

Inheritance

Inheritance is a central concept in the .NET Framework. It provides a way for developers to use existing code in classes. A class can expose both properties and methods that clients can use. Classes that are inherited from a particular base class are said to be *derived* from that class. By inheriting from this class, a developer can reuse the functionality that it exposes without having to rewrite the code.

In addition (and more importantly), a developer using the inherited class can override one or more of the methods exposed by the class in order to provide a specialized implementation of that functionality. This capability will come in handy when you learn about custom server controls.

Windows .NET Server

In much the same way that Microsoft Transaction Server, Microsoft Message Queue Server, Internet Information Server, and Internet Explorer were separately installed products that were eventually folded into the base operating system, the runtime and the .NET Framework class library will become a part of the

Windows operating system. At TechEd 2001, Bill Gates announced that the first version of Windows that will ship with the .NET technologies built in will be Windows .NET Server.

Enterprise Servers

The .NET Enterprise Servers are the first step in the evolution of the Microsoft development platform. Although the .NET Enterprise Servers don't explicitly take advantage of the runtime and the class library, they do form a solid foundation on which you can begin building enterprise-class business solutions.

> ## note
> When you're developing classic ASP applications using the .NET Enterprise Servers, you should do so with ASP.NET in mind. For example, because the default parameter type for Visual Basic .NET is *ByVal*, you should write your classic ASP applications such that they will work without modification under ASP.NET. See Appendix A, "Migrating from ASP to ASP.NET," for more information on coding practices that will make your classic ASP applications easier to migrate.

The .NET Enterprise Servers include the following:

- SQL Server 2000
- Exchange 2000 Server
- Commerce Server 2000
- Host Integration Server 2000
- BizTalk Server 2000
- Internet Security and Acceleration Server 2000
- Application Center 2000

Together, these products provide much of the functionality needed by most large businesses, right out of the box. This section will discuss these products and their features.

SQL Server 2000

SQL Server 2000 is Microsoft's enterprise-class database management system. Building on the success of SQL Server 7.0, SQL Server 2000 is a database that is robust, highly scalable, XML-enabled, and provides the fastest time-to-market for application developers.

Among the features offered by SQL Server 2000 are

- Multiple SQL Server 2000 instances on a single machine
- Side-by-side operation with SQL Server 7.0, including management of both SQL Server 7.0 and SQL Server 2000 from the same instance of SQL Server Enterprise Manager
- Input and output of data as XML
- Integrated OLAP engine
- World-record scalability (as measured by the TPC-C benchmark; see *http://www.tpc.org* for more information and current benchmark results)

For both classic ASP and ASP.NET applications, SQL Server 2000 is a natural choice for developers. In addition to those features, developers can also benefit from MSDE, the desktop edition of SQL Server, which allows for the prototyping of applications against a SQL Server–compatible database engine without the licensing costs of a full version of SQL Server. Once your application is ready to go into production, your MSDE Database can be transferred to SQL Server 2000 without modifications. A named instance of MSDE (under the name *<server-name>\NetSDK*) is installed with the .NET Framework SDK Samples.

Exchange 2000 Server

Exchange 2000 Server is Microsoft's messaging and collaboration tool. In addition to the messaging and collaboration features enjoyed by users of Exchange Server 5.5, Exchange 2000 offers a native XML Web store, a greatly improved version of Outlook Web Access, and integration with Active Directory. For developers who need messaging or workflow features in their applications, Exchange 2000 Server provides a great deal of out-of-the-box functionality that can dramatically reduce time to market.

Commerce Server 2000

Developers who have used Site Server 3.0 Commerce Edition understand that, although it made the development of e-commerce sites substantially faster and easier, it wasn't always the easiest tool in the world to install and use. With Commerce Server 2000, the successor to Site Server 3.0 Commerce Edition, Microsoft has taken great pains to improve the out-of-the-box functionality available to developers.

Using the Commerce Server 2000 starter sites, developers can create a fully functional business-to-consumer e-commerce site simply by importing their product catalog. Although the starter site provides only a basic user interface (UI), as shown in the following figure, it supplies all of the logic necessary to run the navigation, the product searching and browsing, and the shopping cart.

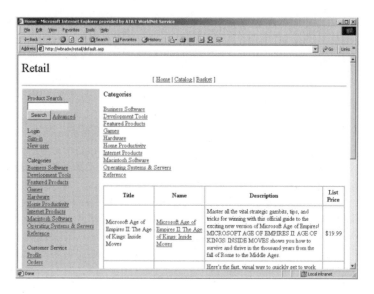

With the additional step of providing a custom UI, developers can very quickly and easily run an e-commerce site with rich UI and back-end functionality, including data and traffic analysis tools (based on the SQL Server 2000 OLAP engine) that allow organizations to track sales, site traffic, and so on.

The new features in Commerce Server 2000 include the following:

- Powerful user registration and profiling system
- Improved catalog management
- Business Internet analytics (using SQL Server 2000 Analysis Services)

Host Integration Server 2000

Host Integration Server 2000 is the successor to Microsoft's SNA Server. It's designed to allow applications written on the Windows platform to access data on and interoperate with programs on legacy back-end systems, such as DB2 on AS/400, CICS and IMS transactional systems, and MQ Series-based messaging environments. Host Integration Server allows COM-based access to programmatic functionality on legacy systems, making it relatively simple for component developers using any COM-compatible language (including .NET components using COM Interop) to take advantage of existing legacy systems.

BizTalk Server 2000

BizTalk Server 2000 is one of the most important of the Enterprise Servers. It lets developers rapidly create effective, robust, and highly interoperable business-to-business e-commerce applications. The features of BizTalk Server 2000 include

- XML-based document transformation
- Business process orchestration
- Document routing and tracking

BizTalk Server lets you send and receive documents (such as purchase orders) in any format using the XML-based transformation functionality of the BizTalk Mapper. The BizTalk Orchestrator lets you quickly and easily diagram a business process and then map each step to scripts or components that will execute that step. Once a process has been diagrammed, BizTalk Orchestrator can create an XML-based document that describes the business process. This document is then used by the BizTalk Orchestrator runtime to execute the process. A distinct advantage of this approach is that it allows rapid development and significantly easier modification of business processes.

Internet Security and Acceleration Server 2000

Designed as a successor to and extension of Microsoft's Proxy Server product, Internet Security and Acceleration Server 2000 (ISA Server) provides both firewall security and caching features that organizations can use to improve the security and performance of their Internet-connected networks. New features in ISA Server include

- Integrated intrusion detection
- Ability to create and enforce Internet usage policies
- Ability to schedule download of content
- Integrated logging and reporting functionality

Application Center 2000

If you've ever built a Web application for a single server and later had to move that application to a Web farm to provide greater scalability, you'll want to take a close look at Application Center 2000. It's designed to simplify the task of creating and managing clusters of Web or application servers. Application Center provides a management console that makes it easy to create a cluster of servers, add new servers to a cluster (including replicating applications and/or content to the new server), shut down or start up servers for upgrades, and so on.

Important features of Application Center 2000 include

- Simple server cluster creation and management
- Automatic failover and server health monitoring
- Dynamic response to performance/health monitoring
- One-click rollout of new servers

Languages and Language Tools

One of the best things about the .NET platform is that, whereas classic ASP restricted developers to scripting languages (with their inherent limitations), ASP.NET lets you work with *any* .NET-compliant language. This means that the code you write in ASP.NET is compiled for better performance, and you can take full advantage of advanced language features.

For the .NET platform, languages (and the tools with which you'll use them) are probably one of the most important topics to discuss, and they're covered throughout this book. For now, let's take a high-level look at some of the languages and tools that will be available for developing .NET applications.

Notepad ".NET"

Believe it or not, many developers, particularly ASP developers, still do much of their development in Microsoft Notepad, which I used to lovingly refer to as "Visual" Notepad. Now I guess I'll have to change to Notepad ".NET". While Notepad has the substantial advantage of being ubiquitous, it's not exactly what you'd call a robust development environment. That said, if you're working with the .NET Framework SDK (rather than Visual Studio .NET), there's no reason you can't use Notepad to do all of your .NET development. The .NET Framework SDK includes command-line compilers for Visual Basic .NET, C# (pronounced "C sharp"), and JScript .NET. So you can create your classes, ASP.NET pages, and so on in Notepad, and then you can either compile them explicitly using the command-line compilers or, in the case of ASP.NET, allow the ASP.NET runtime to dynamically compile the page when it's requested for the first time.

Visual Studio .NET

For simpler and faster development, most developers will probably want to work in Visual Studio .NET. For the first time ever with Microsoft's development platform, Visual Studio .NET provides a single Integrated Development Environment (IDE) for all of Microsoft's .NET languages (see the following figure).

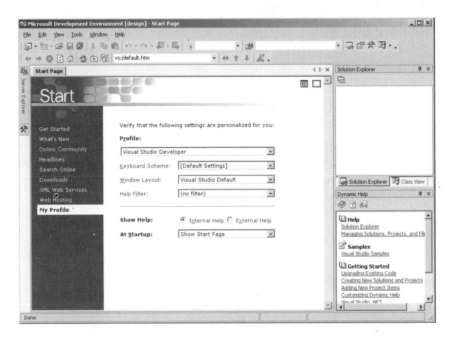

This means that developers of Visual Basic, Visual C++, and C# will all share the same IDE, including the capability to perform debugging and error-handling across languages in the same environment.

Visual Studio .NET provides a substantial number of new features, including

- A single, unified programming model for all .NET languages and for both Windows and Web applications
- Drag-and-drop development for the server using the Server Explorer
- Dynamic Help
- A robust customization and extensibility model for the IDE
- Strong support for XML
- Web services with dramatically easier cross-platform application integration

ASP.NET Overview

Visual Basic .NET

As mentioned earlier, ASP.NET developers are no longer restricted to a watered-down version of Visual Basic like VBScript. They can now take advantage of the full power of the Visual Basic .NET language. And that power has been increased substantially in Visual Basic .NET by adding support for inheritance, structured exception handling, and support for multithreaded programming, just to name a few improvements.

Visual Basic .NET is a managed language, which means that the runtime manages the execution of Visual Basic .NET code. You no longer need to explicitly destroy your object references using *Set object = Nothing*, as you did when using COM components in Visual Basic 6 and earlier. The .NET garbage collector will automatically recover the memory used by the component, once no clients are referencing it.

There are many new features in Visual Basic .NET, but users of VBScript and Visual Basic 6.0 should have little trouble using it once they're familiar with the .NET programming model. There will be plenty of code examples throughout the book to help you get started.

C#

A new member of the Visual Studio family, C#, is a descendent of C. It's much like C++, but designed with greater simplicity and ease of use in mind. Although C# isn't necessarily as easy to learn as Visual Basic, it's far easier than C++ and provides nearly all of the power available to C++ developers. It also doesn't require you to manage the allocation and deallocation of memory, as C++ does. Because C#, like Visual Basic .NET, is a managed language, all of the memory management is taken care of by the runtime. This is an important advantage because memory management is one of the most troublesome areas of C++ development and is responsible for many application crashes.

Developers familiar with C, C++, and Java will quickly become productive using C#. This book will have some code examples in C# that will give you a taste of this exciting new language.

Additional .NET Languages

In addition to Visual Basic .NET and C# (the two languages used in this book), Visual Studio .NET ships with JScript .NET, Visual C++, and the managed extensions for Visual C++, which allow C++ developers to target their applications to the runtime.

Visual Studio .NET also provides an extremely flexible plug-in architecture that allows other languages that are written for or ported to the .NET platform to easily use the power of the Visual Studio IDE.

The current list of third-party languages planned for Visual Studio .NET includes

- APL
- COBOL
- Pascal
- Eiffel
- Haskell
- ML
- Oberon
- Perl
- Python
- Scheme
- Smalltalk
- Many others (17 languages at the time of this writing)

Between the languages that will ship with Visual Studio .NET and the third-party languages that will be available, there should be something to please just about any developer.

ASP.NET Architecture

While there are plenty of familiar features in ASP.NET, there have also been some significant changes made to the ASP.NET architecture, including many improvements and new features. The following section will take a high-level look at what's new in ASP.NET.

Familiar Features

It's important to note that many things in ASP.NET will be familiar to Web developers who've used classic ASP. The much-used *Request* and *Response* objects are still there, as are the *Application*, *Session*, and *Server* objects, albeit with some new properties and methods. You can still use either *<SCRIPT RUNAT= "SERVER">* blocks or the *<% %>* ASP script delimiters to denote server-side script. In fact, for the most part you can write an ASP.NET page exactly the same way you would write a classic ASP page. Once you get used to the new programming model of ASP.NET, though, you'll never go back to coding your ASP applications the way you do today.

Also, you don't need to migrate all of your existing ASP applications at once. ASP.NET is designed to run side by side with classic ASP. So while you're working on your first new ASP.NET application, your current ASP applications can still be running right alongside.

What's New

There's a lot of new stuff in ASP.NET, and it will take time to learn all of it. But once you've learned it, your productivity will be far greater than it was with classic ASP. Let's look at a list of some of the new features of ASP.NET.

- **Web Forms**   This is the new programming model of ASP.NET. Web Forms combines the best of ASP with the ease of development and productivity of Visual Basic. You can drag controls onto a page and then write code to provide interactivity, call business objects, etc. You'll learn about Web Forms in Chapter 9.

- **Server controls**   A major component of the Web Forms programming model, the ASP.NET server controls map approximately to HTML elements (plus some additional controls you'll learn about later) and provide powerful server-side programmability. Server controls are run on the server and can output HTML that's tailored for uplevel browsers, such as Internet Explorer 5.x or later, or for any HTML 3.2–compliant browser. Chapter 10 and Chapter 12 will cover server controls in depth.

- **Web Services**   This is a key part of ASP.NET that allows developers to make programmatic services available to other developers over the Internet (or a local intranet). Web Services are based on the emerging SOAP (Simple Object Access Protocol) standard, so they will allow relatively painless interoperation across diverse platforms. You'll learn more about Web Services in Chapter 13.

- **Caching**   ASP.NET includes a powerful new caching engine that will allow developers to improve the performance of their applications by reducing the Web server and database server processing loads. You'll learn more about caching in Chapter 14.

- **Configuration Improvements**   ASP.NET uses a new method of storing configuration information for Web applications. Instead of having IIS store this information in a hard-to-access database, it's stored in XML-based human- and machine-readable configuration files. You'll look at how these configuration files work in Chapter 7.

■ **State Management Improvements**   If you've had to build an ASP application to run on a Web farm, you know all too well that there were major limitations to state management in classic ASP. ASP.NET overcomes these limitations, providing support for distributing session state across Web servers, persisting state information in a SQL Server database, and providing state management without the use of cookies. You'll learn how to take advantage of these features in Chapter 6.

■ **Security**   This is an extremely important function in today's Web applications. The security model in ASP.NET has been substantially improved, including new and improved authentication methods, code access security, and role-based authorization. You'll look at the ASP.NET security model and how to implement security in your ASP.NET applications in Chapter 8.

■ **Improved Reliability**   ASP.NET contains new features aimed at improving the reliability of Web applications, including proactive restarting of applications and automatic process recycling to resolve deadlock conditions and memory leaks. You'll learn more about these features in Chapter 7.

Conclusion

We've only scratched the surface in describing some of the new offerings of the .NET platform, and the substantial advantages offered by ASP.NET. In subsequent chapters you'll get detailed information on using ASP.NET to create faster, more robust, and more functional Web applications. In the next chapter, you'll learn about the various development tools that you can use to create your Web applications, from simple text editors, to powerful IDEs like Visual Studio .NET.

Using ASP.NET Development Tools

In this chapter, you will learn about

✔ *Notepad ".NET"*

✔ *Other inexpensive or free text editors*

✔ *Visual Studio .NET*

Now that you've learned a little bit about some nifty new features of ASP.NET, the next question is: how do you take advantage of them? Clearly, you're going to need some development tools. Conveniently enough, that's precisely what you're going to learn about in this chapter.

In the world of Visual Basic 6.0 programming, you had only one development tool: the Visual Basic 6 Integrated Development Environment (IDE). You could get it as a stand-alone product or as a part of Visual Studio 6.0, but if you wanted to develop Visual Basic applications, it was pretty much your only choice.

One distinct advantage of classic ASP was that, because the code was interpreted and executed by an ActiveX scripting engine built into Internet Information Services (IIS), you didn't need a compiler or an IDE to create Active Server Pages. All you really needed was a text editor.

What's the point of all this history? Well, ASP.NET pages can also be created with a simple text editor because the language compilers are installed with ASP.NET in the .NET Framework SDK. But instead of being interpreted at runtime, ASP.NET pages are compiled, which means substantially improved performance.

So, if you can write ASP.NET pages with a simple text editor, why would you bother to buy an IDE like Visual Studio .NET? There are many good reasons, including advanced features like IntelliSense statement completion, advanced project file management, rich designer support, and many others.

Still, some people may want to learn about ASP.NET without incurring the expense of a full-featured IDE, while others will settle for nothing less.

Notepad ".NET"

It's not *really* called Notepad ".NET", but just as there were those who affectionately referred to this ubiquitous tool as "Visual" Notepad, calling it Notepad ".NET" is a way of reminding ourselves that sometimes keeping things simple is a good thing. Given that you can find Notepad on just about any Microsoft Windows platform (with the exception of some versions of Microsoft Windows CE), you'd be hard-pressed to name a more convenient development tool.

Still the Cheapest Development Tool Available

One other major advantage of Notepad is its price—it is free. You don't even need to go out and download it. To get started developing with ASP.NET and Notepad, all you really need to do is install the .NET Framework SDK (or the ASP.NET runtime redistributable package).

Once you've installed the SDK, creating an ASP.NET page can be as simple as creating an HTML document using Notepad and saving it with the extension .aspx. That's really all it takes. For example, consider the following HTML code for a very simple ASP.NET page:

```
<html>
  <head>
   <title>First ASP.NET Page!</title>
  </head>
  <body>
   <p>Hello World!</p>
  </body>
</html>
```

If you create a text file in Notepad with this code and save it with an .aspx extension in a valid IIS virtual directory, you'll have a perfectly valid ASP.NET page. (As it happens, this is also a perfectly valid ASP page.) Of course, it doesn't do much yet. You'll fix that soon enough. But first, let's create a virtual directory in IIS for testing ASP and ASP.NET pages.

Creating a Virtual Directory

Creating a Virtual Directory in IIS is a relatively simple process.

1   Click Start, Programs, Administrative Tools, Internet Services Manager to launch the Microsoft Management Console for IIS. (These instructions are for Windows 2000. In Windows NT 4.0, the Internet Service Manager console is located in the Windows NT 4.0 Option Pack program folder.)

2   Expand the node for your computer by clicking the + symbol next to the computer's name.

3   Right-click the Default Web Site node (you can also right-click the node for another Web site if you have one set up) and select New, Virtual Directory. You'll see something like the following figure.

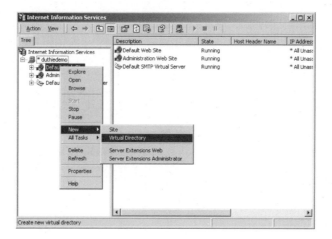

4   On the first page of the Virtual Directory Creation Wizard, click Next.

5   On the second page, enter an alias (name) for the new virtual directory. This name will be used to access the content in the virtual directory from a Web browser. For this example, use the name ASPNETTest. Click Next.

6   Enter the path to the directory in the file system where you'd like to keep the content for the virtual directory. This can be an existing folder or a new folder. If you're using an existing folder or you've already created the new folder for the content, you can use the Browse button to find the folder you want. For this example, use C:\Inetpub\WWWRoot\ASPNETTest. Click Next.

> **note**
>
> In most cases, the file system directories for virtual directories of the default Web site are stored under the C:\InetPub\WWWRoot folder. InetPub is a special folder set up by the IIS installation process, and WWWRoot is a folder set up as the root of all Web server content.
>
> This doesn't mean that you have to use WWWRoot as the parent folder for your Web content folders, but it can be a convenient way of organizing all of your content in a single easy-to-find location. You should keep in mind, however, that using WWWRoot (particularly on the default install location of the C drive) puts all of your applications in a well-known location, which can make life easier for hackers attempting to deface your sites or locate important information to steal.

7   On the Access Permissions page, you can alter the settings that determine how users can access the content in your new virtual directory. The default settings are fine in this case, so click Next.

> **important**
>
> Use caution when altering the access permissions for a virtual directory. Allowing Write, Execute, and/or Browse permissions on your virtual directory can allow unfriendly individuals to alter your content or execute damaging code on your server. Only alter these settings if you understand the implications of doing so.

8   That's it! Your virtual directory is complete. Click Finish.

Now that you've created your ASPNETTest virtual directory, go ahead and save the HTML document listed earlier.

1   Open Notepad. Click Start, Programs, Accessories, Notepad.

2   Type in the HTML code shown on page 18.

3   Save the document to the file system folder that you created to hold the contents of your test virtual directory. Name the file ASPNETHello.aspx.

Now that you've saved the document, you should be able to view it. Open a Web browser and enter the following URL:

http://localhost/ASPNETTest/ASPNETHello.aspx.

Assuming that your Web server is correctly installed and you've created your virtual directory based on the steps earlier in the chapter, you should see something like the following figure.

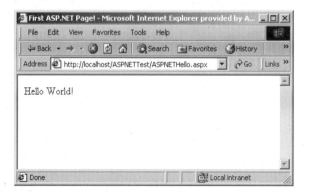

While this page may not be terribly exciting and doesn't do much yet, you've taken the first step toward developing a successful ASP.NET application using Notepad.

note

Localhost is a name that is used in URLs to refer to the local Web server. It's equivalent to the Internet Protocol (IP) address 127.0.0.1, which is the default loopback address for a machine. You can also browse local HTML, ASP, and ASP.NET pages by using the following syntax:

http://<machine name>/<vdir name>/<page name>

where *<machine name>* is the name of the computer you're browsing from, *<vdir name>* is the name of the virtual directory that contains the page you want to browse, and *<page name>* is the name of the page you want to browse. *<page name>* is optional. If *<page name>* is omitted, the Web server will deliver the default page for that virtual directory (usually default.htm, index.htm, or variants of these with the .asp extension), if a default has been specified.

Other Text Editors

Notepad is probably the most common text editor in the Windows world, but it's by no means the only one. In addition to Notepad, there are many third-party text editors that offer many features that were once only available in high-end development tools. Some of these features include the following:

ASP.NET Tools

- **Syntax coloring**   The use of color to indicate various types of keywords in the language you're using for development.
- **Auto-complete**   Suggests possible completions for statements as you type, based on what you've already typed, and how they match with a custom file of the syntax for the language with which you're working.
- **Available source code**   For developers who want to know how to build their own code editor, there are even open-source editors, including one built in the newest .NET language, C#.

If you're only beginning in the world of ASP.NET, one of these text editors may be a good starting point for you. It will allow you to use features you won't find in Notepad without immediately taking on the expense of a professional development tool like Visual Studio .NET.

If you won't settle for anything less than full power, or you want the many extra added features of a true IDE, Microsoft has created Visual Studio .NET, the redesigned version of their Visual Studio development suite. The next section will walk through several simple procedures using the Visual Studio .NET IDE.

Visual Studio .NET

It's certainly possible to create ASP.NET Web applications in Notepad or another text editor, but if you're doing serious ASP.NET or component development, you'll probably want to work within the Visual Studio .NET environment. The advantages of Visual Studio .NET over simple text editors include

- Robust management of project files and multiple projects
- Integration with Microsoft's Visual SourceSafe source-code control environment
- Visual Tools for working with Web services, Web Forms server controls, and database tools
- Packaging and deployment services for Web applications
- Support for multiple languages within a single IDE, including cross-language inheritance and debugging

That's just a brief list. There's much more to the tool than can be covered in a single chapter. So without further ado, let's look at how to create projects and pages in the Visual Studio .NET environment.

Creating an ASP.NET Web Application

One of the first things you're going to want to do in order to work with ASP.NET in Visual Studio .NET is create a new project, or in Visual Studio .NET parlance, a Web application. Here are the steps necessary to create a new Web application:

1   Open Visual Studio .NET.

2   There are three methods of opening the New Project dialog box:

- Click the Create a New Project link on the Visual Studio .NET Start Page (displayed by default when you first open Visual Studio .NET).

- Click the New Project button, located on the toolbar.

- From the File menu, select New, Project.

3   In the New Project dialog box (see the following figure), select the desired project language (in this case, Visual Basic), select the appropriate template (Web Application), and enter the desired project name (ASPNETApp1) and location. (For local projects, the default of *http://<machinename>* works fine, or you can use the localhost alias instead.) Click OK. Visual Studio .NET will create a new Web application along with physical and virtual directories for the project.

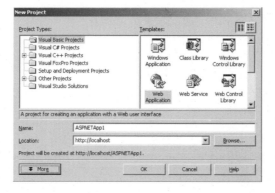

That's it! You've now created your first ASP.NET Web application. Next we'll look at how to add new pages.

Creating a New ASP.NET Page (Web Form)

In your new Web application, you'll notice that Visual Studio .NET has already added a page to the project for you, named WebForm1.aspx, and opened it in the editor. However, since one page is rarely enough for most sites, let's look at how to add a new page to your Web application.

1   As with creating a new project, there are several ways to add a new ASP.NET page (also referred to as a Web Form) to your application. Which one you should use is largely a matter of how you like to work. The methods are

■   In the Solution Explorer window (see the following figure), right-click the application name and then select Add, Add Web Form. You can also select Add New Item and then select Web Form from the Templates selection in the Add New Item Dialog.

■   On the Visual Studio .NET toolbar, click the Add New Item button. You can also click the down arrow next to this button and then choose Add Web Form from the pop-up menu.

■   From the Project menu, select Add Web Form (or Add New Item).

Any of these methods will open the Add New Item dialog box, shown in the following figure.

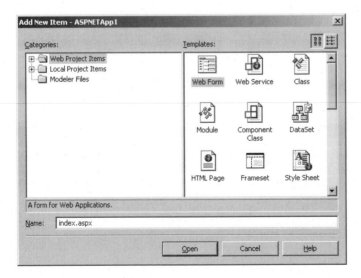

2   In the Add New Item dialog box, select the Web Form template and specify a name for the new page. Since you're going to use this page as the start page for this project, call it index.aspx. Before finishing up, you may want to take a look at some of the other template types that are available, both for Web Projects and for Local Projects. Once you're done looking, click Open. Visual Studio .NET creates the page, adds it to the project, and opens it in the Web Forms Designer (see the following figure).

Adding Controls

Now that you've created a start page for your new application, what can you do with it? Well, let's start by making it do the same thing as the page that you created in Notepad. Only this time, instead of using plain HTML text, use the Label control (one of the ASP.NET server controls) to display the Hello World greeting to the client. Here are the steps to add the Label control to the Web Form:

1   With the Web Form open in design mode, place your mouse over the Toolbox tab. (By default, it's found to the left of the code editor/designer window.)

2   When the Toolbox appears, ensure that the Web Forms palette is active. (The title bar of the active palette is shown immediately above the controls displayed in the Toolbox.) If it isn't active, you can click on its title bar to activate it.

3   With the Web Forms palette active, double-click the Label control entry (see the following figure). Once you've added the label, it should be selected by default.

4   To make the Label control display the text you want, you need to change its Text property. Click to the right of the Text entry in the Properties window, and then change the text (by default, *Label*) to *Hello World!*, as shown in the following figure.

Saving and Browsing Your Page

Now that you've added your Server Control, go ahead and save the page by clicking the Save button on the toolbar. You can also save by selecting Save *<filename>* from the File menu.

Because the Web Form page you used automatically adds a code-behind module for your Web Form, you need to build your project before you can browse the page. (You'll learn more about code-behind in later chapters.) *Building* is the process of compiling all of the code modules in the project so they'll be available to the pages and modules that call them. To build the project, select Build from the Build menu.

Once you've saved the Web Form page and built the application, you can view the page in an embedded browser window by right-clicking the page and selecting View in Browser. The result should look like the following figure.

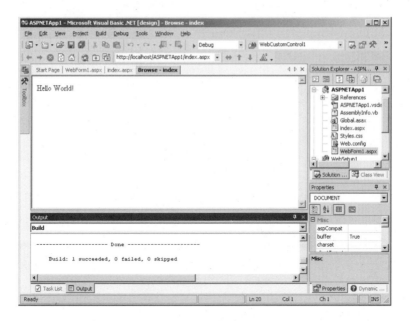

Chapter 2 Quick Reference

To	Do This	Button
Create a Virtual Directory in IIS	Start the Internet Services Manager, right-click the Web site to which you want to add a virtual directory, and then select New, Virtual Directory. Follow the instructions in the Virtual Directory Creation Wizard.	
Create a new project in Visual Studio .NET	Click the New Project Button, select the project language and template, and then provide the name and location for the new project.	
Create a new Web Forms page	Click the Add New Item button (or click the arrow to the right and select Add Web Form). Provide a name for the new Web Form and click OK.	
Save a file	Click the Save button, or select Save *<filename>* from the File menu.	

PART II

ASP.NET Web Development Fundamentals

3

ASP.NET Development Overview

> **In this chapter, you will learn about about**
>
> ✔ *The types of ASP.NET applications and how they map to Visual Studio .NET projects*
>
> ✔ *The file types used in ASP.NET applications and what each one is used for*
>
> ✔ *The available languages for developing ASP.NET applications and why you might use one over another*

In the last chapter, you learned about using some of the development tools available for creating ASP.NET applications. This chapter will delve further into ASP.NET development. We'll also spend some more time looking at Visual Studio .NET and identifying its parts and features so you'll be familiar with them as you read later chapters.

ASP.NET Project Types

There are two basic types of ASP.NET applications, each with a distinct purpose. For a Web application that will provide its own HTML-based UI, there are ASP.NET Web applications. For Web-based functionality that is to be accessed programmatically, there are ASP.NET XML Web services. Both of these application types can be developed with or without Visual Studio .NET, although the Visual Studio environment makes developing either type of application significantly easier and faster. The following figure shows the ASP.NET Web application and ASP.NET XML Web service project templates for Visual Basic .NET.

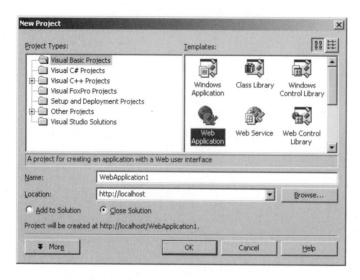

ASP.NET Web Applications

ASP.NET applications, at their simplest, are much like classic ASP applications. A simple ASP.NET application consists of the following four things:

- A virtual directory in IIS, configured as an application root, to hold the files that make up the application and to control access to the files

- One or more .aspx files

- A Global.asax (analogous to the Global.asa file in classic ASP) file to deal with Session and Application start-up and clean-up logic (optional)

- A Web.config file used to store configuration settings (new in ASP.NET and optional)

For Visual Studio .NET users, the good news is that all of the preceding files are created for you when you create a new Web application project.

ASP.NET Web Forms

Web Forms are an important part of any ASP.NET Web application. Put simply, they are ASP.NET pages that use ASP.NET Server Controls. The Web Forms programming model makes it possible (and relatively easy) to develop Web-based applications in much the same way that today's Visual Basic programmers develop Windows-based applications that have a graphical user interface (GUI).

Web Forms in Visual Studio .NET allow you to create rich, interactive applications simply by dragging and dropping controls onto a page and then writing minimal code to handle user interaction, events, etc. In addition, the Visual Studio

.NET environment lets you work on your pages visually, using the Web Forms Designer, or textually, using Visual Studio .NET's powerful source-code editor.

The code that you write in your Web Forms can be written in one of two ways: inline in the .aspx file (as is typical of a classic ASP page), or using a code-behind module. While it's possible to write your application with code in the actual .aspx file and still take advantage of compiled code and the other improvements of .NET, it's recommended that you get in the habit of using code-behind modules.

Code-Behind

Code-behind is a new feature in ASP.NET that allows developers to truly separate the HTML UI code from the code in Visual Basic .NET, C#, or other languages that is used to provide user interaction, validation, etc. There are a number of advantages to using code-behind modules, including the following features.

- **Clean separation of HTML and code**   Code-behind allows HTML designers and developers to do what they do best independently, while minimizing the possibility of messing up one another's work (something that happens all too frequently when developing classic ASP applications).
- **Easier reuse**   Code that isn't interspersed with HTML in an .aspx page can be more easily reused in other projects.
- **Simpler maintenance**   Because the code is separated from the HTML, your pages will be easier to read and maintain.
- **Deployment without source code**   Visual Studio .NET projects using code-behind modules can be deployed as compiled code (in addition to the .aspx pages), allowing you to protect your source code if you wish. This can be very useful if you're creating applications for clients but wish to retain control of your intellectual property.

All in all, it's worthwhile to get into the habit of using code-behind. You'll see examples of the use of code-behind throughout the book. Part IV of the book will discuss Web Forms in detail.

ASP.NET XML Web Services

While no one would deny that Web applications created with ASP.NET (or even with classic ASP) can be very useful, one of the things that has long been missing is an easy way to provide programmatic functionality over the Internet or an intranet without tying the client to a specific UI. This is where ASP.NET XML Web services come in.

An XML Web service, at its simplest, is a chunk of programming code that is accessible over the Web. XML Web services are based on the World Wide Web

Consortium's (W3C) SOAP specification. This allows computers on varying platforms, from Windows servers to UNIX workstations, to offer and consume programmatic services over the HTTP protocol.

> **note**
>
> SOAP can use other protocols, such as FTP or SMTP, but HTTP is the most common protocol used with SOAP and XML Web services because most firewalls allow communication via the HTTP protocol.

ASP.NET makes it remarkably easy to implement XML Web services. In fact, all it takes is adding a declaration to any methods you wish to make available as XML Web services. Visual Studio .NET makes it even easier by taking care of all the work necessary to make your XML Web service available to potential clients. Part V will discuss XML Web services in detail.

ASP.NET File Types

There are a number of new file types you'll see in your ASP.NET applications. To avoid any confusion, let's take a minute to go over the ones you'll see most often and discuss how they're used.

- **.aspx**   The extension you'll see most often is .aspx. It's used for Web Forms pages, and it's analogous to the .asp extension in classic ASP.
- **.ascx**   The extension used for Web Forms user controls is .ascx. User controls provide one of the many ways available in ASP.NET to reuse code. They're somewhat similar to the include files in classic ASP, in that they can be as simple as a few HTML tags or can include complex logic that the author might want to reuse in many pages. User controls are added to a Web Forms page using the @ Register directive, which is discussed in Part IV.
- **.asmx**   The extension used for files that implement XML Web services is .asmx. XML Web services may be accessed directly through .asmx files, or the .asmx file can direct the request to a compiled assembly that implements the Web service.
- **.vb**   The extension for Visual Basic .NET code modules is .vb. All Web Forms pages (.aspx) added to a Visual Studio .NET Web application that are written in Visual Basic .NET will have a corresponding .vb code-behind module with the same name as the Web Form page to which it's related.

- **.cs** The extension for C# code modules is .cs. Like the .vb extension, all Web Forms pages (.aspx) added to a C# Visual Studio .NET Web application will have a corresponding .cs code-behind module with the same name as the Web Form page to which it's related.

- **Global.asax** Like Global.asa in classic ASP, Global.asax is a file used to define Application and Session-level variables and start-up procedures. Note that while Global.asax can be structured like Global.asa, with start-up procedures such as *Session_OnStart* (*Session_Start* in ASP.NET) coded directly in the Global.asax file in a *<script runat="server">* block, Visual Studio implements these procedures in a .vb (or .cs) code-behind module rather than in the Global.asax file itself.

  In addition to the functionality available in a classic ASP Global.asa file, ASP.NET also allows you to import namespaces, link to assemblies, and perform other useful tasks. You'll learn more about Global.asax in Chapter 5.

- **Web.config** Web.config is a new file type in ASP.NET. It's used to solve one of the major hassles with classic ASP applications: configuration. The Web.config file is a human- and machine-readable XML-based file that stores all of the configuration settings for a given application (or segment of an application). Web.config files are interpreted hierarchically; that is, a Web.config file in a subdirectory of your application will override the settings of the Web.config file(s) in its parent directories. The advantage is that configuration settings can be inherited where that is desirable, but you also have very granular control over configuration.

Languages Used in this Book

Although there are several languages to choose from in the Microsoft .NET Framework SDK and Visual Studio .NET, this book will concentrate primarily on Visual Basic .NET and C#. Most code samples will be presented in Visual Basic .NET, but alternate examples using C# will be presented where there are important differences between Visual Basic and C# syntax. This section will help you decide which language is best for you.

Visual Basic .NET

If you've worked with Visual Basic or Visual Basic Scripting Edition (VBScript) but don't have experience with C, C++, or JScript, you'll likely be most comfortable working in Visual Basic .NET. Although there have been substantial changes to the language since Visual Basic 6.0, Visual Basic .NET is similar in syntax. This book isn't intended to be a language tutorial for Visual Basic .NET, but we've made an effort to point out where there are significant differences between the syntax of Visual Basic .NET and its predecessor.

Historically, Visual Basic has not been considered an object-oriented or low-level language, but its longtime critics will be happy to know that the Visual Studio .NET release of the language includes full implementations of inheritance and threading. However, in keeping with the tradition of Visual Basic being OS-safe, Visual Basic .NET doesn't allow unsafe operations such as memory manipulation. Certainly, hardcore low-level enthusiasts will consider this limiting, but ease of use is a good reason to consider this language for most standard applications.

C#

If you've worked with C, C++, JScript, or Java, you may be most comfortable with C#. Like Java, C# is derived from C and C++, so you should have no trouble becoming productive in C# in fairly short order. Unlike C and C++ (and, to an extent, Java), the C# learning curve isn't terribly steep, so developers who are familiar with Visual Basic may wish to take a look at C# as well.

Unlike Visual Basic .NET, C# does allow you to work with unsafe code (pointers and memory manipulation, and so on), although this isn't recommended for beginners. After all, it's not called unsafe code for nothing! If you need to perform direct memory access or work with legacy C or C++ modules, C# will be the better choice for you.

Working with Multiple Languages

As noted in Chapter 1, an advantage of working within the Microsoft .NET Framework is that you're not limited to a single language. If you want to do things that won't work in your language of choice (or that can be implemented more easily in another language), you can always use a different .NET-enabled language to get around that limitation.

For example, let's say your primary language is Visual Basic .NET, but you need to access functionality in a DLL written in C. You can create a class library in C# to access the DLL, and then inherit from that class in Visual Basic .NET (or just use the class from Visual Basic .NET).

Visual Studio .NET Features

The previous chapter looked at how to create a Web application using Visual Studio .NET but didn't examine the Visual Studio .NET environment.

IDE Enhancements

Some of the new enhancements you'll find in the Visual Studio .NET IDE include the following features.

- **Start Page**   This is the default page that's displayed each time you start Visual Studio .NET. It allows you to set up your preferences for the IDE, access recent and existing projects, and create new projects.

- **Multilanguage IDE**   Unlike Visual Studio 6.0, which used different IDEs for each language (although Visual InterDev and Visual J++ shared an IDE), in Visual Studio .NET, all languages share the same IDE. This means that standard features like Find and Replace, debugging, and so on work consistently across different languages. This alone will be a big productivity enhancer.

- **Command window**   A cross between Visual Basic's Immediate window and a command line, the Command window lets you execute Visual Studio commands or code statements, depending on the mode of the window. The following figure shows a Command window that's been switched to immediate mode using the *immed* command. The Command window has two modes:

  - **Command mode**   Allows you to execute Visual Studio commands without using the menu system, or to execute commands that don't appear in any menu.

  - **Immediate mode**   Used in debugging. Allows you to evaluate expressions, check the value of variables, execute program statements and functions, etc.

■ **Tabbed documents**   Designed to simplify the management of multiple files being edited simultaneously, the Tabbed Documents interface allows you to see all of the files you're editing at once. This makes it much simpler to switch back and forth between open editing windows. You can still set up Visual Studio .NET to use the old method used by Visual Studio 6, however. Just select Options from the Tools menu, select the General option in the Environment folder, switch from Tabbed Documents to MDI environment, and then click OK. You'll need to restart Visual Studio .NET for this change to take effect.

■ **Auto-hide**   My personal favorite, auto-hide works much like the feature of the same name in the Windows toolbar. To enable auto-hide for a window, click on the pushpin icon (shown in the margin) in the window's title bar. Now the window will hide itself at the side of the IDE where it's docked when the mouse moves away from the window, leaving only a tab with the window title visible. Mousing over the tab will cause the window to reappear. This is a great feature for preserving the maximum amount of screen real estate for the code window, and it can make life much easier in terms of managing multiple windows in the IDE.

■ **Improved HTML editor**   Like Visual InterDev before it, the Visual Studio .NET HTML editor provides both a design view and an HTML (source) view. Visual Studio .NET has done away with the Quick View window provided by Visual InterDev. Instead, you preview pages in an embedded browser window, which provides a truer view of how a page will really look. The improved editor also supports specifying the HTML schema you're writing for via the *targetSchema* property. Setting *targetSchema* determines which elements will be made available via the editor's statement completion features and allows the IDE to provide you with feedback on syntax that's incorrect in the context of your chosen target schema.

New Features

In addition to the IDE enhancements, there are a number of entirely new features in the Visual Studio .NET IDE.

■ **XML editor**   This allows you to edit XML data (.xml) and schema (.xsd) files in source, data, or schema views, depending on the type of XML file you're editing.

■ **Autogenerated documentation**   An exciting feature that's currently available only in C#, this allows you to generate documentation from comments in your C# code using a special comment delimiter (////) and syntax. Visual Studio can also generate HTML documentation for projects and solutions regardless of the language used by the project.

■ **Dynamic Help**   A feature that provides context-sensitive help while you work in the IDE, it suggests topics of interest as you add files, controls, and code to your project. The following figure shows the Dynamic Help window that appears when you're editing the *<html>* element of a Web Form.

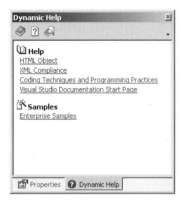

■ **Support for Windows Installer**   Visual Studio now supports this much-improved set-up technology for Windows applications, including support for installation rollback in case of installation issues. You can even create deployment packages for Web applications that will allow you to install and run ASP.NET applications on a machine that does not currently have the .NET Framework installed. The deployment package will install all necessary runtime files for you.

Windows

During your time working with Visual Studio .NET, you'll encounter a wide variety of windows in the IDE, used for a wide variety of purposes. Some are new, like the Dynamic Help window described in the previous section, while some will be familiar to users of previous versions of Visual Studio. This section will take a look at the most commonly used windows.

Development Overview   3

■ **Designer/Source Editor**   The following figure shows the Designer/Source Editor window in the HTML Editing mode. This is where you'll spend most of your time in the Visual Studio environment. This window integrates almost all of the designers and source-code editors that you'll use in Visual Studio, including the Web Forms, XML schema, and HTML designers, as well as a unified source-code editor that provides support for XML, HTML, SQL, Cascading Style Sheets (CSS), and all of the .NET languages. The editor provides enhanced features specific to each language. Two new features of the HTML and CSS editors that are particularly exciting are IntelliSense statement completion for both HTML and CSS, and better control over how (or if) the editor modifies the format of your HTML and CSS documents. To change the formatting settings, select Options from the Tools menu, select the Text Editor folder, select the HTML (or CSS) folder, and select the Format option.

■ **Solution Explorer**   The Solution Explorer window should be familiar to anyone who's used Visual InterDev 6. It's one of the primary tools you'll use to manage project files and resources, including adding, removing, opening, renaming, and moving files, as well as setting a start-up page or project, switching between code and design view for a file, and viewing status information (for example, Source Code Control status) on your files. The following figure shows the Solution Explorer and identifies many of its elements.

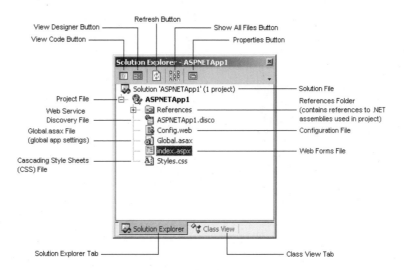

■ **Class View**   The Class View window, shown in the following figure, contains a listing of all classes (contained in .vb or .cs modules) in your projects and the methods, properties, and interfaces implemented in those classes.

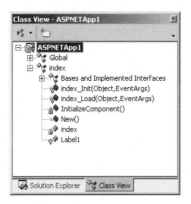

■ **Server Explorer**   The Server Explorer, shown in the following figure, is a new feature of Visual Studio .NET that allows you to view resources on both your local machine and remote servers, including configured data connections, event logs, message queues, and performance counters. The Server

Explorer also lets you drag and drop resources onto Web Forms pages or .NET components, allowing some of the most productive server-side development available to date.

■ **Properties**   The Properties window should be immediately familiar to anyone who's used any of the Visual Studio suite of development tools. It provides access to the properties of the object currently selected in the editor or designer. The following figure shows the Properties window displaying the properties for an ASP.NET Label Server Control. Notice that the Properties window allows you to collapse or expand the properties to better view the categories you're interested in. You can also view the categories by clicking the Alphabetic button, just below the object selection drop-down menu.

■ **The Visual Studio .NET Toolbox** The Visual Studio .NET Toolbox is another element modeled closely on the Visual InterDev environment. It provides access to a wide variety of controls, components, and HTML elements. You can add Toolbox items (essentially, the HTML tags or text elements used to implement controls or components) to Web Forms or components by either double-clicking the item name in the Toolbox (in which case the item is inserted at the current cursor location) or by using drag and drop (allowing you to place the item where desired). Note that some items do not have a visual representation when used in a Web Form. These items will usually be displayed in a separate window area at the bottom of the Designer window. The following figure shows the Toolbox displaying the Web Forms controls.

note

You can add your own items or categories (called tabs) in the Toolbox. To add a tab, simply right-click in the Toolbox, select Add Tab, and give the tab a name. To add your own items, make sure the desired tab is selected, select the desired item in the Designer (or select the desired text in the code editor), and drag it to the Toolbox. If desired, you can give the new item a descriptive name by right-clicking it and selecting Rename.

3

Development Overview

■ **Document Outline**   The Document Outline window, shown in the following figure, displays the outline of Web Forms documents (when in the Design view). It also provides access to a Script Outline view that displays client objects and events that can be scripted, and it can be used to insert JavaScript event handlers for these events.

■ **Task List**   An underrated and often underutilized tool from Visual Inter-Dev, the Task List window allows developers to create, sort, and track tasks to be completed for the current solution. The Task List also can contain tasks automatically generated by Visual Studio to help developers locate and correct build errors. Tasks can be categorized and prioritized according to the developer's needs. Categories include Comment tasks (indicated by comment tokens such as *TODO, UPGRADE_TODO,* etc.), User tasks, Build Errors, Shortcuts (created by right-clicking a line of code in the editor and selecting Add Task List Shortcut), and IntelliSense tasks, which are displayed when IntelliSense detects an error in your code. The following figure shows a Task List with a Shortcut task, a User task, and a Comment task.

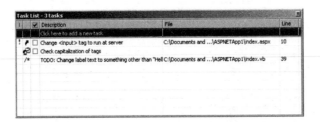

■ **Output**   The Output window will be familiar to developers who've used Microsoft's Visual C++ or Visual J++ tools. One of the primary purposes of the Output window is to display messages related to project builds. (A build is the process of compiling all of the code files that make up a project.) Since

ASP.NET Web applications will need to be built before code modifications will appear, you'll be seeing a lot of this window. The following figure shows the output of a build of a sample project. In this case the build was successful, with no errors or warnings. Had there been build errors or warnings, they would have been displayed in this window.

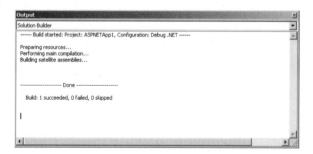

Toolbars

To accomplish tasks in Visual Studio .NET, you'll most likely use a combination of the IDE's toolbars and menus. This section will take a look at the most commonly used toolbars, and the next section will look at the most commonly used menus. You can view the full list of available toolbars by right-clicking any toolbar (or empty toolbar area). In keeping with the customizable nature of the Visual Studio .NET IDE, all toolbars may be customized by adding, removing, or rearranging buttons, moving toolbars, and showing or hiding toolbars.

note

Given the flexibility of the Visual Studio .NET toolbars, it's easy to end up with your toolbars looking nothing like they did when you installed Visual Studio. For some this may be a good thing, but if you want to restore your toolbars to their original configuration, click the toolbar Options button found at the right end of each toolbar, click Add or Remove Buttons, click the menu item for the toolbar name, and finally click Reset Toolbar.

- **Standard** The Standard toolbar, shown in the following figure, contains buttons for common file and project commands, including opening files and projects, creating new files and projects, and accessing various windows in the IDE.

■ **Formatting** The Formatting toolbar, shown in the following figure, contains buttons related to the formatting of text, including font and font size, text alignment options, and background and foreground colors. This toolbar is enabled only when you're entering or editing text in Design view.

■ **Text Editor** The Text Editor toolbar, shown in the following figure, contains buttons related to the operation of the Text Editor, including access to IntelliSense features, indenting and commenting of code, and bookmarks. (You can use these to navigate quickly to specific sections of your code.)

■ **Debug** The Debug toolbar, shown in the following figure, contains buttons related to Debugging commands, from Start, Stop, and Break commands to buttons for accessing the various Debug windows. Note that debugging is covered in Chapter 16.

Menus

There are a great many menus available in Visual Studio .NET, depending on the task you're working on at any given time. While we won't go over all of them here, the menus you'll encounter most frequently in your Visual Studio travels are listed below.

■ **File menu** The File menu is used to create, open, and save files and projects, as well as to print files and to exit the program.

■ **Edit menu** The Edit menu is used for working with text and objects, such as Cut, Copy, and Paste, as well as text-specific commands, such as Find and Replace, and formatting commands, such as Make Uppercase or Make Lowercase.

■ **View menu** The View menu is used to access windows or views that are currently hidden. Use this menu to switch from source code to design view or to open up windows such as the Task List, as well as to choose which toolbars are displayed.

- **Project menu**   The Project menu is used to add items to a project, add references to assemblies or XML Web services, and set the start page and start-up project used for debugging.
- **Build menu**   The Build menu is used for building and rebuilding a project or projects, as well as commands for deploying projects.
- **Debug menu**   The Debug menu is used to start, stop, and pause (break) debugging, and to set breakpoints and access debugging windows.
- **Table menu**   The Table menu is used for working with HTML tables. Use this menu to insert or delete tables, rows, columns, and cells, as well as to merge or split cells.
- **Tools menu**   The Tools menu contains commands related to customizing the IDE and to external tools such as the OLE/COM Object Viewer and Spy++. You can use this menu to access the Customize dialog box discussed earlier, as well as the Options dialog box, discussed in the next section.
- **Query menu**   The Query menu is used for creating and running database queries using Visual Studio's database tools.
- **Window menu**   The Window menu is used to navigate and manage the open document windows being used by the application.
- **Help menu**   The Help menu is used to access the Visual Studio .NET documentation, as well as to access product support. This menu also contains a link to the Visual Studio .NET start page that appears by default when you open Visual Studio. So if you accidentally close it, you can use this menu item to get it back.

note

In addition to these menus, you can create your own custom menus. To create a custom menu, right-click anywhere in the menu bar and select Customize. In the Customize dialog box, click the Commands tab. Under Categories, select New Menu. Under Commands, click and drag the New Menu item to the desired location in the menu bar. Next, right-click the new menu heading and use the Name entry to give your new menu a name. Now you can drag items from the other menu categories to your new menu. To create a submenu, drag another copy of the New Menu item into the desired location on your menu.

Development Overview   3

Options

One of the most dramatic areas of improvement in Visual Studio .NET is in the area of customization. Much of the customization available in Visual Studio .NET is controlled from the Options dialog box, shown in the following figure. As mentioned earlier, you can access this dialog by selecting Tools, Options. Not only has the number of options increased significantly, but the degree of control over particular options has increased as well.

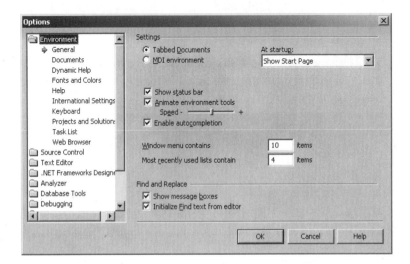

One good example of this increased control is in the area of code formatting. Visual InterDev developers will no doubt remember the frustration of having the VI editor reformat their ASP code when switching from Design to Source view. Visual Studio .NET still performs code formatting, but the developer has language-by-language control over how this formatting is done. (Note that not all languages use auto-formatting, so they won't all have these options.) Go to the Text Editor option folder, choose the language (for example, HTML or CSS), and set the options to your preferred setting. In this way, you can determine how formatting is applied to your code or, for some languages, you can turn off reformatting entirely.

note

One new option that will appeal to longtime BASIC users is having the IDE display line numbers in the text editor. Unlike BASIC, however, the line numbers are only for reference; they're not actually a part of the code file. This option can be turned on or off for individual languages, or it can be turned on globally for all languages.

Chapter 3 Quick Reference

To	Do This
Execute Visual Studio .NET commands or program statements in the Visual Studio .NET IDE	Open the Command Window by clicking View, Other Windows, Command Window or pressing Ctrl+Alt+A.
Modify the properties of an item in Visual Studio .NET	Locate the desired property in the Properties Window and modify its value.
Add an item to a document in the HTML designer	Open the Toolbox, select the desired palette (HTML, Web Forms, etc.), and double-click the desired item.
Add a Shortcut Task to the Task List	Right-click a line of code in the Visual Studio .NET Source Editor and select Add Task List Shortcut.
Change options in the Visual Studio .NET IDE, such as editor fonts, autoformatting options, source-code control options, etc.	Click Tools, Options, select the appropriate option folder, and modify its options.

Understanding Programming Basics

In this chapter, you will learn about

✓ *Expressions, variables, and constants*

✓ *Procedures*

✓ *Flow control*

✓ *Error handling*

✓ *Object-oriented programming*

This chapter is intended for readers who have little or no direct programming experience. It's designed to give a brief overview of some basic programming concepts that will help you better understand the examples presented throughout the book. Readers with programming experience may wish to skip this chapter and move on to Chapter 5.

While this chapter will provide an overview of basic programming concepts, less experienced readers are encouraged to use other resources to supplement this information. These resources include books on programming basics, Web sites such as the Microsoft Developer Network site *(http://msdn.microsoft.com)*, and newsgroups and mailing lists that may be helpful to the inexperienced. (Microsoft maintains a large number of newsgroups on development topics related to Microsoft tools at *http://msnews.microsoft.com.* You can read from and post to these newsgroups using a newsreader such as Outlook Express.) Of course, one of the best (and most overlooked) resources for programming concepts in Visual Basic .NET and C# is the MSDN documentation that ships with Visual Studio .NET (a subset of which is also available as part of the quarterly MSDN library, which can be ordered from *http://msdn.microsoft.com/subscription*). The MSDN documentation contains samples, tutorials, language references, and specifications for Visual Basic .NET, C#, managed extensions for C++, and JScript .NET.

This chapter will discuss how these basic programming concepts apply to ASP.NET, and how you can use them to create effective ASP.NET applications. Although most of these concepts aren't language-specific, there are some subtle differences in how they're implemented in different languages. Where appropriate, we'll point out these differences using code samples in both Visual Basic .NET and C#.

note

In ASP.NET, all code is contained in either Web Forms pages, code-behind modules, or modules that make up class libraries that are external to your ASP.NET applications. The term *module* in this sense refers to the .cs or .vb file that contains the code, while *module* as referred to by the Visual Basic .NET documentation is a container of code that is made available to other classes and modules within the same namespace. Unless otherwise specified, the term *module* in this book has the former meaning rather than the latter.

A class, as you'll see in "Using Classes as Containers for Code" on page 74, is a special type of code container that provides a number of useful features. Classes are contained within modules (that is, files with the extension .cs or .vb).

Expressions, Variables, and Constants

Expressions, variables, and constants are some of the most basic building blocks of computer programs, and you'll use them all extensively in your ASP.NET applications.

Expressions

Expressions are central to virtually all computer programs. Expressions let you

- Compare values to one another
- Perform calculations
- Manipulate text values

An expression can be as simple as the following:

```
1 + 1
```

An expression like this isn't very useful by itself, however. Unlike people, who can easily recognize "one plus one" and fill in the blank ("equals two"), computers aren't capable of that kind of leap of logic. In order for the expression to be useful, it needs to tell a computer not just to add one and one, but to store the result somewhere so that we can make use of it later (either by displaying it to the user or using it in another expression later). This is where variables come in.

Variables

As with the preceding example, at some point during the execution of most programs, you'll need to store values of some sort. Examples include the results of mathematical operations (as in the preceding example), accepting text input from users, and the results of comparisons. Simply put, *variables* are storage areas for data. This data can be numeric, text, or one of a number of special types. The kind of data that can be stored by a variable is determined by its data type.

Data Types

The *data type* of a variable defines the type of data that can be stored in it, as well as the format in which that data is stored (and the amount of memory that the system needs to allocate for the variable). The following table lists the data types supported by Visual Basic .NET and C#, as well as the .NET Framework SDK types to which they map. The data types marked with an asterisk don't have a native representation. You can still access these data types by using the appropriate *System* type when declaring the variable.

The data type of a variable is determined at the time the variable is declared. This will be discussed further in the section entitled "Declaring Variables" on page 56.

Data Type Comparison			
VB Data Type	**C# Data Type**	**.NET Data Type**	**Size**
Boolean	bool	System.Boolean	1 byte
Byte	byte	System.Byte	1 byte
*	sbyte	System.SByte †	1 byte
Char	char	System.Char	2 bytes
Date	*	System.DateTime	8 bytes
Decimal	decimal	System.Decimal	12 bytes
Double	double	System.Double	8 bytes

(continued)

| Data Type Comparison *(continued)* | | | |
VB Data Type	C# Data Type	.NET Data Type	Size
Integer	int	System.Int32	4 bytes
*	uint	System.UInt32 †	4 bytes
Long	long	System.Int64	8 bytes
*	ulong	System.UInt64 †	8 bytes
Object	object	System.Object	4 bytes
Short	short	System.Int16	2 bytes
*	ushort	System.UInt16 †	2 bytes
Single	float	System.Single	4 bytes
String	string	System.String	10 bytes, plus (2 x string length)
User-Defined Type	struct	System.ValueType (inherited)	Sum of member sizes

* These data types do not have a language-specific representation. If you need to use these types, you can use the equivalent .NET data type.

† These data types do not comply with the Common Language Specification (CLS).

important

ASP.NET contains both framework-specific data types and language-specific data types for specific .NET languages, such as Visual Basic .NET and C#. In order to take advantage of some of the multilanguage features of the .NET environment, you need to limit your use of data types to those supported by the Common Language Specification (CLS), a subset of the data types supported by the common language runtime. In the preceding table, data types marked with a † are not CLS-compliant. Avoid using them in classes that you wish to make available for use with other .NET languages.

Value Types vs. Reference Types

In .NET development, there are two categories of data types: value types and reference types. Although understanding the distinction between these types isn't absolutely necessary if you want to develop ASP.NET applications, it may help you to better understand how these data types operate and how to deal with error messages resulting from coding errors. (Not that those ever happen, right?)

Value types are data types that store their data directly as values in memory. They include all the numeric types (*int32*, *short*, *single*, etc.), structures (custom data types based on *System.ValueType*), and enumerations (custom types that represent a defined set of values), as well as *boolean*, *char*, and *date* types. Value types are accessed directly, as in the following example:

```
Dim myInt as Integer 'Visual Basic.NET declaration for an int32
'Expression to assign the value 123 directly to the variable
myInt = 123
```

Reference types are data types that store a reference to another memory location that contains the data, which is usually based on a class, such as the *String* class in the Framework. Reference types include *Object* (which acts as a replacement for Visual Basic's *Variant* type, no longer supported in .NET), *String*, and all *Arrays*, as well as instances of custom classes. Reference types are accessed through members of the class to which the type holds a reference, as in the following example:

```
' Define a class
Class myClass
    Public myInt As Integer
End Class

'Create an instance of the class
Dim myClassInstance As New myClass()
'Expression to assign the value 123 to myClass member myInt
myClass.myInt = 123
```

note

Conversion between value and reference types is accomplished through a process called boxing and unboxing. *Boxing* is the process of creating an instance of the reference type object and assigning the value of a value type to the object (as well as storing information on the value's data type). *Unboxing* is the process of assigning the value of the boxed object type to a variable of the appropriate type (or a compatible type, such as assigning a boxed *int16* to a variable of type *int32*).

Declaring Variables

Before you can use variables in your programs, you need to declare them. *Variable declaration* is the process of specifying the characteristics of the variable (data type, lifetime, scope, and visibility) so that the runtime system knows how much storage space to allocate for the variable, which actions to allow on the variable, and who can take those actions. A variable declaration takes the following form in Visual Basic .NET:

```
Dim x As Integer 'Declares a variable of type Integer
```

The same declaration in C# would take the following form:

```
int x; // Declares a variable of type int
```

> **note**
>
> The examples above use *x* as the name of the variable. While this is perfectly acceptable as far as the language compilers are concerned, you should consider giving your variables more meaningful names, such as *FirstName* (for a string variable holding a first name), *LoopCount* (for a numeric variable used in a looping structure), or *Person* (for a reference to a class representing data on a person). This naming convention makes it much easier to remember the purpose of a variable, and it will make your code much easier to maintain.

Both of the preceding declarations specify a variable of type *Integer* (or *int*, both of which map to the *System.Int32* type). In both cases, the variables would be accessible only within the module in which the declarations appeared. In addition to simple declarations like these, you can use the placement of the declarations, as well as Visual Basic .NET and C# keywords, to modify the lifetime, scope, and accessibility of your variables.

Lifetime

Lifetime refers to the span of time from when the variable is declared to when it is destroyed. The lifetime of a variable depends on where it is declared. For example, the lifetime of a variable declared inside a procedure is limited to the execution of the procedure. Once the procedure has finished executing, the variable is destroyed and the memory it occupied is reclaimed. An example is shown here:

```
'Visual Basic.NET Sub procedure
Sub HelloWorld()
    'Declare procedure-level string variable
    Dim HelloString As String
```

```
    HelloString = "Hello World!"
    'Write HelloString to browser
    Response.Write(HelloString)
    'Lifetime of HelloString will end after next line
End Sub
```

When this procedure completes, the variable *HelloString* no longer exists. Its lifetime has ended. If *HelloString* had been declared outside the procedure, its lifetime would be until the instance of the class containing it was destroyed.

```
'Declare module-level string variable
Dim HelloString As String

'Visual Basic.NET Sub procedure
Sub HelloWorld()
    HelloString = "Hello World!"
    'Write HelloString to browser
    Response.Write(HelloString)
    'Lifetime of HelloString will not end after next line
End Sub
```

note

The Visual Basic .NET documentation recommends using whole words when naming your variables. You should use mixed case, with the first letter of each word capitalized, as in *HelloString*. This is one of many possible naming conventions you can use for variables and other elements in your programs. *Naming conventions* are simply agreed-upon standards for how elements will be named in a program. The particular naming convention you choose isn't important, but you must choose one and use it consistently. Doing so will make it easier for you to maintain your code and will help others understand what it's doing.

You can extend the lifetime of a procedure-level variable through the substitution of the Visual Basic .NET *Static* keyword for the *Dim* keyword used earlier. (In C#, you would use the *static* modifier.) In the following example, *HelloString* is declared within the procedure, but because it's declared as *Static*, its lifetime continues until the class or module containing the procedure has finished running:

```
'Visual Basic.NET Sub procedure
Sub HelloWorld()
    'Declare static string variable
    Static HelloString As String
```

```
    HelloString = "Hello World!"
    'Write HelloString to browser
    Response.Write(HelloString)
    'Lifetime of HelloString will not end after next line
End Sub
```

Scope

Related to the lifetime of a variable is its *scope*. Scope, also known as visibility, refers to the region of code in which a variable may be accessed. The scope of a variable depends on where the variable is declared, and in Visual Basic .NET it can include the following levels.

- **Block-level**   Variables declared within an *If...Then*, *For...Next*, or *Do...Loop* block. Although the scope of block-level variables is limited to the block in which they're declared, their lifetime is that of the procedure in which the block appears.
- **Procedure-level**   Also known as local variables, these are visible only within the procedure in which they're declared.
- **Module-level**   In modules, classes, or structures, any variable declared outside of a procedure is referred to as a module-level variable. The accessibility of module-level variables is determined by any accessibility keywords used in their declaration (see "Accessibility" on page 59).
- **Namespace-level**   Variables declared at module level, but given public accessibility (*Public* or *Friend*), are referred to as namespace-level variables. They're available to any procedure in the same namespace that contains the module in which the variable is declared.

The important distinction between lifetime and scope is that a variable may be out of scope (that is, unavailable) without having reached the end of its lifetime. The preceding example of a *Static* variable that's declared within a procedure is a good example of this. In that example, the variable *HelloString* will continue to exist even after the procedure in which it's declared has completed, but because it has procedure-level scope, it's only accessible within the procedure. Here are some good programming practices to follow:

- Limit your variables to the narrowest possible scope that will allow you to accomplish your objectives.
- Avoid using the same name for variables of different scope within the same module. Using the same name in such situations can lead to confusion and errors.

Namespaces

A namespace is a container used for scoping. Namespaces can contain classes, structures, enumerations, interfaces, and delegates. By using namespaces, you can have more than one class in a given program with the same name, so long as the classes reside in different namespaces.

Namespaces are declared in Visual Basic .NET using the *Namespace…End Namespace* syntax, where these statements bracket the classes, structures, and so on to be contained within the namespace. C# uses the *namespace { }* syntax, where the classes and other types to be contained within the namespace are bracketed by the curly braces.

Namespaces can also be nested within other namespaces, forming a hierarchical tree. This structure allows you to combine classes in logical groupings, making it easier for those using your namespaces to find the classes they're looking for.

Following these guidelines will make your application more memory efficient and will make maintaining your code easier.

- Since module-level and *Static* variables all continue to consume memory as long as the class or module is running, you should use them only when necessary.

Accessibility

The last important concept in variable declaration is accessibility. The accessibility of a variable determines whether it can be accessed from outside the module (or application) in which it's declared. In Visual Basic .NET, accessibility is determined through the substitution of one the following keywords for the *Dim* keyword.

- *Public*   Variables declared with the *Public* keyword are accessible from anywhere in the same module (or class) in which they're declared, the namespace containing that module, and any other applications that refer to the application in which they're declared. They can only be used at the module or class level.
- *Friend*   Variables declared with the *Friend* keyword are accessible from anywhere in the same module (or class) in which they're declared, as well as the namespace containing that module.

■ *Protected*   Variables declared with the *Protected* keyword are accessible only within the class in which they're declared or a class that inherits from that class. (See "Using Inheritance" on page 74.) The *Protected* keyword can be combined with the *Friend* keyword and can be used only to declare class members.

■ *Private*   Variables declared with the *Private* keyword are accessible only from the module, class, or structure in which they're declared. In classes or modules, declaring a variable with *Dim* or *Private* has the same effect on the variable's accessibility, but *Private* makes your intentions more explicit. The *Private* keyword cannot be used within a procedure.

note

In C#, all variables must be declared before they can be used. Failure to declare a variable will result in a compiler error. In Visual Basic .NET, it's possible (but not advisable) to use variables without first declaring them. Using variables that have not been explicitly declared is a major source of bugs in Visual Basic programs and should be avoided.

The Visual Basic *Option Explicit* statement (placed at the top of a module or class) requires that all variables in that module must be explicitly declared.

```
Option Explicit On 'turns Option Explicit on
Option Explicit Off 'turns Option Explicit off
```

To further protect your code from inadvertent bugs, you can also use the new *Option Strict* statement. When *Option Strict* is on, conversions between data types that would result in data loss are disallowed, as are conversions between strings and numeric types.

```
Option Strict On 'turns Option Strict on
Option Strict Off 'turns Option Strict off
```

Following these guidelines can help reduce the number of bugs in your code, and more importantly, the time you spend tracking them down.

The *Option Strict* statement includes all of the restrictions of *Option Explicit*, so it is not necessary to use both.

Constants

Constants are similar to variables, except for one important detail: Once a constant has been declared and initialized, its value may not be modified. Constants are very useful when you have a literal value that you want to refer to by name. For example, if you're a fan of Douglas Adams, you might want to create a constant to refer to the literal value *42*.

```
Const TheAnswer As Int = 42
```

Anywhere within your program (subject to the same scope, lifetime, and accessibility rules as variables) you can use the constant name *TheAnswer* instead of the literal value *42*.

Constants are particularly handy in place of literal values used as the arguments to methods of components you may use. For example, in classic ADO (ActiveX Data Objects), the data types of stored procedure parameters were represented by numeric values. Trying to remember all of those values would be unrealistic, so the developers of ADO also made it possible to use constants (*adInteger*, *adVarChar*, etc.) in place of the literal values.

In other words, constants let you substitute easy-to-remember names for difficult-to-remember literal values. This can make your code easier to write and maintain.

Procedures

Procedures are an important tool in ASP.NET development because they allow you to determine at the time that you write the code the order in which sections of code will run at runtime. Procedures also allow you to better organize your code into discrete units based on the functionality provided by each one. For example, if you write code that multiplies two numbers and returns the result, that code is much more useful if it's wrapped in a procedure. Using a procedure allows the code to be called from more than one place in your application as necessary, which allows you to reuse the code rather than rewriting it each time you need to multiply two numbers.

In Visual Basic .NET, there are two main types of procedures that you'll use: *Sub* procedures and *Function* procedures. (C# has functions only.)

Sub Procedures

A *Sub* procedure executes code but doesn't return a value. Code contained in a *Sub* procedure is delimited by the *Sub* and *End Sub* statements, as follows:

```
'Sub procedure that writes output to the browser
Sub WriteHello()
    Response.Write("Hello World!)
End Sub
```

A Visual Basic .NET *Sub* procedure is equivalent to a C# function declared with the *void* modifier. The same procedure would look like the following in C#:

```
// C# procedure that writes output to the browser
void WriteHello()
{
    Response.Write("Hello World!);
}
```

Receiving Input Parameters

Note that in both the Visual Basic .NET *Sub* procedure and C# Function, the name of the procedure is followed by a set of empty parentheses. These parentheses have a purpose other than simply taking up space. You can place code between these parentheses to define one or more parameters that users must pass when they call the procedure. Parameters can be passed either by value (a copy of the value is passed to the procedure) or by reference (a reference to the location of the value is passed to the procedure, which allows the procedure to modify the original value). You use the keywords *ByVal* or *ByRef* to specify which way the parameters are to be passed. If no keyword is used, the parameters will be passed by value. The following code shows some examples:

```
' ByVal example
Sub ModifyInt(ByVal myInt As Integer)
    'Add 42 to myInt
    myInt = myInt + 42
    'If you don't do anything here, the modified value
    ' will not be available outside the procedure
End Sub
```

```
' ByRef example
Sub ModifyInt(ByRef myInt As Integer)
   'Add 42 to myInt
   myInt = myInt + 42
   'The modified value will be available outside the procedure
End Sub


'Implicit ByVal example
Sub ModifyInt(myInt As Integer)
   'Add 42 to myInt
   myInt = myInt + 42
   'If you don't do anything here, the modified value
   ' will not be available outside the procedure
End Sub
```

You can pass more than one parameter to a procedure simply by separating each parameter with a comma, as in the following example:

```
Sub WriteHello(ByVal Name1 As String, ByVal Name2 As String)
   Response.Write("Hello to both " & Name1 & " and " & Name2)
End Sub
```

important

In Visual Basic 6, the default for a parameter definition without the *ByVal* or *ByRef* keywords is to pass the parameter by reference. Because this behavior is the opposite of that in the vast majority of languages, the Visual Basic development team has changed this behavior in Visual Basic .NET.

In Visual Basic .NET, parameters defined without the *ByVal* or *ByRef* keywords are passed by value.

Whether you're writing Visual Basic 6 code that may need to be upgraded to Visual Basic .NET or writing native Visual Basic .NET code, it's a good programming practice to always use *ByVal* and *ByRef* to explicitly declare how your parameters should be passed.

Note that you explicitly type the parameters by declaring the data type of each parameter as *String*. If any data type other than *String* is passed to the procedure, an exception will be thrown.

You can make one or more of the parameters of your procedure optional (meaning the caller decides whether the parameter will be passed or not) by preceding them with the *Optional* keyword.

```
Sub WriteHello(Optional ByVal Name1 As String = "Bob")
    Response.Write("Hello, " & Name1 & "!")
End Sub
```

When you use optional parameters, you must supply a default value for each one, as in the preceding example. Also, once you've declared an optional parameter, all subsequent parameters for that procedure must also be optional.

Finally, you can change the accessibility of *Sub* procedures using the *Public*, *Private*, *Friend*, and *Protected* keywords. *Sub* procedures are public by default, which means they can be called from anywhere within your application.

Function Procedures

Function procedures in Visual Basic .NET are just like *Sub* procedures, except for one important detail—they can return a value. This allows your procedure to

- Return a numeric value representing an error or success code
- Return data in the form of an array or an ADO.NET dataset
- Return True or False to indicate the results of some conditional test

The following code example takes two string parameters, concatenates them, and then returns the result to the caller as a string:

```
Function ConcatStrings(ByVal String1 As String, _
    ByVal String2 As String) As String
    ConcatStrings = String1 & String2
End Function
```

Notice that since the *Function* procedure itself is declared as a string, you don't need to create a local variable to hold the result of concatenating the two strings. Instead, simply assign the result to the function name to return it to the caller.

Flow Control

Another important piece of any program is flow control, which allows you to determine at runtime which sections of your code will run, and in what order. Flow control statements are the foundation of business logic and consist of conditional logic (including *If* and *Case* statements), looping structures (*For...* and *Do...* loops), and error-handling statements.

If Statements

If statements are the form of conditional logic, also known as decision structures, that you will probably use most in your programs. They allow you to look for a defined condition in your program and execute a specific block of code if that condition is true. The following code checks a *Session* variable for the logged-in username (set in the login page) to prevent a user who has not logged into your ASP.NET application from viewing pages that require a login:

```
If Session("LoggedInUserName") = "" Then
    Response.Redirect("Login.aspx")
End If
```

In Visual Basic .NET, an *If* statement always requires an accompanying *End If* statement to denote the close of the *If* block. You can also provide code that will execute if the defined condition is false by adding the *Else* statement, and you can test for more than one condition by using one or more *ElseIf* statements. These techniques are shown in the following example:

```
If Session("LoggedInUserName") = "" Then
    Response.Redirect("Login.aspx")
ElseIf Session("LoggedInUserName") = "SuperUser" Then
    Response.Write("You are a superuser!")
Else
    Response.Write("Hello, " & Session("LoggedInUserName") & "!")
End If
```

> **note**
>
> Visual Basic .NET also supports single-line *If* statements, such as the following:
>
> ```
> If 1 < 2 Then Response.Write("1 is less than 2")
> ```
>
> This syntax should only be used for very simple *If* statements, as it is inherently harder to read and debug single-line If statements.

Select Case Statements

Another form of conditional logic you'll use frequently is the *Select Case* statement. This statement is useful in situations where you can reasonably expect the defined condition you're testing to evaluate to one of a limited number of values (or ranges of values). For example, the following code checks to see which item of a listbox was chosen by a user, and then it takes appropriate action.

```
Dim ColorString As String

ColorString = Request.Form("Colors")

Select Case ColorString
    Case "Red"
        Response.Write("<font color='" & ColorString & "'>")
        Response.Write("You chose Red")
        Response.Write("</font>")
    Case "Green"
        Response.Write("<font color='" & ColorString & "'>")
        Response.Write("You chose Green")
        Response.Write("</font>")
    Case "Blue"
        Response.Write("<font color='" & ColorString & "'>")
        Response.Write("You chose Blue")
        Response.Write("</font>")
End Select
```

You can also add a *Case Else* statement in order to execute specific code when the tested expression doesn't match any of your listed values, as the following code demonstrates:

```
Select Case ColorString
    Case "Red"
        ...
    Case "Green"
        ...
    Case "Blue"
        Response.Write("<font color='" & ColorString & "'>")
        Response.Write("You chose Blue")
        Response.Write("</font>")
    Case Else
        Response.Write("<font color='Black'>")
        Response.Write("You did not choose a color")
        Response.Write("</font>")
End Select
```

It's good programming practice to always have a *Case Else* statement, just in case there are unexpected values for the expression you're testing (such as *ColorString* in this example).

Looping Statements

Looping statements are useful features that allow you to perform actions repeatedly, by either specifying explicitly at design time the number of times the code should loop, deciding at runtime how many times to loop, or looping through a collection of objects and taking a specific action on each item. There are several different types of looping statements, each of which has its own particular syntax and is useful for a different situation. Loop types include

- *For...* loops
- *For Each...* loops, a special case of *For...* loops
- *Do...* loops, which include *Do While...* and *Do Until...* loops
- *While...End While* loops

> **note**
>
> Visual Basic 6 supported the *While...End* syntax for *While...* loops. In Visual Basic .NET, this syntax is no longer supported. You should use the *While...End While* syntax instead.

Using For... Loops

For... loops are useful for repeating a given set of statements a number of times. The number of times the statements are executed can be determined either explicitly or by evaluating an expression that returns a numeric value. The following example (from the *ASP.NET QuickStart Tutorial*) uses a *For...* loop that counts from 1 to 7 and, for each pass of the loop, outputs a message with a font size equal to the counter variable:

```
<% For i = 0 To 7 %>
   <font size="<%=i%>">Welcome to ASP.NET</font><br>
<% Next %>
```

You can also use the *Step* keyword to loop by steps greater than 1, or even to loop backward by specifying a negative number, as follows:

```
<% For i = 7 To 0 Step -1 %>
   <font size="<%=i%>">Welcome to ASP.NET</font><br>
<% Next %>
```

You can also use a *For...* loop to loop through the elements of an array by specifying the length of the array as the loop count expression, as follows:

```
<%
   Dim s(5) As String
   s(0) = "A"
   s(1) = "B"
   s(2) = "C"
   s(3) = "D"
   s(4) = "E"
   For i = 0 To s.Length - 1 %>
   <font size="<%=i%>"><%=s(i)%></font><br>
<% Next %>
```

note

In Visual Basic .NET, all arrays are zero based. Therefore, to use the *Length* property of the array for a looping statement, you should use *Length – 1*.

Using For Each... Loops

For Each... loops are a specialization of *For...* loops that allow you to loop through a collection or group of elements and take action on each item. The following example demonstrates looping through the items in an array of dates:

```
Dim Dates(2) As Date
Dim DateItem As Date

Dates(0) = Now.Date
Dates(1) = Now.AddDays(7).Date
Dates(2) = Now.AddYears(1).Date

For Each DateItem In Dates
    Response.Write("Date is: " & DateItem.ToString & ".<br/>")
Next
```

This code outputs each date to the browser using *Response.Write*. Note that when declaring the *Dates* array, you use the upper bound of 2, not the number of items desired, to size the array.

Using Do... Loops

Do... loops allow you to execute a set of statements repeatedly for as long as a test condition remains true. *Do...* loops (also known as *Do...While* loops) come in several variations. The most basic of these is shown in the following example:

```
<%
'Do While…Loop syntax:
Dim i as Integer = 1
Do While i <= 5
%>
    <font size="<%=i%>">Welcome to ASP.NET</font><br>
<%
    i = i + 1
Loop
%>
```

The statements within the loop will be executed as long as the variable *i* is less than or equal to 5. If, for whatever reason, *i* is greater than or equal to 5 the first time the *Do* statement is executed, the statements within the loop will not be executed. If you want to ensure that the statements within the loop will execute at least once, you can move the *While* expression to the end of the loop, as follows:

```
<%
'Do…Loop While syntax:
i = 0
Do
    i = i + 1
%>
    <font size="<%=i%>">Welcome to ASP.NET</font><br>
<%
Loop While i < 5
%>
```

You can also use the *Until* keyword in place of *While* to test for a condition, which would give you the opposite result of *While*.

Ultimately, the only real difference between *While* or *Until* is that *While* will loop as long as its test condition evaluates to True, whereas *Until* will loop as long as its test condition evaluates to False.

Using While...End While Loops

While...End While loops do essentially the same thing as *Do While...* loops, letting you execute a given set of statements while a given condition is true. *While...* loops are not as flexible as *Do...* loops because they don't offer the *Until* keyword or allow the condition to be placed at the end of the loop rather than the beginning. An advantage of *While...End While* loops is that the simpler syntax may be easier for beginning programmers to use more consistently. A *While...* loop that does the same thing as the preceding *Do...* loops would look like the following:

```
<%
'While...End While syntax:
Dim i as Integer = 1
While i <= 5
%>
    <font size="<%=i%>">Welcome to ASP.NET</font><br>
<%
    i = i + 1
End While
%>
```

Most programs will use a variety of loop types. No matter which loop type you choose, the important thing is that you use it correctly and consistently for a given task. This will make your code easier to read and maintain.

Error Handling

In any application, one challenge faced by developers is dealing with the inevitable errors that pop up. Application errors come in three varieties:

- **Syntax Errors**   These include misspelled or missing keywords (such as a missing *End If* statement), or other mistakes relating to the syntax of the language you're using. Syntax errors are typically flagged by the IDE and may be easily fixed at design time.

- **Runtime Errors**   These are errors that appear once your code is compiled and running. Runtime errors are caused by code that appears correct to the compiler, but that cannot run with certain values. For example, code that divides one integer variable by another will appear to be correct to a compiler, but it will cause a runtime error if the second variable is zero.

- **Logic Errors**   These are errors in which a program that works correctly under some (or most) circumstances gives unexpected or unwanted results based on certain input values. This type of error can be extremely difficult to track down and fix because it doesn't stop the execution of the program.

One thing that all three types of errors have in common is that they must all be handled in some fashion, lest they provoke grave dissatisfaction on the part of your users. An important first step is prevention. In Visual Basic .NET, two steps you can take to prevent errors are using *Option Explicit* and *Option Strict* in your applications. (They're both turned on by default in the Visual Studio .NET IDE.) Using *Option Explicit* will raise a syntax error if you attempt to use a variable before declaring it, which can help greatly if you have a habit of misspelling variable names. Using *Option Strict* will raise a syntax error if you attempt an implicit data type conversion that would result in a loss of data. *Option Strict* also implicitly includes *Option Explicit*, so *Option Strict* will also raise a syntax error on any attempt to use an undeclared variable.

The following example demonstrates the use of *Option Strict*:

```
Option Strict On

Dim MyInt As Integer
Dim MyDouble As Double

MyDouble = 3.14159
MyInt = MyDouble 'This line will cause an error at compile time
```

Both *Option Explicit* and *Option Strict* must come before any other code in the module in which they appear.

Using the On Error Statement

Once you've taken the preventive steps of using *Option Explicit*, or better yet, *Option Strict*, it's time to look at handling those inevitable errors. Error handling, also known as exception handling, is another type of flow control that allows you to execute code that you specify when an error or exception occurs. In Visual Basic 6, the only available option for error handling was setting up an error handler using the *On Error* statement. That option still exists in Visual Basic .NET.

```
Sub ExampleSub(Arg1, Arg2)
    On Error GoTo ErrorHandler
        'Code that might cause an error
    Exit Sub
ErrorHandler:
        'Error handling code
    Resume Next
End Sub
```

The *On Error* statement transfers execution to the section of code indicated by the *ErrorHandler* label. Once the error-handling code has executed, the *Resume*

Next statement causes execution to return to the statement immediately following the line that caused the error. The *Exit Sub* statement appearing just prior to the *ErrorHandler* label prevents the error handler from running if no error occurs.

The *On Error* statement is an example of unstructured error handling. Applications using unstructured error handling are generally more difficult to debug and maintain. Fortunately, Visual Basic .NET now also supports structured exception handling using the *Try...Catch* syntax.

note
You may see the terms *error* and *exception* used interchangeably. In .NET, exceptions are unexpected events that occur during the execution of your code. They differ from errors in that each exception is represented by an instance of an exception class (there are many types of exception classes, each derived from the base *System.Exception* class), which provides developers with properties and methods that allow them to deal with the exception.

Using Structured Exception Handling: Try...Catch...Finally

The *Try...Catch...Finally* form of exception handling, also known as structured exception handling, should be familiar to C++ and Java developers. C#, a language with origins in C/C++, also supports structured exception handling. This form of exception handling is new to Visual Basic developers.

In Visual Basic .NET, the *Try...Catch...Finally* syntax allows you to enclose code that may cause an exception in such a way as to catch and deal with specific exceptions and/or provide generic exception handling. The following code shows a simple *Try...Catch* block:

```
Dim a, b As Integer
Dim c As Single
Try 'Start monitoring for exceptions
   'Code that may cause an exception
   a = 1
   b = 0
   c = a / b
Catch DivideByZeroException
   'Code to handle exception
Finally
   'Code that executes after any code in the Catch block(s)
End Try
```

You can define *Catch* blocks for as many specific errors as you wish to handle. The *Finally* block can be used for any code you want to run after the exception-handling code, including clean-up code, such as code to close a file. You'll see more examples of exception handling throughout the book.

Understanding Object-Oriented Programming Basics

Something that will probably be new to many Visual Basic programmers, as well as those new to programming entirely, is object-oriented programming. This section will provide an overview of object-oriented programming, particularly as it relates to the .NET development platform. Object-oriented programming is a substantial topic, so it's highly recommended that you do some additional reading to supplement the material provided here. The Visual Studio .NET documentation for Visual Basic contains an entire section on object-oriented programming that is a good place to start. There are also many books on both object-oriented programming and *design patterns*, a related subject.

In the simplest terms, an *object* is an instance of a class in an object-oriented language such as C++, C#, and now Visual Basic .NET. Objects typically mirror their real-world counterparts: employees, invoices, and purchase orders are all examples of real-world entities that can be modeled as objects in your programs. Objects typically provide both *properties*, which describe some attribute of the object (for example, an employee might have an *EmployeeID* property), and *methods*, which allow actions to be taken by the object (for example, an *Invoice* object might expose a *Process* method). Properties and methods make it easier for programmers to know how to use a given object.

In addition to properties and methods, object-oriented programming offers three helpful features: inheritance, polymorphism, and encapsulation.

Inheritance is the ability to create new classes that are derived from existing classes. A derived class "inherits" all of the properties and methods of the class from which it is derived (referred to as the *parent class*). Programmers can then add additional properties and methods to the derived class, or in some cases override the implementation of an existing method inherited from the parent class.

Polymorphism lets programmers have identically named methods on different classes, and it allows the correct method to be executed based on the context of the call. For example, a programmer could define an *Invoice* class with a *Process* method. The programmer could then define separate *TimeInvoice* and *Materials-Invoice* classes that derived from the *Invoice* class, but which might or might not use the same implementation of the *Process* method exposed by the parent class.

Encapsulation allows objects to be treated as "black boxes" in that only the properties and methods defined by the programmer as publicly available are visible outside of the object. Internal object state and the implementation of the publicly available methods are hidden by encapsulation. This limited visibility lets developers freely modify the internal state and implementation of their objects, as long as they don't change the publicly defined interface used to access the object.

Using Classes as Containers for Code

Classes are the basic unit of an object-oriented application. A class in Visual Basic .NET or C# typically contains property and method definitions, as well as event handlers (a special class of methods). Classes are often grouped into useful collections through the use of namespaces. *Namespaces* can contain classes and other namespaces. For example, the *System.Web* namespace defined by the .NET Framework SDK contains not only classes such as the *HttpRequest*, *HttpResponse*, and *HttpServerUtility* classes (which provide the equivalent functionality of the ASP *Request*, *Response*, and *Server* intrinsic objects), but also a number of namespaces, including the *System.Web.UI*, *System.Web.Caching*, and *System.Web.SessionState* namespaces, each of which also contains classes and/or namespaces.

By using classes as containers for code and namespaces, the .NET architecture makes it very easy to create a rich, yet intuitive application hierarchy that can make your code easier to use, debug, and maintain.

note

When you develop applications in the Visual Studio .NET environment, a root namespace will be created with the same name as your project. If you specify additional namespaces within your code modules, these will become child namespaces of the root namespace. You can change the root namespace, if desired, by right-clicking your project in the Solution Explorer window and selecting Properties. The Root Namespace property appears under Common Properties, General.

Using Inheritance

Now that you know a bit about object-oriented programming, let's take a look at a simple example of how to put it to use. First, let's define a class based on a real-world entity, an animal.

```
Public Class Animal

    Overridable Public Sub Eat()
        Console.WriteLine("Yum!")
    End Sub

    Overridable Public Sub Sleep()
        Console.WriteLine("Zzzzz…")
    End Sub

End Class
```

Next, create a more specific animal class, *Cat*, that derives from the *Animal* class. Note the use of the *Inherits* keyword on the second line. Inheriting from another class is really that simple. This class will override the behavior of the *Eat* method, but not the *Sleep* method, as follows:

```
Public Class Cat
    Inherits Animal

    Overrides Public Sub Eat()
        Console.WriteLine("Yum, Yum…Meow, Meow!")
    End Sub

End Class
```

You'll also create a *Dog* class that derives from *Animal* and that overrides the *Sleep* method, but not the *Eat* method, as follows:

```
Public Class Dog
    Inherits Animal

    Overrides Public Sub Sleep()
        Console.WriteLine("Zzzzz…woofwoofwoofwoof…zzzzz!")
    End Sub

End Class
```

Finally, use the *Cat* and *Dog* classes in the following code. Note that you use the *Imports* statement to access the members of the *Animals* namespace without fully qualified names (such as *Cat* instead of *Animal.Cat*).

```
Imports Animals

Public Class UseAnimals

    Public Shared Sub Main()
        Dim MyCat As New Cat
        Dim MyDog As New Dog

        MyCat.Eat
        MyCat.Sleep
        MyDog.Eat
        MyDog.Sleep


    End Sub

End Class
```

This code, when run from a command line, provides the following output:

```
Yum, Yum…Meow, Meow!
Zzzzz…
Yum!
Zzzzzz…woofwoofwoofwoof…zzzzzz!
```

Even though you called the same two methods on both the *Cat* and *Dog* classes, when you overrode a method of the parent *Animal* class, you got the behavior that you specified for the particular animal. When you didn't override, the output shows that you got the behavior inherited from the parent *Animal* class. You can find the full source code for this example, as well as a batch file for compiling the classes used, in the source folder for this chapter on the CD-ROM accompanying the book.

Inheriting from the .NET Base Classes

The preceding example may not seem terribly useful, and admittedly, creating your own *Cats* and *Dogs* by inheriting from *Animal* won't help you much in your development efforts. Fortunately, the same principles demonstrated in that example apply to the classes that make up the .NET framework. Many of these classes can be used to derive your own specialized classes. You'll see specific examples of this in Chapter 12.

Inheriting Across Languages

Another nifty feature of the .NET Framework and the common language runtime is that they allow you to inherit from classes written in other languages. Why is this important? Because it means that development teams can make better use of the existing skill sets of their developers, as well as the company's existing code base. For example, a company with experienced Visual Basic developers (and existing code in Visual Basic) can have those developers continue to write in Visual Basic .NET. If the company also has a group of skilled Java developers, they can easily make the transition to C# and use the existing class resources created by the VB developers through inheritance.

Chapter 4 Quick Reference

To	Do This	Example
Declare a variable in Visual Basic .NET	Use the *Dim* keyword, along with the desired data type.	`Dim MyInt As Integer`
Declare a variable in C#	Use the data type, followed by the variable name.	`int MyInt`

Modify the accessibility of a variable or procedure in Visual Basic .NET	Use the *Public, Private, Friend*, or *Protected* keywords.	`Public Sub MySub()`
		
		`End Sub`

Modify the accessibility of a variable or procedure in C#	Use the *public, private, internal*, or *protected* keywords.	`public void myProc()`
		`{`
		`}`

Use structured exception handling in Visual Basic .NET	Create a *Try...Catch...Finally* block.	
Use Structured Exception Handling in C#	Create a *Try...Catch...Finally* block.	

Inherit from a base class in Visual Basic .NET	Use the *Inherits* keyword.	`Class Dog`
		`    Inherits Animal`
		`End Class`

Inherit from a base class in C#	Append the base class name to the name of the derived class, separated by a colon.	`class Dog : Animal`
		`{`
		`}`

PART III

ASP.NET Web Applications

Creating an ASP.NET Web Application

In this chapter, you will learn how to

✔ *Create an ASP.NET Web application with Visual Studio .NET*

✔ *Create and configure an IIS Virtual Directory*

✔ *Create an ASP.NET Web Form*

✔ *Create Global.asax and Web.config files*

This chapter will walk you through the steps necessary to create an ASP.NET Web application, using both the Microsoft .NET Framework SDK and Visual Studio .NET. While it's simple to create a Web application in Visual Studio .NET, it's also a good idea to know how to create a Web application manually if the need arises.

Creating a Web Application with Visual Studio .NET

To create a Web application in Visual Studio .NET follow these steps:

1 Start the Visual Studio .NET IDE by selecting Programs from the Start menu. Select Microsoft Visual Studio .NET 7.0 and click on Microsoft Visual Studio .NET 7.0.

2 From the File menu, select New and then choose Project.

3   In the New Project dialog box, choose a language and project type (in this case, Web Application), provide a name and location for the new project, and click OK.

4   Visual Studio .NET creates all of the necessary files and an Internet Information Services (IIS) virtual directory for the project.

As simple as this process appears, there is quite a bit of activity behind the scenes. The next section will show you how to create a Web application on your own, without Visual Studio .NET help.

Creating a Web Application with the .NET SDK

Although the .NET Framework SDK provides everything you need to run an ASP.NET application, creating a Web application with the SDK is a bit more involved than it is with Visual Studio .NET. Still, creating a new Web application is relatively straightforward. The process consists of the following steps:

- Creating an application root
- Creating subdirectories
- Creating .aspx pages
- Creating a Global.asax file
- Creating a Web.config file

Creating an Application Root

An *application root*, a special type of virtual directory in IIS, serves as the boundary for the Web application, both from a standpoint of files contained within the application and from a standpoint of any COM+ services your application may use. The application root also contains the Global.asax and Web.config files, if your application uses these optional files. Additionally, all files and folders under the application root are considered a part of the application.

To create an application root follow these steps:

1   Open the IIS management tool by selecting Programs from the Start menu. Select Administrative Tools and then choose Internet Services Manager.

2   Expand the node representing your machine to display the Web sites and other Internet services on your machine. The result will look similar to the following figure.

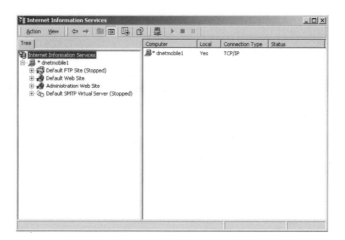

3   Right-click the Web site underneath which you want to create the application root, select New, and choose Virtual Directory.

4   Click Next on the first page of the Virtual Directory Creation Wizard, as shown in the following figure.

5   On the second page of the wizard, shown in the following figure, enter an alias for the application root. The alias is the name that you'll use to access the application. (If you create an application root on the default Web site with an alias of MyWebApp, you could access that application with the URL *http://localhost/ MyWebApp*.) Once you've entered an alias, click Next.

Creating Web Apps   5

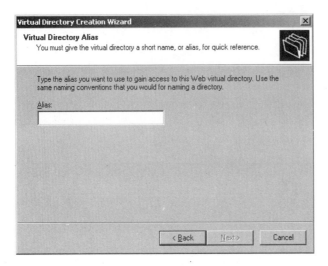

6 On the third page of the wizard, shown in the following figure, enter or browse to the path for the file system folder that will contain the files in the application. If this folder doesn't exist yet, create it now. Content folders for virtual directories or application roots under the default Web site are most commonly stored in the \InetPub\wwwroot folder, which is usually located on the C: drive. While it's possible to put your content anywhere within the file system, keeping your content folders under \InetPub\wwwroot makes it easier to keep track of all of your Web content. Once you've entered the path to your content folder, click Next.

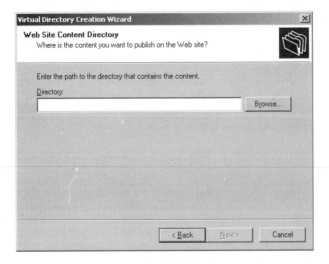

7 On the fourth page of the wizard, shown in the following figure, select the actions you wish to allow on this virtual directory. For most applications, the default of Read and Run Scripts (Such As ASP) is sufficient. When you're finished selecting permissions, click Next.

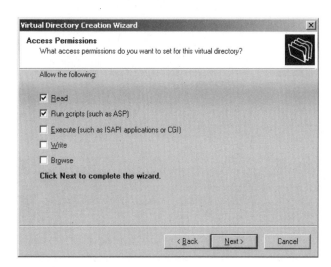

8 Click Finish to exit the wizard.

 Once you've finished with the wizard, you should make sure that your application root has been created correctly. The application root should be represented by the icon shown at left.

 By way of contrast, a virtual directory that is *not* an application root is represented instead by the icon shown at left.

If you accidentally create a virtual directory when you wanted to create an application root, you can turn the virtual directory into an application root with a few simple steps.

1 Right-click the virtual directory name in the Tree pane of Internet Services Manager, and then choose Properties.

2 On the Virtual Directory tab, shown in the following figure, click the Create button.

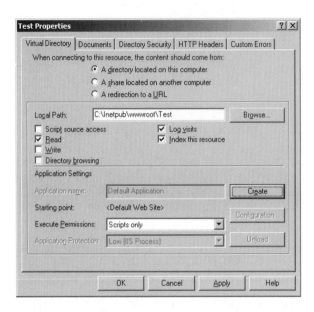

3   You can configure the application as desired using the options accessed by the Configuration button. For more information on IIS configuration options, view the IIS documentation by entering *http://localhost/iisHelp/iis/misc/default.asp* in your Web browser.

4   You can create a virtual directory from an application root by clicking the Remove button (which replaces the Create button when the application root is created).

Creating Subdirectories

If all you need is a subfolder, rather than a virtual directory, you can create a new folder in the file system underneath the folder of an existing virtual directory and then add content to it. Your folder and content will be displayed under your application root (or virtual directory) when you refresh the Internet Services Manager window.

Creating .aspx Pages

Once you've created your application root and configured the IIS application settings as desired, you'll probably want to start creating some content. If you've installed the .NET Framework SDK and you've created your application root correctly, any pages you create with the .aspx extension will be executed by the ASP.NET runtime engine.

Access Permissions

Before you select Execute, Write, or Browse permissions, you should make sure that you understand the security implications of each one. These settings can make your application vulnerable to attacks by hackers if used improperly. The following list explains the purpose of each available access permission and when it's appropriate to use.

- **Read**   Clients can read files with this permission set. This is selected by default.
- **Run Scripts**   This allows scripts in files such as ASP files to be executed, but does not allow executables (.exe, .dll) to be run.
- **Execute**   This allows executable file types such as .exe and .dll applications to be executed, as well as Common Gateway Interface (CGI) applications.
- **Write**   Clients can write to a directory with this permission set. Use this permission only when necessary.
- **Browse**   Clients entering a URL that doesn't specify a file name or a default document (such as index.htm or default.asp) will receive a listing of the files in the directory they're browsing. Because this information can help malicious users compromise your application, the Browse permission should be limited to situations where browsing is the intended behavior.

Some of these permissions should be used rarely, if at all, on production systems. More importantly, you should avoid certain combinations of permissions, such as Write and Run scripts or Write and Execute. These combinations could allow a malicious user to upload and execute scripts or other executable content that would compromise your server or data. If you need to allow Write permissions, always set up a separate folder that doesn't allow Run Scripts or Execute permissions.

As noted in Chapter 2, all you need to form a valid ASP.NET page is a valid HTML file with the extension .aspx. Of course, such a page wouldn't be especially useful, so you probably want to take a few more steps. The first step is choosing a development language for the page.

> **note**
>
> You might be wondering what the difference is in IIS between a directory and a virtual directory. A *directory* is any file system folder or directory within the home directory of your application root or virtual directory. A *virtual directory* allows you to map a file system folder or directory outside your home directory so that it appears to clients to be residing within the home directory.
>
> For example, the default home directory for the default Web site is C:\InetPub\wwwroot\. Content within this folder can be accessed locally via the URL *http://localhost/*. To make content residing in C:\MyWebApp available via the URL *http://localhost/MyWebApp/*, you would need to create a virtual directory (or an application root, if you wanted MyWebApp to define an application boundary) in the default Web site that maps the MyWebApp alias to the folder C:\MyWebApp\.

Choosing a Page Language

Unlike developing in Visual Studio .NET, creating your own ASP.NET pages from scratch gives you the freedom to write your pages in any .NET language, regardless of whether other pages in your Web application use a different language. In all likelihood, using multiple languages in the same application will make your code more difficult to maintain, but you're free to do it. Once you've chosen the language for your page, you can make your choice known to ASP.NET by adding the following line to the top of your HTML file:

```
<%@ Page Language="languagechoice" %>
```

> **note**
>
> Before you start creating pages and other content, take a moment to think about how you plan to organize that content. For example, consider using an /images folder to keep the images for your Web application separate from the rest of your content.
>
> Something else to consider if you're planning to use your own custom components is that, by default, ASP.NET will load any .NET assemblies found in a bin folder under your application root. So if you want your ASP.NET pages to be able to locate your custom .NET components, you need to create a bin folder and ensure that your assemblies are located there.

Here, *languagechoice* is the language you want to develop the page in. If you want to develop in Visual Basic .NET, the @ *Page* declaration would look like the following:

```
<%@ Page Language="VB" %>
```

In C#, the declaration would be

```
<%@ Page Language="C#" %>
```

So a page like the one you looked at in Chapter 2, with the @ *Page* directive, would look like the following code:

```
<%@ Page Language="C#" %>
<html>
  <head>
    <title>First ASP.NET Page!</title>
  </head>

  <body>
    <p>Hello World!</p>
  </body>

</html>
```

Any code located in either *<script>* blocks or <% %> render blocks in the preceding code will be assumed to be C# code.

Code Location Options

Another important choice to make when creating ASP.NET pages from scratch is whether to place the code in the .aspx file itself or use a code-behind module. Using code-behind modules has the advantage of providing much better separation of code from presentation (HTML). This can make it easier to debug your code, and it also makes it easier for teams of UI designers and developers to work together without breaking one another's work. Since code-behind allows you to create .aspx files that consist solely of HTML tags and tag-based server and user controls, it's much easier for UI designers to work with the .aspx files without breaking the code behind them.

> **note**
>
> While the theoretical benefit of separating code from presentation using code-behind modules is substantial, the practical benefit may be limited by the tools being used by the UI design team. It's reasonable to expect that many, if not most, Web design tools will eventually recognize and support custom ASP.NET tags (such as those used for server controls and user controls). However, at the time of this writing, many of these tools don't recognize these tags and may respond with error messages when you try to edit the files.
>
> Many Web design and development tools and editors post updated syntax and dictionary files on their Web sites. If your development tool doesn't support ASP.NET server control tags out of the box, check its manufacturer's Web site to see if an update is available.

If you choose to use code-behind for your ASP.NET code, you'll need to add the *src* attribute to the @ *Page* directive to tell ASP.NET where to find your code module, as follows:

```
<%@ Page Language="C#" src="filename.cs" %>
```

You'll also need to add the *inherits* attribute to tell ASP.NET which namespace and class the code-behind file exposes.

```
<%@ Page Language="C#" src="filename.cs" inherits="MyClass" %>
```

You'll learn more about code-behind and its use in ASP.NET Web Forms in Chapter 9.

Creating a Global.asax File

In addition to creating your application root and adding subfolders and content, you can also add a file called Global.asax to your Web application. Global.asax (which is added to Visual Studio .NET Web applications by default) is a file that is primarily used to provide application and session (per-user) start-up and clean-up code, as well as to set options that are to apply to the application as a whole. In Global.asax, you can

- Respond to selected application and session events.
- Respond to events of custom *HttpModules* you have created for your application.
- Import namespaces into the application using the @ *Import* directive. You can then use the members of the namespace from any code within your application without needing to import the namespace on each page.

■ Register assemblies for use in your application using the @ *Assembly* directive.

■ Create instances of application-level objects using the *<object runat="server">* tag syntax.

Using the OnStart and OnEnd Event Handlers

One downside of manually adding a Global.asax file to your project instead of having it added for you by Visual Studio .NET is that you then need to add each of the appropriate application and session event handlers manually. However, the benefit is that you can selectively add only the event handlers you actually use, rather than having handlers for all of the available events. The set of events that Visual Studio .NET automatically handles in Global.asax are as follows:

■ *Application_OnStart*   This event is fired when the first request for any .aspx page in your application is received. It can be used to initialize application-level variables necessary to your application or to execute other start-up code.

■ *Session_OnStart*   This event is fired when a request comes from a user who does not have a current session in your application. (By default, this is determined by whether a *SessionID* cookie is passed with the request.) It can be used to initialize session-level variables or to execute per-user start-up code.

■ *Application_BeginRequest*

■ *Application_EndRequest*

■ *Session_OnEnd*

■ *Application_OnEnd*

A typical set of Global.asax event handlers in Visual Basic .NET would look like the following:

```
<script language="VB" runat=server>
  Sub Application_OnStart()
    ' Application start-up code goes here…
  End Sub
  Sub Session_OnStart()
    ' Session start-up code goes here…
  End Sub
  Sub Session_OnEnd()
    ' Session clean-up code goes here…
  End Sub
  Sub Application_OnEnd()
    ' Application clean-up code goes here…
```

5

Creating Web Apps

```
End Sub
Overrides Sub HandleError(ErrorInfo as Exception)
   ' Application error occurs
End Sub
</script>
```

You can also handle events exposed by custom *HttpModules*, which are classes that inherit the *IHttpModule* interface and participate in processing ASP.NET requests. Handling events exposed by custom HttpModules is essentially the same as handling the application and session events. Events exposed by the Http-Module must use the naming pattern *modulename_eventname(eventargs)*.

Importing Namespaces in Global.asax

Importing a namespace into your ASP.NET pages allows you to refer to the members of that namespace without having to fully qualify the member names. For example, you could refer to *Color* instead of *System.Drawing.Color*. While it's easy enough to use the @ *Import* directive in your individual ASP.NET pages, you can save yourself some typing by using @ *Import* in Global.asax for namespaces that you use in most or all of your pages. For example, if you wanted to be able to call members of the *System.Web.UI* namespace in any ASP.NET page in your application, you could simply add the following line:

```
<%@ Imports Namespace="System.Web.UI" %>
```

There are two things you should keep in mind.

- If two or more namespaces that you've imported contain members with the same names, you'll still need to qualify the names in your code to avoid conflicts.
- While it's useful to avoid having to type extra code (especially in a large application), keep in mind that by not explicitly importing the namespaces used in each page, you make your code somewhat less readable and main-tainable. That is, someone who hasn't looked at your Global.asax file may not immediately grasp why the names in your pages are not fully qualified, and he or she may have more difficulty figuring out which namespace a par-ticular class or structure comes from.

Creating Components in Global.asax

If there are components that are used throughout your application, you may want these components to run in application scope (shared across all users of your application) or session scope (shared across all pages in your application for a single user). For example, you may have a dictionary component that you use to store information to be shared across user sessions. You can instantiate such a component in Global.asax using the *<object runat="server">* tag syntax. This syntax can be used with a *progid=* or *classid=* attribute to instantiate a classic COM component, or with a *class=* attribute to instantiate a .NET component. The following example would create an instance of the *System.Data.DataSet* class that could be used throughout the application:

```
<object runat="server" class="System.Data.DataSet"
  scope="Application">
```

If you omit the *scope* attribute, the default scope for server-side objects created in Global.asax with the *<object>* tag is AppInstance, which means that the object is local to Global.asax, but you should always use the *scope* attribute to explicitly control whether the component is given Application, Session, or AppInstance scope.

The following are some things to keep in mind with components you instantiate in Global.asax.

- Limit the number of components you instantiate at Application or Session level to those you absolutely need. Remember that these objects will be consuming resources (such as memory) for the entire lifetime of the Application (or Session). This consumption level can be a problem for applications requiring high scalability.

- Any components instantiated by the *<object>* tag should be multithreaded. In the .NET world, this isn't a major difficulty, but you should avoid things like instantiating classic COM components written in Visual Basic 6 with this syntax.

- Components created with the *<object>* tag syntax are not instantiated immediately, but at the time when they're first called on a page.

Creating a Web.config File

Another optional file you can add to your application is called Web.config. This is an XML-based, human- and machine-readable file that contains the configuration options for your application. The reason that this Web.config file is optional is that if you don't include it, your application will inherit the settings of the machine-level configuration file Machine.config. If you add a Web.config file to your application root, the configuration settings contained in that file will apply throughout your application. You can override these settings in specific areas of your application by setting up child folders in your application that contain their own Web.config files. In this way, you can set up a hierarchy of configuration settings for your application.

Among the configuration options that are controlled by Web.config are

- **HttpModules and HttpHandlers**   Process specific types of requests and are similar to ISAPI filters
- **Session state settings**   Determine whether session state is in process, out-of-process (shared across multiple machines), or stored by SQL Server
- **Browser capabilities**   Customize the properties returned by the *HTTPBrowserCapabilities* class when it encounters a given browser
- **Security**   Determines the settings for authentication, authorization, and identity
- **Compilation**   Determines the settings used for compiling the code in an ASP.NET application, including which external assemblies are included in the compilation of the application
- **Trace**   Provides configuration settings for ASP.NET application tracing (See Chapter 16 for more information on application tracing.)

Several more areas of configuration are available to the Web.config file. A more detailed discussion of ASP.NET configuration can be found in Chapter 7.

Chapter 5 Quick Reference

To	Do This
Create a new project in Visual Studio .NET	Click the New Project button, select the project language and template, and then provide the name and location for the new project. Alternatively, you can go to the File menu, select New, and choose Project.
Create a Virtual Directory in IIS	Start the Internet Services Manager, right-click the Web site you want to add the Virtual Directory to, and then select New and choose Virtual Directory. Follow thwe instructions in the Virtual Directory Creation Wizard.
Create a new Web Forms page	Add the @ *Page* directive with a *Language=* attribute to the top of an HTML page and save it with the .aspx extension. Add code using either *<script>* blocks with the *runat="server"* attribute or <% %> render blocks.
Handle application and session-level events	Create a Global.asax file in the application root with the appropriate event handlers.
Configure application settings	Create a Web.config file with the appropriate configuration sections. You can modify configuration settings for sections of your application by partitioning it into separate folders and placing a Web.config file in each folder that needs its own configuration settings.

Creating Web Apps

5

Managing Application State

In this chapter, you will learn about

- ✔ *Using application state*
- ✔ *Using session state*
- ✔ *Configuring state storage*
- ✔ *Using client-side cookies for state storage*
- ✔ *State and scalability*
- ✔ *ASP.NET server control state*

Most applications of any significance will use pieces of data, or variables, that need to be maintained across a series of requests or shared between multiple users of an application. This data is referred to as *state*. In a rich client application, it's relatively simple to maintain individual user state simply by allocating space in memory on the client machine. In Web applications, managing user and application state is more challenging. The primary reason for this is that the Hypertext Transfer Protocol (HTTP), the protocol used to send and receive requests through a Web browser, is inherently stateless. That is, HTTP doesn't inherently provide a way for the Web server to identify a series of requests as coming from the same user, making it difficult for the Web server to maintain state and associate it with an individual user.

In classic ASP, this limitation was overcome through an in-memory collection of key-value pairs associated with the *Session* intrinsic object. The *Session* collection, however, had a number of important limitations of its own, which are discussed later in this chapter.

In addition to individual user state, many applications need to store and retrieve *application-level* state information that is global to all users of the Web application. Classic ASP exposed a collection similar to that of the *Session* collection on the *Application* intrinsic object.

Using Application State

Application state refers to any data that you wish to share among multiple users of your application. This can include connection string information for databases (although this information is often better limited to the business tier of an application), shared variables, and cached datasets (although these may be better stored using the ASP.NET cache engine, which is discussed in more detail in Chapter 14). In fact, one of the difficulties in managing application state is choosing from the many available options for storing such state.

Like classic ASP, ASP.NET provides a collection of key-value pairs that developers can use to store values and object instances. This collection can be accessed in much the same way as in classic ASP (note the slight difference in syntax between VB.NET and C# in accessing the *Application* collection).

```
'VB.NET
Application("MyApplicationVar") = "MyValue"
MyLocalVar = Application("MyApplicationVar")
```

```
// C#
Application["MyApplicationVar"] = "MyValue";
MyLocalVar = Application["MyApplicationVar"]
```

Application state storage in ASP.NET is supplied by the .NET *HttpApplication-State* class, an instance of which is exposed as the *Application* property of the *Page* class. Because every ASP.NET page inherits from the *Page* class, you can access the *Application* property as if it were an inherent property of the page, as shown in the preceding code.

For backward-compatibility with classic ASP, the ASP.NET *Application* object exposes a *Contents* property that can be used to access individual values, using the appropriate key.

```
' VB.NET
Application.Contents("MyApplicationVar") = "MyValue"
MyLocalVar = Application.Contents("MyApplicationVar")
```

New in ASP.NET is the ability to add items to the *Application* collection using the *Add* method exposed by the *Application* object. You can use the *Remove* method (exposed by the *Application.Contents* collection in classic ASP) to remove items from the *Application* collection.

```
' VB.NET
Application.Add("MyApplicationVar", "MyValue")
Application.Remove("MyOtherApplicationVar")
```

```
// C#
Application.Add("MyApplicationVar", "MyValue");
Application.Remove("MyOtherApplicationVar");
```

You can also clear the contents of the *Application* collection by using the *Clear* method exposed by the *Application* object (or the *RemoveAll* method, which is provided for backward-compatibility with classic ASP).

```
' VB.NET
' Either line below will clear the application state
Application.Clear()
Application.RemoveAll()
```

The *Application* object exposes several other ways to access and modify the values stored in the *Application* collection, as shown in the following table.

Application Object Methods and Properties	
Method or Property	**Use**
AllKeys property	Returns a collection of all of the keys by which *Application* collection values can be accessed.
Count property	Returns the number of objects stored in the *Application* collection.
Get method	Returns an item from the *Application* collection by key or by index.
Set method	Updates an item in the *Application* collection by key or by index.
GetKey method	Returns the key for an item based on a supplied index.
ToString method	Returns a string that represents an item in the *Application* collection. Useful when a string value is required, rather than an object reference.

In addition to storing values in the *Application* collection, you can instantiate and store references to .NET components in application state using the *<object runat="server">* tag syntax in the Global.asax file (or its associated code-behind file), as described in the previous chapter. These objects then become part of the application's *StaticObjects* collection and can be referenced in your ASP.NET Web Form pages by referring to the *id* attribute associated with the object.

```
'Global.asax
<object runat="server" id="MyClassInstance" class="MyClassName"
    scope="Application">
</object>


'Web Forms page
Response.Write("Value = " & MyClassInstance.MyValue)
```

Note that Global.asax (or its associated code-behind file) is the only mechanism for creating object instances with *Application* scope.

important

When you're using either the *Application* or *Session* collections, it's a good idea to initialize the variables you're using to a default value (such as " " for a string or *0* for a numeric) in the *Application_Start* and *Session_Start* event handlers in Global.asax. You can then test for the default value as a way of determining whether it has been altered.

Synchronizing Access to Application State

One challenge in managing state information that's shared between multiple users is ensuring that no two users can attempt to update the state information simultaneously, which could lead to corruption of the data being stored. Like classic ASP, the ASP.NET *Application* object provides *Lock* and *Unlock* methods that developers can use to ensure that only a single user can update application state information at any given time. Developers should call *Application.Lock()* prior to modifying any data stored in the *Application* collection, and call *Application. Unlock()* once the modification is complete. Keep in mind that while the application is locked, no other users can modify data stored in the Application collection, which can cause scalability problems. For this reason, you should make sure to keep the application locked for the shortest time possible, and perform as little work as possible while the application is locked.

Recommendations for Application State

Information stored in application state can be easily shared between all users of an application. This can make it very tempting to use application state to store all manner of data, from application settings such as database connection strings to cached datasets containing frequently used data. In many cases, there are more efficient means of storing this data than application state. The following table shows some examples of when you may or may not want to store information in application state, as well as alternatives for storing such information.

Application State Recommendations		
State Information	**Issues**	**Alternative**
Database connection strings or other application configuration settings	Typically, these settings are accessed infrequently. Storing this information in application state is not very efficient.	Use the Web.config configuration file to store this information, and retrieve with the *GetConfig* method of the *Context* object, as discussed. (See Chapter 7.)
Datasets containing frequently read data	Caching frequently used data at the application level can be efficient, but there's little automatic control over when the data is refreshed.	Use the ASP.NET cache engine to cache expensive or frequently read data. The ASP.NET cache engine provides fine-grained control over how and when data is refreshed or purged from the cache. (See Chapter 14 for more information.)
Shared application flags or counter variables	Shared values that may be updated by multiple users of an application can present major scalability issues, as discussed in "State and Scalability" on page 107.	Consider storing shared application flags in a database, which will provide finer-grained control over the reading and updating of individual values.
References to object instances	Storing references to objects with the wrong threading model (such as legacy COM components created with Visual Basic) can have a severe impact on the scalability of an application.	If it's absolutely necessary to store a reference to an object instance, ensure that the class from which the object is created is thread safe.

6

Application State

Limitations of Application State

Application state has several limitations that you should consider when deciding how to manage your state information.

- **Durability**   Application state lasts only as long as the Web application is running. If the Web application or Web server is shut down or crashes, any state information stored at the application level will be destroyed. Any information that needs to persist between application restarts should be stored in a database or other persistent storage.

- **Web farms**   Application state is not shared across multiple servers in a Web farm (nor across multiple processors in a Web garden). If you need to store values that must be available to all users in these scenarios, application state is not an appropriate choice.

- **Memory**   Any given server has only a limited amount of physical memory available. Overuse of application state may result in information being swapped to virtual memory (a location on a hard drive used to provide supplemental "memory" storage). This can reduce performance significantly.

> **note**
>
> Web farms are groups of identically configured servers that share the load of serving user requests for a given Web application. Each server contains the same content and can fulfill any request. Requests are routed to individual servers by a hardware- or software-based load-balancing algorithm that either determines which server is least loaded or assigns requests to a given server randomly.
>
> Web gardens are a new concept in ASP.NET in which an application can be set to run on specific processors on a multiprocessor server.

Using Session State

As challenging as it can be to manage application-state information, the statelessness of HTTP makes maintaining state for individual users even more challenging. First, the Web server needs to be able to identify a series of requests as coming from a single user. Then the Web server must associate these requests with the state information for that specific user.

In classic ASP, these challenges were met with the *Session* intrinsic object. Each user had his or her own session instance, identified by a session ID, which could be used to store per-user state information. The session ID, a unique generated value for that run of the application, was then stored in a cookie on the client machine. It would then be passed back to the server with each subsequent request, allowing the server to identify the session associated with that user.

Unfortunately, session state in classic ASP had several inherent limitations that made it less than ideal, particularly for applications requiring high scalability. These included the following:

- **Web farms**   In classic ASP, session state could not be scaled across multiple servers in a Web farm, limiting its usefulness in high-scalability situations.
- **Durability**   In classic ASP, session state would be destroyed by a server restart or crash. This made it a poor choice for such uses as shopping carts, whose contents should survive such events.
- **Cookie reliance**   Classic ASP offered no inherent solution for supporting session state with browsers that could not or would not accept cookies. Although aftermarket solutions were available, they often involved unacceptable performance trade-offs.

ASP.NET solves each of these limitations, providing per-user state storage that's scalable, reliable, and available on browsers that don't support cookies (or for users who choose not to accept cookies). For more information on the available options for ASP.NET session state and how they solve these limitations, see "Configuring Session State Storage" on page 108.

As with the ASP.NET *Application* object, the ASP.NET *Session* object is exposed as a property of the *Page* class, from which all ASP.NET pages inherit. This allows access to the *Session* object using the *Session* keyword.

```
' VB.NET
Session("MySessionVar") = "MyValue"
MyLocalVar = Session("MySessionVar")

// C#
Session["MySessionVar"] = "MyValue";
MyLocalVar = Session["MySessionVar"]
```

note

When accessing the *Session* or *Application* collections directly using a key, you must use square brackets with C#, as shown in the preceding code . When calling methods, such as the *Add* or *Remove* methods, parentheses are used for VB.NET and C#.

Application State

6

The *Session* object functionality is provided by the *HttpSessionState* class, an instance of which is created for each user session for which session state has been enabled.

Like the *Application* object, the *Session* object exposes a *Contents* collection for backward-compatibility with classic ASP. Any values stored in the *Session* collection can also be accessed through the *Contents* collection alias.

```
' VB.NET
Session.Contents("MySessionVar") = "MyValue"
MyLocalVar = Session.Contents("MySessionVar")
```

The *Session* collection can also be used to store references to object instances, using similar syntax to that used to store object references at the application level. These objects then become part of the session's *StaticObjects* collection and can be referenced in your ASP.NET Web Form pages by referring to the *id* attribute associated with the object.

```
'Global.asax
<object runat="server" id="MyClassInstance" class="MyClassName"
    scope="Session">
</object>


'Web Forms page
Response.Write("Value = " & MyClassInstance.MyValue)
```

The following table lists some of the additional properties and methods provided by the *Session* object to retrieve and manipulate *Session* collection values.

Session Object Properties and Methods	
Method or Property	Use
Keys property	Returns a collection of all of the keys by which *Session* collection values can be accessed.
Count property	Returns the number of objects stored in the *Session* collection.
SessionID property	Returns a string containing the session ID for the current session.
Timeout property	Returns an Int32 value representing the current *Session Timeout* setting.

Session Object Properties and Methods	
Method or Property	**Use**
Abandon method	Destroys the current user session.
Clear method	Removes all items from the *Session* collection.
RemoveAt method	Removes a specific item from the *Session* collection, based on its index within the collection.
ToString method	Returns a string that represents an item in the *Session* collection. Useful when a string value is required rather than an object reference.

Enabling Session State

Unlike application state, which is always available to Web applications, session state must be enabled before you can use it. The good news is that the default configuration file at the server level (Machine.config) automatically enables session state, so you don't need to take any additional steps to enable it. Nonetheless, you should be aware that the settings in the Machine.config configuration file, as well as in the Web.config configuration file for your application, determine whether session state is enabled or disabled. The pertinent settings are detailed in Chapter 7.

If you want to delay the creation of a session until it's necessary, you can add the *EnableSessionState* attribute to the @ *Page* directive of all pages not requiring session state.

```
<%@ Page EnableSessionState="False" %>
```

Any attempt to access the *Session* object from a page on which *EnableSession-State* has been set to *False* will result in an error. Note that once a session has been created for a given user, setting the *EnableSessionState* attribute to *False* doesn't result in the destruction of the existing session. It only prevents access to the *Session* object from that page.

You can set the session state to read-only for a given page by setting the *EnableSessionState* attribute to *ReadOnly*. Any attempts to update values stored in the *Session* collection from that page will be ignored.

Enabling Session State in Visual Studio.NET

Visual Studio.NET makes it even easier to enable (or delay enabling) session state in your applications by exposing the *enableSessionState* attribute as a property of the *Document* object. This allows you to view and modify its value using the Visual Studio.NET Properties window, shown in the following figure.

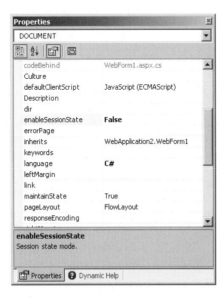

To change its setting, select the *enableSessionState* entry in the Properties window, click the drop-down list containing the values, and select the desired value.

Recommendations for Session State

Session state's ease of use makes it easy to overuse or abuse. The following table lists examples of when you may or may not want to store information in session state, as well as alternatives for storing such information.

Session State Recommendations		
State Information	**Issues**	**Alternative**
User-specific settings	Depending on how frequently these values are accessed, session state may not be the most efficient way to store these settings.	For infrequently accessed values, consider storing user-specific settings in a database.

Session State Recommendations		
State Information	Issues	Alternative
Datasets containing frequently read data	Caching frequently used data at the session level can be efficient, but there's little automatic control over when the data is refreshed. It's very important to consider the cost of storing a dataset for each user session over the cost of retrieving the dataset from the database.	Use the ASP.NET cache engine to cache expensive or frequently read data. The ASP.NET cache engine provides fine-grained control over how and when data is refreshed or purged from the cache. See Chapter 14 for more information on caching.
References to object instances	Storing references to objects with the wrong threading model (such as legacy COM components created with Visual Basic) can severely affect the scalability of an application. It's important to consider the cost of storing a reference to an object for each user session.	If it's absolutely necessary to store a reference to an object instance, ensure that the class from which the object is created is thread safe.

Limitations of Session State

Thanks to a number of new features in ASP.NET, the primary limitation of session state in ASP.NET is that of memory. As with application state, session state is limited by the memory available on the Web server. Once the available physical memory on the Web server has been exhausted, information will be stored in much slower virtual memory.

State and Scalability

How and where you choose to store state information for your application can have a major impact on how scalable your application is. *Scalability* refers to the ability of an application to service requests from increasing numbers of users without any significant decrease in performance or response time.

Some of the factors affecting application scalability that result from poor decisions in state management include the following conditions.

■ **Failure to disable session state when not used**   If you're not using session state within your application, disable it by changing the *mode* attribute of the *sessionState* configuration section of Web.config to *"off"*. For applications that make limited use of session state, ensure that any pages that don't use session state include the *EnableSessionState="false"* attribute as a part of the page's @ *Page* directive.

- **Misuse of *Application.Lock()*** The *Application.Lock()* method prevents access to all application values for any user other than the user whose request resulted in the call to *Application.Lock()*. This continues until the *Application.Unlock()* method is called. You should minimize the time that these values are locked by calling *Application.Lock()* immediately prior to updating a value and calling *Application.Lock()* immediately afterward.

- **Storing references to single (or apartment) threaded objects** Storing references to non-free-threaded objects at application or session level can interfere with IIS thread management capabilities and can result in severe scalability problems. Avoid storing non-free-threaded objects at application or session level.

- **In-process session state** In order to scale a Web application beyond a certain point, it's often necessary to use a Web farm to allow multiple servers to handle requests. In-process session state, the default, is not available to all servers on a Web farm. To use session state with a Web farm, you should set your application's *Session* mode to either *"StateServer"* or *"SQLServer"* as described in the next section.

- **Overuse of session or application storage** Storing numerous object references or large datasets at the application level, and particularly at the session level, can rapidly exhaust the physical memory on a Web server, causing it to substitute virtual memory for storing additional information. This can have a dramatic effect on the performance of an application. You should always ensure that any use of application state (and more importantly, session state) will not exceed the physical memory resources available on the Web server. Also remember that other applications will be using some of these resources.

Configuring Session State Storage

ASP.NET provides several new possibilities for storing session state. Each is designed to overcome one or more of the limitations of session state in classic ASP. The available settings include the following:

- **In-process *(InProc)*** This is the default setting. Its behavior is essentially the same as in classic ASP.

- **Out-of-process *(StateServer)*** This setting specifies that session state will be stored by a server running the ASP.NET state NT service. The state server to connect to is specified by an attribute, as described in the section "Storing Session State Out-of-Process."

- **SQL Server** *(SQLServer)* This setting specifies that session state will be stored in a SQL Server database. The SQL Server to connect to is specified by an attribute, as described in the section "Storing Session State in SQL Server" on page 111.

- **Cookieless Sessions** This setting allows you to maintain session state even for users whose browsers cannot handle cookies.

The following sections describe how to configure each of these settings.

Storing Session State In-Process

By default, Web applications, whether created in Visual Studio .NET or created manually, will store session state in-process. As noted, this setting has several inherent limitations, including lack of scalability and durability. For applications requiring neither scalability beyond a single server nor durability of session state across server restarts or crashes, however, this setting may work just fine. And it's the simplest to deal with because it doesn't require any changes to the application configuration file.

Storing Session State Out-of-Process

The first solution to the problems of scalability and durability for session state is to store session state out-of-process in a dedicated ASP.NET state process provided by an NT service. One advantage of this method is that the ASP.NET state service can service requests from multiple servers, making it possible to scale session state across a Web farm. Another advantage is that the ASP.NET state service runs in a separate process (or even on a separate machine), so state information can survive restarts or crashes of a specific Web application process. Note that session state information stored by the ASP.NET state service does *not* survive a restart or crash of the machine on which it's running.

To store session state out-of-process follow these steps:

1 Open the Web.config configuration file for your application and locate the *sessionState* configuration section.

2 Change the *mode* attribute from *"InProc"* to *"StateServer"*.

3 Modify the *stateConnectionString* attribute so that it reflects the server name (or IP address) of the state server and the port that the ASP.NET state service is monitoring (by default, this is 42424).

6

Application State

4   The complete *sessionState* configuration section that uses the ASP.NET state service on the local machine would look like the following code. (Note that the *sqlConnectionString* attribute, which is not used in this example, and the *cookieless* and *timeout* attributes have been omitted. The full list of attributes is available in Chapter 7.)

```
<sessionState
    mode="stateserver"
    stateConnectionString="tcpip=127.0.0.1:42424"/>
```

5   Start the Services Microsoft Management Console (MMC) snap-in by clicking Start, Programs, Administrative Tools, Services.

6   Start the ASP.NET state service on the desired server from the Services MMC snap-in.

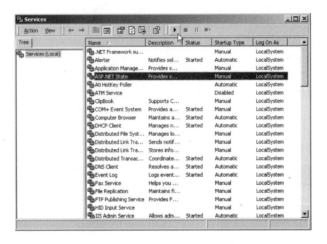

ASP.NET will automatically connect to the specified state server to store session state for your application. If the state service on the specified server is not running, you will receive an error message.

Keep in mind that although storing session state in a dedicated server process can improve the overall scalability of your application, there are inherent performance implications of moving session state out of process. Retrieving state information from a different process (and especially from a different machine) is significantly more costly than retrieving it from within the same process. You should test the impact on the type and amount of session data you plan to store before implementing this type of session state storage in a production application.

Storing Session State in SQL Server

The second solution to the problems of scalability and durability for session state is to store it out-of-process in a SQL Server database. One advantage of this method is that the specified SQL Server can service requests from multiple servers, making it possible to scale session state across a Web farm. Also, the session state information is stored in a SQL Server database, so state information can survive restarts or crashes of any Web application process, any Web server, or even the SQL Server itself.

To store session state in SQL Server follow these steps:

1   Set up the SQL Server session state database by running the InstallSqlState.sql batch (located in the .NET Framework install directory, by default %windir%\Microsoft.NET\Framework\%version%) against the SQL Server you plan to use. (For more information on running batch statements, check with your database administrator or the SQL Server Books Online.)

2   Open the Web.config configuration file for your application and locate the *sessionState* configuration section.

3   Change the *mode* attribute from *"InProc"* to *"SQLServer"*.

4   Modify the *sqlConnectionString* attribute so that it reflects the IP address of the desired SQL Server and the user ID and password used to access the SQL Server.

5   The complete *sessionState* configuration section that uses a SQL Server on the local machine would look like the following (note that the *stateConnectionString* attribute and the *cookieless* and *timeout* attributes have been omitted).

```
<sessionState
  mode="SQLServer"
  sqlConnectionString="data source=127.0.0.1;user id=sa;password="/>
```

> **note**
>
> There are security implications to placing the SQL Server user ID and password in the connection string in Web.config. A better practice, where possible, is to use a trusted connection to SQL Server. Chapter 11 describes the steps necessary to use a trusted connection with SQL Server, as well as other connection techniques. Chapter 8 further explores the topic of security in ASP.NET, including good practices for storing connection string information.

Application State

Using Cookieless Sessions

One ongoing challenge for Web developers using classic ASP is how to handle session state for users whose browsers can't or won't accept cookies. Classic ASP provided no intrinsic solution for this situation. In ASP.NET, it's relatively simple.

1   Open the Web.config configuration file for your application and locate the *sessionState* configuration section.

2   Change the *cookieless* attribute from *"false"* to *"true"*.

3   The complete *sessionState* configuration section would look like the following (note that the *stateConnectionString*, *sqlConnectionString*, and *timeout* attributes have been omitted).

```
<sessionState
    cookieless="true"/>
```

When the *cookieless* attribute is set to *"true"*, ASP.NET will automatically embed the *SessionID* value in the URL for all requests. For best results, always use relative URLs for internal links within your application. Relative URLs contain only the path and file information for the requested resource, and not the protocol and domain, which are assumed to be the same as the current page.

Formatting URLs for Cookieless Sessions

ASP.NET provides automatic embedding of session IDs in the relative URLs within your application, but not for absolute URLs, nor for URLs from applications outside yours. If a request for a page within an application set up for cookieless sessions is received that doesn't contain an embedded session ID, ASP.NET will create a new session ID and embed it in the URL for that request.

In order to prevent this problem, you can manually format URLs by calling the *ApplyAppPathModifier* method of the *Response* intrinsic object, and passing it a virtual path. The method will return an absolute URL containing the embedded SessionID for use with cookieless sessions. An absolute URL includes the protocol, domain, path and file name necessary to request a given resource. The syntax for this method is as follows:

```
Dim myAbsoluteURL As String
myAbsoluteURL = Response.ApplyAppPathModifier("foo.aspx")
```

Using Client-Side Cookies for State Storage

A discussion of state management would be incomplete without at least a brief mention of another option for storing application state: client-side cookies. This method doesn't work with users whose browsers cannot handle cookies (or who have turned off cookies), but it's the most lightweight method for storing certain types of state data because it requires no resources on the Web server.

Follow these steps to store user state in a nonpersistent cookie:

1   Create a new instance of the *HttpCookie* class.

```
Dim MyCookie As New HttpCookie("MyCookieName")
```

2   Set the *Value* property of the cookie to the desired value.

```
MyCookie.Value = "MyValue"
```

3   Add the cookie to the *Cookies* collection of the *Response* object (exposed by the *Page* class).

```
Response.Cookies.Add(MyCookie)
```

This sets a cookie called *"My Cookie"* that lasts until the user closes the browser.

Using Persistent Cookies

To store user state that will persist across multiple browser sessions, you need to use persistent cookies. In order for a cookie to be persistent, its expiration must occur in the future. To make the cookie created in the previous example persist for two days, add the following line of code, just prior to adding the cookie to the *Response.Cookies* collection:

```
MyCookie.Expires = Now.AddDays(2)
```

Here are some things to consider about using persistent cookies.

- Cookies have a bad reputation due to their misuse by some Web companies to track the surfing habits of Web users. It's a good idea to explain to your users exactly how and why you're using persistent cookies, and describe the benefits of accepting those cookies.

- Keep the expiration of persistent cookies within a reasonable amount of time. For most sites, cookie expiration should be measured in hours or days, or at most months. Setting your cookie expiration to years in the future is likely to result in more users refusing your cookie.

■   *Never* store user data, such as credit card numbers or other data that could be at risk if intercepted or otherwise compromised, in a cookie.

important

Although it may seem obvious to avoid storing information such as credit card numbers in cookies, it's equally important to consider the security implications of storing such information on the server side, whether in session state in memory, or in a database server. Although there's no single right answer to how to store sensitive data, here are some guidelines you should follow:

■   Store sensitive data only if you must, and then only for the minimum length of time necessary.

■   Encrypt sensitive data to better protect it from being compromised.

■   When possible, archive sensitive data on systems that are not connected to the Internet (and are thus less vulnerable to being compromised).

■   Make sure that you follow good security practices on all of your servers, particularly those exposed to the Internet. (We'll cover security in greater detail in Chapter 8.)

Although following these guidelines won't guarantee that your Web applications will never be compromised by crackers, they'll help you limit the damage.

ASP.NET Server Control State

Finally another kind of state that is managed by ASP.NET is server control state. Developers who used classic ASP to create data-driven applications had to figure out how to maintain the state of the various HTML form elements on their ASP pages from one page to the next, or even between submissions of a page that submits to itself. HTML provides no built-in mechanism for maintaining the state of individual form elements, so developers were left to come up with their own methods of maintaining and restoring this information.

ASP.NET provides a solution to this challenge with the server control architecture. All ASP.NET server controls are capable of maintaining their own state through a mechanism known as ViewState. ViewState is maintained on a page-by-page basis as a hidden form field that contains all of the state information for all of the form elements on that page.

ViewState and server controls are discussed in detail in Chapters 10 and 12.

Chapter 6 Quick Reference

To	Do This	Example
Store information in the *Application* collection	Use either the *Application* object or the *Application.Contents* collection to add the item to the collection, or use the *Application.Add* method.	*Application(key) = value* *Application.Contents(key) = value* *Application.Add(key,value)*
Modify information in the *Application* collection	Use the *Application* object to access and modify the item by its key or index, or use the *Application.Set* method to access and modify the item by its key.	*Application(key) = newvalue* *Application(index) = newvalue* *Application.Set(key, newvalue)*
Create and store an object in the *Application StaticObjects* collection	Add an *<Object>* tag in Global.asax with the *runat="server"* attribute and the *scope= "application"* attribute.	*<object runat="server" id="myObject" scope="Application" class="myClassName"> </object>*
Store session state in a dedicated server process	Modify the *sessionState* configuration section of your application's Web.config file, changing the *mode* attribute to *"StateServer"* and the *stateConnectionString* attribute to the appropriate IP address and TCP port for the state server being used.	*<sessionState mode="StateServer" stateConnectionString= "tcpip=127.0.0.1:42424"/>*

6

Application State

Chapter 6 Quick Reference

To	Do This	Example
Store session state in a SQL Server database	Modify the *sessionState* configuration section of your application's Web.config file, changing the mode attribute to *"SQLServer"* and the *sqlConnectionString* attribute to the appropriate data source name, user ID, and password for the SQL Server being used.	*<sessionState mode="SQLServer" sqlConnectionString= "data source=127.0.0.1; user id=sa; password="/>*
Provide support for session state without cookies	Modify the *sessionState* configuration section of your application's Web.config file, changing the *cookieless* attribute to *"true"*.	*<sessionState cookieless="true"/>*

Configuring an ASP.NET Application

Configuring Apps

In this chapter, you will learn

✓ *ASP.NET configuration elements*

✓ *Retrieval of custom configuration settings from ASP.NET pages*

One of the most important new features of ASP.NET, given the advantages it provides developers, is the new configuration system it provides ASP.NET. This configuration system uses human- and machine-readable XML-based files to store configuration information. This chapter will look at how these configuration files work and how you can use them in your applications.

Understanding ASP.NET Configuration

Configuration in ASP.NET is based on a series of XML-based files that are hierarchical in nature. Each server contains a master (or root) configuration file called Machine.config that is stored at the path c:*windir*\Microsoft.NET\ Framework*version*\CONFIG\Machine.config (see the following figure). This master configuration file contains the default settings for all ASP.NET applications on that server. This file also contains settings for machine-wide configuration (such as assembly binding and remoting channels), as well as other settings. Use caution when you edit this file, to avoid inadvertently making changes that affect other applications.

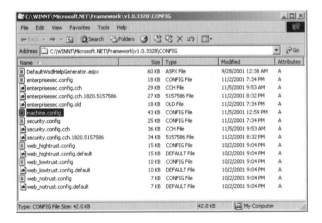

In addition to Machine.config, each ASP.NET Web application may have one or more files called Web.config in its folders. Each Web.config file must reside in its own folder, and each file overrides any settings of the configuration files in parent folders. Settings in Web.config apply only to content within the folder in which the file resides, and any content in child folders. This allows you to set up a hierarchy of configuration files that lets you set application-wide configuration options at the highest levels, while still allowing you to override those settings at a lower level. For example, if you have a group of files whose access must be restricted, you can place those files in a separate folder within your application and then add a Web.config file that implements tighter security restrictions. You'll see how to do this later in this chapter.

note

If you decide to use multiple levels of configuration files within your application, you should consider using comments to make it clear where you're overriding settings from parent Web.config files or from Machine.config. This way, those who need to maintain the application can understand your intent. Comments in ASP.NET configuration files use the same syntax as HTML comments: <!-- -->.

Keep in mind also that many of the settings configured in Web.config and Machine.config can also be overridden at the page level using attributes of the @ Page directive. Take care to ensure that all developers on a project (as well as those who will maintain the application) understand this, to avoid confusion.

Changes to configuration file settings are detected automatically by the ASP.NET runtime and integrated into the cached configuration settings for the application.

When a change is made, all new requests for resources within the scope of a given configuration file use the new configuration settings automatically.

Introducing Web.config

Like the Machine.config file, Web.config is XML based. This means that each Web.config file is made up of tags and attributes, similar to HTML. (XML is a markup language based on Structured Generalized Markup Language or SGML, the same language on which HTML was based.) Unlike Machine.config, however, most Web.config files will not contain elements for every available configuration setting. In fact, an ASP.NET application doesn't actually require a Web.config file in order to function. If Web.config is omitted from an application, it simply inherits its configuration settings from the master configuration file, Machine.config.

A Web.config file has the following basic structure:

```
<?xml version="1.0" encoding="utf-8" ?>
<configuration>
   <system.web>
      <elementName1>
         <childElementName1
            attributeName1=value
            attributeName2=value
            attributeNameN=value />
      </elementName1>
      <elementName2
            attributeName1=value
            attributeName2=value
            attributeNameN=value
      </elementName2>
      <elementNameN
            attributeName1=value
            attributeName2=value
            attributeNameN=value />
   </system.web>
</configuration>
```

Each Web.config file should begin with the standard XML declaration, though it will work without it. The file also contains opening and closing *<configuration>* tags. Nested within those tags are the opening and closing *<system.web>* tags, indicating that the content within is ASP.NET-specific configuration information. This configuration information is supplied in tags referred to as *elements*. Each element consists of either an opening and closing tag with one or more child elements to provide specific configuration values, or a tag pair with one or more attributes to provide specific configuration values. If an element doesn't have child elements, you can omit the closing tag by adding the / character at the end of the opening tag. (This is standard XML syntax.) You'll see this format in action in "ASP.NET Configuration Elements" on page 123.

note

Many developers found it frustrating when Visual InterDev 6 reformatted code according to its preferred style. That feature was difficult, if not impossible, to turn off. In Visual Studio .NET, not only can you control how code is validated and formatted, but in most cases you can turn off autoformatting entirely.

To view or change the formatting settings for a given language, from the Tools menu select Options, and then click the Text Editor folder. Click the folder for the language of your choice (see the following figure). Note that for some languages, the formatting settings appear on more than one option page. For example, HTML/XML formatting options are set on the Format page, the HTML Specific page, and the XML Specific page, all under the HTML/XML folder.

Editing Configuration Files

At the time of this writing, the Visual Studio .NET environment's tools for editing configuration files are limited to syntax coloring, XML validation, and code formatting. Because the ASP.NET configuration files are XML-based, you can use your favorite XML editor (or text editor) to edit ASP.NET configuration files.

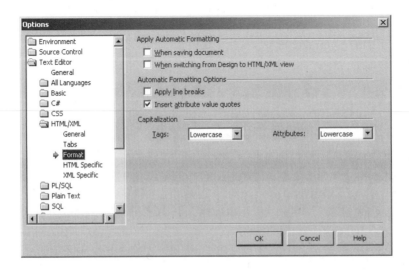

In addition to syntax coloring and validation, Visual Studio .NET also provides a default Web.config file for each new Web application project that you create. This default file contains the most commonly used elements, as well as comments that explain the available options for each element. The default Web.config file is useful as a template for any additional Web.config files you want to place in subfolders of your Web application. Keep in mind that when you're using configuration files in subfolders of your application, it's a good idea to only include the elements for the configuration settings from the parent file that you want to override. This helps prevent overriding a configuration setting by accident, and it may help reduce parsing overhead for the configuration of your application.

Editing the Master Configuration File

Not only does the master configuration file, Machine.config, contain the default settings for all ASP.NET applications on the machine, but it has machine-wide configuration settings as well. Be cautious when editing this file. It is prudent to create a backup copy of the file before you edit it. Also keep in mind that unless you're the only one who uses the machine on which you're developing, any changes that you make to Machine.config will also affect other ASP.NET developers using the machine. Unless you enjoy dealing with unhappy colleagues, you should discuss any proposed changes with them first.

Configuring an ASP.NET Application

At the time of this writing there are no GUI tools available for editing the Web.config files and modifying configuration settings. Fortunately, the default Web.config file created by Visual Studio .NET Web Applications, shown in the following figure, contains comments specific to the most commonly used settings. These comments provide guidance for using the available parameters for a given configuration element (although not all configuration elements appear in the default Web.config file).

In addition to the comments found in the Web.config file generated by Visual Studio .NET, the Machine.config file also contains comments with specific settings for certain elements. These comments can guide you when you make configuration changes. These elements and their settings are described in "ASP.NET Configuration Elements" on page 123.

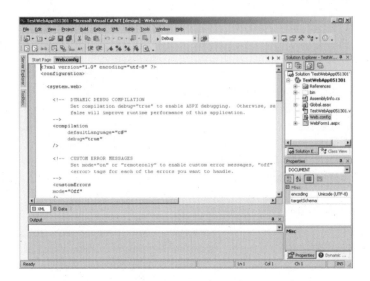

Overriding Configuration Settings for Subdirectories

Once you've created the application-level Web.config file and modified its settings to suit your needs, you may want to modify the configuration settings for a subset of your application. For example, you may want to apply more stringent security requirements to a particular set of files. In ASP.NET, it's simple to override the application-level configuration settings. It takes only the following three steps:

1 Create a subfolder in your application, and place in it the content to which the new configuration settings will apply.

2 Create a new Web.config file in the new folder.

3 Add the configuration settings you want to override to the new Web.config file.

Include only the configuration settings that you want to override in the new Web.config file. All other settings are inherited from the Web.config file of the parent folder or, if that file doesn't exist (or doesn't contain settings for all available configuration elements), from the Machine.config file for your Web server.

Locking Down Configuration Settings

Clearly, there will be times when Web developers or administrators want to configure settings for an entire server or site, and prevent them from being overridden. This might be desirable in the case of authentication and authorization settings, or to prevent the overriding of security policy settings. Fortunately, ASP.NET provides the *<location>* tag for just this purpose.

The *<location>* tag has two attributes: *path* and *allowOverride*. The *path* attribute allows you to specify a path to which the settings within the *<location>* tag pair apply. This attribute allows you to use a single configuration file, such as Machine.config, to apply configuration settings for multiple applications, virtual directories, or files on the same machine. Some settings may only be set at the machine or application level. If you attempt to apply these settings at the directory or file level using the path attribute, an exception will be thrown.

> ## note
>
> When you're using the *path* attribute to apply configuration settings to multiple locations, use comments to clarify the intended purpose of each set of *<location>* tags. In shared server environments, use comments to note the person responsible for a given set of configuration settings.

The *allowOverride* attribute determines whether the settings within the *<location>* tag pair can be overridden by settings applied in a child configuration file. If this attribute is set to *false*, any attempt to change the specified setting in a child configuration file will result in an exception.

To use the *<location>* tag to lock down configuration settings

1   Open the configuration file (Web.config or Machine.config) from which you want to lock down a particular setting.

2   Add the following code within the *<configuration>* and *</configuration>* tags:

```
<location path="path to lock down" allowOverride="false">
  <system.web>
  </system.web>
</location>
```

3   Add the desired configuration elements between the *<system.web>* and *</system.web>* tags.

ASP.NET Configuration Elements

Now that you've looked at the location and structure of the ASP.NET configuration files and how to override the settings of one Web.config file with another, let's look at the individual configuration elements for configuring ASP.NET applications. This section lists the syntax for each configuration element and describes the attributes and child elements available for that element (where applicable).

Configuring Apps

7

The names of configuration elements and their attributes are case sensitive and are in what is referred to as *camel case*. The entire first word of a name is lowercase, and the initial letter of each additional word in the name is capitalized. For example, the *sessionstate* configuration element becomes *sessionState*. Remember to use camel case with both configuration element names and attribute names, or you'll get an error when you try to access a page in the application.

\<trace\>

The *\<trace\>* element allows you to enable or disable application-wide tracing (see Chapter 16 for more on this useful feature), as well as set the parameters for the tracing functionality. When tracing is enabled, you can review information about requests received by the Web server with the special URL *http://\<servername\>/ \<appname\>/trace.axd*. The *\<trace\>* element has the following syntax:

```
<trace
    enabled="true|false"
    localOnly="true|false"
    pageOutput="true|false"
    requestLimit="integer"
    traceMode="SortByTime|SortByCategory" />
```

For information on *\<trace\>* element attributes, consult the following table.

\<trace\> Element Attributes		
Attribute	**Description**	**Options**
enabled	Determines whether application-level tracing is enabled for the application.	*true* Turns on application-level tracing. *false* Turns off application-level tracing. The default is *false*.
localOnly	Determines whether trace information is viewable by computers other than the local Web server.	*true* Trace output can be viewed only from the local Web server. *false* Trace output is viewable from any machine. The default is *true*.

<trace> Element Attributes		
Attribute	**Description**	**Options**
pageOutput	Determines whether trace output is appended to each ASP.NET page in the application or is available only through *trace.axd*.	*true* Trace output is appended to each page within the scope of the configuration file. *false* Trace output is available only by browsing the special *trace.axd* URL. The default is *false*.
requestLimit	Determines the number of requests that are stored for review through the trace.axd URL. Once this limit has been reached, the current trace must be cleared by browsing *trace.axd* in order to collect information on additional requests.	The default is *10*, but the higher this number, the more overhead is involved in tracing. Set this number as small as is feasible.
traceMode	Determines the sort order of the requests stored.	*SortByTime* Sorts trace information by the order in which events are processed. *SortByCategory* Sorts trace information alphabetically by category. When used with the *Trace.Write* method, this can be useful for grouping *Trace.Write* statements using the same category argument. The default is *SortByTime*.

<globalization>

The *<globalization>* element controls globalization settings for ASP.NET applications. This includes the encoding used for requests, responses, and files, as well as settings for specifying the culture to be associated with Web requests and local searches. The *<globalization>* element has the following syntax:

```
<globalization
    culture="any valid culture string"
    fileEncoding="any valid encoding string"
    requestEncoding="any valid encoding string"
    responseEncoding="any valid encoding string"
    uiCulture="any valid culture string" />
```

Configuring Apps

7

For information on *<globalization>* element attributes, consult the following table.

<globalization> Element Attributes		
Attribute	**Description**	**Options**
culture	Determines the culture (such as language defaults) used to process incoming Web requests.	This attribute must be set to a valid culture string. For a list of valid culture strings, see the .NET Framework documentation entry for the *System.Globalization.CultureInfo* class.
fileEncoding	Determines the type of character encoding used for parsing ASP.NET application files (.aspx, .asmx, and .asax).	This attribute must be set to a valid encoding string. If this attribute is not included in either Machine.config or Web.config, encoding is based on the machine's Regional Options setting in Control Panel.
requestEncoding	Determines the type of character encoding used to process incoming Web requests.	This attribute must be set to a valid encoding string. If this attribute is not included in either Machine.config or Web.config, encoding is based on the machine's Regional Options setting in Control Panel. The default is *utf-8*.
responseEncoding	Determines the type of character encoding used to encode outgoing responses.	This attribute must be set to a valid encoding string. If this attribute is not included in either Machine.config or Web.config, encoding is based on the machine's Regional Options setting in Control Panel. The default is *utf-8*.
uiCulture	Determines the culture (such as language defaults) used to process searches that are culture- or locale-specific.	This attribute must be set to a valid culture string. For a list of valid culture strings, see the .NET Framework documentation entry for the *System.Globalization.CultureInfo* class.

`<httpRuntime>`

The *<httpRuntime>* element controls several aspects of the ASP.NET HTTP Runtime engine. The *<httpRuntime>* element has the following syntax:

```
<httpRuntime
    appRequestQueueLimit="number of requests"
    executionTimeout="seconds"
    maxRequestLength="kbytes"
    minLocalRequestFreeThreads="number of threads"
    minFreeThreads="number of threads"
    useFullyQualifiedRedirectUrl="true|false" />
```

Fully Qualified vs. Relative URLs

There are two basic types of URLs used for creating hyperlinks in Web pages: fully qualified URLs and relative URLs. Fully qualified URLs, also known as absolute URLs, contain all of the information necessary for the browser (or other client program) to locate the resource named in the URL. This includes the protocol moniker being used (*ftp://*, *http://*, *https://*, etc.), the server's domain name or IP address (on local Windows networks, the machine name may also be used), and the path to the resource. A typical fully qualified URL would look like the following:

http://localhost/quickstart/aspplus/default.aspx

Relative URLs provide only the information necessary to locate a resource relative to the current document (known as document relative) or current server or domain (known as root relative). A document relative URL used to link to the previously referenced page from another page in the same virtual directory would look like the following:

default.aspx

A root relative URL would look like the following:

/quickstart/aspplus/default.aspx

Because some controls or applications may not know how to use relative URLs, there may be times when you need to use a fully qualified URL.

For information on *<httpRuntime>* element attributes, consult the following table.

<httpRuntime> Element Attributes		
Attribute	**Description**	**Options**
appRequestQueueLimit	Specifies the number of requests that ASP.NET will queue when no threads are available to process them, before returning a "503 - Server Too Busy" error message.	Increasing this value may result in unacceptably long wait times for users, so use caution and test carefully when making adjustments to this value. The default is *100*.
executionTimeout	Determines amount of time, in seconds, that an ASP.NET request may continue executing before being shut down.	This attribute, which is similar to classic ASP's *Server.ScriptTimeout* property, can be used to prevent hung or long-running requests from consuming more resources than necessary. This attribute should be set somewhere higher than the average time it takes to process requests, but not so high as to allow processor overutilization by errant or inefficient pages. The default is *90 seconds*.
maxRequestLength	Determines maximum size of incoming file uploads, in kilobytes.	This attribute is designed to help prevent denial of service attacks mounted by uploading large files to a server. Set it to the smallest size feasible for files you expect your users to upload. The default is *4,096 kbytes*.
minFreeThreads	Configures the minimum number of threads ASP.NET will keep free for processing new requests.	The default is *8*.

| <httpRuntime> Element Attributes | | |
Attribute	Description	Options
minLocalRequestFreeThreads	Configures the minimum number of threads ASP.NET will keep free for processing requests coming from the local machine. Maintaining these free threads can help prevent deadlocks in multi-threaded processing.	The default is *4*.
useFullyQualifiedRedirectUrl	Determines whether relative or fully qualified URLs are used for client-side redirects. This attribute allows developers to support certain mobile controls that require fully qualified URLs for client-side redirects.	*true* Client-side redirects are fully qualified. *false* Client-side redirects are relative. The default is *true*.

<compilation>

With ten attributes and two child elements, the *<compilation>* element is one of the more extensive ASP.NET configuration elements and contains settings that determine how ASP.NET compiles code in your Web applications and Web Services. The settings you'll see most frequently are the *debug* and *defaultLanguage* attributes, which are placed in your application's Web.config file by default when you're using Visual Studio .NET. Other settings, such as the *<assemblies>* and *<namespaces>* child elements, are equally important but usually are inherited from the settings in Machine.config, unless overridden by a developer.

The *<compilation>* element has the following syntax:

```
<compilation
   batch="true|false"
   batchTimeout="seconds"
   debug="true|false"
   defaultLanguage="language"
   explicit="true|false"
   maxBatchSize="number of pages"
   maxBatchGeneratedFileSize="kbytes"
   numRecompilesBeforeAppRestart="number"
```

```
strict="true|false"
tempdirectory="directory" >

<compilers>
  <compiler
    extension="file extension"
    language="language"
    compilerOptions="compiler options"
    type=".NET type"
    warningLevel="number" />
</compilers>

<assemblies>
  <add assembly="assembly name" />
  <remove assembly="assembly name" />
  <clear />
</assemblies>

</compilation>
```

For information on *<compilation>* element attributes, consult the following table.

<compilation> Element Attributes			
Element	**Attribute**	**Description**	**Options**
<compilation>		Determines compiler options for the application. Supports the *<compilers>* and *<assemblies>* child elements.	
	batch	Determines whether the application supports batch compilation of ASP.NET pages. When batch compilation is enabled, ASP.NET will attempt to compile all ASP.NET pages within the application directory on the first request. This prevents later page requests from having to be compiled on request.	*true* Batch compilation is supported. *false* Pages will be compiled one by one as they are requested. The default is *true*.

Configuring Apps 7

`<compilation>` Element Attributes *(continued)*			
Element	**Attribute**	**Description**	**Options**
	batchTimeout	Determines the amount of time, in seconds, before timeout of batch compilation. If the timeout is exceeded, the compiler will switch to per-request compilation mode.	This setting will vary depending on the size of an application, and the amount of time you are willing to allow for batch compilation. The default is *15 seconds*.
	debug	Determines whether debug information is included in compiled assemblies for ASP.NET pages and Web Services. This attribute should always be set to *false* in a production application because debug assemblies are larger and don't perform as well as release-type assemblies.	*true* Assemblies are compiled with debug info. *false* Assemblies are compiled without debug info. The default is *false*.
	defaultLanguage	Determines the language(s) to be used during dynamic compilation.	This attribute is the name of a language, as specified by one of the *<compiler>* child elements. The default is *vb*.
	explicit	Determines whether ASP.NET compiles pages written in Visual Basic .NET using the Visual Basic *Option Explicit* compiler option (which forces explicit declaration of variables). Enabling this setting makes it easier to locate and fix common problems, such as misspelled variable names, that otherwise wouldn't be discovered until runtime.	*true* Enabled. *false* Disabled. The default is *true*.

(continued)

Element	Attribute	Description	Options
\<compilation\> Element Attributes *(continued)*			
	numRecompiles BeforeApp Restart	Determines how many times application resources can be dynamically recompiled before the application is automatically restarted. This setting can be configured at the application level and at the global level through Machine.config.	The default is *15*.
	strict	Determines whether ASP.NET compiles pages written in Visual Basic .NET using the Visual Basic *Option Strict* compiler option (which prevents type conversions that would result in data loss, late binding, and other error-prone coding habits) to your .aspx files before compilation.	*true* Enabled. *false* Disabled. It's a good practice to turn this on, through either Machine.config or Web.config, through the Visual Studio .NET properties dialog for the project (the Build choice under Common Properties), or by adding *Option Strict* to the page or module you're working on. This makes it easier to fix common problems, such as overflows or rounding errors, that otherwise wouldn't be discovered until runtime. The default is *false*.
	tempDirectory	Determines the directory in which the temporary ASP.NET files resulting from dynamic compilation will reside.	Any valid directory.
\<compilers\>		Child element containing individual *\<compiler\>* child elements.	

<compilation> Element Attributes *(continued)*			
Element	**Attribute**	**Description**	**Options**
<compiler>		Determines options for specific language compilers. One or more of these child elements may be contained within the *<compilers>* element.	
	extension	Determines the file extension used by dynamically compiled code-behind modules for a specific compiler. The extensions for the three most commonly used ASP.NET languages (Visual Basic .NET, C#, and JScript .NET) are included in Machine.config, so you don't need to set them yourself unless you want to add additional extensions for one of these languages.	String representing the file extension (.vb, .cs, etc.). Multiple extensions should be delimited by semicolons. This setting should match the language specified in the language attribute. This attribute is required.
	language	Determines the list of language names to be handled by a specific compiler. The names for the three most commonly used ASP.NET languages (Visual Basic.NET, C#, and JScript .NET) are included in Machine.config, so you don't need to set them yourself unless you want to add additional names for one of these languages.	String representing the language name (*vb;visualbasic; vbscript*). Multiple names should be delimited by semicolons. This setting should match the language specified in the *extension* attribute. This attribute is required.
	compilerOptions	Determines any compiler-specific options to be passed along during compilation.	Consult the .NET Framework SDK documentation to determine available options.

(continued)

<compilation> Element Attributes *(continued)*			
Element	**Attribute**	**Description**	**Options**
	type	Determines which .NET class and/or assembly is used to compile resources using the language specified in the language attribute, or with the extension in the extension attribute. The types for the three most commonly used ASP.NET languages (Visual Basic .NET, C#, and JScript .NET) are included in Machine.config, so you don't need to set them yourself unless you want to modify the type for one of these languages (not recommended).	This attribute is a comma-delimited list that can include the class name, assembly name, and version information. The Machine.config file contains good examples of the syntax for this attribute. This attribute is required.
	warningLevel	Determines the compiler warning levels, which determine the types of warning messages (and the severity) that are emitted by the compiler.	The value for this attribute depends on the language compiler being configured. The default for C# is *1*.
<assemblies>		Child element containing one or more of the *<add/>*, *<remove/>*, or *<clear/>* child elements.	The child elements of the *<assemblies>* element are used to add references to assemblies to be used during compilation. ASP.NET automatically links in the assemblies specified here during dynamic compilation.
<clear>		Specifies that all current or inherited assembly references should be removed.	

<compilation> Element Attributes *(continued)*			
Element	**Attribute**	**Description**	**Options**
<add>	*assembly*	Specifies an assembly, by its assembly name, to be referenced during dynamic compilation.	This setting should be the assembly name, not the DLL name, of the desired assembly. You can also use the wildcard * to add all assemblies from the application's private assembly cache (by default, in the bin subdirectory).
<remove>	*assembly*	Specifies an assembly, by its assembly name, to be removed from use during dynamic compilation.	The assembly name used must match exactly the name of an assembly added by a previous *add* directive (for example, from a parent Web.config). You may not use wildcards for this attribute.

<pages>

The *<pages>* element allows you to set the defaults for the page-level attributes that are more commonly associated with the attributes of the @ *Page* ASP.NET directive. The settings in this element apply to all pages for which specific attributes of the @ *Page* directive do not appear. If these attributes do appear in an ASP.NET page, their settings will override those in either the Machine.config or Web.config configuration files. As such, the *<pages>* element provides a great way of configuring the *SessionState*, *ViewState*, and other settings at an application or subfolder level, giving you a great deal of control over your application.

The *<pages>* element has the following syntax:

```
<pages
    autoEventWireup="true|false"
    buffer="true|false"
```

```
enableSessionState="true|false|ReadOnly"
enableViewState="true|false"
enableViewStateMac="true|false"
pageBaseType="typename, assembly"
smartNavigation="true|false"
userControlBaseType="typename" />
```

For information on *<page>* element attributes, consult the following table.

<page> Element Attributes

Attribute	Description	Options
autoEventWireup	Determines whether support for page events (*Page_Load*, etc.) is automatically provided in an application's ASP.NET pages.	*true* Event support is provided automatically. *false* Event support is not provided. Event handlers must be manually wired by developers. The default is *true*.
buffer	Determines whether responses are buffered before being sent to the client. This setting is analogous to the classic ASP *Response.Buffer* property.	*true* Buffering is enabled. Page output will be buffered until the page is completely processed, or until either the *End* or *Flush* method of the *HTTPResponse* class is called. *false* Buffering is not enabled. Page output is sent to the client as it is rendered. The default is *true*.
pageBaseType	Provides the type or assembly name of a class from which ASP.NET pages should inherit. In the absence of this attribute, the default is to inherit from the *Page* class of the *System.Web.UI* namespace).	You can use this attribute to provide a class derived from the *Page* class if you want to provide additional functionality not included in the base *Page* class. This is a simple yet powerful way to extend ASP.NET applications.

Configuring Apps 7

\<page\> Element Attributes *(continued)*

Attribute	Description	Options
userControlBaseType	Provides the type or assembly name of a class from which ASP.NET User Controls (.ascx files) should inherit. In the absence of this attribute, the default is to inherit from the *UserControl* class of the *System.Web.UI* namespace.	
enableSessionState	Determines whether a new session is created by default for the current user by an ASP.NET page. Note that if the user already has a session from a prior page in which this attribute is set to *false*, this attribute will not affect that session. However, if it's set to *ReadOnly*, it will prevent the page from modifying values set in previous pages.	*true* If the user does not have a current session when he requests a page, a new session will be created for him. *false* If the user does not have a current session, one will not be created. If the user does have a session, it will not be affected, but its values cannot be accessed from pages where this attribute is *false*. *ReadOnly* If the user does not have a current session, one will not be created. If the user does have a session, its values may be read from within a page where this attribute has been set to *ReadOnly*, but they may not be modified. The default is *true*.
enableViewState	Determines whether *ViewState* (the method by which ASP.NET Server Controls store their state between page requests) is enabled.	*true* *ViewState* is enabled. Server Controls will maintain their values from one request to the next. *false* *ViewState* is not enabled. Server control state will be reset with each request.

(continued)

\<page\> Element Attributes *(continued)*		
Attribute	**Description**	**Options**
enableViewStateMac	Determines whether a Machine Authentication Check (MAC) is performed on *ViewState* data when a Web Form is posted back to the server. The MAC can help identify client-side tampering with the *ViewState* hidden field.	*true* MAC is enabled for *ViewState*. *false* MAC is not enabled for *ViewState*.

\<customErrors\>

The *\<customErrors\>* element allows you to customize how your ASP.NET application responds to error conditions. In this element, you can specify whether the raw error messages generated by ASP.NET should be visible to local or remote clients, or whether to redirect the client to either a custom error page or a page specific to the error that occurred (based on the status code of the error). The *\<customErrors\>* element supports one child element, *\<error\>*, and has the following syntax:

```
<customErrors
    defaultRedirect="url"
    mode="on|off|RemoteOnly">
    <error
        redirect="url"
        statusCode="status code"/>
</customErrors>
```

For information on *\<customErrors\>* element attributes, consult the following table.

\<customErrors\> Element Attributes			
Element	**Attribute**	**Description**	**Options**
\<customErrors\>		Determines how ASP.NET errors are handled.	
	defaultRedirect	Determines the page to which a user is redirected if an error occurs.	The page to which this URL points can be either an .aspx page, in which you attempt to clean up or recover from the error, or a static HTML page, to inform the user of the error and offer guidance on what to do.

`<customErrors>` Element Attributes *(continued)*			
Element	**Attribute**	**Description**	**Options**
	mode	Determines whether raw ASP.NET error messages are sent to the client.	*On* Custom errors are enabled. When an error occurs, the client, whether on the local Web server or remote, will be redirected to the custom error page specified by the *defaultRedirect* attribute (or to a page specified in an *<error>* child element). *Off* Custom errors are not enabled. When an error occurs, the client will see the error page generated by ASP.NET. Note that depending on how your application is designed, this can expose proprietary information to clients, so you should rarely use this setting. *RemoteOnly* Custom errors are enabled for remote clients. When an error occurs, remote clients will be redirected to a custom error page, while clients on the local Web server will see the error page generated by ASP.NET. This allows developers to track down errors without having clients see raw error pages.
<error>		Determines redirect page for a specific error type, based on the HTTP status code for the error.	Adding *<error>* tags provides finer-grained control over how errors are handled.
	redirect	Determines the page to which a user is redirected if an error of the type specified in the *statusCode* attribute occurs.	

(continued)

<customErrors> Element Attributes *(continued)*			
Element	**Attribute**	**Description**	**Options**
	statusCode	Determines the HTTP status code (*404-Not Found*, etc.) that is handled by this *<error>* child element.	

<authentication>

The *<authentication>* element controls configuration of authentication in ASP.NET. You can choose from one of three authentication methods, and you can set appropriate parameters for the method you choose or choose no authentication at all. The *<authentication>* element supports two child elements, *<forms>* and *<passport>*. Additionally, the *<forms>* element supports one child element, *<credentials>*, which in turn supports one child element, *<user>*, as shown in the following example:

```
<authentication mode="Windows|Forms|Passport|None">

    <forms
        loginUrl="url"
        name="name"
        path="/"
        protection="All|None|Encryption|Validation"
        timeout="number">

        <credentials passwordFormat="Clear|MD5|SHA1">
            <user name="username" password="password" />
        </credentials>

    </forms>

    <passport redirectUrl="url" />

</authentication>
```

For information on *<authentication>* element attributes, consult the following table.

<authentication> Element Attributes

Element	Attribute	Description	Options
<authentication>		Determines how ASP.NET authentication is handled.	
	mode	Determines the authentication mode to be used. This will be discussed in greater detail in Chapter 8.	*Windows* ASP.NET will use Windows authentication by default. Works with IIS' Basic, Digest, NTLM, or Certificate-based authentication methods. *Forms* ASP.NET will use Forms-based authentication, which provides basic support for "roll-your-own" security scenarios, by default. *Passport* ASP.NET will use Microsoft Passport as the default authentication method. *None* No authentication will be performed by ASP.NET.
<forms>		Determines the parameters associated with Forms-based authentication.	
	loginUrl	Determines the URL where a user is redirected if he doesn't have a valid authentication cookie.	This can be any page in your ASP.NET application that allows a user to log in. The default is *login.aspx*.
	name	Determines the name of the cookie used for authenticating a user.	Default is *.ASPXAUTH*.

(continued)

<authentication> Element Attributes *(continued)*			
Element	**Attribute**	**Description**	**Options**
	path	Determines the path to set for the authentication cookie.	Default is /. This is to prevent the possibility of missing cookies due to browser case sensitivity with respect to URL paths and cookies.
	protection	Determines the methods used to protect the authentication cookie from being compromised. Your choice of which method to use, or whether to use any at all, will depend on your security needs vs. the amount of resources you're willing to devote to security. Generally, the higher the level of security, the greater the performance overhead.	*All* (default) Both encryption and data validation will be used to protect the cookie. This is the recommended setting. *Encryption* The authentication cookie will be encrypted, but will not be validated. This leaves the cookie vulnerable to certain types of attacks. *Validation* The authentication cookie's contents will be validated to ensure that they haven't been changed between the browser and the server. *None* Neither encryption nor validation are used. Not recommended.
	timeout	Determines the amount of time, in minutes, until the authentication cookie expires.	Default is *30*. You should set this value to the minimum amount that will allow users to use your site effectively. If you use persistent cookies with forms authentication, they will not time out.

Element	Attribute	Description	Options
<authentication> Element Attributes *(continued)*			
<credentials>		In conjunction with the *<user>* child element, allows you to define credentials to authenticate against within a configuration file.	If you use this method to store credentials in a Web.config file within your application scope, and your application is compromised, it may be possible for intruders to gain the passwords stored there, even if they're encrypted. Remember that no encryption method is perfect.
	passwordFormat	Determines the encryption used for stored passwords.	*Clear* No encryption is used. Not recommended. *MD5* Passwords are encrypted using the MD5 hash algorithm. *SHA1* Passwords are encrypted using the SHA1 hash algorithm.
<user>		Determines the username and password of a single user. Use one *<user>* child element for each set of credentials you want to store in the configuration file.	
	name	Specifies the username of the user to authenticate against.	

(continued)

Configuring Apps

7

<authentication> Element Attributes *(continued)*			
Element	**Attribute**	**Description**	**Options**
	password	Specifies the password of the user to authenticate against.	This value should be an encrypted version of the password created with the hash algorighm specified by the *passwordFormat* attribute of the *<credentials>* tag.
<passport>		Child element used to set the parameters for Microsoft Passport-based authentication.	
	redirectUrl	Determines the URL where the user will be redirected if he has not been authenticated.	

<identity>

By default, requests made by ASP.NET applications for resources requiring authentication, such as files secured by NT Access Controls Lists (ACLs), are made in the context of either the IUSR_MACHINENAME or IWAM_MACHINENAME accounts, depending on whether the application is configured to run in-process or out-of-process relative to IIS. The *<identity>* element allows ASP.NET applications to use impersonation, in which an application takes on the security context of the user making a request, or of a specified account. The *<identity>* element has the following syntax:

```
<identity
    impersonate="true|false"
    userName="username"
    password="password" />
```

For information on *<identity>* element attributes, consult the following table.

<identity> Element Attributes		
Attribute	**Description**	**Options**
impersonate	Determines whether ASP.NET applications will use impersonation.	*true* Enables impersonation of security accounts by ASP.NET applications. *false* Disables impersonation of security accounts by ASP.NET applications.
userName	Specifies a user account that the affected ASP.NET application will impersonate.	Any valid user account. You should ensure that the account that you choose has access to only the desired resources. For example, as a rule, it is not a good idea to have an ASP.NET application impersonate an account in the Administrators group. If omitted, ASP.NET will impersonate the account of the logged on user (as provided by IIS).
password	Specifies the password for the account named in the *userName* attribute.	

<authorization>

The *<authorization>* element lets you specify which accounts or roles (groups) are authorized to access resources within the scope of the configuration file. The *<authorization>* element supports two child elements, *<allow>* and *<deny>*, each of which has three attributes. The *<authorization>* element has the following syntax:

```
<authorization>
   <allow
      users="userlist"
      roles="rolelist"
      verbs="verblist" />
   <deny
      users="userlist"
      roles="rolelist"
      verbs="verblist" />
</authorization>
```

For information on *<authorization>* element attributes, consult the following table.

<authorization> Element Attributes			
Element	**Attribute**	**Description**	**Options**
<authorization>		Determines authorization settings for an application or directory. Contains one or more *<allow>* or *<deny>* child elements.	
<allow>		Allows access to resources based on user account, group membership, or HTTP request method.	
	users	List of users (NT user accounts) granted access to the resource(s).	This attribute takes a comma-delimited list. Access to anonymous users is allowed using the *?* wildcard, and access to everyone is allowed using the * wildcard.
	roles	List of roles (NT groups) granted access to the resource(s).	This attribute takes a comma-delimited list.
	verbs	List of HTTP verbs (*GET*, *POST*, etc.) granted access to the resource(s).	This attribute takes a comma-delimited list. Verbs available are *GET*, *HEAD*, *POST*, and *DEBUG*.
<deny>		Denies access to resources based on user account, group membership, or HTTP request method.	
	users	List of users (NT user accounts) denied access to the resource(s).	This attribute takes a comma-delimited list. Access to anonymous users is denied using the *?* wildcard, and access to everyone is denied using the * wildcard.

<authorization> Element Attributes			
Element	**Attribute**	**Description**	**Options**
	roles	List of roles (NT groups) denied access to the resource(s).	This attribute takes a comma-delimited list.
	verbs	List of HTTP verbs (*GET, POST*, etc.) denied access to the resource(s).	This attribute takes a comma-delimited list. Verbs available are *GET, HEAD, POST*, and *DEBUG*.

<machineKey>

The *<machineKey>* element allows you to specify the keys used for encryption and decryption of cookie data in Forms-based authentication. This element can be used at the machine level through Machine.config, as well as at the site and application levels through Web.config files, but it may not be used at the sub-directory level. The *<machineKey>* element has the following syntax:

```
<machineKey
    decryptionKey="autogenerate|value"
    validation="autogenerate|value"
    validationKey="3DES|MD5|SHA1" />
```

For information on *<machineKey>* element attributes, consult the following table.

<machineKey> Element Attributes		
Attribute	**Description**	**Options**
decryptionKey	Determines whether the decryption key to be used is auto-generated, or specifies a key value to be used.	*autogenerate* (default) ASP.NET will generate a random key for decryption. *value* This represents a string of characters (minimum 40, maximum 128) to be used as a decryption key. Note that 128 characters is the recommended length. For shorter-length keys, you should ensure that the key is randomly generated. This setting is necessary in Web farms to ensure that all servers are using the same keys, providing transparent user access while still taking advantage of encryption.

(continued)

Configuring Apps

<machineKey> Element Attributes *(continued)*		
Attribute	**Description**	**Options**
validation	Determines the type of encryption to be used by ASP.NET.	*3DES* Data is encrypted using Triple-DES (3DES) encryption. *MD5* Data is encrypted using the MD5 hash algorithm. *SHA1* (default) Data is encrypted using the SHA1 hash algorithm.
validationKey	Determines whether the validation key to be used is autogenerated, or specifies a key value to be used.	*autogenerate* (default) ASP.NET will generate a random key for validation. *value* This represents a string of characters (minimum 40, maximum 128) to be used as a validation key. Note that 128 characters is the recommended length. For shorter-length keys, it is recommended to ensure that the key is randomly generated. This setting is necessary in Web farms to ensure that all servers are using the same keys, providing transparent user access while still taking advantage of encryption.

<securityPolicy>

The *<securityPolicy>* element allows you to specify one of several named security policies, or a custom policy, for code-access security based on the *name* and *policyFile* attributes of its *<trustLevel>* child element. The *<trust>* element, described in the next section, specifies which of the named policies is implemented for a given site or application. The *<securityPolicy>* element supports one child element, *<trustLevel>*, with two attributes, and has the following syntax:

```
<securityPolicy>
   <trustLevel
      name="value"
      policyFile="value" />
</securityPolicy>
```

For information on *<securityPolicy>* element attributes, consult the following table.

<securityPolicy> Element Attributes			
Element	**Attribute**	**Description**	**Options**
<securityPolicy>		Determines the available named security policies for sites and/or applications.	
<trustLevel>		Each *<trustLevel>* child element sets up an available named policy based on its *name* and *policyFile* attributes.	
	name	Specifies the name to use for the policy.	The name specified by this attribute is also used by the *<trust>* element to implement the named policy.
	policyFile	Specifies the file name of the file that contains the code-access security settings to be used under the named policy.	The file name specified by this attribute is relative to the location of the Machine.config file.

<trust>

The *<trust>* element is used to implement one of the named security policies created by the *<securityPolicy>* element. This element can be used at the machine level through Machine.config, as well as at the site and application levels through Web.config files. However, it can't be used at the subdirectory level. The *<trust>* element has the following syntax:

```
<trust
    level="Full|High|Low|None|custom name"
    originUrl="url" />
```

For information on *<trust>* element attributes, consult the following table.

`<trust>` Element Attributes		
Attribute	**Description**	**Options**
level	Determines the applicable trust level, based on a named security policy.	*Full* Code-access security is based on the *Full* named policy set up by default in Machine.config. *High* Code-access security is based on the *High* named policy set up by default in Machine.config. *Low* Code-access security is based on the *Low* named policy set up by default in Machine.config. *None* Code-access security is based on the *None* named policy set up by default in Machine.config. *custom name* Code-access security is based on a custom named policy set up in either Machine.config or a Web.config file at the site or application level.
originUrl	Specifies the origin URL for an application.	*Optional* This attribute can be used to support permissions for Socket and WebRequest requests that allow connectivity to the origin host.

`<sessionState>`

The *<sessionState>* element is used to configure the Session State HttpModule, including the type of state management to be used (in-process, out-of-process, or SQL Server), the default session timeout, and whether or not to use cookies for associating requests with user sessions. The *<sessionState>* element has the following syntax:

```
<sessionState
    connectionString="IP address:port number"
    cookieless="true|false"
    mode="Off|Inproc|StateServer|SQLServer"
    sqlConnectionString="sql connection string"
    timeout="number" />
```

For information on *<sessionState>* element attributes, consult the following table.

<sessionState> Element Attributes		
Attribute	**Description**	**Options**
connectionString	Specifies the server and port number to connect to when the mode attribute is set to *StateServer*.	This attribute is required when the mode is set to *StateServer*. The default is *tcpip=127.0.0.1:42424*.
cookieless	Determines whether user sessions are mapped to requests by using cookies or by adding a user's *SessionID* to the URL string for requests by that user.	*true* SessionIDs are added to request URLs, and cookies are not used. *false* Cookies are used to map user requests to sessions. The default is *false*.
mode	Determines the type of session state management that applications will use.	*Off* Session state is disabled. *Inproc* Session state is stored in-process with the application, as in classic ASP. *StateServer* Session state is managed by an out-of-process NT Service, allowing multiple servers in a Web farm to share a single state store. *SQLServer* Session state is managed by SQL Server database, allowing multiple servers in a Web farm to share a single state store. This mode has the added advantage of providing persistent state storage in the event of a Web server crash. The default is *InProc*.
sqlConnectionString	Specifies the connection string used to connect to a SQL Server database where state information is stored.	This attribute is required when the mode is set to *SQLServer*.
timeout	Specifies the amount of time, in minutes, before the user's session expires.	Like the classic ASP *Session.Timeout* property, this attribute uses sliding expiration. Each request by the user resets the amount of time before his session expires. The default is *20 minutes*.

Configuring Apps

\<httpHandlers\>

The *\<httpHandlers\>* element allows you to assign requests of certain types or for certain resources to specific handler classes. For example, in Machine.config, the handling of ASP.NET pages (requests with the .aspx extension) is assigned to the *System.Web.UI.PageHandlerFactory* class. The *\<httpHandlers\>* element can also be used to prevent HTTP access to certain types of files by assigning them to the *System.Web.HttpForbiddenHandler* class, as is done by default for configuration files (*.config) and source files (*.vb and *.cs, for example).

The *\<httpHandlers\>* element supports three child elements, *\<add\>*, *\<remove\>*, and *\<clear\>*, and has the following syntax:

```
<httpHandlers>
    <add
        path="path"
        type="type, assembly name"
        validate="true|false"
        verb="verblist" />
    <remove
        path="path"
        verb="verblist" />
    <clear />
</httpHandlers>
```

For information on *\<httpHandlers\>* element attributes, consult the following table.

\<httpHandlers\> Element Attribute			
Element	**Attribute**	**Description**	**Options**
\<httpHandlers\>		Determines the assignment of requests to *httpHandlers* for ASP.NET applications.	
\<add\>		Each *\<add\>* child element maps a specific type of request to a given *httpHandler*.	

<httpHandlers> Element Attribute			
Element	**Attribute**	**Description**	**Options**
	path	Specifies the URL path this *httpHandler* will handle.	This can be a single URL, as in the case of the default mapping of the *trace.axd* URL to *System.Web.Handlers.TraceHandler*, or may use a wildcard to specify that the *httpHandler* should handle all requests of a given type (such as *.aspx or *.asmx).
	type	Specifies the .NET class that should handle the requests specified by the *path* and *verb* attributes.	This is a string containing a comma-separated list with the class name and other information, such as version and public key, that enables ASP.NET to locate the class in either the application's bin directory or the global assembly cache.
	verb	Specifies the HTTP verbs for which the *httpHandler* will handle requests.	Comma-separated list of verbs (*GET*, *POST*) or a wildcard (such as *, which specifies that all verbs should be handled).
<remove>		Removes an *httpHandler* mapping, based on the *path* and *verb* attributes specified.	
	path	Specifies path of the *httpHandler* to be removed.	This attribute must exactly match the path attribute of an *httpHandler* added by a previous *<add>* child element.
	verb	Specifies verb(s) of the *httpHandler* to be removed.	This attribute must exactly match the verb attribute of an *httpHandler* added by a previous *<add>* child element.
<clear>		Removes all *httpHandler* mappings, either those configured by the current file or those inherited from parent configuration files.	

Configuring Apps

\<httpModules>

HttpModules are classes that implement the *IHttpModule* interface and are used to provide functionality to ASP.NET applications. For example, by default, the Machine.config file adds *HttpModules* for output caching, session-state management, authentication, and authorization. The *\<httpModules>* element allows you to add *HttpModules* to ASP.NET applications.

The *\<httpModules>* element supports three child elements, *\<add>*, *\<remove>*, and *\<clear>*, and has the following syntax:

```
<httpModules>
    <add
        name="name"
        type="type\ assembly name" />
    <remove
        name="name"
    <clear />
</httpModules>
```

For information on *\<httpModules>* element attributes, consult the following table.

\<httpModules> Element Attributes			
Element	**Attribute**	**Description**	**Options**
\<httpModules>		Determines the *httpModules* available for ASP.NET applications within the scope of the configuration file.	
\<add>		Each *\<add>* child element adds a specified *httpModule*.	
	name	Specifies a name that can be used by ASP.NET applications to refer to the module identified by the *type* attribute.	

<httpModules> Element Attributes *(continued)*			
Element	**Attribute**	**Description**	**Options**
	type	Specifies the .NET class that implements the desired *httpModule*.	This is a string containing a comma-separated list with the class name and other information, such as version and public key, that enables ASP.NET to locate the class in either the application's bin directory or the global assembly cache.
<remove>		Removes an *httpModule*, based on the *name* and *type* attributes specified.	
	name	Specifies the name of the *httpModule* to remove.	This attribute must exactly match the *name* attribute of an *httpModule* added by a previous *<add>* child element.
<clear>		Removes all *httpModules*, either those configured by the current file or those inherited from parent configuration files.	

<processModel>

The *<processModel>* element configures settings related to how ASP.NET applications run, and it provides access to a number of features geared towards improving the availability of applications. These include automatic restart (which can be configured based on elapsed time or number of requests), allowed memory size, and Web garden, in which applications can be associated with specific processors in a multiprocessor machine. Note that when ASP.NET is running under IIS 6.0 in native mode, the settings in the *<processModel>* element are ignored in favor of the settings configured by the IIS administrative UI.

The *<processModel>* element has the following syntax:

```
<processModel
    clientConnectedCheck="time"
    comAuthenticationLevel="Default|None|Connect|Call|Pkt|
        PktIntegrity|PktPrivacy"
    comImpersonationLevel="Default|Anonymous|Identify|Impersonate|
        Delegate"
    cpuMask="number"
    enable="true|false"
    idleTimeout="time"
    logLevel="loglevel"
    maxIoThreads="number"
    maxWorkerThreads="number"
    memoryLimit="number"
    pingFrequency="hh:mm:ss"
    pingTimeout="hh:mm:ss"
    requestLimit="number"
    requestQueueLimit="number"
    responseDeadlockInterval="Infinite|hh:mm:ss"
    responseRestartDeadlockInterval="Infinite|hh:mm:ss"
    restartQueueLimit="number"
    serverErrorMessageFile="filename"
    shutdownTimeout="time"
    timeout="time"
    webGarden="true|false"
    username="user name"
    password="password" />
```

For information on *<processModel>* element attributes, consult the following table.

<processModel> Element Attributes		
Attribute	**Description**	**Options**
clientConnectedCheck	Determines the frequency with which ASP.NET checks if the client is still connected while a request is queued.	This attribute takes a time value in the format *hrs:min:sec*. The default is *0:00:05*. This attribute can be useful for preventing processor resources from being wasted on queued requests for which the client has disconnected.

\<processModel\> Element Attributes *(continued)*

Attribute	Description	Options
comAuthenticationLevel	Specifies the DCOM authentication level.	*Default* DCOM will determine authentication level based on its normal security negotiation algorithm. *None* No authentication. *Connect* DCOM authenticates the credentials of the client at the time the connection is established. *Call* DCOM authenticates the credentials of the client with each remote procedure call. *Pkt* DCOM authenticates that all received data is coming from the expected client. *PktIntegrity* Same as *Pkt*, but also verifies that data has not been modified in transport. *PktPrivacy* Same as *PktIntegrity*, but adds encryption. The default value is *Connect*.
comImpersonationLevel	Specifies the COM authentication level.	*Anonymous* Client is anonymous. Not supported in the current release. *Identify* Server can obtain the client's identity and impersonate the client for ACL checking, but cannot access system objects using the client's identity.

(continued)

<processModel> Element Attributes (continued)

Attribute	Description	Options
		Impersonate Allows the server to impersonate the client and access system resources using the client's security context, but this context can only be passed across a single machine boundary.
		Delegate Same as *Impersonate*, but the impersonation token may be passed across multiple machine boundaries.
cpuMask	Specifies the processors (on a multiprocessor server) that are allowed to run the ASP.NET application. This attribute works with the *webGarden* attribute. When *webGarden* is set to *true*, *cpuMask* determines the eligible processors for the application.	The default is *0xffffffff*.
enable	Enables or disables the *processModel* settings for ASP.NET applications.	*true* *processModel* settings are enabled. *false* *processModel* settings are disabled.
idleTimeout	Determines the amount of time, in minutes, before ASP.NET shuts down an inactive worker process.	Default is *Infinite*, in which case the process will not be shut down when idle.

<processModel> Element Attributes *(continued)*		
Attribute	**Description**	**Options**
logLevel	Specifies the types of process events that will be written to the event log.	*All* All process events are logged. *Errors* Only unexpected shutdowns, memory limit shutdowns, and deadlock shutdowns are logged. *None* No events are logged. The default is *Errors*.
maxIoThreads	Specifies the maximum number of IO threads per CPU.	Any value from *5* to *100* is valid. The default is *25*.
maxWorkerThreads	Specifies the maximum number of worker threads per CPU.	Any value from *5* to *100* is valid. The default is *25*.
memoryLimit	Determines the maximum allowable memory size for an ASP.NET application.	This attribute takes a number representing the percentage of the total system memory that the application's worker processes can consume. If this value is exceeded, ASP.NET will launch a new process, reassign existing requests to it, and then shut down the old process.
pingFrequency	Determines how often the ASP.NET ISAPI extension pings the worker process to see if it is running. If the process does not respond in the interval specified by *pingTimeout*, the worker process will be restarted.	The format of this value is *hh:mm:ss*. The default is *30 seconds*.

(continued)

`<processModel>` Element Attributes *(continued)*

Attribute	Description	Options
pingTimeout	Determines the time interval after which an unresponsive worker process is restarted.	The format of this value is *hh:mm:ss*. The default is *5 seconds*.
responseDeadlockInterval	Determines the time interval after which the process will be restarted when there are queued requests, and no responses have been generated for this interval.	The format of this value is *hh:mm:ss*. The default is *3 minutes*.
responseRestartDeadlockInterval	Determines the time interval that must elapse before a second restart to cure a deadlock (as specified by *responseDeadlockInterval*) can occur.	The format of this value is *hh:mm:ss*. The default is *9 minutes*.
requestLimit	Determines the number of requests an application can fulfill before ASP.NET launches a new worker process and shuts down the old one.	Default is *Infinite*, in which case the process will not be shut down, regardless of the number of requests. This setting can be used to restart the application after a given number of requests, and it can help deal with problems such as memory leaks in legacy COM components used by an application or blocked processes.
requestQueueLimit	Determines the number of requests that may be queued before ASP.NET returns the "503 - Server Too Busy" status error.	Default is *5000*.

\<processModel> Element Attributes *(continued)*		
Attribute	**Description**	**Options**
restartQueueLimit	Specifies the number of requests that are kept in the queue while the process is restarting.	Default is *10*.
serverErrorMessageFile	Provides custom message for *Server Unavailable* error condition.	Path and file name to the desired file. If omitted, the default *Server Unavailable* message is used.
shutdownTimeout	Determines the amount of time that an ASP.NET worker process is given to shut itself down.	This attribute takes a time value in the format *hrs:min:sec*. If the time specified by this attribute is exceeded, ASP.NET will force the shutdown of the worker process. The default is *0:00:05*.
timeout	Determines the amount of time, in minutes, before ASP.NET launches a new worker process and shuts down the old one.	This setting can be used to restart the application after a given period of time, and it can help deal with problems such as memory leaks in legacy COM components used by an application or blocked processes.
webGarden	Determines whether Web gardening is enabled.	*true* Web gardening is enabled. *false* Web gardening is disabled.
password	Specifies a password for the user account specified in the *username* attribute.	Default is *autogenerate*, which can be used with either the *SYSTEM* or *MACHINE* special accounts.

(continued)

`<processModel>` Element Attributes *(continued)*		
Attribute	**Description**	**Options**
username	Determines the identity under which ASP.NET worker processes are run.	Default is *MACHINE*, which runs worker processes as an unprivileged ASP.NET service account called *ASPNET*. This provides a higher level of security than the beta releases of ASP.NET (which used the more privileged *SYSTEM* account), but may make certain techniques, such as using trusted connections with SQL Server, more difficult because the *ASPNET* account is not trusted. You can also use another special account, *SYSTEM*, to run the ASP.NET worker processes, but for security reasons, this is not recommended.

`<webControls>`

The *<webControls>* element allows you to specify the location of script files used by client-side implementations of ASP.NET Server Controls, such as the validation controls. The *<webControls>* element has the following syntax:

```
<webControls
    clientScriptsLocation="path" />
```

For information on *<webControls>* element attributes, consult the following table.

`<webControls>` Element Attributes		
Attribute	**Description**	**Options**
clientScriptsLocation	Determines where ASP.NET will look for client-side scripts for use with ASP.NET Server Controls.	This attribute is relative to the root Web of the Web server.

\<clientTarget\>

The *\<clientTarget\>* element allows you to set up aliases to be used by the *ClientTarget* property of the *Page* class. The *\<clientTarget\>* element supports one child element, *\<add\>*, and has the following syntax:

```
<clientTarget>
  <add
     alias="aliasname"
     userAgent="true|false" />
</clientTarget>
```

For information on *\<clientTarget\>* element attributes, consult the following table.

\<clientTarget\> Element Attributes		
Element	**Attribute**	**Description**
\<clientTarget\>		Creates aliases for specific browser user agents that can then be specified from the *Page.ClientTarget* property.
\<add\>		Maps a specific user agent string to an alias name.
	alias	Specifies the name of the alias.
	userAgent	Specifies the browser user agent that the alias looks for.

\<browserCaps\>

The *\<browserCaps\>* element contains settings used by ASP.NET to provide the functionality of the browser capabilities component (accessible via the *Request.Browser* property). It provides filtering processes that allow the browser capabilities component to populate its properties with information on the capabilities of a user's browser, based on the information contained in the user agent string passed by the browser. The *\<browserCaps\>* element supports three child elements, *\<result\>*, *\<use\>*, and *\<filter\>*. The *\<filter\>* element supports one child element, *\<case\>*. The *\<browserCaps\>* element has the following syntax:

```
<browserCaps>
    <result type="System.Web.HttpBrowserCapabilities" />
    <use var="HTTP_USER_AGENT" />
```

```
list of default property values

<filter>
   <case match="string1|string2|stringN">
      property=value
   </case>
</filter>
</browserCaps>
```

For information on *<browserCaps>* element attributes, consult the following table.

<browserCaps> Element Attributes			
Element	Attribute	Description	Options
<browserCaps>		Allows filtering and mapping of strings within the browser user agent string to properties of the browser capabilities component.	
<result>		Specifies the result type of the configuration element.	
	type	.NET class used as the result type.	The default is *System.Web.HttpBrowserCapabilities.*
<use>		Determines the server variables used while evaluating *<filter>* and *<case>* elements.	
	var	Server variable used in evaluating *<filter>* and *<case>* elements.	The default is *HTTP_USER_AGENT.*

<browserCaps> Element Attributes			
Element	**Attribute**	**Description**	**Options**
<filter>		The *<filter>* – contains one or more *<case>* child elements to search for specific strings within the user agent string.	
<case>		Each *<case>* child element searches for a specific string or strings within the user agent string.	
	match	Specifies the string or strings (separated by | characters) to look for in the code.	If a specified string is found, the property assignment enclosed by the *<case></case>* tags is executed.

Setting and Retrieving Custom Application Settings

The final configuration element is a special one because it allows you to configure your own custom application settings, which can then be easily retrieved from within your ASP.NET applications.

<appSettings>

The *<appSettings>* element allows you to create your own configuration settings as key/value pairs. You can use this configuration element to store configuration information such as DSNs for data access, and then retrieve them in your application using the following syntax:

```
Dim DSN As String
DSN = ConfigurationSettings.AppSettings("dsn")
```

This is assuming that you've stored the DSN using *"dsn"* as the key.

The *<appSettings>* element has the following syntax:

```
<appSettings
    key="string"
    value="string" />
```

For information on *<appSettings>* element attributes, consult the following table.

<appSettings> Element Attributes	
Attribute	**Description**
key	Specifies the key by which the value in the *appSettings* hash table will be retrieved.
value	Specifies the value to be retrieved by the specified key.

Chapter 7 Quick Reference

To	Do This
Configure an ASP.NET application	Add the desired configuration element to the application's Web.config file, and set its attributes and child elements to the appropriate values.
Configure all ASP.NET applications on a machine	Add the desired configuration element to the applications on a Machine.config file, and set its attributes and child elements to the appropriate values.
Store application-specific configuration settings	In either Web.config or Machine.config, add the *<appSettings>* element, setting its *key* and *value* attributes to the desired values.
Lock down configuration settings	Wrap the settings you wish to lock down in a *<location></location>* tag pair, setting the *allowOverride* attribute of the *<location>* tag to *false*. You can optionally set the *path* attribute to apply the settings to a specific file or folder in the application.

Security in ASP.NET

In this chapter, you will learn about

✔ *The importance of security in Web applications*

✔ *Some security best practices*

✔ *Security features offered by ASP.NET*

✔ *Implementing security in your applications*

In days gone by, there were primarily two types of applications: single-user applications in which presentation, business logic, and any necessary data handling all occurred on the client machine of the user, and client/server applications, which removed much or all of the data handling to a separate database server. Back then, security was largely a matter of making sure that in a client/server situation, users only made modifications to data that they were authorized to change. Issues such as denial of service attacks, port sniffing, and so on were seldom faced by the typical application developer.

The Internet has changed all that forever. Applications that are exposed to the Internet are inherently vulnerable to a host of issues, ranging from attempts at stealing data to the defacing of Web sites to denial of service attacks. No matter what operating system or other software you run, that vulnerability will never go away entirely. Software is an imperfect science, and unfortunately, there has yet to be an operating system that is invulnerable to attack.

The good news is that most software, including Windows 2000, Windows XP, and IIS, can be made quite secure if you follow best practices (a recognized set of recommended procedures and policies) for security, such as keeping track of and installing security patches as soon as they are released. One of the remarkable things about security practices in our industry is just how many servers (both Microsoft-based and otherwise) are sitting out there exposed to the Internet, without patches installed that have been available for months, or even years!

The Importance of Security

Security is one of the first concerns a Web developer thinks about when designing and implementing an application (if it's not, it certainly should be). In many ways, designing an application without *considering* security is the same as designing an application *without* security. It is much harder to add security to an application after the fact than it is to do so up front.

That said, there are different levels and types of security. The type and level you need for your application will vary depending on what your application does, the type and value of data (if any) that you store, the amount of risk you are comfortable with, and the amount of time, effort, and money you are willing to expend to have a secure application. The security needs of a personal home page, for example, are very different from those of a corporate intranet site or a retail e-commerce site. The following table describes the kinds of threats that are out there and the consequences of being underprepared for them.

> **note**
>
> A more complete discussion of this topic is available in the article "Web Security" by William Stallings on Microsoft TechNet (*http://www.microsoft.com/ technet/security/website/chaptr14.asp*), excerpted from Stallings' book, *Cryptography and Network Security: Principles and Practice, Second Edition*, published by Prentice Hall, PTR (1998).

Security Threats		
Type of Threat	**Primary Target**	**Consequence**
Web server compromise ● Defacement ● Substitution of incorrect or misleading information for valid information ● Unauthorized access to internal networks ● Installation of Trojan or Distributed Denial of Service (DDoS) code	All Web sites	This threat may be embarrassing for an individual, but can be costly to a corporation, not only in terms of repairing damages, but also in the cost to the company's reputation of having its site defaced or, worse yet, having inaccurate or misleading information posted. Compromised systems may also be used to mount DDoS attacks on other systems—a potential source of liability.
Denial of Service	Higher-profile sites	A denial of service attack can prevent users from using your site by flooding it with illegitimate requests, among other techniques. These attacks can be difficult to prevent.
Data loss or compromise ● Data compromised through packet sniffing ● Server data compromised user impersonation or data forgery	All sites transmitting and receiving sensitive data	Consequences of not addressing this threat include compromise of credit card or other sensitive data, and illicit modification of server data.

Security Basics

With so many potential threats against Internet applications, it's often difficult to know just where to start in designing a secure application. This section will discuss some of the strategies you can use to get started.

- **Server set-up and application design**   Preventing Web server and/or data compromise due to insecure server settings and poor application design

- **Patching**   Preventing Web server compromise due to vulnerabilities in server software

- **Access control**   Preventing Web server and/or data compromise due to inappropriate access settings

- **Auditing and logging**   Tracking who is hitting your site, what they're doing, and when

- **Using SSL and other cryptographic security tools**   Preventing data compromise

Server Setup and Application Design

One of the first areas to concentrate on is how you set up your server. Designing an application that implements authentication and authorization properly is futile if someone can simply bypass all that security through some vulnerability that you haven't applied the patch for. This section will discuss a number of good practices for server set-up and application design, but it's no substitute for a solid understanding of IIS security. You should consult other sources for IIS security, such as the Microsoft Technet site (*http://www.microsoft.com/technet/*) and the security guides for Windows 2000 offered by the NSA (which include a guide to securing IIS 5, available at *http://nsa2.www.conxion.com/win2k/download.htm*). An especially good source of information on IIS (and Web application) security are the books of Michael Howard, who has been a security program manager for Microsoft IIS 4.0 and 5.0 and also has been on the Microsoft Windows XP team. His books include *Designing Secure Web-based Applications for Microsoft Windows 2000* (2000) and the recently released *Writing Secure Code* (2002), both from Microsoft Press.

Choosing an OS

When you're choosing an operating system, the first thing to ask yourself is just how much security you need. As with many questions related to the design of a Web application, there are trade-offs to be made between security and cost. Although client operating systems such as the Windows 9x series may be able to act as Web servers on a limited basis through Personal Web Services (PWS), they are not acceptable when security is an important factor.

Workstation or server operating systems, such as Windows NT 4.0 and Windows 2000, offer more robust scalability and better security features, including better access control (see "Access Control" on page 186), logging, and encryption.

> **important**
>
> One reason to choose Windows NT or Windows 2000 to host a Web application is that these server operating systems can use the NTFS file system, where the Windows 9x series cannot. NTFS allows you to provide robust access control at both the file and folder level, and it also provides built-in support for file encryption (in Windows 2000). FAT and FAT32 (available in the 9x series) are poor choices for Web applications requiring robust security.

Server operating systems offer the most robust security features, as well as better scalability, greater ease of configuration, and better features for developers.

Choosing between Windows NT and Windows 2000 is fairly easy for a new application. Windows 2000 should be the hands-down choice because of its improved reliability, security features, and performance over NT 4.0. If you're working in an existing NT 4.0 environment, however, you may have to take that into account when deciding whether to continue development on that platform or migrate to Windows 2000 for new projects and upgrades of existing Web applications.

Ultimately, your choice of operating system comes down to the following three factors:

- Features (in this case, security features)
- Cost
- Existing environment

Your evaluation should include an analysis of all of these factors, with the goal of determining which OS meets your security needs (features), while allowing you to work within the constraints of cost and existing environment (if any).

important

Windows 2000 provides a number of major security improvements, including built-in support for file system encryption, security policies and templates (discussed later in this section), and a Security Configuration and Analysis tool. This tool can be very useful in determining whether your system will meet your security needs as configured, and can help you easily configure it if it doesn't. For these reasons, Windows 2000 (or later) should be the default choice for secure Web applications on the Microsoft platform.

Choosing a Purpose

Another important point to consider when choosing your operating system is the purpose of the server. For smaller applications with low scalability requirements, it may be acceptable to run your Web server, database server, and components all on the same machine. Because IIS and most databases make significant demands on both RAM and processor power, this model does not scale particularly well for larger applications. More importantly, however, placing a database on a Web server that is exposed to the Internet greatly increases the security risks to the data stored in that database. This can also be true for other server and application software, from mail server software to productivity applications such as Microsoft Office. The important point is that as you add more purposes to a server, you are also adding more security exposure. Keep all of this in mind as you configure your servers and decide the purpose for each one.

Too Much Service

The next important set of decisions comes when you install your operating system of choice (Windows 2000, for example), or when you add on services to be used by your application (as with Windows NT, for which IIS 4.0, Microsoft Transaction Server, and ASP are add-ons to the operating system). This choice concerns which services will be installed.

Unused running services can be a significant security risk. For example, if you install the FTP or SMTP services and have not protected the ports those services use, an attacker could detect the services and attempt to use them to compromise your server through various known vulnerabilities. (You can also reduce the risk of compromise through diligent application of patches. See "Patching" on page 185 for more information.)

If you are not using a service, you should avoid installing it, or use Add/Remove Programs to remove it. The following steps show how:

1   Click Start, Settings, Control Panel.

2   Double-click the Add/Remove Programs icon.

3   In the left side of the window, click the Add/Remove Windows Components button.

4   Review the list of installed components (shown in the following figure). Of particular interest is the IIS node. Select that node and click the Details button.

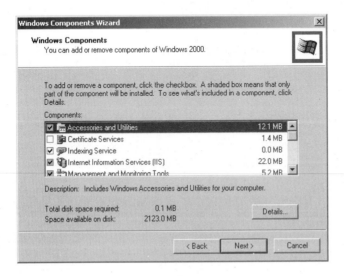

5   To remove a service or component, uncheck (deselect) the check box next to it, as shown in the following figure. Click OK to close the detail dialog.

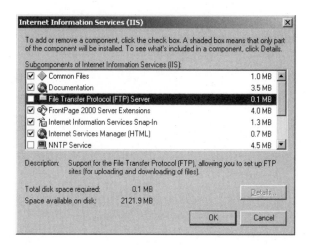

6   Click Next to apply your changes.

7   Click Finish to complete the process.

Also, if you need to install services that are not used all the time, you should set them to be started manually rather than automatically. This way, you have control over when these services are running.

Be a Policy Maker

One unheralded feature of the Windows 2000 operating system family is a robust set of tools for setting up a machine's security settings quickly and relatively painlessly. A full discussion of these tools is beyond the scope of this book (and could take up a book of its own), but let's look at a couple of them.

The Security Templates tool and the Security Configuration and Analysis tool, when used together, let you create, edit, and apply templates for defining security policies, from minimum password length to file system auditing policy. Both tools, shown in the following figure, are implemented as Microsoft Management Console (MMC) snap-ins.

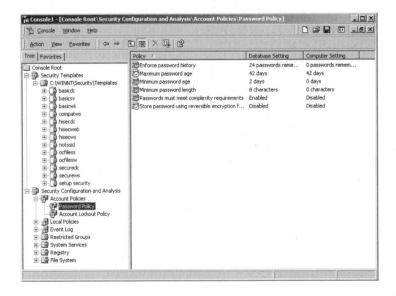

note

You can also define security policies manually by using the Local Security Policy editor, which you can find by clicking Start, Programs, Administrative Tools, Local Security Policy. This tool allows you to adjust individual local security policy settings, as well as apply security templates to the local machine.

To access the Security Templates tool, perform the following steps:

1 Either open an existing MMC console or create a new one by clicking Start, Run. Then type *mmc* and click OK.

2 From the Console menu, select Add/Remove Snap-in (Ctrl+M). Then click the Add button.

3 From the list of available snap-ins, select the Security Template snap-in. Then click the Add button.

4 Click the Close button to close the Add Standalone Snap-in dialog. Then click OK to close the Add/Remove Snap-in dialog.

5 If desired, save your new or modified MMC console by selecting Save (Ctrl+S) or Save As from the Console menu.

> **note**
>
> One of the least used but most useful features of the MMC is creating and saving custom consoles that contain the MMC snap-ins you use most frequently. You can use the same procedure outlined in the preceding list to add the Security Configuration and Analysis snap-in (or any other snap-in) to a console.

The advantage of using the Security Templates tool to create and edit your security templates is that it allows you to create security policy templates separately from applying the template to the local machine. To create a new security template, perform the following steps:

1 Right-click the template path folder for the path where you want to store your new template. Then select New Template.

2 Enter a name and description for the new template and click OK. The new template will be displayed under the path folder you selected in step 1.

3 Expand the node for your new template by double-clicking it, or click the + sign next to it to display the options available for configuration with the template.

4 Using the same technique as in step 3, expand the policy area you want to customize, such as the Password Policy (which can be found under the Account Policies node). Select the policy area to view its available attributes in the right pane of the console window.

5 Double-click the attribute you want to modify.

6 Check the Define This Policy Setting in the template check box, as shown in the following figure. Then edit the value to your desired value.

7   Click OK to close the Template Security Policy Setting dialog and apply your change to the template.

8   After making any additional desired changes to the template, save it by right-clicking its name and selecting Save.

Of course, once you've created your custom template, you may want to use it to configure security for one or more machines. This can be accomplished using the Security Configuration and Analysis tool, which can also be used to determine which settings on the local machine are not in compliance with the template you've defined (or one of the predefined templates).

You can also use templates to define security settings for development, staging, and production security requirements. A development or staging server's security requirements are usually less restrictive than those for a production server environment, where the completed application ultimately will be deployed. Unfortunately, when an application is moved to the more restrictive environment of the production server, the application may not work due to security restrictions. By defining security templates for development, staging, and production environments, you can apply those templates to your development and/or staging servers to test whether the application will work with the greater restrictions of those environments. Once testing is complete, you can restore the previous template to continue development work.

important

Because the Security Templates tool can affect a large number of security settings on a machine, it is very important that you configure and test your templates on development or staging systems before applying them to production systems. Certain security restrictions can prevent Web applications from functioning properly (for example, by restricting access to accounts used by the application), so you should always make sure your application works properly under the security policy defined by the template before applying the template to a production system.

To apply a template to the local machine

1   Open a console containing the Security Configuration and Analysis MMC snap-in.

2   Before selecting a new template, you may want to save your current settings as a template so you can restore them after applying a different template. To save a template containing the current settings, right-click the Security Configuration and Analysis node, select Export Template, provide a name for the exported template, and click Save.

3   Right-click the Security Configuration and Analysis node and select Import Template.

4   Select the desired template from the dialog and click OK. For this example, select the built-in hisecws.inf template.

> ## note
>
> Microsoft has made a template called hisecweb.inf available for configuring a high-security Web server. This template can be used as a starting point for creating your own security templates. You can download it from the following URL:
>
> *http://download.microsoft.com/download/win2000srv/SCM/1.0/NT5/ EN-US/hisecweb.exe*

5   To compare the settings in the template to those currently configured on the local machine, right-click the Security Configuration and Analysis node, select Analyze Computer Now, and then click OK in the Perform Analysis dialog.

6   Expand the Account Policies node to display the Password Policy node. Then select the Password Policy node to view its settings, as shown in the following figure. Where local settings match the template, there's a green check mark. Where settings do not match, there's a red X.

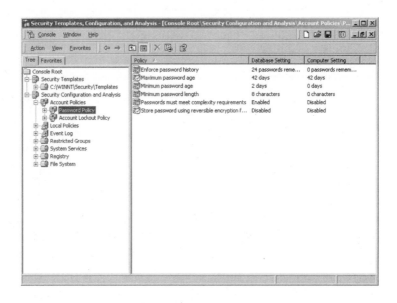

7 To configure the local machine with the settings specified in the template, right-click the Security Configuration and Analysis node, select Configure Computer Now, and then click OK in the Configure System dialog.

8 If you want to view the settings modified by the template, you will need to reanalyze the computer as described in step 5.

Keep in mind that only settings for which a value has been defined in the template will be applied. All other settings will remain as they were previously configured. Also note that when a server that you're configuring is part of a Windows 2000 domain, any settings configured in the domain-wide security policy will override settings in the local security policy.

Passwords, Please

One of the most common (and dangerous) areas overlooked in Web server security is password protection. Problems in this area include weak or nonexistent passwords for sensitive information or services, and placing passwords in plaintext files such as ASP and ASP.NET pages, Global.asa or Global.asax files, or configuration files in the Web space.

Weak or Blank Passwords

A simple rule of thumb for sensitive information on your Web server is that it should be protected by a password, and a strong one. Too often, developers wrongly assume that it's sufficient to put Web pages that are to be accessed only by certain authorized users (or other sensitive content) in a separate directory that is only accessible by entering the URL directly. Worse, Web developers who are not sufficiently familiar with SQL Server (or its desktop equivalent, MSDE, which is installed with the .NET Framework QuickStart samples) may install these databases on a Web server or another server on their network without understanding the security ramifications.

SQL Server and MSDE both contain an extended stored procedure called *xp_cmdshell* that allows command-line commands to be run on the server. Why is this important? Because in many cases, people still install SQL Server or MSDE with a blank password for the *sa* (system administrator) account. For a server connected to the Internet, this is like begging to be hacked. In fact, one Web hosting company that hosts a site devoted to ASP and ASP.NET articles fell prey to precisely this problem (due to the default configuration of MSDE in the Beta 2 .NET Framework QuickStart samples, which included a blank *sa* password). This highlights the inherent risk of both beta software and of samples, which are rarely designed for high security. The result was that some malcontents used *xp_cmdshell* to delete much of the content on the affected server. The Web hosting company was fortunate enough to have backups of the content and was able to restore the server, but the damage could have been much worse.

> ## important
>
> It cannot be emphasized strongly enough: you must have a strong password on the *sa* account of any SQL Server or MSDE databases on your network. A malicious user with access through the *sa* account can do anything to your server that he could accomplish from a command line, including adding or deleting user accounts, installing and executing malicious code, and deleting content or system files.

If you have MSDE installed (which is part of the install process for the ASP.NET QuickStart samples), ensure that the *sa* account does not have a blank password.

1   On the machine where MSDE is installed, open a command prompt.

2   Enter the following, which attempts to connect to the \NetSDK named instance of MSDE that is installed by the QuickStart samples using the *osql* command-line utility:

```
osql -S(local)\NetSDK -U sa -P
```

3   If the connection is successful, you'll see the following prompt (if the login fails, you'll get a failure message):

```
1>
```

4   If the logon is successful, enter the following commands to modify the password for the *sa* account. Make sure that you memorize the new password so you won't forget it. (Avoid writing it down if possible. But if you must, make sure you put it somewhere secure so prying eyes won't find it.) Replace *<new password>* with the new password you've chosen, and follow the *go* command by pressing the Enter key:

```
1> sp_password NULL, '<new password>', 'sa'
2> go
```

5   If the result is successful, you should see the message shown in the following figure. Also note that, in this example, a password containing letters, numbers, and symbols has been chosen.

You can also use the SQL Server Enterprise Manager utility, if it is available, to modify the login accounts and passwords for an MSDE database.

Almost as bad as blank passwords are passwords that are weak (easily guessable), such as

- Names or places
- Dates, such as birthdays or anniversaries
- Words found in a dictionary
- Short passwords (8 characters or fewer)
- All letters, all lowercase, all uppercase, or all numeric

Weak passwords make it much easier for someone trying to hack a server to guess the password for an account. So-called *dictionary attacks* use a dictionary of common terms or words to rapidly attempt to log in to an account. *Brute force attacks* attempt every possible value until they find the correct one. While a strong password won't necessarily eliminate brute force attacks, it can increase the time needed for such an attack to succeed. In combination with appropriate auditing and logging, this can give you time to deal with the attack.

Strong passwords meet minimum requirements for length and complexity. You can require secure passwords using a security template, such as the hisecweb.inf template, using the Security Configuration and Analysis tool as described earlier in this chapter. The hisecweb.inf template sets minimum and maximum password age, enforces password history (preventing users from reusing old passwords), sets minimum password length to eight characters, and requires passwords to meet minimum complexity requirements, including requiring passwords to include three of the following four categories of characters:

- Uppercase characters
- Lowercase characters

- Numeric characters
- Non-alphanumeric symbols (such as punctuation, special characters like *, #, and $, etc.)

Note that these settings only control passwords for NT security accounts. If you use your own authentication credentials in your application, you will need to implement your own solution for enforcing strong passwords, such as using the RegularExpressionValidator Server Control to perform pattern matching. (See Chapter 10 for more information on validation controls.)

Unsafe Storing of Passwords

Another common problem in Web applications is the storing of passwords or other sensitive data in unsafe locations: plain-text files such as ASP and ASP.NET pages, Global.asa or Global.asax files, and configuration files in the Web space (those that are accessible by HTTP requests to the Web server). The problem usually occurs when developers place database login information, including the password, in a plain-text file on the Web server. These developers assume that since users are prevented from viewing the source of .asp, .aspx, .asa, and .asax files by default, this information will be safe.

Unfortunately, this is true only if the Web server is not compromised by a security vulnerability. If a server is compromised, a malicious user may be able to read any file in the Web space for an application and gain the password(s) stored there.

Sensitive information, such as database passwords, can be protected using one of the following options.

- If you're using SQL Server or MSDE, use a trusted connection to connect to your database. This method uses the *Trusted_Connection* attribute of a connection string to tell SQL Server to use the current user's NT login information to log in. This is most useful in intranet scenarios where users log in to your application via NTLM with an NT username and password. This method has the advantage of not needing to store a password at all.
- Store the connection string information in the Machine.config file, which is not directly in the Web space of the application, using the appSettings configuration section (described in Chapter 15). Although this method is still not ideal because password information is still being stored in plain text, the fact that the Machine.config file is stored outside of the Web space makes it that much harder for a malicious user to get to this file. For better security with this method, the directory containing Machine.config and the directory containing your Web application should reside on different drives.

In addition, you can also use such methods as encryption to make a would-be hacker's job more difficult. The bottom line is that there is really no place that you can store passwords that is 100% secure, but some methods are more secure than others. Balance your need for security against other factors when choosing how and where to store sensitive information.

> **note**
> Using a trusted connection with SQL Server requires either using Windows authentication and impersonation, as described in "Using Impersonation" on page 203, or setting up the default ASPNET account (the account used to run the ASP.NET worker processes) as a login account in the SQL Server database being accessed. This process is described in Chapter 11.

Limit Those Accounts

Account limitations are an important security strategy from the standpoint of Windows 2000 accounts, database accounts, and any custom accounts you may create for your application. You should configure each account to have only the capabilities necessary for the type of user it represents. For example, it is usually a good idea to set up a database account with read-only access for pages (or components) in your application that only need to read and display data.

A good example of this practice is Microsoft's decision to change the default account for running ASP.NET worker processes. The default account used to be the SYSTEM account, which has numerous privileges and can perform almost any action on a machine. Now the default is the ASPNET account (specified by the *MACHINE* value for the *username* attribute of the *<processModel>* configuration element in Web.config), which has very few privileges on the system. This change makes certain techniques more difficult to use, but it also reduces the likelihood that a single compromised application would compromise an entire system or an entire network.

No Samples, Thank You

Another area of danger for the unwary IIS administrator or Web developer is sample applications. By default, some versions of IIS are installed with a set of sample applications designed to help developers learn to develop applications on an IIS server. The .NET Framework SDK also has samples that may be installed to help developers learn to develop .NET applications. These and other sample applications have their place, but *not* on a production Web server.

Sample applications are not designed to run on production servers, so typically they do not use best practices to prevent servers or applications from being compromised. One example is that samples installed with one version of IIS included a utility that allowed users to view the source of ASP pages. Unfortunately, if this utility was installed on a server containing production applications, it could be used to view the source code and make them vulnerable to attack.

As mentioned earlier, the .NET QuickStart samples install an instance of the MSDE database software. In the Beta 2 release, this instance was installed with a blank password for the *sa* account. If these samples were installed on a server that is exposed to the Internet, this would result in a major vulnerability.

Additionally, some sample applications demonstrate extremely poor practices when it comes to security. In earlier versions, the QuickStart samples used the *sa* account with a blank password for database connections. This is an extremely bad practice. Not only does it reinforce the bad habit of leaving the *sa* account with no password, but it also uses an account for data access that has much wider permissions than are necessary for data access alone. The good news is that the current versions of the QuickStart samples follow the best practice of using an MSDE account created especially for the sample applications. This account only has permission to access the databases used by the samples, and only the permissions on those databases necessary for the samples.

Although the changes in the .NET Framework QuickStart samples indicate that Microsoft is committed to demonstrating better security practices in sample applications, they still should not be installed on a production server (or any other server that is exposed to the Internet, for that matter) without a very clear understanding of the risks entailed, and without undertaking efforts necessary to mitigate those risks.

You Need Validation

Validation is another area that is often overlooked in Web application security. For example, developers may include validation code to ensure that users enter an e-mail address or phone number in the correct format. But they might not consider that other text fields, particularly large text fields or those that may be used for display elsewhere in the application, may expose the application to unacceptable risks.

The problem with not validating all text input by the user is that a malicious user can enter text, such as script commands, ASP.NET <% %> render blocks, or other text that, in the wrong context, could be allowed to execute rather than being treated as plain text to be displayed. Additionally, input fields used to construct SQL statements for data access may be vulnerable to unexpected commands being entered. Validation can help you prevent this problem, as well as prevent nuisance problems such as users attempting to post profanity in guest book or discussion list applications built with ASP.NET. In fact, ASP.NET makes it very easy to implement robust validation using a set of server controls designed specifically for this purpose. These controls are discussed further in Chapter 10.

The important thing to remember is that you should always treat any input from a user as suspect until it has been proven otherwise. Validate that the input from the user is what you're expecting *before* you use, store, or display it.

Mind Those Ports!

Internet applications communicate via the TCP/IP protocol, which is the basis for all communication between computers on the Internet. TCP/IP uses two pieces of information to find the endpoints for a given communication: the IP address, which is a unique number assigned to a given machine, and a TCP port number, which for most applications is a well-known number used consistently by all applications of that type. For example, all Web servers use TCP port 80 as the default port for HTTP (Web) communications. The well-known nature of these port numbers and the services found on them makes it much easier for Web servers and clients to find one another.

Other well-known ports include File Transfer Protocol (FTP, port 21), Simple Mail Transport Protocol (SMTP, port 25), and POP3 (port 110). The full list of well-known ports and the services assigned to them can be found at *http:// www.iana.org/assignments/port-numbers*.

Why is this important to the discussion of security and Web server set-up? Because the very ease of discovery that well-known port numbers makes possible also presents a security risk for the unwary. For example, on Windows 2000, the ports for services such as FTP, SMTP, and POP3 (among others) are left open by default. This gives hackers an engraved invitation to probe these ports and see if the software behind them is vulnerable to attack. Given the many vulnerabilities discovered in FTP, SMTP, and other Internet-based services, it is essential to close all ports that are not in use by your application.

Closing ports can be accomplished in a number of ways, the most common being packet filtering (either through firewall software or a hardware router) or using the Windows 2000 IPSecurity Policy Management MMC snap-in. For many applications, the preferred solution is to set up a hardware firewall between the Web server and the Internet that only allows traffic on port 80 (HTTP), and optionally port 443 (HTTPS) if secure sockets Web traffic is required. (See "Using SSL to Protect Communications" on page 188 for more information on Secure Sockets Layer communication.) Then a second firewall is added between the Web server and the internal network that only allows traffic on ports necessary for the Web server to reach other servers (such as the database server), and that blocks ports 80 and 443 (and any other ports open in the other firewall). This method places the Web server in what is referred to as a DMZ (demilitarized zone), which is designed to prevent direct communication between the Internet and an internal network. This protects servers on the internal network from attack.

important

Whichever method you use to close unused ports on your Web server, it is imperative that you block traffic to any ports that your application or applications do not use. Remember, however, that the ports that remain open are still a security risk. Effective logging of server activity, frequent monitoring of logs, and prompt patching of vulnerabilities in software operating on the open ports are all important means of defending your server(s) from attacks.

A full discussion of packet filtering, routing, and IPSec management is beyond the scope of this chapter. Consult the manual for your firewall or router, or the Windows 2000 Help files, for more information on implementing these solutions.

Patching

Once your server is set up correctly and securely, and you've considered how the design of your application affects security, you might think you're home free. Not so! Even the most securely configured server and securely designed application can be compromised by a lax attitude toward ongoing maintenance. One of the most important aspects of ongoing maintenance of servers and applications is staying on top of patches released by vendors of any software you're using.

In an ideal world, the software we use would be perfect from the start. However, the reality is that there are few, if any, programs that do not contain vulnerabilities. When these vulnerabilities are discovered, typically the vendor of the program will issue a patch designed to correct the problem. Unfortunately, many server administrators do not apply these patches consistently, leaving their servers vulnerable to attack.

This is inexcusable. Most patches can be applied easily, and there are many ways that you can be notified automatically about new ones for Microsoft software. These include the following sources of information about patches.

■   The Windows Update site (*http://windowsupdate.microsoft.com/*) lets you analyze the updates available for a given system and determine which of them are currently installed. Windows 98 and later and Windows 2000 and later install a link to Windows Update in the Start menu by default.

■ The Microsoft Product Security Notification service lets you sign up for e-mail notification of vulnerabilities and available patches. This method is useful for administrators who need to keep track of patches without visiting multiple machines. You can sign up for this service at *http://www.microsoft.com/technet/treeview/default.asp?url= /technet/security/bulletin/notify.asp*.

■ The Network Security Hotfix Checker is a command-line utility that will scan the local machine, or machines on the local network, for uninstalled patches for Windows NT 4.0, Windows 2000, IIS 4.0 and 5.0, SQL Server 7.0 and 2000 (and MSDE), and IE 5.01 and later. The Network Security Hotfix Checker is downloadable from *http://www.microsoft.com/ downloads/release.asp?releaseid=31154*. You can find more information on using the Network Security Hotfix Checker at *http://support.microsoft.com/ directory/article.asp?ID=KB;EN-US;q303215*.

Access Control

Access control is the process of determining who can access resources on your server. This includes both authentication (determining the identity of a user making a request) and authorization (determining whether that user has permission to take the action requested). For an ASP.NET application, there are several different authentication and authorization methods. You'll learn how to implement authentication and authorization in ASP.NET later in this chapter.

It is important not to forget that access control also includes physical access to the machine being secured. The best authentication, authorization, and password practices won't help you a bit if someone can gain physical access to a machine and circumvent your security barriers, or simply damage the machine beyond repair. Any machine that has value to you should be secured physically, as well as via software, from unauthorized use.

Auditing and Logging

As mentioned earlier in this chapter, even the best security practices and strongest passwords cannot provide 100 percent protection against attacks. For this reason, it is imperative to enable auditing and logging on exposed servers.

Auditing is the process of monitoring certain activities, such as logon attempts, for success or failure, and then logging the results of this monitoring to the Windows event log. Auditing (and proper monitoring of the logs) allows you to determine when someone is attempting to attack your machine, such as by trying numerous incorrect passwords. In this case, by auditing login failures, you would be able to see the failed login attempts in the Security event log and take appropriate action to foil the would-be intruder (such as disabling the account being attacked). As with many of the other settings discussed in this chapter, the auditing policy for a Windows 2000 machine can be set using a security template via the Security Configuration and Analysis MMC snap-in.

Logging is the process of writing information about the activities being performed on a machine to a known location for later review. For our purposes, the most important logging (after the logging of audit information) is done by IIS for the Web, FTP, and SMTP services. Logging is performed at the site level. To enable logging in IIS, use the following steps. (They're for enabling logging for a Web site, but the steps for FTP, SMTP, and other IIS services are similar.)

1   Open the Internet Services Manager MMC snap-in by clicking Start, Programs, Administrative Tools, Internet Services Manager.

2   Select the server you want to manage, and expand the tree to find the site you want to manage. Right-click the desired site and select Properties. The following dialog will be displayed.

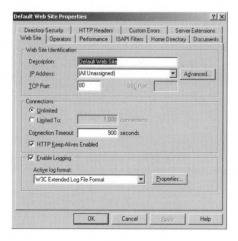

3   In the *<sitename>* Properties dialog, ensure that the Enable Logging checkbox is checked.

4   You can modify the format of the logs using the Active log format drop-down, and you can click the Properties button to modify where logs are kept, how frequently a new log file is created, and the specific information that is logged.

> **note**
>
> It is considered a good practice to modify the location of the Web server logs from their default of *%WinDir%\System32\LogFiles* because that makes it more difficult for a hacker who gains access to your system to cover his tracks. If the log files are in their default location, a hacker can easily alter them or delete them to hide their activity.

Using SSL to Protect Communications

By default, information sent via HTTP requests and responses is sent as clear text. This means that someone could capture the packets that make up these requests and responses and then recreate them, including any data passed from form fields on a submitted page. If such a form contained sensitive data, such as passwords or credit card numbers, this data could be stolen.

Encryption is an important tool for keeping this kind of information secure. The most commonly used form of encryption in Web applications is the Secure Sockets Layer (SSL) protocol. SSL is used by sites requiring secure communications between the Web server and the browser to create and exchange a key used to encrypt communications between the client and server, which helps protect this information from prying eyes. This is typically done by e-commerce sites to protect credit card information, for example. SSL can also be useful for protecting other information, including SessionID cookies and login information when using basic authentication, or ASP.NET Forms-based authentication. (See "Enabling Authentication" on page 191 for more information on basic authentication.)

By default, SSL communications occur on port 443 (as opposed to non-SSL Web communications, which are on port 80 by default), using the *https://* prefix for URLs that use SSL. Enabling SSL for your Web server requires obtaining a server certificate and binding that certificate to the Web sites on which you want to use SSL. To request a server certificate from a certification authority, follow these steps:

1   Open Internet Services Manager.

2   Right-click the site you want to protect via SSL and then select Properties.

3   On the Directory Security tab, shown in the following figure, click the Server Certificate button. This will start the Web Server Certificate Wizard.

4   Use the Web Server Certificate Wizard to create a new certificate request. This method is useful if you want to create a certificate request to send to a third-party certificate authority, such as Verisign or Thawte, who will verify the information in the request and send you a server certificate. Alternately, if you have Certificate Services installed on a machine on your network, you can use it to create a certificate. (Note that your clients must have your Certificate Services CA listed in their browser as a trusted certificate authority in order to use this method.) See the Certificate Services documentation for more information on creating and installing your own certificates.

note

No matter which method you use to generate a certificate request, the common name of the certificate (identified by the Certificate Services Web request pages as Name) must match the fully qualified domain name of the site the certificate will be installed on. Otherwise, users will get a warning that the server's certificate is valid but the name on the certificate doesn't match the requested URL.

Once you've received the response from the certificate authority containing your certificate, follow these steps to install the certificate for use in IIS:

1   Locate the certificate file you received from the certificate authority. Right-click the file and select Install Certificate.

2   Open Internet Services Manager.

3   Right-click the site you want to protect via SSL and select Properties.

4   On the Directory Security tab, click the Server Certificate button. This will again start the Web Server Certificate Wizard.

5   Click Next to advance to the second page of the wizard.

6   On the Server Certificate page of the wizard, shown in the following figure, select Assign an existing certificate and then click Next.

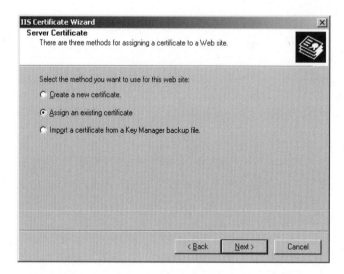

7   The Available Certificates page should list all of the certificates on the current machine, including the certificate you just installed. Select the desired certificate and then click Next.

8   Review the Certificate Summary information to ensure you are assigning the correct certificate. Then click Next.

9   Click Finish to complete the wizard.

Once you've installed the certificate for a given site, you can use SSL to encrypt communications on any of the virtual directories under that site by having users request pages with *https://* rather than *http://*. To ensure that pages cannot be viewed without SSL, however, you must require SSL for the page or directory you want to protect.

1   Open Internet Services Manager.

2   Right-click the site, virtual directory, or file you want to protect and then select Properties.

3   On the Directory Security or File Security tab, click the Edit button, which should now be available. This will open the Secure Communications dialog, shown in the following figure.

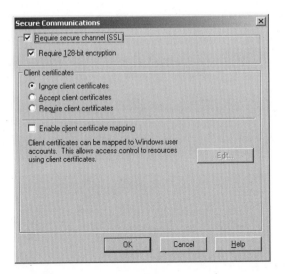

4   In the Secure Communications dialog, check the Require secure channel (SSL) check box. You can check the Require 128-bit encryption checkbox for greater security, but this requires that the client browser support 128-bit encryption.

5   Click OK to close the Secure Communications dialog, and then click OK again to close the Properties dialog for the site, directory, or file you are protecting. The resource should now be accessible only by using *https://*.

Enabling Authentication

As discussed earlier in this chapter, authentication is the process of validating the identity of the user making the current request. ASP.NET applications work with IIS to carry out authentication based on one of several authentication types, which are discussed in the following section.

Authentication and authorization in ASP.NET work hand-in-hand and operate on two distinct levels: the operating system/IIS level and the ASP.NET level. The next several sections discuss how these levels interact.

Selecting an Authentication Type

There are three basic types of authentication available for ASP.NET applications: Windows-based, Passport, and Forms-based authentication. The authentication method you choose will depend on the types of clients you're dealing with, the level of control you have over the client browser choice, and a number of other factors. The next several sections will discuss the available methods, how they're implemented, and why you might choose one particular method over another.

important

The interaction between IIS and ASP.NET in terms of authentication and authorization may be somewhat confusing if you're inexperienced with these features. Until you understand how the various options work, you should practice the techniques and procedures discussed in this section on a machine that is not exposed to the Internet or other potential sources of compromise.

Requests for resources in an ASP.NET application go through two distinct levels of authentication: the IIS level and the ASP.NET application level. The type of authentication you choose determines which of these levels is used to determine whether the request is properly authenticated. As mentioned earlier, authorization also occurs on two levels, so it is important to choose the appropriate authorization method for the authentication type you're using.

The authentication type is determined by the *<authentication>* tag in the Web.config file for an application. The syntax of the *<authentication>* tag is explained in Chapter 7.

Using Windows-Based Authentication

In Windows-based authentication, ASP.NET relies on IIS to authenticate the incoming request using one of its available authentication methods:

- **Basic authentication**   This is compatible with most browsers, but the password is sent in clear text. Use this only if you can protect the communication with SSL encryption.

- **Digest authentication**   This authentication method was introduced as a feature of HTTP 1.1, so it may not be supported by all browsers. It sends a hashed value instead of a clear-text password, making it more secure than basic authentication. This method requires a Windows 2000 Domain Controller. You have to store a clear-text version of the password on the Domain Controller used to validate the password, so the Domain Controller must be secured from physical and network intrusions. If no Windows 2000 Domain Controller is available, this option will be unavailable, as seen in the Authentication Methods dialog box shown later in this chapter.

- **Integrated Windows (NTLM) authentication**   This is available only with Internet Explorer. It's the most secure method because it never sends the username or password over the network. Use this method if you require your clients to use Internet Explorer to access your application. Note also that Integrated Windows authentication will not work over an HTTP proxy connection, which may make it impossible for clients on a corporate network using a proxy to log in to an application over the Internet. It also requires each person that logs on to your site to have an NT account either on the Web server or on a domain controller trusted by the Web server.

If more than one authentication type checkbox is checked, Digest and Integrated Windows authentication will always take precedence over basic authentication.

Once IIS has authenticated the user, it passes the authenticated identity to ASP.NET, which can then use that information to allow or deny access to resources within the application. See "Authorizing Users and Roles" on page 201 for more information on this type of authorization.

To change the authentication method used by IIS, follow these steps:

1   Open Internet Services Manager.

2   Right-click the site, virtual directory, or file for which you want to modify the authentication method. Select Properties.

3   In the Anonymous access and authentication control section of the Directory Security tab (or the File Security tab for files), click the Edit button. This will open the Authentication Methods dialog.

4   In the Authentication Methods dialog, uncheck the Anonymous access checkbox. Then check the checkbox for the desired authentication method, as shown in the following figure.

5   Click OK to close the Authentication Methods dialog, and then click OK to close the Properties dialog for the resource you selected in step 2.

To select Windows authentication as the authentication type used by ASP.NET

1   Open the Web.config file for the application in your preferred text editor or Visual Studio .NET. (Note: Visual Studio .NET color-codes configuration files.)

2   Modify the *<authentication>* configuration section as follows. (Note: you can set the authentication method only at the application or server level. Attempting to add the *<authentication>* tag to a Web.config in a subdirectory will result in an error.)

```
<authentication mode="Windows" />
```

3   If desired, you can have ASP.NET impersonate the logged-in user (so that resource requests are made in the security context of the logged-in user) by adding an *<identity>* section as follows (see "Using Impersonation" on page 203 for more on impersonation):

```
<identity impersonate="true">
```

4   Save and close the Web.config file.

Once you have set the authentication mode to Windows, you need to set the desired authorization method to protect the desired resources.

Using Passport Authentication

Passport authentication uses the centralized Passport authentication service provided by Microsoft. Passport authentication gives users a single login to use with any Passport-enabled site. In order to use Passport authentication with ASP.NET, you must download and install the Passport SDK, which is available at *http://www.passport.com/business*. ASP.NET provides a wrapper around the Passport authentication service, so you can use it simply by setting the appropriate value for the Web.config *<authentication>* tag.

To configure ASP.NET to use the Passport authentication method

1   Open the Web.config file for the application in your preferred text editor or Visual Studio .NET. (Note: Visual Studio .NET color-codes configuration files.)

2   Modify the *<authentication>* configuration section as follows:

```
<authentication mode="Passport" />
```

3   If desired, you can set up an internal redirect URL for Passport authentication by adding a *<passport>* section as follows:

```
<passport redirectUrl="<URL>">
```

4   Save and close the Web.config file.

note

To download and install the Passport SDK and use Passport authentication on your site, you will need to register on *http://www.passport.com/business* and pay a license fee.

Using Forms-Based (Cookie) Authentication

Forms-based authentication (which was called cookie authentication in ASP.NET Beta 1) allows developers to easily implement "roll-your-own" security in their applications. Whereas in classic ASP you would need to add an include file or component to every page to look for an authentication cookie, and then redirect to a login page if the cookie didn't exist, ASP.NET Forms-based authentication takes care of all this for you.

All you need to do is create the login page, tell ASP.NET where to find it (via settings in Web.config), and set the desired authorization restrictions. In your login page, you can verify the username and password credentials entered by the user against a database, Windows 2000 Active Directory, or another credential store of your choice. Once you've verified the user's credentials, you can use the methods exposed by the *FormsAuthentication* class to set or remove an authentication cookie, redirect the user to the original page they requested, or renew the authentication cookie.

important

In Forms-based authentication, the username and password are sent as clear text. To ensure the security of this information, you should always use an SSL-enabled connection for your login page.

Let's take a look at an example. First use the following steps to create a new IIS virtual directory and add a test page and a login page to it:

1   Create a new virtual directory called Chapter8 in IIS. (See Chapter 2 for directions on how to do this.) Leave the Internet Services Manager open for now.

2   Create two new files in the physical directory associated with the virtual directory: test.aspx and login.aspx. The content of both of the files is shown in the following listing.

Test.aspx

```
<%@ Page Language="VB" %>
<%@ Import Namespace="System.Web.Security " %>
<html>
<head>
   <script runat="server">
      Sub Page_Load
         User.Text = "Username is " & Page.User.Identity.Name & "."
      End Sub

      Sub Logout_Click(Src As Object, E As EventArgs)
         FormsAuthentication.SignOut
         Response.Redirect("login.aspx")
      End Sub
   </script>
</head>
<body>
   <asp:label id="User" runat="server" />
   <br/>
   <form runat="server">
      <asp:button id="logout" text="Log Out" OnClick="Logout_Click"
         runat="server" />
   </form>
</body>
</html>
```

Login.aspx

```
<%@ Page Language="VB" %>
<%@ Import Namespace="System.Web.Security " %>
<html>
<head>
   <script runat="server">
      Sub Login_Click(Src As Object, E As EventArgs)
         'NOTE: The user name and password are stored below for
         ' the sake of simplicity for our example. In production code,
         ' these values would be pulled from a database, Active
         ' Directory, or some other secure location.
         If Username.Value = "charliebrown" And _
            Password.Value = "rats" Then
         FormsAuthentication.RedirectFromLoginPage(Username.Value, _
            persist.Checked)
```

```
                   Else
                       Msg.Text = "Incorrect Username or Password: Try again."
                   End If
              End Sub
         </script>
    </head>
    <body>
       <form runat="server">
          <table>
             <tr>
                <td>Username:</td>
                <td>
                    <input id="UserName" type="text" runat="server" />
                </td>
             </tr>
             <tr>
                <td>Password:</td>
                <td>
                    <input id="Password" type="password" runat="server" />
                </td>
             </tr>
             <tr>
                <td>Persist Authentication Cookie:</td>
                <td>
                    <asp:checkbox id="persist" runat="server" />
                </td>
             </tr>
             <tr>
                <td>
                    <asp:button id="login" text="Login"
                    OnClick="Login_Click" runat="server" />
                </td>
                <td>
                    <input type="reset" text="Reset Form" runat="server">
                </td>
             </tr>
          </table>
          <asp:Label id="Message" ForeColor="red" runat="server" />
       </form>
    </body>
</html >
```

3   Next, add a Web.config file to the directory, with the content shown here:

```
<!-- web.config -->
<configuration>
   <system.web>
      <authentication mode="Forms">
         <forms name="formsauth" loginUrl="login.aspx" protection=
            "All" timeout="60" />
      </authentication>
      <authorization>
         <deny users="?" />
      </authorization>
   </system.web>
</configuration>
```

4   Save all three files.

5   In the Internet Services Manager, locate the test.aspx file, right-click it, and select Browse to browse the page. You should see something like the following figure. Note the *ReturnUrl* querystring argument. This allows ASP.NET to return the user to the originally requested page once he's authenticated.

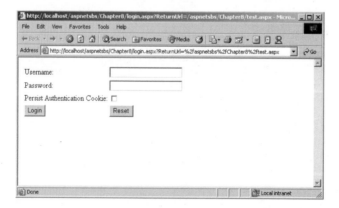

6   Enter *charliebrown* for the username and *rats* for the password, and then click Login. If you check the Persist Authentication Cookie checkbox, the cookie will be saved to disk (if your browser settings allow this) rather than being removed as soon as the browser is closed. Once you've clicked Login, you should see something like the following figure.

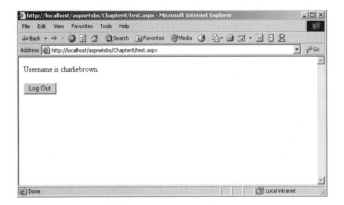

Test.aspx uses the *User* property of the *Page* object to access the identity of the current user. From the identity, you use the *Name* property to display the name of the authenticated user.

7 Click the Log Out button. This calls the *SignOut* method of the *FormsAuthentication* helper class, which removes the authentication cookie. Now, if you attempt to browse test.aspx again, you will need to log in again.

note

In this example Web.config file, the URL for the login page is specified with the *loginUrl* attribute of the *forms* tag. (For more information on all of the attributes of the form tag, see Chapter 7.) However, if you leave this attribute out, ASP.NET supplies the same name, login.aspx, as a default.

ASP.NET also supplies a default value of default.aspx for the redirect page when *FormsAuthentication.RedirectFromLoginPage* is called, if no *RedirectUrl* *querystring* argument is found. So in the preceding example, if you call the login page directly and authenticate successfully, ASP.NET will attempt to redirect you to default.aspx. If there's no such page, you'll get a "file not found" error.

Using Authorization

After you've authenticated the user making the request, the next step is to authorize the request. Authorization means deciding whether to permit the user to access the requested resource.

Authorization in ASP.NET takes two major forms: authorization against NTFS Access Control Lists (ACLs) and URL-based authorization.

Using NTFS ACLs for Authorization

ACL-based authorization is useful when you're using Windows-based authentication in ASP.NET. With ACL-based authorization, you use tools such as the Properties dialog for a file or folder in Windows Explorer to set the list of users or groups that are allowed to access a given resource, and what rights (read, write, execute, etc.) each one has. The primary advantage of using ACL-based authorization with Windows-based authentication is that it does not require writing any security-specific code in your ASP.NET application. All security settings can be taken care of administratively.

When a request for a resource (such as an ASP.NET page) comes in, IIS authenticates the request, using whichever method (basic, digest, integrated Windows) has been configured for the application. IIS passes the identity of the logged-in user to ASP.NET, which then impersonates the identity of the user and checks the ACL for the requested resource to see if the user has the required permission. If so, ASP.NET fulfills the request.

To take advantage of ACL-based authorization, you need to do the following:

1   Configure your ASP.NET application to use Windows authentication, and to impersonate the logged-in user, by adding the following sections to the application's Web.config file.

```
<authentication mode="Windows" />
<identity impersonate="true" />
```

2   Using Windows Explorer, right-click a file or folder in your application's physical directory that you want to restrict access to, and select Properties.

3   Click the Security tab and add or remove users or groups as desired. Note that you should remove the Everyone group if it is present. If you want ASP.NET to be able to access a resource when not impersonating, the SYSTEM account should be given access to the resource. When you're finished applying permissions, click OK to close the dialog.

4   Browse to the protected resource. You should be prompted to log in using your Windows username and password. If you enter credentials for one of the accounts you configured in step 3, you should be able to access the resource.

Using URL-Based Authorization

URL-based authorization, which is new in ASP.NET, lets you grant or deny access to resources in your application based on their URL (thus the name) using the *<authorization>* tag. Unlike the *<authentication>* tag, which cannot be used in or applied to a subdirectory of an application, the *<authorization>* tag can be applied to subdirectories and even individual files, either by creating Web.config

files in the subdirectories or by using the *path* attribute of the *<location>* tag to
specify the URL for the resource to be protected. URL-based authentication also
allows you to specify the HTTP method for which a particular rule applies.

Authorizing Users and Roles

The most basic form of ASP.NET URL-based authorization looks like this:

```
<configuration>
   <system.web>
      <authorization>
         <allow users="Andrew" />
         <deny users="*" />
      </authorization>
   </system.web>
</configuration>
```

When the *<authorization>* section is added to the Web.config for an application,
it allows Andrew to access resources in the application's root directory, and in any
subdirectories that do not have conflicting *<authorization>* permissions set, as
well as denying access to all other users. The *users* attribute of the *<allow>* and
<deny> tags allows you to specify comma-separated lists of users to be allowed or
denied access to the URL being protected. (Note that if no path is specified,
ASP.NET will apply the settings to the directory in which the Web.config containing the settings resides, as well as its children.) ASP.NET provides the following
two wildcards for allowing and denying access:

- ■ *   This wildcard lets you allow or deny all users
- ■ ?   This wildcard lets you allow or deny anonymous users

You can also specify a comma-separated list of roles (equivalent to NT groups) to
allow or deny by adding the roles attribute to an *<allow>* or *<deny>* tag:

```
<allow roles="Administrators, Users">
```

Note that authorization settings for child directories override those of the parent,
unless the parent settings are locked down using the optional *allowOverride*
attribute of the *<location>* tag. To prevent the preceding authentication settings
from being overridden, you would modify the Web.config file as follows:

```
<configuration>
   <location allowOverride="false">
      <system.web>
         <authorization>
            <allow users="Andrew" />
```

```
            <deny users="*" />
        </authorization>
    </system.web>
</location>
</configuration>
```

Note that the *location* tag also has a *path* attribute that allows you to specify the path to which the settings contained between the *location* tags apply. This can be a very convenient way to specify the authorization settings for multiple files or directories in an application from a single Web.config file, allowing the developer or administrator to decide which settings may or may not be overridden by child Web.config files. This is an especially useful feature in shared server or shared hosting situations. A server administrator can place master permissions in the Machine.config file for the server and use the *location* tag to prevent overriding of these permissions.

Allowing or Denying Specific HTTP Methods

In addition to the *users* attribute, the *allow* and *deny* tags also expose a *verbs* attribute, which allows you to specify the HTTP verb type to allow or deny for the specified user(s) or role(s). Following the preceding example, you could prevent all users from making *POST* requests, while still allowing them other access, by modifying your Web.config file as follows:

```
<configuration>
    <location allowOverride="false">
        <system.web>
            <authorization>
                <allow users="Andrew" />
                <deny verbs="POST" users="*" />
            </authorization>
        </system.web>
    </location>
</configuration>
```

Limiting the request types to those necessary for a page or pages in your application can be an important way to prevent hackers from compromising your site. If a hacker is unable to make a *POST* request, it is that much more difficult for him to take advantage of a vulnerability that requires sending data in an HTTP request body. You can restrict HTTP verb access for a page or set of pages by adding the *path* attribute to the *location* tag, as described in the previous section.

Using Impersonation

Impersonation is the process by which ASP.NET takes on the security context of the user making the request. This allows ASP.NET (and components called by ASP.NET) to gain access to resources that the user is authorized to access.

In classic ASP, impersonation was used by default. If the user making the request had not been authenticated by IIS using basic or NTLM authentication, ASP requests ran with the security context of the IUSR_MACHINENAME built-in account. In ASP.NET, impersonation must be turned on explicitly by using the *impersonation* attribute of the *<identity>* tag. Without impersonation, ASP.NET runs as the built-in SYSTEM account. (Although you can use the *<processModel>* configuration section to configure ASP.NET to run as a different account that has fewer privileges, such as the MACHINE built-in account.)

For example, you might want to take advantage of impersonation to use trusted connections with SQL Server. Trusted connections use Windows security to connect to a SQL Server database without the need for a SQL Server username and password. As discussed earlier in this chapter, one of the challenges facing ASP.NET developers is where to store database login information to reduce the risk of it being compromised. With trusted connections, this is not a problem because the login information is never stored by the application.

To make a trusted connection to SQL Server work, you must do the following:

1   Configure your application to use Windows authentication, as described earlier in this chapter.

2   Add the *<identity>* tag to your configuration file to make ASP.NET impersonate the identity of the client making the request.

```
<identity impersonate="true">
```

3   Add the desired Windows accounts to the SQL Server security database.

4   In the connection string used to connect to the database, specify *Trusted_Connection=yes*. The full connection string would look something like the following:

```
"server=(local)\NetSDK;database=pubs;Trusted_Connection=yes"
```

5   Using one of the accounts that you added to the SQL Server security database, log in to the ASP.NET application. You should be able to access the data on the SQL Server database.

> **note**
>
> If you are unable to use Windows authentication and impersonation in your ASP.NET application, you may still be able to take advantage of trusted connections by configuring the default ASPNET account (used to run the ASP.NET worker processes) as a SQL Server login account. Keep in mind, though, that this will allow anyone who can access any ASP.NET application to change the database according to the permissions you have set up for the ASPNET account. The process of setting up the ASPNET account as a SQL Server login is described in Chapter 11.

Understanding Code Access Security

Another new security feature in ASP.NET is code access security. A full discussion of code access security is beyond the scope of this chapter, but here's an overview.

Code access security is Microsoft's answer to the challenge of preventing untrusted code from performing actions on your system that might result in the damage or compromise of data. It allows ASP.NET developers and/or server administrators to specify the level of trust a given application should have, using the *<securityPolicy>* and *<trust>* tags in Web.config. (See Chapter 7 for more information on these tags.) ASP.NET comes preconfigured with a set of code access security templates that are mapped to trust levels in Machine.config. Depending on the level of trust specified in the *<trust>* tag, the proper set of code access security permissions are applied to the application. This can include such permissions as whether the application can read from parts of the file system outside its Web space, can write to its file space, is restricted to only reads, or is only allowed to execute.

Like the *<location>* tag that allows the lockdown of configuration settings at a machine level, code access security and the templates used to apply its permissions are ideal in shared server environments in which you want to allow users to create their own ASP.NET applications, but want to be able to choose which actions can be taken by code written by different users.

Security Resources

The following are some URLs to keep handy when securing your application.

- *http://www.microsoft.com/technet/security*   This is the starting point for finding security-related information for Windows, IIS, and other Microsoft products. There is a host of good information on improving the security of your servers and applications to be found here.

- *http://www.microsoft.com/technet/security/iis5chk.asp*   This is the Secure Internet Information Services 5 Checklist. Prepared by Michael Howard of the Windows 2000 and IIS security teams, this document provides recommendations and best practices for securing IIS 5.

- *http://www.microsoft.com/technet/treeview/default.asp?url=/technet/ itsolutions/security/tools/tools.asp*   This is a list of security tools available through the Microsoft Technet Web site.

- *http://nsa2.www.conxion.com/win2k/download.htm*   This is the download site for the Windows 2000 Security Recommendation Guides prepared by the National Security Agency (NSA).

- *http://www.microsoft.com/technet/treeview/default.asp?url=/technet/ columns/security/10imlaws.asp*   This is the 10 Immutable Laws of Security, a list of the many ways to lose control of your computer.

- *http://www.microsoft.com/technet/treeview/default.asp?url=/technet/ columns/security/10salaws.asp*   This is the 10 Immutable Laws of Security Administration, a list of sage advice for those who have the onerous task of securing their systems.

Chapter 8 Quick Reference

To	Do This
Remove unused services	Open the Control Panel, double-click the Add/Remove Programs icon, and then click the Add/Remove Windows Components button.
Create a Windows 2000 security template	Open the Security Templates MMC snap-in, right-click the folder for the new template, and select New Template.
Apply a security template	Open the Security Configuration and Analysis MMC snap-in, import the desired template by right-clicking the Security Configuration and Analysis node and selecting Import Template. Apply the imported template by right-clicking the Security Configuration and Analysis node and selecting Configure Computer Now.
Change the blank *sa* password of a default install of MSDE	Use the *osql* command-line utility to run the *sp_password* stored procedure. You can also add logins, remove logins, and perform many other tasks with *osql* and the system stored procedures.

Chapter 8 Quick Reference

To	Do This
Enable logging for a Web site	Open the Internet Services Manager, navigate to the site you want to configure, right-click, and then select Properties. In the Properties dialog for the site, click the Web Site tab and ensure that the Enable Logging checkbox is checked.
Enable SSL communications for a site	Use the Web Server Certificate Wizard to create a certificate request (or follow the procedures recommended by the certification authority of your choice). Once you have received and installed your certificate, open the Internet Services Manager, navigate to the site to be configured for SSL, and access the Properties dialog for the site. On the Directory Security tab, click the Server Certificate button and use the Assign an existing certificate option in the Web Server Certificate Wizard to assign the newly installed certificate to the site. You can require SSL communications by using the Edit button on the Directory Security tab.
Enable ASP.NET to use Windows authentication	Set the mode attribute of the *<authentication>* tag in Web.config to *Windows*.
Enable ASP.NET to use Passport authentication	Set the mode attribute of the *<authentication>* tag in Web.config to *Passport*. Install the Passport SDK and follow the instructions to configure.
Enable ASP.NET to use Forms authentication	Set the *mode* attribute of the *<authentication>* tag in Web.config to *Forms*. Add the *<forms>* tag with the desired attributes, such as *loginURL* and *timeout*.
Lock down authorization settings	Wrap the *<authentication>* tags in a *<location>* tag pair with the *allowOverride* attribute set to *false*.

PART IV

ASP.NET Web Forms

9

Creating Web Forms

In this chapter, you will learn about

✔ *Creating Web Forms pages*

✔ *How the various parts of a Web Form work together to produce their magic*

✔ *Automatic handling of postbacks*

✔ *Using code-behind classes to separate executable code from HTML markup and server control tags*

"Let's start from the very beginning, a very good place to start. When you read you begin with A... B... C... when you..."

No, that won't do at all. But you don't have to channel Julie Andrews in *The Sound of Music* to figure out Web Forms. And you *will* start at the beginning... the beginning of the page, that is.

Anatomy of an ASP.NET Web Form

In previous chapters, you saw some examples of very simple ASP.NET pages, and you've seen some more complicated examples as well. The simplest ASP.NET page consists of plain HTML and is named with the .aspx extension. While that's perfectly valid, it's also missing a lot of what makes ASP.NET pages and what makes them Web Forms.

Web Forms go beyond what classic ASP pages offered, adding new directives, new reusability options in the form of user controls and server controls, and a new server-side data-binding syntax, to name a few. This section will explore how a page is put together and how you can use these new features in your Web Forms.

The following listing shows an example of a relatively simple Web Forms page.

HelloSimple.aspx

```
<%-- Example of the @ Page directive --%>
<%@ Page Language="vb" ClassName="Hello" %>
<html>
<head>
    <script runat="server">
        'this is a script code declaration block
        Private _name As String = "Andrew"

        Public Property Name As String
           Get
               Return _name
           End Get
           Set
               _name = Value
           End Set
        End Property

        Sub SayHello()
           Label1.Text = "Hello, " & _name & "!"
        End Sub

        Sub Page_Load(Sender As Object, E As EventArgs)
           If IsPostBack Then
               If NameTextBox.Text <> "" Then
                   Name = NameTextBox.Text
               End If
               SayHello
           End If
        End Sub

    </script>
</head>
<body>
    <!-- this is a server side form -->
    <form runat="server">
        <!-- a Server Control -->
        <asp:Label id="NameLabel" runat="server">Name: </asp:Label>
        <!-- a Server Control -->
```

```
            <asp:textbox id="NameTextBox" runat="server"/>
            <!-- a Server Control -->
            <asp:button id="NameButton" text="Submit" runat="server"/>
        </form>
        <!-- a Server Control -->
        <asp:Label id=Label1 runat="server"/>
    </body>
</html>
```

This example contains a directive, HTML markup, a *<script>* code declaration
block, a server-side form, and several server controls. The following sections
describe all of these elements, as well as other elements that may be used in a
Web Form page.

Understanding Page Elements

HelloSimple.aspx (the preceding listing) shows examples of many of the elements
that may be used in an ASP.NET Web Form. The elements used in
HelloSimple.aspx include server-side comments, the *@ Page* directive, static
HTML, a server-side *<script>* code-declaration block containing both event handlers and methods, and several ASP.NET server controls. The following table
describes the elements that may be used in an ASP.NET page.

ASP.NET Page Elements	
Element	**Description**
Static HTML tags	These standard HTML elements are treated by ASP.NET as literal controls, and are rendered to the client browser as represented in the source file.
HTML comments	Syntax: *<!-- -->*. HTML comments allow descriptive text to be added to a page. This text is sent to the client but is not rendered by the browser.
Directives	Directives, such as the *@ Page* directive, provide the ASP.NET runtime with information about how to process the page. Using directives, you can control such ASP.NET features as session state, wiring up of events, and output caching, as well as importing namespaces and registering custom controls for use within a page.

(continued)

Creating Web Forms

9

ASP.NET Page Elements *(continued)*

Element	Description
Server-side code	Code can be contained in either server-side *<script>* code declaration blocks or <% %> render blocks. See "Writing Code in Web Forms" on page 228 for information on using code declaration and render blocks. ASP.NET supports server-side code in any language that targets the runtime.
Event handlers	Event handlers are procedures in *<script>* code declaration blocks that handle page or server control events, such as *Page_Load* or *control Click* events. Most ASP.NET code should be written in or called from event handlers, rather than being written in render blocks.
<script> code declaration blocks	These blocks are used to contain page-level procedures and to declare variables that are global to the page. Executable code, other than global variable declarations in code declaration blocks, must be contained within a procedure declaration. Server-side code declaration blocks must have the *runat="server"* attribute, as shown in HelloSimple.aspx.
<% %> render blocks	These blocks are used to contain executable code not contained within procedures. Overuse of render blocks can result in code that is difficult to read and maintain.
Client-side *<script>* blocks	These blocks are used to contain script code to be executed on the client, usually in response to a client-side event. Choice of language (set by the language attribute) is dictated by the languages supported by the target browser. JavaScript is the most common choice for cross-browser compatibility in client scripts.
Server-side comments	Syntax: <%-- --%>. Server-side comments allow descriptive text to be added to a page. Unlike HTML comments, this text is not sent to the client.
User controls	These are custom controls that are defined declaratively in files with the .ascx extension. They provide a simple and straightforward mechanism for reuse of UI and UI-related code, and can contain most of the same elements as Web Forms pages.

ASP.NET Page Elements *(continued)*	
Element	**Description**
ASP.NET server controls	This set of built-in controls provides ASP.NET developers with a programming model that mimics that of Visual Basic. Controls are added to a page, and programmers write code to handle events raised by users' interaction with the controls at runtime. ASP.NET provides two sets of built-in controls: the HTML controls, which provide a 1-to-1 mapping of server-side controls for most HTML elements; and the Web controls, which provide a set of controls that are very similar to the Visual Basic UI controls.
Custom server controls	Custom server controls are another mechanism for reuse in ASP.NET. They're defined in class files (.cs or .vb files) and are precompiled into managed assemblies before use.

Understanding Page Lifetime

The goal of the ASP.NET Web Forms programming model is to provide an experience similar to that of a Visual Basic rich client event-driven application, in which user actions, such as selecting an item from a list or clicking a button, cause server-side code to be executed. This is accomplished through *postbacks*.

The first time that an ASP.NET Web Forms page is executed, the code contained within the page (and any code-behind class associated with the page) is compiled into a class that inherits from the *Page* base class. The following figure shows the relationship between the page, its code-behind class (if any), and the compiled assembly. Once compiled, the class is executed, the resulting HTML is rendered to the browser, and the class is removed from memory.

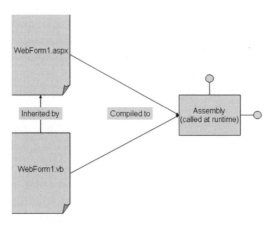

Each ASP.NET Web Forms page contains a server-side *<form>* tag that directs the page to post back to itself when the form is submitted by the user. Many ASP.NET server controls also render JavaScript to the client, allowing actions such as selecting an item in a drop-down list to cause a postback. The ASP.NET runtime also renders a hidden form field to the page that allows the page to maintain its state between requests.

The postback and hidden field are key, because when the client is interacting with the page, there is no code running on the server at all. The postback and hidden field allow the page to be reconstituted on the server. Also, they allow code to be executed in response to the event raised by the user action, and based on any changes to the form fields. Once the page has been processed and the output rendered to the browser, the page and its controls are again discarded. The steps in this process are as follows:

1   The user requests the page from the browser.

2   The page and controls are loaded and initialized.

3   If the page request is the result of a postback, the control state is loaded from the viewstate (hidden form field), and any changes submitted by the user are applied. (Note that both the original values in the viewstate and the updated values are available to server-side code.)

4   Page event handlers and event handlers for events triggered by user actions are executed.

5   Control state is saved to viewstate (hidden form field).

6   HTML output from the page is rendered to the browser.

7   The page and controls are unloaded.

It's important to note that while most server controls save their state to viewstate automatically, the same is not true for properties that you define in your pages, or in user controls or custom server controls. You'll learn how to use viewstate for storing custom control state in Chapter 12.

Using Directives

If you've developed a classic ASP page, you've worked with directives. There were few directives in classic ASP, but they were important. Most prominent were the @ *Language* directive and the *#Include* directive. The @ *Language* directive, which appeared at the top of every classic ASP page, told the ASP runtime which language engine to use in interpreting script found in <% %> render blocks in the page. The *#Include* directive told the ASP interpreter to include a particular file inline with the current ASP page.

Directives are simply ways for developers to declaratively determine how certain aspects of a program will operate. In classic ASP, this was somewhat limited. In fact, there were only the following four @ directives in classic ASP, in addition to the @ *Language* directive:

- @ *Codepage* Used in globalization to set the code page for an ASP page
- @ *EnableSessionState* Used to disable session state for a page
- @ *LCID* Used to set the locale identifier for a page
- @ *Transaction* Used to specify whether and how the page participates in COM+ transactions

ASP.NET greatly expands the use of directives, adding a number of useful directives for everything from controlling page behavior and configuration to caching page output. In addition, @ directives in ASP.NET have attributes, which increase their power and flexibility. The classic ASP directives listed previously are represented in ASP.NET as attributes of the @ *Page* directive, which is described in the next section.

@ Page

The @ *Page* directive, which is allowed in .aspx files only, defines page-specific attributes that are used by ASP.NET language compilers and the runtime to determine how the page will behave. The default values for a few of these attributes are set in the *Pages* configuration section in Machine.config. Some of the attributes, including *AutoEventWireup*, are set or overridden in pages created by Visual Studio .NET. The attributes available for the @ *Page* directive are listed in the following table.

@ Page Attributes		
Attribute	**Values**	**Purpose**
AspCompat	*true/false*	Provides compatibility with COM components created with Visual Basic 6.0 (or earlier) by forcing the page to be run in an STA (Single Threaded Apartment). Also provides the component with access to unmanaged instances of the ASP intrinsics (Session, Application, Request, etc.). This setting will likely degrade performance, so use it only when necessary. Default is *false*.

(continued)

Creating Web Forms

9

@ Page Attributes *(continued)*		
Attribute	**Values**	**Purpose**
AutoEventWireup	*true/false* Default is set in the *<pages>* section of Machine.config or Web.config.	Determines whether or not handlers for events such as *Page_Load* are set up automatically. See "Event Handling" on page 240 for more information. Default is *true*.
Buffer	*true/false* Default is set in the *<pages>* section of Machine.config or Web.config.	Determines whether rendered output is buffered before being sent to the client or is sent as it is rendered. Default is *true*.
ClassName	Any valid class name.	Determines the name of the page generated by dynamically compiling the page. This attribute works with or without *Codebehind*, and with either the *Src* or *Codebehind* attributes. The default behavior if this attribute is omitted is for the page name to be in the form *filename*_aspx.
ClientTarget	Any valid *UserAgent* string. Available values are set in the *<clientTarget>* section of Machine.config or Web.config.	Determines the target browser for which server controls should render output. The User Agent string should be one recognized by the server controls being used.
Codebehind	File name of *code-behind* class.	This attribute is used in Visual Studio .NET to locate *code-behind* classes to be compiled during a build operation. It is not used by the ASP.NET runtime.
CodePage	Any valid code page value.	Same as in classic ASP.
CompilerOptions	String containing valid compiler options.	Allows developers to pass compiler options for the page to the compiler. For Visual Basic .NET and C#, this can be any valid sequence of command-line switches for the compiler.

@ Page Attributes *(continued)*

Attribute	Values	Purpose
ContentType	Any valid MIME type (such as *"text/html"* or *"application/ vnd.ms-excel"*).	Sets the MIME type for the page output. This attribute is useful when returning binary content (such as images) to the client.
Culture	Any valid culture string (such as *en-US* for US English).	Determines the culture setting for the page.
Debug	*true/false* Default is set by the *debug* attribute of the *<compilation>* section of Machine.config or Web.config.	Determines whether pages are compiled with debug symbols or without. This setting affects performance, so production applications should have this set to *false*. The default is *false*.
Description	Any string.	Provides a text description of the page. This attribute is ignored by the ASP.NET runtime.
EnableSessionState	*true/false/readonly* Default is set in the *<pages>* section of Machine.config or Web.config.	Determines whether a request to the page will initiate a new session, and whether or not the page can access or modify data stored in an existing session. Default is *true*.
EnableViewState	*true/false* Default is set in the *<pages>* section of Machine.config or Web.config.	Determines whether or not viewstate is enabled for the page. *ViewState* allows server controls to save their current state from request to request. Default is *true*.
EnableViewStateMac	*true/false* Default is set in the *<pages>* section of Machine.config or Web.config.	Determines whether ASP.NET runs a Machine Authentication Check (MAC) on the content of the hidden form field that is used to store viewstate, to ensure that it has not been altered on the client. Default is *false*.

(continued)

Creating Web Forms

9

@ Page Attributes *(continued)*		
Attribute	**Values**	**Purpose**
ErrorPage	Any valid URL.	Specifies a page to which the client is redirected if there is an unhandled exception in the page.
Explicit	*true/false* Default is set in the *<compilation>* section of Machine.config or Web.config.	Determines whether code written in Visual Basic is subject to the *Option Explicit* rule when compiled. Default is *true*.
Inherits	Any class derived from the *Page* class. Format is *"namespace-name.classname"* or *"classname"*.	Specifies a code-behind class for the page. Any code contained in the page is combined with the code in the code-behind class into a single class.
Language	Any valid string for an installed .NET language (such as *"vb"/ "visualbasic"*, *"c#"/ "cs"/"csharp"*, etc.) Default is set in the *<compilation>* section of Machine.config or Web.config.	Specifies the language compiler to be used to compile the page. -Default is *vb*.
LCID	Any valid locale identifier.	Same as classic ASP.
ResponseEncoding	Any valid encoding string. Default is set in the *<globalization>* section of Machine.config or Web.config.	Used in globalization to set the character encoding for the HTTP response. Default is *utf-8*.
Src	File name of code-behind class	Specifies the name of a code-behind class file to be compiled dynamically at runtime.

@ Page Attributes *(continued)*		
Attribute	**Values**	**Purpose**
Strict	*true/false*	Determines whether code written in Visual Basic is subject to the *Option Strict* rule when compiled. Default is *false*.
Trace	*true/false* Default is set in the *<trace>* section of Machine.config or Web.config.	Determines whether the page includes trace output. Default is *false*.
TraceMode	*SortByTime/SortBy-Category* Default is set in the *<trace>* section of Machine.config or Web.config.	Determines how the trace output is sorted when tracing is enabled. Default is *SortByTime*.
Transaction	One of the following: *NotSupported* *Supported* *Required* *RequiresNew*	Determines whether and how the page will participate in COM+ transactions. Default is *NotSupported*.
WarningLevel	*0 – 4*	Specifies the warning level at which the compiler should abort page compilation. Lower numbers allow compilation to continue through warnings of greater severity. Levels 2–4 apply to C# only.

@ Page Examples

In this section, we'll take a look at a couple of examples of using the @ *Page* directive. The first example will show how to enable debugging of ASP.NET pages, and the second will show how to enable page-level tracing.

Enabling Debug Information

By default, ASP.NET pages are compiled without debug symbols. This is good for performance, but one of the major advances that ASP.NET offers is much richer error information than was available in classic ASP. However, this functionality requires debug symbols to be included when your page is compiled, so you may wish to turn this option on while you are developing. (Just remember to turn it back off before you deploy your application, for better performance.) Here's how to enable the insertion of debug symbols on a page-by-page basis:

1   Open the desired page in a text editor, or in Visual Studio .NET.

2   Add the *debug* attribute to the @ *Page* directive, with a value of *true*.

```
<%@ Page debug="true" %>
```

3   Save and close the file. Now if you encounter an unhandled error in the page, ASP.NET will provide you with debug information, including the source file in which the error occurred, the error message, and the line of the error, as shown in the following figure.

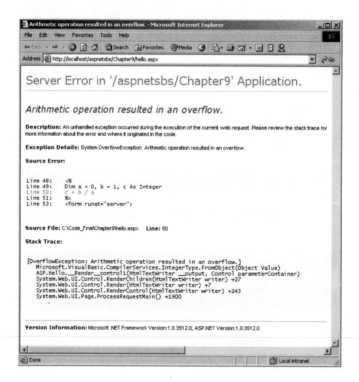

Enabling Tracing

By default, the *trace* functionality is not enabled for ASP.NET pages. As with the default setting for the *debug* attribute, this is good for performance, since there is overhead associated with tracing. Tracing enables you to view information about the current request, including the collections (cookies, forms, headers, query-strings, and server variables) associated with the request. Here's how to enable tracing on a page-by-page basis:

1 Open the desired page in a text editor, or in Visual Studio .NET.

2 Add the *trace* attribute to the @ *Page* directive, with a value of *true*.

```
<%@ Page trace="true" %>
```

3 Save and close the file. When you request the file from a browser, you'll be able to see the trace information appended to the page output, as shown in the following figure.

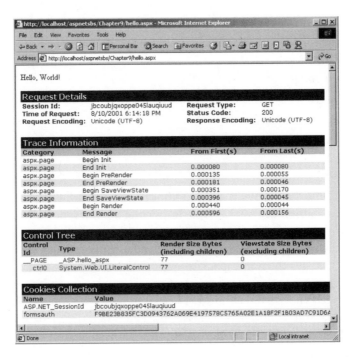

For more information on tracing and its uses in debugging ASP.NET applications, refer to Chapter 16.

@ Control

The @ *Control* directive, which is allowed in .ascx files only, performs the same function as the @ *Page* directive. However, instead of setting attributes for pages, it sets the attributes for user controls, which are reusable snippets of code named with the .ascx file extension. The attributes exposed by the @ *Control* directive are a subset of those exposed by the @ *Page* directive, and their purpose and values are the same as in the @ Page Attributes table beginning on page 215. The attributes available for the @ *Control* directive are as follows:

- *AutoEventWireup*
- *ClassName*
- *Codebehind*
- *CompilerOptions*
- *Debug*
- *Description*
- *EnableViewState*
- *Explicit*
- *Inherits*
- *Language*
- *Strict*
- *Src*
- *WarningLevel*

@ Import

The @ *Import* directive is used to import either a .NET Framework namespace or a custom namespace into a page. Importing a namespace allows you to write code against the members of that namespace without explicitly specifying the namespace each time. The @ *Import* directive has only one attribute, *Namespace*, which specifies the namespace to import. Each @ *Import* directive can have only one *Namespace* attribute, so you must use a separate @ *Import* directive for each namespace you wish to import. For example, to use the .NET Framework *SmtpMail* and *MailMessage* classes to send e-mail from an ASP.NET page, you would need to add the *System.Web.Mail* namespace to your page, as follows:

```
<%@ Import namespace="System.Web.Mail" %>
```

Then, to create an instance of the *MailMessage* class, you would use the following:

```
Dim myMail As New MailMessage
```

Without the @ *Import* directive, you would need to use the following:

```
Dim myMail As New System.Web.Mail.MailMessage
```

@ Implements

The @ *Implements* directive is used to implement a defined interface from within an ASP.NET page. An interface provides an abstract definition of a set of methods and properties. When you implement an interface, you commit to supporting the methods and properties defined by the interface, and you must create matching method and property definitions in your .aspx file, using *<script>* blocks. The @ *Implements* directive can't be used to implement interfaces in a code-behind file. It has one attribute, *interface*, which specifies the interface being implemented.

@ Register

The @ *Register* directive is used with both user controls and custom server controls to register them for use within a page. The @ *Register* directive's attributes are listed in the following table.

@ Register Attributes		
Attribute	**Value**	**Purpose**
Assembly	Any valid assembly name. The assembly name should not contain a file extension.	Specifies the precompiled assembly for a custom server control. Used with the *Namespace* and *TagPrefix* attributes. The assembly named needs to be available to the application, either by being placed in the bin subdirectory of the application or by being installed into the global assembly cache.
Namespace	Any valid namespace name.	Specifies the namespace to be associated with the tag prefix specified by the *TagPrefix* attribute.
Src	Any valid path to a user control (.ascx) file Accepts either relative or absolute URLs.	Specifies the location of a user control associated with a *TagName/TagPrefix* pair.
TagName	Any string (must be valid for XML).	Specifies an alias for a user control to be used in implementing the user control within the page. Must be used with the *TagPrefix* attribute.
TagPrefix	Any string (must be valid for XML).	Specifies an alias for a tag prefix for a user control or custom server control to be used in implementing the control within the page. If used without the *TagName* attribute, as with a custom server control, the tag name is the same as the class name defined in the server control assembly specified by the *Assembly* and *Namespace* attributes.

For examples of the use of the @ *Register* directive, please see "Creating and Using User Controls" on page 231 and "Using Server Controls" on page 236.

@ Assembly

The @ *Assembly* directive is used to link an assembly into a page at compilation time. This allows developers to use all of the classes, methods, and so forth exposed by the assembly as if they were part of the page. The @ *Assembly* directive's attributes are listed in the following table. Only one of the *Name* and *Src* attributes of the @ *Assembly* directive may be used at a time.

@ Assembly Attributes		
Attribute	**Value**	**Purpose**
Name	Any valid assembly name.	Specifies the name of a compiled assembly to be linked to when the page is compiled.
Src	Any valid path to a class source file (.vb, .cs, etc.).	Specifies the path to a source file to be dynamically compiled and linked to the current page.

Note that it is not necessary to use the @ *Assembly* directive to link in assemblies residing in the bin subdirectory of your application. These assemblies are automatically linked in by default, based on the *<assemblies>* subsection of the *<compilation>* section of the Machine.config configuration file, which contains the following tag:

```
<add assembly="*"/>
```

This specifies that ASP.NET should link in any assemblies in the bin subdirectory. Note also that any other assemblies specified by an *<add>* tag in the *<assemblies>* subsection do not require linking with the @ *Assembly* directive.

@ OutputCache

The @ *OutputCache* directive is used to specify that the rendered output of the page or user control in which it appears should be cached, and it specifies the attributes that determine the duration of caching, the location of the cached output, and the attributes that determine when a client will receive freshly rendered content rather than the cached content. Output caching in user controls can be especially useful when some of the content in a page is relatively static, but other content is frequently updated, making it a poor candidate for caching. In a case like this, you could move the static content into a user control and use the @ *OutputCache* directive to cache its content, while leaving the rest of the page to be dynamically generated with each request.

The @ *OutputCache* directive's attributes are listed in the following table.

@ OutputCache Attributes		
Attribute	**Value**	**Purpose**
Duration	Number of seconds. (Required.)	Specifies the time, in seconds, for the page or control to be cached.
Location	One of the following: *Any* *Client* *Downstream* *None* *Server* (Required.)	Specifies the location where cached output should be stored.
VaryByCustom	Any valid text string.	Specifies a custom string by which to vary the output cache. If *browser* is used, output caching will vary based on the browser name and major version. If you want to vary by HTTP request data other than the requesting browser, you will need to override the *GetVaryByCustomString* method of the *HttpApplication* class in Global.asax in order to implement your custom string.
VaryByHeader	List of valid HTTP headers, separated by semicolons.	Specifies one or more HTTP headers to be used to vary the output cache. When a request is received with a value for the specified HTTP header(s) that does not match that of any of the cached pages, a new version of the page will be rendered and cached. This attribute may not be used with user controls.
VaryByParam	List of querystring keys or form field names, separated by semicolons, or one of the following: *none* * (Required.)	Specifies one or more names of either querystring keys passed with a *GET* request, or form field names passed with a *POST* request to be used to vary the output cache. When a request is received with a value for one of the specified parameters that does not match that of any of the cached pages, a new version of the page will be rendered and cached. If the value of this attribute is set to *none*, the output cache will not vary based on *GET* and *POST* parameters. If the value is set to *, the output cache will vary by all *GET* and *POST* parameters.

(continued)

9

Creating Web Forms

@ OutputCache Attributes *(continued)*		
Attribute	**Value**	**Purpose**
VaryByControl	List of properties exposed by a user control, separated by semicolons.	Specifies one or more properties exposed by a user control to be used to vary the output cache. When a request is received with a value that does not match the specified property of any of the cached pages, a new version of the page will be rendered and cached. This attribute may only be used for output caching with user controls, not with ASP.NET pages.

Enabling Output Caching

For pages or user controls whose content does not change frequently, output caching can provide a simple and powerful way to improve the performance of your application. With output caching enabled, requests that match the parameters of the cached pages will be served from the cache, which is much faster than rendering the page again. Use these steps to enable output caching on an Web Forms page:

1   Open the desired page in a text editor, or in Visual Studio .NET.

2   Add the @ *OutputCache* directive with, minimally, the required *Duration*, *Location*, and *VaryByParam* attributes.

```
<%@ OutputCache duration="60" location="Any" VaryByParam="*" %>
```

3   Save the file. With these values for the attributes, the output of the page will be cached for 60 seconds. Any *GET/POST* requests with parameters that do not match an existing cached version of the page will be served a freshly rendered version of the page, which will then be cached.

For more information on output caching and using the ASP.NET cache engine to store arbitrary data, refer to Chapter 14.

@ Reference

The @ *Reference* directive allows you to dynamically load user controls by referencing the file name of the desired control and then using the *Page.LoadControl* method to load the control at runtime. The @ *Reference* directive directs the ASP.NET runtime to compile and link the specified control to the page in which it is declared. You'll see an example of using the @ *Reference* directive later, when this chapter discusses user controls.

The Page Class

The *Page* class provides much of the functionality of an ASP.NET page. Pages can take advantage of this functionality because every page derives from the *Page* class and inherits all of the methods and properties that it exposes. Some of the more notable members of the *Page* class, which resides in the *System.Web.UI* namespace, are included in the following list.

- The ASP *Intrinsic* objects (*Application*, *Session*, *Request*, *Response*, *Server*, and *Context*) are implemented in ASP.NET as class instances, which are exposed as properties of the *page* object. For example, the *Server* functionality is provided by a class called *HttpServerUtility*. Because the instance of *HttpServerUtility* is exposed as the *Server* property of the *Page* class, you can call its methods (*Server.Transfer*, for example) just as you could in classic ASP.

- The *Controls* collection provides access to the collection of controls defined for the page. As you'll see later in this chapter, you can use this collection to add or modify controls on a page using this collection.

- The *IsPostBack* property allows you to determine whether the current request is a *GET* request or a *POST* request resulting from the current page being posted back to itself. This property is very useful in deciding what to do when loading a Web Forms page, as you'll see later in this chapter.

- The *User* property provides access to information about the currently logged-in user.

- The *Cache* property provides access to the ASP.NET cache engine, allowing data to be cached for later retrieval.

- The *FindControl* method allows you to locate a control contained in the page's *Controls* collection by specifying its *ID* property.

- The *ViewState* property provides access to a state dictionary (based on the *StateBag* class) that allows you to store information in *Key/Value* pairs. This information is passed with each request as a hidden HTML form field.

- The *ClearChildViewState* method allows you to delete all viewstate information for any child controls on the page. This is useful if you want these controls to maintain their state most of the time, but you want to clear the state programmatically under specific circumstances.

Many other properties and methods are exposed by the *Page* class. A substantial number of these are inherited from the *Control* class, from which the *Page* class is derived, or the *Object* class, from which the *Control* class (and ultimately, every other class) is derived. This is an example of how inheritance allows you to build a very rich object model.

There are two methods by which an ASP.NET page is inherited from the *Page* class. The first is adding the @ *Page* directive to an .aspx file, which automatically makes all of the properties and methods of the *Page* class available to any code written in the page. The second method, which is discussed in more detail later in this chapter, is inheriting from the *Page* class in a code-behind class that is associated with the page by either the *Src* or *Inherits* attribute. This not only makes all of the members of the *Page* class available to the code-behind class, but it also allows ASP.NET to combine the code in the Web Form's .aspx file with the code in the code-behind class file into a single compiled class at compile time. This single compiled class contains all of the methods and properties exposed by the *Page* class, as well as any methods and properties implemented by your code.

Any of the members of the *Page* class can be called within code in a page without explicitly using the page name. For example, to write text to the browser using the *Write* method of the *Response* object, you would use the following code:

```
<%
    Response.Write("Hello, World!")
%>
```

You could also use

```
<%
    Page.Response.Write("Hello, World!")
%>
```

But it is not necessary to add the *Page* property because the *Response* property and the other *Page* members are exposed directly.

Writing Code in Web Forms

One of the strengths of classic ASP was that it gave you a lot of flexibility in writing your code. You could write your code inline with the HTML markup, as a part of <% %> render blocks. You could write your code in subroutines in render blocks. And you could write your code in *<script>* declaration blocks, either as arbitrary code or as subroutines.

While this flexibility made it very easy to create ASP pages, it was also a major weakness of classic ASP because it allowed for some sloppy coding. It was far too easy to write unmanageable spaghetti code, with some code inline, some code in subroutines, etc. In addition, although code in render blocks in classic ASP was executed in a linear fashion, arbitrary code (code not contained in a subroutine) in a *<script>* block was not. This often resulted in confusion, because sometimes this code was executed out of sequence with what developers expected.

ASP.NET solves these problems by imposing limitations on what types of code may be written, and where. As with classic ASP, there are still two ways to write code within a Web Forms page: *<script>* blocks and <% %> render blocks.

Using <script> Code Declaration Blocks

As mentioned, in classic ASP, you could write pretty much any code you wanted (property and method definitions, arbitrary code, etc.) in a *<script>* block using the *runat="server"* attribute. The problem was that you couldn't be sure when any arbitrary code in the *<script>* block would execute, relative to the code in the rest of the page. For this reason, ASP.NET does not allow you to use arbitrary code within *<script>* blocks, which are now referred to as code declaration blocks, to emphasize their purpose of declaring properties and methods.

So if you want to call *Response.Write* within a code declaration block, you need to wrap that call within a method declaration. The following code will work:

```
<script language="vb" runat="server">
   Sub SayHello
      Response.Write("Hello, World!")
   End Sub
</script>
```

The following code will cause an error:

```
<script language="vb" runat="server">
      Response.Write("Hello, World!")
</script>
```

Likewise, you can declare a local member variable in a declaration block, but you may not assign to it outside of a defined method. So the following code will work:

```
<script language="vb" runat="server">
   Dim Name As String
   Sub SetName
      Name = "Andrew"
   End Sub
</script>
```

But the following will cause an error:

```
<script language="vb" runat="server">
   Dim Name As String
   Name = "Andrew"
</script>
```

There is one exception to the variable assignment rule. You can initialize the value of a variable by assigning a value as part of the variable declaration, as follows:

```
<script language="vb" runat="server">
   Dim Name As String = "Andrew"
</script>
```

The *language* attribute of the *<script>* block is optional. If it is omitted, the value will default to the language specified by the @ *Page* directive's *language* attribute. If no *language* attribute has been specified for the @ *Page* directive, the value will default to *VB*.

Using ASP <% %> Code Render Blocks

Like *<script>* blocks, <% %> render blocks in classic ASP were pretty much "anything goes." In many cases, this led to sloppy programming habits and hard-to-maintain code. ASP.NET solves these problems by not allowing anything other than inline code and expressions in render blocks. This means that you can no longer place method definitions in a render block. So the following code will cause a compiler error:

```
<%
Sub SayHello
   Response.Write("Hello, World!")
End Sub
%>
```

Whereas the following code will work fine:

```
<%
   Response.Write("Hello, World!")
%>
```

Compatibility with Classic ASP

Clearly, one of the issues that arises from these changes is that a good deal of code written in classic ASP will not be compatible with the restrictions on the use of code declaration and render blocks. For this reason, it is a good idea to examine any classic ASP code that you are considering migrating to ASP.NET for these incompatibilities, so that you can address them before making the migration. (And discovering too late that the code won't work!)

Creating and Using User Controls

User controls are a new feature of ASP.NET that provides a simple and fast method for getting reuse out of your presentation code. User controls can also dramatically increase performance when used in conjunction with the *OutputCache* directive described previously. They are sometimes referred to as *declarative* controls (as opposed to server controls, which are *compiled* controls).

At their simplest, user controls consist of HTML markup and/or ASP.NET code persisted in a file with the .ascx file extension. As you saw earlier in this chapter, developers of user controls can also add the @ *Control* directive to specify aspects of how the user control will behave. Unlike Web Forms pages, user controls cannot be called directly. Instead, they must be used in an existing page.

User controls can contain most, but not all, of the same elements that can be used in Web Forms pages. For example, user controls should not contain *<html>*, *<body>*, or *<form>* elements because presumably they already exist in the page in which the user control is used. It's also a good idea to at least add the @ *Control* directive, along with its *ClassName* attribute, as follows:

```
<%@ Control ClassName="MyClass" %>
```

Adding the *ClassName* attribute allows the user control to be strongly typed when added to a page programmatically (as opposed to declaratively).

Creating a User Control

Creating a user control is fairly straightforward.

1   Using your favorite text editor, create a new file called Hello.ascx and save it to a folder that is set up as an IIS virtual directory.

2   Add the following code to the file:

```
<%@ Control ClassName="Hello" %>
<script language="vb" runat="server">
    Private _name As String = ""

    Public Property Name As String
      Get
        Return _name
```

```
        End Get
        Set
            _name = Value
        End Set
    End Property

    Public Sub SayHello()
        Label1.Text = "Hello, " & _name & "!"
    End Sub
</script>
<asp:Label id=Label1 runat="server"></asp:label>
```

3   Save the file.

This code declares a private string variable called *_name*; a *Property* procedure called *Name* that will be used to set and retrieve the value of the *_name* variable from outside the user control; and a *Sub* procedure called *SayHello* that sets the *Text* property of the *Label* server control defined in the last line of the user control code.

In order to use this control, you need to add it to a Web Forms page. There are two ways to do this: declaratively and programmatically. The declarative method is simpler, but the programmatic method gives you better runtime control.

Adding a User Control to a Page Declaratively

To use a user control in a Web Forms page, you need to make the control available to the page, and implement the control on the page. As described in "Using Directives" on page 214, user controls can be made available to a page using either the @ *Register* directive or the @ *Reference* directive, depending on whether you are adding the control declaratively or programmatically. If you want to add the control declaratively, you need to use the @ *Register* directive to set up the tag syntax for the control.

1   Create a new Web Forms page called HelloContainer.aspx and save it in the same folder as Hello.ascx.

2   Add the following code to the file:

```
<%@ Page Language="vb" %>
<%@ Register TagPrefix="ASPNETSbS" TagName="Hello"
    Src="hello.ascx" %>
<html>
<head>
</head>
```

```
<body>

</body>
</html>
```

3 Save the file, but don't close it. You'll be adding to it in a moment.

Using the @ *Register* directive allows you to declare a user control instance (thus, declarative) using a tag-based syntax similar to HTML. The *TagPrefix* and *TagName* attributes in the @ *Register* directive determine the syntax for the tag. Here's how to add an instance of the Hello.ascx user control to the page:

1 Add the following line to the <*body*> section of the HelloContainer.aspx page:

```
<body>
    <ASPNETSBS:Hello id="MyHello" runat="server"/>
</body>
```

2 Save the file, but again, don't close it.

This tag adds an instance of the user control defined in Hello.ascx to the page and gives it the ID *MyHello*. It also provides a placeholder in the page for any output generated by the user control.

The last thing you need to do is set the *Name* property of the user control and call its *SayHello* method, which you'll do by adding a *Page_Load* method to the page. Note that you can also define a *Page_Load* method in the user control to have the user control take care of setting its property and calling its method. To set the property and call the method when your Web Forms page is loaded, follow these steps:

1 Add the following code in the <*head*> section of the HelloContainer.aspx page, as shown here:

```
<head>
    <script runat="server">
        Sub Page_Load(Sender As Object, E As EventArgs)
            MyHello.Name = "Andrew"
            MyHello.SayHello
        End Sub
    </script>
</head>
```

2 Save the page.

3   Browse HelloContainer.aspx. You can do this either by entering the URL for the virtual directory in which you saved the file, plus the file name, into the browser address box, or by opening Internet Services Manager, locating the folder containing the page, right-clicking the page, and selecting Browse, as shown in the following figure.

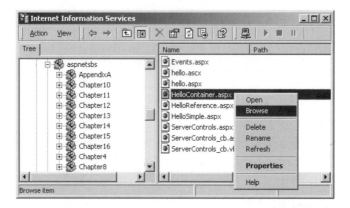

The output should appear similar to that in the following figure.

Adding a User Control to a Page Programmatically

The steps for adding a control to a page programmatically are somewhat similar, but a bit more involved than adding a control declaratively. You still need to make the control available to the page. For controls that are to be added programmatically, you can do this with either the @ *Register* directive, as in the previous example, or the @ *Reference* directive. Since the @ *Register* directive is more commonly used for declarative controls, use the @ *Reference* directive.

1   Create a new Web Forms page called HelloReference.aspx and save it in the same folder as Hello.ascx.

2   Add the following code to the file:

```
<%@ Page Language="vb" %>
<%@ Reference Control="hello.ascx" %>
```

```
<html>
<head>
</head>
<body>
</body>
</html>
```

3   Save the file, but don't close it.

The @ *Reference* directive tells ASP.NET to compile and link the user control hello.ascx with the page when it is compiled. This makes the control available to be added to the page. Since you're not going to be adding a tag within the HTML markup for the control's output, take advantage of a special server control called the *Placeholder* control. As the name suggests, this allows you to put a placeholder in the HTML markup to which you can add controls later. In this way, you can decide precisely where you want the output from the control to appear. Here's how to add the *Placeholder* control:

1   Add the following line to the *<body>* section of the HelloReference.aspx page:

```
<body>
    <asp:placeholder id="HelloHolder" runat="server"/>
</body>
```

2   Save the file, but don't close it yet.

Finally we need to add the control to the page, and add it to the *Controls* collection of the *Placeholder* control, which will place the output of the control where we want it. Then we'll set the *Name* property of the control, and call the *SayHello* method, just as we did before.

1   Add the following code in the *<head>* section of the HelloReference.aspx page:

```
<head>
    <script runat="server">
        Sub Page_Load(Sender As Object, E As EventArgs)
            Dim MyHello As Control = LoadControl("hello.ascx")
            HelloHolder.Controls.Add(MyHello)
            CType(MyHello, Hello).Name = "Andrew"
            CType(MyHello, Hello).SayHello
        End Sub
    </script>
</head>
```

2   Save the page.

Creating Web Forms

9

3   Browse HelloReference.aspx. Either type the URL for the virtual directory in which you saved the file, plus the file name, into the browser address box, or use the Internet Services Manager as shown in the previous example. The output of the page should be the same as in the previous figure.

Comparing User Controls to Include Files

User controls perform a similar function to server-side includes in classic ASP, but they're considerably more powerful because of the level of integration with the page model. A user control can have its own controls, and it can save the viewstate of its controls or its own viewstate. This allows the user control to maintain its state across multiple calls without any effort on the part of the page containing the user control. User controls can expose both properties and methods, making them easy to understand for developers who are used to components.

Include files are still available in ASP.NET, mainly for backward compatibility with classic ASP. For new applications, it makes more sense to use user controls, given their advantages.

Using Server Controls

Like user controls, ASP.NET *server controls* allow developers to reuse functionality. ASP.NET comes with a wide variety of built-in server controls that provide a great deal of functionality that developers can reuse in their applications. These include controls that provide server-side equivalents of standard HTML controls, more advanced controls that mimic Visual Basic–style controls, and validation controls that allow powerful and robust validation of data entry. Developers can also create custom server controls to provide their own reusable functionality.

The code for adding a server control to a page is simple and straightforward, particularly for the built-in server controls. This section demonstrates how to add an HTML control (a server control from the *System.Web.HtmlControls* namespace), a Web control (a server control from the *System.Web.WebControls* namespace), and a custom server control to a page. The differences between HTML controls and Web controls are discussed in detail in Chapter 10. The creation of custom server controls is discussed in Chapter 12.

One of the advantages of the built-in server controls is that they are available from any Web Forms page. You don't need to make them available via the

@ *Register* or @ *Reference* directives, as is necessary with user controls (as well as with custom server controls, as you'll see later in this section). This means that to use a server control, you need only add the appropriate tag to your page.

Adding an HTML Control to the Page

HTML controls use the same syntax as client-side HTML elements, with one addition: the *runat="server"* attribute. So in order to add an *HtmlInputButton* control (a server control that maps to the HTML *<input type="submit">*, *<input type="button">*, or *<input type="reset">* elements) to a page, follow these steps:

1 Using your favorite text editor, create a new page in the same folder as the previous examples. Name the page ServerControls.aspx.

2 Add the following code to the page:

```
<%@ Page Language="vb" %>
<html>
<head>
</head>
<body>
    <form runat="server">
        <input id="NameButton" type="submit" runat="server"/>
    </form>
</body>
</html>
```

3 Save the page, but don't close it. You'll use this page for further examples.

By adding the *runat="server"* attribute to the HTML *<input>* element, you've created a full-fledged server control that can now be manipulated programmatically through server-side code. Note that to make it easier to program against your server controls, you should always give them an *id* attribute, which specifies the name you'll use to identify the control in server-side code. You've also added a server-side *<form>* to wrap your server control, which causes the page to be posted back to the server when the button is clicked.

Adding a Web Control to the Page

Web controls use a slightly different syntax than HTML controls. It's similar to the syntax used for adding a user control to the page declaratively, except that instead of defining your own tag prefix, all Web controls use the prefix *asp*. For example, the tag for adding a *TextBox* Web control to the page would be *<asp:TextBox id="myTextBox" runat="server"/>*.

> **note**
>
> If you're familiar with XML namespaces, you may notice the similarity between the tag prefixes used for Web controls, user controls, custom server controls, and XML namespaces. This is no coincidence, since the implementation of the tag syntax for server controls and user controls is based on XML namespaces.
>
> Likewise, user control and server control tags must also follow the syntax rules for XML tags, which require an opening and closing tag for any tag that contains text or child tags, such as the *Label* Web control, which allows you to set its *Text* property by placing the desired text between the opening and closing *<asp:label>* tags. A closing / in a single tag may be used for tags that do not contain text or child tags, such as the *HtmlInputButton* HTML control.

To add a *TextBox* Web control and two *Label* Web controls, follow these steps:

1   Add the following tags to the server-side form of the ServerControls.aspx page created in the previous example:

```
<asp:Label id="NameLabel" runat="server">Name: </asp:Label>
<asp:TextBox id="NameTextBox" runat="server"/>
```

2   Add another *Label* control just below the closing *</form>* tag. Set the *id* attribute to *"HelloLabel"*. Use the single-tag syntax. The finished *<body>* section of the page should look like the following:

```
<body>
   <form runat="server">
    <asp:Label id="NameLabel" runat="server">Name: </asp:Label>
    <asp:TextBox id="NameTextBox" runat="server"/>
    <input id="NameButton" type="submit" runat="server"/>
   </form>
   <asp:Label id="HelloLabel" runat="server"/>
</body>
```

3   Save the page, but don't close it.

Having added this code, you can enter text in the *TextBox* control and submit the page by clicking the button. But you still must add code to process text entered in the textbox. See "Event Handling" on page 240 for more information.

Server-Side Forms, Postbacks, and ViewState

The term *postback* describes the ability of an ASP.NET page to make an HTTP *POST* request to itself, usually in response to a user clicking a button server control or interacting with another server control that initiates a postback. Postbacks are very useful because they allow a single page to both display UI elements, such as form fields for a user to fill in, and process the data entered by the user. The page developer can check the page-level *IsPostBack* property to determine whether the current request is the result of a postback, and then take appropriate action.

By default, server controls such as the *TextBox* and *DropDownList* Web controls automatically save their state from request to request using the viewstate facility built into ASP.NET.

Both the postback and viewstate facilities require the use of a server-side *<form>* to function. HTML controls and Web controls may be added to a Web Forms page without the a server-side *<form>* element wrapping the controls, and the controls will still function and can still be manipulated programmatically. But these controls will not be able to participate in postbacks, nor will they be able to save their state in the page's viewstate. For this reason, when using server controls, most often you'll want to wrap the controls in a server-side *<form>*.

Adding a Custom Server Control to the Page

Custom server controls use essentially the same tag syntax as user controls, but a slightly different form of the @ *Register* directive to make the custom control available to the page. Whereas the @ *Register* directive for a user control contains *TagPrefix* and *TagName* attributes to specify the tag that will be used to invoke the user control, and an *Src* attribute that points to the .ascx file containing the user control, the @ *Register* directive for a custom server control contains only the *TagPrefix* attribute, while the tag name for the control is supplied by the class name of the class that defines the server control. The location of the custom server control is supplied by an *Assembly* attribute containing the name of the compiled

9

Creating Web Forms

assembly containing the control definition. This assembly must reside either in the Web application's bin subdirectory or in the global assembly cache. The @ *Register* directive for a custom server control also requires a *Namespace* attribute with the namespace that contains the class defining the custom control.

Assuming you had a custom server control with a class name of *MyControlClass* in a namespace called *MyNS* in an assembly called MyControl.dll, the @ *Register* directive for the control would look like the following:

```
<%@ Register TagPrefix="MyPrefix" Namespace="MyNS"
    Assembly="MyControl" %>
```

The tag used to invoke the control would look like the following:

```
<MyPrefix:MyControlClass id="MyControlID" runat="server"/>
```

For more information on the standard server controls included with ASP.NET, refer to Chapter 10. Creating and using custom server controls is covered in much greater detail in Chapter 12.

Event Handling

One of the biggest differences between classic ASP and ASP.NET is the execution model. In classic ASP, pages were executed in a top-to-bottom fashion. That is, with the exception of detours to execute functions defined in the page, classic ASP pages were procedural rather than event-driven, like Visual Basic programs.

ASP.NET changes that by bringing event-driven programming to Web development through server controls and postbacks. At runtime, the code in a Web Form, as well as in any code-behind class associated with that Web Form, is compiled into an assembly. When executed, the code in that assembly fires events that you can handle, both those exposed by the *Page* class and those that are fired by server controls that have been added to the page.

Some events, such as those fired by the page, are fired automatically as certain stages of page processing occur. Others, such as those associated with server controls, are actually triggered on the client (such as a user clicking a button server control) but are fired and handled on the server when the page is posted back to the server. Because the page is reloaded and the control state is restored with each postback, to the client it appears as though the page is there throughout the client's interaction with it, and the application appears to operate much like a Visual Basic form-based application.

Page Processing Stages

A Web Forms page goes through the following processing stages:

- **Init** Page and control settings are initialized as necessary for the request.
- **LoadViewState** Server control state that was saved to viewstate in an earlier request is restored.
- **LoadPostData** Any data returned in server control form fields is processed, and the relevant control properties are updated.
- **Load** Controls are created and loaded, and control state matches the data entered by the client.
- **RaisePostDataChangedEvent** Events are raised in response to changes in control data from the previous request to the current request.
- **RaisePostBackEvent** The event that caused the postback is handled, and the appropriate server-side events are raised.
- **PreRender** Any changes that need to be made prior to rendering the page are processed. Any processing after this point will not be rendered to the page.
- **SaveViewState** Server control state is saved back to the page's viewstate prior to tearing down the controls.
- **Render** Control and page output is rendered to the client.
- **UnLoad** The page and its constituent controls are removed from memory on the server.

Of these stages, you can add page-level event handlers for the *Init*, *Load*, *PreRender*, and *UnLoad* events. These handlers are typically named *Page_Init*, *Page_Load*, *Page_PreRender*, and *Page_UnLoad*, respectively. For other stages, such as the *LoadViewState*, *SaveViewState*, and *Render* stages, you can override the appropriate method to customize the processing of these stages. Overriding these methods is discussed in Chapter 12.

Handling Page Events

Each stage in the processing of a Web Forms page fires an event that allows you to perform processing of your own during that stage.

To illustrate this concept, let's finish up the ServerControls.aspx page that you started in the previous example by adding an event handler to use the text the user enters in the *TextBox* server control.

1   If it's not already open, open the ServerControls.aspx page you created earlier.

2   Add the following code to the *<head>* section of the page:

```
<head>
<script runat="server">
    Sub Page_Load(Sender As Object, E As EventArgs)
        If IsPostBack Then
            HelloLabel.Text = "Hello, " & _
                Server.HtmlEncode(NameTextBox.Text) & "!"
        End If
    End Sub
</script>
</head>
```

3   Save the page, and then browse to it by entering the appropriate URL in a browser window, as shown in the following figure, or using Internet Services Manager.

4   Enter a name in the textbox, and then click the Submit Query button. After the page is posted back, the output should look similar to the following figure.

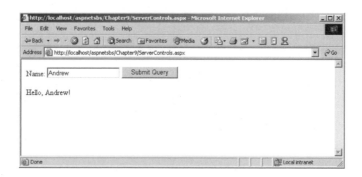

In the preceding code, you added an event handler for the *Page_Load* event. This event handler is called when the *Load* stage of the page processing is reached. In the event handler, you check the page-level property *IsPostBack* to determine if the page has been posted back as a result of a client action (clicking the button in this case). If it has, you set the *Text* property of *HelloLabel* to the desired text, which includes the text the user entered in the textbox. Notice that you use the *Server.HtmlEncode* utility method to encode the text entered by the user. This helps prevent nasty users from entering *<script>* tags or other HTML content to do something you don't want them to do. Using the *HtmlEncode* method means that any such content will be written out using HTML entity equivalents of characters such as less than (<), greater than (>), and quotation marks.

important

The preceding code assumes that the *AutoEventWireup* attribute of the page has been set to *true*. Normally, you won't need to set this manually, since this is the default setting that is inherited from the *<pages>* configuration section in Machine.config. However, pages created by Visual Studio .NET have the *AutoEventWireup* attribute in their @ *Page* directive set to *false*. This means that all event handlers in these pages must be manually wired to the events that they are to handle. You'll learn about manually wiring events in Chapter 10.

Handling Control Events

Handling events raised by controls is fairly straightforward. There are two steps. The first is similar to the way that you handle page events, only instead of naming the event handler *Page_eventname*, you use the syntax *controlname_eventname*.

This is similar to how event handlers are constructed in Visual Basic. The second step is to map the event raised by the control to the event handler using an attribute of the control's tag.

For example, if you wanted to add an event handler to ServerControls.aspx to handle the *TextChanged* event of the *TextBox* server control, you would add the following code to the *<script>* block in ServerControls.aspx:

```
Sub NameTextBox_TextChanged(Sender As Object, E As EventArgs)
    HelloLabel.Text &= " This text is different!"
End Sub
```

And then you would add the following attribute to the *NameTextBox* server control tag:

```
<asp:TextBox id="NameTextBox" onTextChanged="NameTextBox_TextChanged"
    runat="server"/>
```

Notice that here you use the &= operator to add text to the *Text* property of *HelloLabel*. The &= operator is shorthand for the following:

```
HelloLabel = HelloLabel & " This text is different!"
```

If you add this code to ServerControls.aspx and run it, the output when the text is changed will look like the following figure.

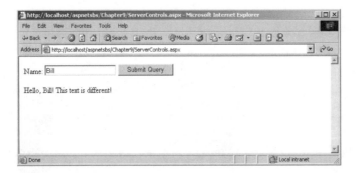

Handling Page Errors

While using structured exception handling may be useful for catching exceptions that are expected (see Chapter 4), there are times when you want to handle errors at the page level. This is possible through a special event handler called *Page_Error*. The *Page_Error* event is raised whenever a page encounters an unhandled exception. Within the *Page_Error* event handler, you can examine the exception that occurred using the *Server.GetLastError* method and take appropriate action or display a friendly message to the user.

Page Runtime Structure

As discussed earlier, at runtime ASP.NET combines the code in the page and any associated code-behind class into a single class, and then it compiles that class and executes it on the server. In the process, ASP.NET builds a control tree containing all of the controls on the page, including *LiteralControl* server controls for each section of HTML text.

important

When compiling a page, ASP.NET automatically creates controls that represent the HTML markup in the page, using the *LiteralControl* server control class. This allows the HTML markup to be easily manipulated at runtime, and also allows greater flexibility in adding controls at runtime. If the page contains <% %> render blocks, however, ASP.NET will not create controls to encapsulate the HTML markup. If you want to be able to manipulate the markup as *LiteralControls*, don't use <% %> render blocks.

At the top of the control tree is the control that represents the page, which has the ID *__PAGE*. Beneath that are any child controls that belong to the page's *Controls* collection. Each child control, depending on the type of control, may in turn have its own *Controls* collection containing child controls, and so on. This structure makes it much easier to find and manipulate controls at runtime.

Viewing the Page Control Tree

The easiest way to view the control tree for a page is to turn on tracing for the page. To view the control tree for the ServerControls.aspx page you created earlier, follow these steps:

1   Open ServerControls.aspx in a text editor.

2   Add the *Trace* attribute to the @ *Page* directive and set its value to *true*. The completed directive is as follows:

```
<%@ Page Language="vb" Trace="true" %>
```

3   Save the file and browse the page. The control tree section of the Server-Controls.aspx trace output is shown in the following figure. Notice that where a control has been given an explicit ID through its *id* tag attribute, that ID is used in the control tree.

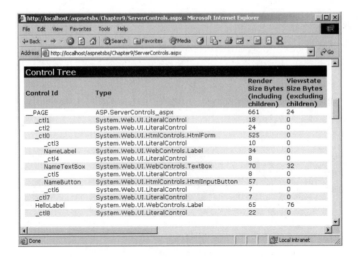

Adding and Manipulating Controls at Runtime

Thanks to the control tree built by ASP.NET at runtime, you can easily add, remove, or manipulate controls at runtime, even if you don't know the name of a control. For example, you can use the *Add* method of the page's *Controls* collection to add a new control to the page at runtime.

```
Dim MyTextBox As New TextBox
Page.Controls.Add(MyTextBox)
```

If you want to place the new control at a particular position in the control tree, you can use the *AddAt* method instead.

```
Dim MyTextBox As New TextBox
Page.Controls.AddAt(2, MyTextBox)
```

To remove a control by name, you can use the *Remove* method.

```
Page.Controls.Remove(MyTextBox)
```

And to remove a control by index, you can use *RemoveAt*.

```
Page.Controls.RemoveAt(2)
```

To locate a particular control by ID, you can use the *FindControl* method of the page or control containing the control you're looking for.

```
MyControl = Page.FindControl("MyTextBox")
```

Note that because *FindControl* returns an object of type *Control* (rather than of the specific type of control used), you will need to cast to the appropriate control type before using properties or methods that are specific to that control type.

Using Code-Behind in Web Forms

In addition to the changes in *<script>* blocks and <% %> render blocks in ASP.NET that make it easier to write clean code, ASP.NET introduces an entirely new concept called *code-behind*, which allows developers to entirely separate executable code from their HTML markup and server control tags.

A code-behind for a Web Form consists of a file containing a class derived from the *Page* class, and optionally contained within a namespace. The Web Form page then inherits from the code-behind class at runtime, allowing both the Web Form and its code-behind class to be compiled into a single assembly for execution.

Separating Code from UI

To show you how this works, let's use the ServerControls.aspx page one last time. To use code-behind with this page, follow these steps:

1   Open ServerControls.aspx in a text editor.

2   Using a text editor, create two new files, ServerControls_cb.aspx and ServerControls_cb.vb.

3   Copy all of the text from ServerControls.aspx and paste it into ServerControls_cb.aspx, and then close ServerControls.aspx.

4   Cut all of the code contained within the *<script>* block in ServerControl_cb.aspx and paste it into ServerControls_cb.vb, and then remove the *<script>* tags.

5   Add *Src* and *Inherits* attributes to the @ *Page* directive in ServerControls_cb.aspx to help ASP.NET locate the code-behind class file.

```
<%@ Page Language="vb" Src="ServerControls_cb.vb"
    Inherits="ServerControls" %>
```

6   Save ServerControls_cb.aspx. The final page should look like the following:

```
<%@ Page Language="vb" Src="ServerControls_cb.vb"
    Inherits="ServerControls" %>
<html>
<head>
</head>
<body>
   <form runat="server">
    <asp:Label id="NameLabel" runat="server">Name: </asp:Label>
      <asp:TextBox id="NameTextBox"
       onTextChanged="NameTextBox_TextChanged" runat="server"/>
       <input id="NameButton" type="submit" runat="server"/>
   </form>
```

```
      <asp:Label id="HelloLabel" runat="server"/>
</body>
</html>
```

7   Add the following code to ServerControls_cb.vb, before the text that you pasted in step 4:

```
Imports System
Imports System.Web
Imports System.Web.UI
Imports System.Web.UI.WebControls

Public Class ServerControls
    Inherits Page
    Public HelloLabel As Label
    Public NameTextBox As TextBox
```

8   Add an *End Class* statement to ServerControls_cb.vb, after the text that you pasted in step 4. The finished code should look like the following:

```
Imports System
Imports System.Web
Imports System.Web.UI
Imports System.Web.UI.WebControls

Public Class ServerControls
    Inherits Page
    Public HelloLabel As Label
    Public NameTextBox As TextBox

    Sub Page_Load(Sender As Object, E As EventArgs)
        If IsPostBack Then
            HelloLabel.Text = "Hello, " & _
                Server.HtmlEncode(NameTextBox.Text) & "!"
        End If
    End Sub

    Sub NameTextBox_TextChanged(Sender As Object, E As EventArgs)
        HelloLabel.Text += " This text is different!"
    End Sub
End Class
```

9   Save both files, and browse ServerControls_cb.aspx. The output should be the same as in the previous figure.

In this example, you've separated the event handling code into a code-behind class file. To make this work, you've had to take some extra steps. You added the *Imports* statements to the code-behind file to allow you to use the names of classes such as *Label* and *Textbox* without explicitly adding their namespaces. This is essentially the same as using the @ *Import* directive described earlier in this chapter. One difference is that unlike Web Forms pages, code-behind class files must explicitly import any of the namespaces for classes to be used in the file (unless all class references use the fully qualified name for the class).

You also added the *Class* statement, to define the class *ServerControls*, and the *Inherits* statement, which specifies that you want the *ServerControls* class to be derived from the *Page* class. Then you declared two *Public* variables, one for each server control that you want to access in your event-handler code. Finally, you wrapped up the code-behind with an *End Class* statement to close out the class.

In the Web Form, you associated ServerControls_cb.vb with ServerControls_cb.aspx by adding the *Src* and *Inherits* attributes to the @ *Page* directive. The *Src* attribute tells ASP.NET where to locate the class file for the code-behind, and the *Inherits* attribute tells ASP.NET which class (or namespace and class) you want to inherit from in the code-behind file.

While there are a few more steps involved in creating a page that uses code-behind compared to writing all of your code in a Web Form, the resulting code is generally much easier to maintain and update. For complicated pages, this alone can make it well worthwhile to use code-behind.

Creating Web Forms

Chapter 9 Quick Reference

To	Do This
Modify the runtime behavior of an ASP.NET Web Form	Add the @ *Page* directive to the page and set the desired attributes.
Use classes by name without explicitly specifying their namespace	In a Web Form, add the @ *Import* directive, with the namespace attribute specifying the namespace to import.
	In a Visual Basic .NET code-behind file, add the *Imports* statement with the desired namespace.
	In a C# code-behind file, add the *using* statement with the desired namespace (such as *using System.Web;*).
Make a user control or custom server control available for use on a Web Form	Add the @ *Register* directive to the page, and set the appropriate attributes.
Enable output caching	Add the @ *OutputCache* directive to the page, and set the desired attributes.
Create a user control	Create a file with the .ascx extension containing the desired HTML markup, server controls and code. User controls should not contain *<html>*, *<body>*, or *<form>* elements.
	Optionally, add the @ *Control* directive to modify the runtime behavior of the control.
Write server-side functions in a Web Forms page	Create a *<script>* block with the *runat="server"* attribute and place the functions within it.
Handle page-level events	Add an event handler with the appropriate signature (such as *Page_eventname*) to the server *<script>* block.

Using Server Controls

In this chapter, you will learn about

✔ *The purposes of the two main types of server controls: HTML controls and Web controls*

✔ *How to use specialized Web controls, such as the* Calendar *control and the* Validation *server controls*

✔ *How to perform data binding on server controls*

✔ *How to manipulate server controls programmatically at runtime*

✔ *How to handle server control events*

Chapter 9 looked at how Web Forms pages are constructed, including some simple uses of server controls. This chapter will take an in-depth look at using server controls in your application.

Types of Controls

As discussed briefly in the previous chapter, the built-in server controls in ASP.NET are divided into two groups, HTML controls and Web controls, each of which is contained in its own namespace. This section will discuss the available controls in each group and show examples of when and how to use each type of control. It will also discuss some of the specialized Web controls, including the *Calendar* and *AdRotator* controls, as well as the *Validation* server controls.

HTML Controls

The HTML controls map 1-to-1 with the standard HTML elements. However, some HTML elements don't map directly to a specific HTML control. Why would you want to use an HTML control instead of just coding HTML?

You do this because you can easily manipulate the look and functionality of the page at runtime by changing the control's attributes programmatically.

The HTML controls reside in the *System.Web.UI.HtmlControls* namespace, which is available to Web Forms pages automatically. The HTML elements for which there is direct mapping are shown in the following table.

Mapping of HTML Elements to HTML Controls		
HTML Element	**Control Type**	**Purpose**
<a>	*HtmlAnchor*	Allows programmatic access to the HTML anchor element. Exposes the *ServerClick* event.
<button>	*HtmlButton*	Allows programmatic access to the HTML button element. This element is defined in the HTML 4.0 spec and is only supported by Internet Explorer 4.0 and higher. Exposes the *ServerClick* event.
<form>	*HtmlForm*	Allows programmatic access to the HTML form element. Acts as a container for other server controls. Any controls that need to participate in postbacks should be contained within an *HtmlForm* control.
<img>	*HtmlImage*	Allows programmatic access to the HTML image element.
<input type="button"> *<input type="submit">* *<input type="reset">*	*HtmlInputButton*	Allows programmatic access to the HTML input element for the *button*, *submit*, and *reset* input types. Exposes the *ServerClick* event.
<input type="checkbox">	*HtmlInputCheckBox*	Allows programmatic access to the HTML input element for the *checkbox* input type. Exposes the *ServerChange* event.
<input type="file">	*HtmlInputFile*	Allows programmatic access to the HTML input element for the *file* input type.

Mapping of HTML Elements to HTML Controls		
HTML Element	**Control Type**	**Purpose**
<input type="hidden">	*HtmlInputHidden*	Allows programmatic access to the HTML input element for the *hidden* input type. Exposes the *ServerChange* event.
<input type="image">	*HtmlInputImage*	Allows programmatic access to the HTML input element for the *image* input type. Exposes the *ServerClick* event.
<input type="radio">	*HtmlInputRadioButton*	Allows programmatic access to the HTML input element for the *radio* input type.
<input type="text"> *<input type="password">*	*HtmlInputText*	Allows programmatic access to the HTML input element for the *text* and *password* input types. Exposes the *ServerClick* event.
<select>	*HtmlSelect*	Allows programmatic access to the HTML select element. Exposes the *ServerChange* event.
<table>	*HtmlTable*	Allows programmatic access to the HTML table element. Note that some table subelements (such as *<col>*, *<tbody>*, *<thead>*, and *<tfoot>*) are not supported by the *HtmlTable* control.
<td> and *<th>*	*HtmlTableCell*	Allows programmatic access to HTML table cell elements.
<tr>	*HtmlTableRow*	Allows programmatic access to HTML table row elements.
<textarea>	*HtmlTextArea*	Allows programmatic access to the HTML text area element. Exposes the *ServerChange* event.
<body>, *<div>*, *<span>*, *<font>*, etc.	*HtmlGenericControl*	Allows programmatic access to any HTML element not specifically represented by its own HTML control class.

Each HTML control class is derived from the generic *HtmlControl* class. This class provides methods and properties common to all HTML controls, such as the *Attributes* collection, which provides a collection of name/value pairs for any attributes contained in the tag definition for the control (such as *id="myControl"* or *border="1"*). The individual control classes then expose additional methods and properties that are specific to the HTML element that they represent. For example, the *HtmlAnchor* control exposes an *Href* property that allows you to programmatically modify the URL to which the anchor tag is linked, as well as a *Target* property, which allows you to modify the target of the anchor tag.

important

Because the HTML controls do not expose a strongly typed control equivalent for every HTML element, you can use the *Attributes* collection to add tag attributes to any HTML control programmatically. This allows you to set properties of tags that are not exposed declaratively by the HTML control classes.

Many of the HTML controls also expose events to which you can respond (above and beyond the standard events inherited from *HtmlControl*). There are two events exposed by HTML controls, *ServerClick* and *ServerChange*. The table that begins on page 252 lists which controls support which events.

note

Unlike the server controls in the Web control namespace, which only handle server-side events, HTML controls can handle both server-side events and any client-side events that exist for the HTML element to which they map. For example, the *HtmlInputButton* control supports both the server-side *ServerClick* event and the client-side *Click* event.

To handle both events, you'd use the following tag declaration:

```
<input type="submit" onclick="client_handler"
    onserverclick="server_handler" runat="server"/>
```

This allows you to perform actions on the client before the page is posted back to the server, if desired.

Because of their close mapping to individual HTML elements, HTML controls provide the fastest and easiest path for moving from static HTML to the power of ASP.NET server controls.

> ## note
> In Web Forms pages, there are three basic rules of the game when it comes to case sensitivity.
>
> ■ Namespaces and class names are case sensitive. For example, namespaces imported using the @ *Import* directive will cause an error if the correct case is not used. This is a common cause of errors for those just getting started with ASP.NET.
>
> ■ Tag names and attributes are not case sensitive. This also applies to server control properties expressed as tag attributes.
>
> ■ Control names used in *<script>* blocks or in code-behind classes may or may not be case sensitive, depending on whether the language you're using is case sensitive. C# is case-sensitive, for example, so using the incorrect case for a control name or property in C# code can lead to errors.
>
> When you're working with a case-sensitive language, or when you receive errors such as "The Namespace or type *<namespace>* for the Import 'System.<namespace>' cannot be found," it's usually a good idea to check for incorrect case in control, class, or namespace names.

HTML Control Examples

To demonstrate the simplicity and power of HTML controls, let's take a look at some examples. Let's say you have the following static HTML page:

```
<html>
<body>
<font>Hello, World!</font>
</body>
</html>
```

By simply adding the *runat="server"* attribute and an *id* attribute to the *<body>* and *<font>* elements, you can turn these elements into *HtmlGenericControls*.

```
<html>
<body id="Body" runat="server">
<font id="HelloFont" runat="server">Hello, World!</font>
</body>
</html>
```

Once you've converted the elements to HTML controls, it is fairly simple to manipulate them in server-side code.

```
<html>
<head>
<script language="vb" runat="server">
   Sub Page_Load(Sender As Object, E As EventArgs)
      Body.Attributes("bgcolor") = "Red"
      HelloFont.Attributes("size") = "7"
      HelloFont.Attributes("color") = "Blue"
   End Sub
</script>
</head>
<body id="Body" runat="server">
<font id="HelloFont" runat="server">Hello, World!</font>
</body>
</html>
```

If you save and run this code, the output should look like the following figure.

HTML controls are useful for dynamically adding and removing HTML table rows or *<select>* items. In the following example, you'll see how to dynamically add and remove items in a drop-down list created by an *HtmlSelect* control:

1   Create a new text file called HtmlSelect.aspx in your favorite text editor.

2   Add the following HTML markup to the file:

```
<html>
<body>
```

```
<form>
    What's your favorite ice cream?<br/>
    <select id="IceCream" size="1">
        <option>Chocolate</option>
        <option>Strawberry</option>
        <option>Vanilla</option>
    </select>
    <input id="Enter" type="button" value="Enter">
    <h3><span id="Fave"></span></h3>
</form>
</body>
</html>
```

3   Add *runat="server"* attributes to the *<form>*, *<select>*, *<input>*, and *<span>* elements to transform them into HTML controls. After this step, the page should look like the following:

```
<html>
<body>
    <form runat="server">
        What's your favorite ice cream?<br/>
        <select id="IceCream" size="1" runat="server">
            <option>Chocolate</option>
            <option>Strawberry</option>
            <option>Vanilla</option>
        </select>
    <input id="Enter" type="button" value="Enter" runat="server">
        <h3><span id="Fave" runat="server"></span></h3>
    </form>
</body>
</html>
```

4   Add *Page_Load* and *Enter_Click* event handlers to the page to add new items to the *HtmlSelect* control and to display the choice of the user. (The following code should go between the first *<html>* tag and the *<body>* tag that follows it.)

```
<head>
<script language="vb" runat="server">
    Sub Page_Load()
        If Not IsPostBack Then
            IceCream.Items.Add("Pistachio")
            IceCream.Items.Add("Rocky Road")
            'We don't like Strawberry
            IceCream.Items.Remove("Strawberry")
```

```
        End If
    End Sub
    Sub Enter_Click(Sender As Object, E As EventArgs)
      Fave.InnerHtml = "Your favorite is " & IceCream.Value & "!"
    End Sub
</script>
</head>
```

5   Finally add an *OnServerClick* attribute to the *<input>* tag to route the *HtmlInputButton* control's *ServerClick* event to your event handler. The complete tag is shown here:

```
<input id="Enter" type="button" value="Enter"
    OnServerClick="Enter_Click" runat="server">
```

6   Save the page, and then browse it. The output should look similar to the following figure.

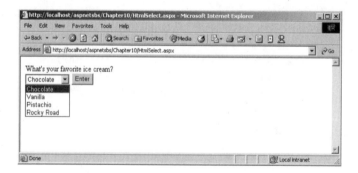

Web Controls

Web controls are truly the gem in the crown of ASP.NET. These server controls give you an unprecedented level of productivity by providing a rich, event-driven programming model, similar to that of Visual Basic. The Web controls reside in the *System.Web.UI.WebControls* namespace, which is available to all Web Forms pages automatically.

The Web controls run the gamut of functionality, from simple controls like the *Button*, *TextBox*, and *Label* controls, to the richer *ListBox* and *DropDownList* controls, to the even richer *Calendar* and *AdRotator* controls. There are even special controls that are especially designed for data binding, including the *DataGrid*, *DataList*, and *Repeater* controls. You'll see examples of these types of controls in later sections.

> **note**
>
> Although the *System.Web.UI.WebControls* and *System.Web.UI.HtmlControls*
> namespaces are available to Web Forms pages automatically, the same is not
> true of code-behind pages associated with Web Forms pages. If you want to use
> controls in either of these namespaces without using the fully qualified class
> name, you need to add the appropriate statement (*Imports* for Visual Basic;
> *using* for C#) to your code-behind class to import the namespace.

Adding Server Controls to a Page

As you saw in the last chapter, adding server controls to a page is fairly easy.
There are two different ways to add controls to a page, declaratively and programmatically. Either way allows you to set properties of the control as desired,
and either one can be used to place a control where you want it on the page.

Adding Controls Declaratively

As you saw earlier in this chapter, the ASP.NET HTML controls use essentially
the same syntax as standard HTML elements, with the exception of the *runat*
attribute, which is always set to *server*. Web controls also use a tag-based syntax,
but are prefaced with *asp:*. So, you'd declare an *HtmlInputButton* server control
with the following syntax:

```
<input id="Enter" type="button" value="Enter"
    OnServerClick="Enter_Click" runat="server">
```

You would declare an ASP.NET *Button* server control with the following syntax:

```
<asp:button id="Enter" Text="Enter" OnClick="Enter_Click"
    runat="server" />
```

Notice that in the second example, a / character is added before the closing >
character. This is required when you do not use a complete closing tag. Here's an
example of a closing tag:

```
<asp:label id="myLabel" runat="server">Hi there!</asp:label>
```

You enclose the literal text *Hi there!* between an opening and closing tag. The
literal text becomes the *Text* property of the *Label* control. The *Label* control,
which renders as a *<span>* on the client side, is one of a number of controls that
allow you to enclose literal text for the *Text* property, or some other property of
the control, between the opening and closing tags. Other controls include the
Literal, *Panel*, *PlaceHolder*, and *TextBox* controls.

Choosing the Right Control

Because there are two distinct sets of server controls to choose from, you may wonder how to choose the right control for a given application. In general, if you are interested in handling client-side events or are converting HTML elements to server controls, you should look at the HTML controls. If you're familiar with the Visual Basic programming model, the Web controls provide a model that maps very closely to that. The Web controls also provide additional functionality, such as validation, and provide a strong basis for customization.

You could also accomplish the same result by using a single-tag syntax.

```
<asp:label id="myLabel" text="Hi there!" runat="server"/>
```

When you add a control to the page declaratively, you are doing two things: giving the control enough information to be created and initialized properly, and setting the properties for the control. The first part is accomplished by the *asp:* prefix and the tag *(control)* name, plus the *id* and *runat* attributes. Only the prefix/tagname and *runat* attribute are required to create a server control, but the *id* attribute is required if you want to refer to the control in server-side code.

Once you've provided this minimum information, you can set additional properties by adding attributes to the tag declaration corresponding to the property you want to set. For example, if you wanted to set the *Visible* property of a *Label* control to *false* (to set up a message declaratively and show it by making it visible later in server-side code), you would modify the declaration as follows:

```
<asp:label id="myLabel" text="Hi there!" visible="false"
    runat="server"/>
```

Some of the more feature-filled controls, such as the *DataGrid* control, use a combination of attributes in the main tag definition and subtags that declare additional controls or set properties (such as the *ItemStyle* and *AlternatingItemStyle* tags that can be used with the *DataGrid* or *DataList* controls) to define the properties for the control. You'll see examples of these in this chapter.

Adding and Manipulating Controls Programmatically

Although adding controls to the page declaratively is probably the most straightforward approach, you can also add controls to the page and manipulate them programmatically. This gives you greater control because you can choose how and if to add controls at runtime.

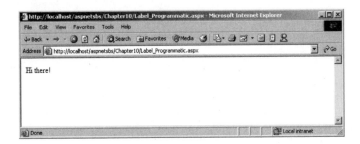

Adding a control programmatically is as simple as declaring a new instance of the control class and adding it to the page's *Controls* collection, as follows:

```
Dim myLabel As New Label
'You can also just use Controls, but the Page reference makes it
'    clear what you intend, which is always a good idea.
Page.Controls.Add(myLabel)
myLabel.Text = "Hi there!"
```

The output of this code, when added to the *Page_Load* event of a Web Forms page, produces the output shown in the following figure.

As you can see, the code successfully creates the *Label* control and sets its text property to *Hi there!*. There's just one problem. As written, the code adds the control to the end of the page's *Controls* collection, which is actually after the closing *<body>* and *<html>* tags, which ASP.NET treats as *Literal* controls on the server. The code that is sent to the browser is shown here:

```
<html>
<head>
</head>
<body>
</body>
</html>
<span>Hi there!</span>
```

While this output will still be rendered in most browsers, it's not ideal because it's incorrect HTML syntax. This presents even more of a problem when you are dealing with both declarative and programmatically created controls. Creating controls out of order may produce unintended results. So what do you do?

One option is to call the *AddAt* method of the *Controls* collection, instead of *Add*. *AddAt* takes two arguments: an integer representing the location in the collection where the control should be added, and the name of the control to add.

```
Page.Controls.AddAt(3, myLabel)
```

The only problem is that in order to render the control where you want it in the page, you have to know exactly where the control should appear in the collection. This is not always practical.

An easier way to ensure that programmatically created controls appear where you want them to is to use a *PlaceHolder* control to locate the control in the page. The *PlaceHolder* control has no UI of its own. All of the content within a *PlaceHolder* control is rendered based on the controls in its *Controls* collection. So, to make sure that the control in the previous example is displayed within the body of the HTML document sent to the browser, you can use the following code:

```
<%@ Page Language="vb" %>
<html>
<head>
<script runat="server">
    Sub Page_Load()
        Dim myLabel As New Label
        myPH.Controls.Add(myLabel)
        myLabel.Text = "Hi there!"
    End Sub
</script>
</head>
<body>
    <asp:placeholder id="myPH" runat="server" />
</body>
</html>
```

This produces the following HTML output:

```
<html>
<head>
</head>
<body>
    <span>Hi there!</span>
</body>
</html>
```

Multiple controls can be added to the same placeholder, and multiple place-holders can be used in the same page.

Adding Controls with Visual Studio .NET

Of course, the easiest way to add ASP.NET server controls to a Web Forms page (and to discover all of the properties available for a control) is to use the Visual Studio .NET Toolbox to add a control to the page. The Web Forms tab of the Toolbox is shown in the following figure.

Follow these steps to add a server control to a Web Forms page in Visual Studio .NET:

1   Open Visual Studio .NET and open the solution containing the page you want to edit.

2   Open the page to which you wish to add a server control by double-clicking it in the Solution Explorer window.

3   Make sure the page is displayed in Design mode by clicking the Design button that appears directly below the text/design editor pane.

4   Open the Toolbox window by moving the mouse pointer over the Toolbox tab in the IDE, and select the Web Forms tab of the Toolbox by clicking it.

5   Double-click the desired server control. The control will be inserted into the page at the location of the cursor if the page is in FlowLayout mode, or at the top-left corner of the page if the page is in GridLayout mode. In GridLayout mode, you can also select a control from the Toolbox and draw it on the form as you would a Visual Basic–style control.

6   Save the page.

Applying Styles to Controls

Once you've added your controls to the page, eventually you'll probably want to make changes to how those controls are displayed. For example, you may want to make the text of a *Label* control red. Simply set the *ForeColor* property of the control to *Red*, as follows:

```
<asp:label id="myLabel" forecolor="red" runat="server">
    Hi there!
</asp:label>
```

But what if you want to do something more complicated? While controls such as the *Label* control expose properties like *ForeColor* and *BackColor*, there are times when this will not be sufficient. Let's say you want to apply a Cascading Style Sheet (CSS) class defined elsewhere (either in a *Style* block at the top of the page or in a linked style sheet) to a server control. Or maybe you just want to use CSS styles directly in your control tag.

For these occasions, the *CssClass* and *Style* properties defined in the *WebControl* base class (and inherited by all *WebControl* classes) come in handy. With the *CssClass* property, you can set up a CSS class such as the following:

```
<style type="text/css">
.mylabel { font-size:24pt; font-weight:bold; color:red;}
</style>
```

You can use this to format your control as follows:

```
<asp:label id="myLabel" cssclass="mylabel" runat="server">
    Hi there!
</asp:label>
```

This technique works fine for linked style sheets as well.

The *Style* property can be used to specify CSS styles directly as follows:

```
<asp:label id="myLabel"
    style="font-size:24pt; font-weight:bold; color:red;"
    runat="server">
    Hi there!
</asp:label>
```

Note that whether you set the color of a *Label* control with the *ForeColor* property or use the *CssClass* or *Style* properties declaratively, the result is rendered as a class or style attribute on the resulting *<span>* tag, which is the client-side representation of the *WebControl* control.

> **note**
>
> Although you can set most control properties declaratively by using the property name as an attribute of the tag used to declare the control, some compound properties (properties that are represented by another class) require that you use a slightly different attribute syntax.
>
> A good example of this is the *Font* property (defined in the *WebControl* base class), which returns an instance of the *FontInfo* class. In order to modify the font of a control that inherits from *WebControl* (such as the *Label* control), you use attributes in the form *font-<propertyname>*, as follows:
>
> ```
> <asp:label id="myLabel" font-name="arial"
>     runat="server>
> ```
>
> You can also access these properties programmatically, using the form *<controlname>.Font.<propertyname>*, as follows:
>
> ```
> myLabel.Font.Name = "Arial"
> ```

Finally, you can also apply styles to your controls based on the client-side representation of the control. As noted, *Label* controls are rendered on the client as *<span>* tags, so if you define a style that applies to all *<span>* elements, your *Label* controls will also use this style. As long as you know the client-side representation of a particular control (which you can get by viewing the source of the page from the browser), you can create a style sheet to format that control.

Additional Web Control Examples

Web controls are quite easy to use and provide a great deal of flexibility. So far, you've used only simple examples. This section will look at a few more complex examples to demonstrate the use of various Web controls. The first example will show you how to use server controls to set up a form for sending e-mail from an ASP.NET Web Form via the Simple Mail Transport Protocol (SMTP). The second example will show you how to use *Panel* controls to simulate a wizard-style multipage interface within a single Web Forms page.

Sending Mail

A common task for many Web applications is sending e-mail to customers or visitors. Often, this e-mail is generated automatically, without the need for specific data entry. But site operators may also want a way to send a quick e-mail through the site. Web controls, in combination with the .NET *SmtpMail* and *MailMessage* classes, can make it quick and easy to add this functionality to a Web site.

> **note**
>
> This example assumes that you have access to an SMTP server from which to send your e-mail. Windows 2000, Windows XP Professional, and Windows .NET Server come with an SMTP service that is part of the services provided by IIS. The SMTP service is relatively easy to install and configure. Details for setting up the SMTP service can be found at *http://msdn.microsoft.com/library/en-us/dnduwon/html/d5smtp.asp*.

To add this functionality, follow these steps:

1   First set up an IIS virtual directory for the page, or choose an existing Web application for the page. Once you've done that, create a new file using your favorite text editor, and save the empty file as SmtpEmail.aspx.

2   Add the following to the file and save it (you may want to save a separate file with these elements to use as a template for your Web Forms pages):

```
<%@ Page Language="vb" %>
<html>
<head>
</head>
<body>
</body>
</html>
```

3   The first thing you'll add is a server-side form to contain all of your server controls. This will give you automatic handling of postback data and state for the controls. Add the following between the *<body>* tags in the file:

```
<form runat="server">
</form>
```

4   Next add an HTML table to the *<form>* to ensure that your controls line up nicely on the page.

```
<table>
  <tr>
    <td>
    </td>
    <td>
    </td>
  </tr>
  <tr>
```

```
        <td>
        </td>
        <td>
        </td>
    </tr>
    <tr>
        <td>
        </td>
        <td>
        </td>
    </tr>
    <tr>
        <td>
        </td>
        <td>
        </td>
    </tr>
    <tr>
        <td>
        </td>
        <td>
        </td>
    </tr>
</table>
```

5   Now add a *Label* control and a *TextBox* control to each row of the table (except the last one, which will be saved for another set of controls).

```
<table>
    <tr>
        <td>
            <asp:label id="ToLabel" text="To:" runat="server"/>
        </td>
        <td>
            <asp:textbox id="ToText" runat="server"/>
        </td>
    </tr>
    <tr>
        <td>
            <asp:label id="CCLabel" text="CC:" runat="server"/>
        </td>
        <td>
```

```
               <asp:textbox id="CCText" runat="server"/>
            </td>
         </tr>
         <tr>
            <td>
               <asp:label id="BCCLabel" text="BCC:" runat="server"/>
            </td>
            <td>
               <asp:textbox id="BCCText" runat="server"/>
            </td>
         </tr>
         <tr>
            <td>
         asp:label id="SubjectLabel" text="Subject:" runat="server"/>
            </td>
            <td>
               <asp:textbox id="SubjectText" runat="server"/>
            </td>
         </tr>
         <tr>
            <td>
              <asp:label id="BodyLabel" text="Body:" runat="server"/>
            </td>
            <td>
               <asp:textbox id="BodyText" runat="server"/>
            </td>
         </tr>
         <tr>
            <td>
            </td>
            <td>
            </td>
         </tr>
      </table>
```

6   To complete the user interface for the page, add a *Button* control and an *HtmlInputButton* to the last row of the table. Set the *type* attribute of the *HtmlInputButton* to *reset* so that it allows you to reset the form fields on the client without a round-trip to the server:

```
<tr>
   <td>
      <asp:button id="Send" text="Send" runat="server"/>
   </td>
   <td>
      <input id="reset" type="reset" value="Reset Form"
         runat="server"/>
   </td>
</tr>
```

7   If you save and browse the file, the output will look something like the
following figure.

8   The only real problem with this output is that the *Body* text box is a little small
for typing the body of an e-mail. You can solve this by adding a few attributes to
the *Body TextBox* control.

```
<asp:textbox id="Body" textmode="multiline" rows="10"
   columns="60" runat="server"/>
```

9   Now that you've completed the UI, you need to add code to send the mail when
the Send button is clicked. Start by adding a server-side *<script>* block, which
goes between the *<head>* and *</head>* tags:

```
<script runat="server">
</script>
```

10   Next add an event handler for the *Click* event of the *Button* control.

```
<script runat="server">
   Sub Send_Click(Sender As Object, e As EventArgs)
      'Code to handle the event goes here
      Response.Write("Send Clicked!")
   End Sub
</script>
```

11 Add an attribute to the *Button* control to map the event to the event handler, and then save the file.

```
<asp:button id="Send" text="Send" onclick="Send_Click"
    runat="server"/>
```

12 If you refresh the page now and then click the Send button, the output should look like the following figure. (If you get the Send Clicked! message, you know the event handler works.)

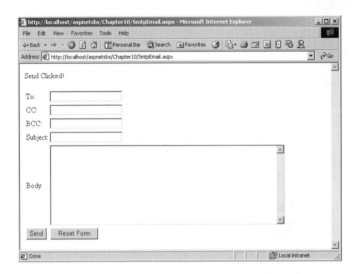

13 The last part of the process is adding the code to send an e-mail using the data entered by the user. First, add an @ *Import* directive to import the *System.Web.Mail* namespace so you can refer to its classes without using the namespace name each time. This directive should go directly below the @ *Page* directive at the top of the page.

```
<%@ Import Namespace="System.Web.Mail" %>
```

14 Finally replace the *Response.Write* statement in the event handler with the following code. It creates an instance of the *MailMessage* class, sets the necessary properties, and then sends the message using the *Send* method of the *SmtpMail* class. (Because the *Send* method is a *Static* method, it is not necessary to create an instance of *SmtpMail* to use the method). Once the mail has been sent, the code then hides all of the form controls by setting the *Visible* property for each control to *False*, and it adds a *HyperLink* control to link back to the original page to send another e-mail, if desired. Note that you need to set *Mail.From* to a valid e-mail address and *SmtpMail.SmtpServer* to the name of an available server running SMTP (unless the local machine is running SMTP, in which case this line may be removed).

```
'Create MailMessage instance, set properties, and send
Dim Mail As New MailMessage
Mail.To = ToText.Text
Mail.CC = CCText.Text
Mail.BCC = BCCText.Text
Mail.Subject = SubjectText.Text
Mail.Body = BodyText.Text
Mail.From = <valid email address>
SmtpMail.SmtpServer = <local SMTP server>
SmtpMail.Send(Mail)

'Use the first label to display status
ToLabel.Text = "Mail Sent"

'Hide the rest of the controls
ToText.Visible = False
CCLabel.Visible = False
CCText.Visible = False
BCCLabel.Visible = False
BCCText.Visible = False
SubjectLabel.Visible = False
SubjectText.Visible = False
BodyLabel.Visible = False
BodyText.Visible = False
Send.Visible = False
Reset.Visible = False

'Add a Hyperlink control to allow sending another email
Dim Link As New HyperLink
Link.Text = "Click here to send another email."
Link.NavigateUrl = "SmtpEmail.aspx"
Page.Controls.Add(Link)
```

15 Save and refresh the page. You should now be able to send an e-mail by filling out the fields (at a minimum, you must have an e-mail address in the To, CC, or BCC field) and clicking the Send button. The output should look something like the following figure, and the link should take you back to the form.

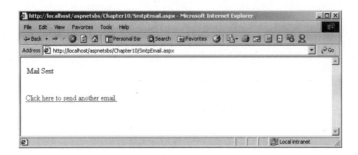

This example shows how simple it can be to send e-mail using server controls on a Web Form, but it does have a couple of shortcomings. One is that if you don't enter an address in the To, CC, or BCC field, you'll get an error. Another is that it takes a fair amount of code to hide all the controls once you've sent the e-mail. You can fix this second shortcoming by adding another *Label* control outside the table, and then turning the table into an *HtmlTable* control by adding the *runat="server"* attribute. You can then hide all of the controls in the table by setting the *Visible* property of *HtmlTable* to *False*. Make sure you save the example file because we'll be taking another look at it later in this chapter. The full code for this example is shown in the following listing.

SmtpEmail.aspx

```
<%@ Page Language="vb" %>
<%@ Import Namespace="System.Web.Mail" %>
<html>
<head>
<script runat="server">
    Sub Send_Click(Sender As Object, e As EventArgs)
        'Create MailMessage instance, set properties, and send
        Dim Mail As New MailMessage
        Mail.To = ToText.Text
        Mail.CC = CCText.Text
        Mail.BCC = BCCText.Text
        Mail.Subject = SubjectText.Text
        Mail.Body = BodyText.Text
        Mail.From = <valid email address>
```

```
SmtpMail.SmtpServer = <local SMTP server>
SmtpMail.Send(Mail)

'Use the first label to display status
ToLabel.Text = "Mail Sent"

'Hide the rest of the controls
ToText.Visible = False
CCLabel.Visible = False
CCText.Visible = False
BCCLabel.Visible = False
BCCText.Visible = False
SubjectLabel.Visible = False
SubjectText.Visible = False
BodyLabel.Visible = False
BodyText.Visible = False
Send.Visible = False
Reset.Visible = False

'Add a Hyperlink control to allow sending another email
Dim Link As New HyperLink
Link.Text = "Click here to send another email."
Link.NavigateUrl = "SmtpEmail.aspx"
Page.Controls.Add(Link)
    End Sub
</script>
</head>
<body>
<form runat="server">
<table>
    <tr>
        <td>
            <asp:label id="ToLabel" text="To:" runat="server"/>
        </td>
        <td>
            <asp:textbox id="ToText" runat="server"/>
        </td>
    </tr>
    <tr>
        <td>
            <asp:label id="CCLabel" text="CC:" runat="server"/>
```

```
          </td>
          <td>
             <asp:textbox id="CCText" runat="server"/>
          </td>
       </tr>
       <tr>
          <td>
             <asp:label id="BCCLabel" text="BCC:" runat="server"/>
          </td>
          <td>
             <asp:textbox id="BCCText" runat="server"/>
          </td>
       </tr>
       <tr>
          <td>
           <asp:label id="SubjectLabel" text="Subject:" runat="server"/>
          </td>
          <td>
             <asp:textbox id="SubjectText" runat="server"/>
          </td>
       </tr>
       <tr>
          <td>
             <asp:label id="BodyLabel" text="Body:" runat="server"/>
          </td>
          <td>
             <asp:textbox id="BodyText" textmode="multiline" rows="10"
                columns="60" runat="server"/>
          </td>
       </tr>
       <tr>
          <td>
             <asp:button id="Send" text="Send" onclick="Send_Click"
                runat="server"/>
          </td>
          <td>
             <input id="Reset" type="reset" value="Reset Form"
                runat="server"/>
          </td>
       </tr>
    </table>
```

```
</form>
</body>
</html>
```

Registration Wizard

Another common need in Web applications is providing users with an easy way to register. Registration allows you to provide personalized services, saved shopping carts, and other valuable services for your visitors. In order to make this as simple as possible, you might want to use a multipage format similar to a Windows Wizard interface. This type of interface will be immediately familiar to Windows users. The following listing shows the code for a simple registration wizard implemented as an ASP.NET Web Form.

RegWiz.aspx

```
<%@ Page Language="vb" %>
<html>
<head>
<script runat="server">
   Sub Page_Load()
      If Not IsPostBack Then
         Step1.Font.Bold = True
      End If
   End Sub
   Sub Next_Click(Sender As Object, e As EventArgs)
      Select Case Sender.Parent.ID
         Case "Page1"
            Page1.Visible = False
            Step1.Font.Bold = False
            Page2.Visible = True
            Step2.Font.Bold = True
         Case "Page2"
            Page2.Visible = False
            Step2.Font.Bold = False
            Page3.Visible = True
            Step3.Font.Bold = True
            ReviewFName.Text += FirstName.Text
            ReviewMName.Text += MiddleName.Text
            ReviewLName.Text += LastName.Text
            ReviewEmail.Text += Email.Text
            ReviewAddress.Text += Address.Text
            ReviewCity.Text += City.Text
```

```
                    ReviewState.Text += State.Text
                    ReviewZip.Text += Zip.Text
            End Select
        End Sub
        Sub Previous_Click(Sender As Object, e As EventArgs)
            Select Case Sender.Parent.ID
                Case "Page2"
                    Page2.Visible = False
                    Step2.Font.Bold = False
                    Page1.Visible = True
                    Step1.Font.Bold = True
                Case "Page3"
                    Page3.Visible = False
                    Step3.Font.Bold = False
                    Page2.Visible = True
                    Step2.Font.Bold = True
            End Select
        End Sub
    </script>
    <style type="text/css">
    div
    {
        background:silver;
        width:400px;
        border:2px outset;
        margin:5px;
        padding:5px;
    }
    </style>
    </head>
    <body>
        <form runat="server">
            <asp:label id="RegWiz" text="Registration Wizard"
                font-bold="true" font-size="16" font-name="verdana"
                runat="server"/>
            <br/>
            <asp:label id="Step1" text="Step 1: Enter Personal Info"
                font-name="verdana" runat="server"/>
            <br/>
            <asp:label id="Step2" text="Step 2: Enter Address Info"
                font-name="verdana" runat="server"/>
```

```
<br/>
<asp:label id="Step3" text="Step 3: Review"
    font-name="verdana"
    runat="server"/>
<br/>
<asp:panel id="Page1" runat="server">
    <table align="center">
        <tr>
            <td>
                <asp:label id="FirstNameLabel" text="First Name:"
                    runat="server"/>
            </td>
            <td>
              <asp:textbox id="FirstName" runat="server"/>
            </td>
        </tr>
        <tr>
            <td>
                <asp:label id="MiddleNameLabel" text="Middle Name:"
                    runat="server"/>
            </td>
            <td>
                <asp:textbox id="MiddleName" runat="server"/>
            </td>
        </tr>
        <tr>
            <td>
                <asp:label id="LastNameLabel" text="Last Name:"
                    runat="server"/>
            </td>
            <td>
                <asp:textbox id="LastName" runat="server"/>
            </td>
        </tr>
        <tr>
            <td>
                <asp:label id="EmailLabel" text="Email:"
                    runat="server"/>
            </td>
            <td>
                <asp:textbox id="Email" runat="server"/>
```

```
                        </td>
                    </tr>
                    <tr>
                        <td colspan="2" align="center">
                            <asp:button id="P1Previous" Text="Previous"
                                enabled="false" onclick="Previous_Click"
                                runat="server"/>
                            <asp:button id="P1Next" Text="Next"
                                onclick="Next_Click" runat="server"/>
                            <input id="P1Reset" type="reset" runat="server"/>
                        </td>
                    </tr>
                </table>
            </asp:panel>
            <asp:panel id="Page2" visible="false" runat="server">
                <table align="center">
                    <tr>
                        <td>
                            <asp:label id="AddressLabel" text="Street Address:"
                                runat="server"/>
                        </td>
                        <td>
                            <asp:textbox id="Address" runat="server"/>
                        </td>
                    </tr>
                    <tr>
                        <td>
                            <asp:label id="CityLabel" text="City:"
                                runat="server"/>
                        </td>
                        <td>
                            <asp:textbox id="City" runat="server"/>
                        </td>
                    </tr>
                    <tr>
                        <td>
                            <asp:label id="StateLabel" text="State:"
                                runat="server"/>
                        </td>
                        <td>
                            <asp:textbox id="State" runat="server"/>
```

```
            </td>
         </tr>
         <tr>
            <td>
               <asp:label id="ZipLabel" text="Zip Code:"
                  runat="server"/>
            </td>
            <td>
               <asp:textbox id="Zip" runat="server"/>
            </td>
         </tr>
         <tr>
            <td colspan="2" align="center">
               <asp:button id="P2Previous" Text="Previous"
                  onclick="Previous_Click" runat="server"/>
               <asp:button id="P2Next" Text="Next"
                  onclick="Next_Click" runat="server"/>
               <input id="P2Reset" type="reset" runat="server"/>
            </td>
         </tr>
      </table>
   </asp:panel>
   <asp:panel id="Page3" visible="false" runat="server">
      <table align="center">
         <tr>
            <td colspan="2">
               <asp:label id="ReviewFName" text="First Name: "
                  runat="server"/>
            </td>
         </tr>
         <tr>
            <td colspan="2">
               <asp:label id="ReviewMName" text="Middle Name: "
                  runat="server"/>
            </td>
         </tr>
         <tr>
            <td colspan="2">
               <asp:label id="ReviewLName" text="Last Name: "
                  runat="server"/>
            </td>
```

```
            </tr>
            <tr>
               <td colspan="2">
                  <asp:label id="ReviewEmail" text="Email: "
                     runat="server"/>
               </td>
            </tr>
            <tr>
               <td colspan="2">
                  <asp:label id="ReviewAddress" text="Address: "
                     runat="server"/>
               </td>
            </tr>
            <tr>
               <td colspan="2">
                  <asp:label id="ReviewCity" text="City: "
                     runat="server"/>
               </td>
            </tr>
            <tr>
               <td colspan="2">
                  <asp:label id="ReviewState" text="State: "
                     runat="server"/>
               </td>
            </tr>
            <tr>
               <td colspan="2">
                  <asp:label id="ReviewZip" text="Zip: "
                     runat="server"/>
               </td>
            </tr>
            <tr>
               <td colspan="2">
                  <asp:button id="P3Previous" Text="Previous"
                     onclick="Previous_Click" runat="server"/>
                  <asp:button id="P3Next" Text="Next" enabled="false"
                     onclick="Next_Click" runat="server"/>
                  <input id="P3Reset" type="reset" disabled="true"
                     runat="server"/>
               </td>
            </td>
```

```
        </tr>
      </table>
    </asp:panel>
  </form>
</body>
</html>
```

The keys to the functionality of the registration wizard are the three *Panel* controls and the *Next_Click* and *Previous_Click* event handlers. The *Panel* controls contain *Label*, *TextBox*, and *Button* Web controls (as well as an *HtmlInput-Button* control for resetting the form fields), which are formatted using standard HTML table elements. When the user clicks the Next button or the Previous button (depending on which one is enabled for that page), the event handlers hide the currently visible panel, show the next (or previous) panel, and update the *Label* controls that tell the user which step in the process they are on currently.

Since ASP.NET takes care of maintaining the state of the controls from request to request, it is simple to display the data entered by the user on the third panel by simply accessing the *Text* property of the *TextBox* controls on the other panels. Notice that the caption text of the controls on the third panel is set declaratively in the tag, and then the text that the user entered is appended to this text programmatically in the event handler using the &= operator. The first page of the registration wizard is shown in the following figure.

Specialty Controls

In addition to the standard suite of Web controls that provide functionality much like that of the Visual Basic GUI controls, ASP.NET also offers a set of richer specialty controls that reside in the *System.Web.UI.WebControls* namespace. Currently, these include the *AdRotator*, *Calendar*, and *Xml* controls. This section will describe the purposes of these controls and show some examples.

note

The *<style>* block that you defined takes care of formatting for the *Panel* controls by defining the desired style for the *<div>* HTML element. Note that since the *Panel* control is rendered as a *<div>* on Internet Explorer and as a *<table>* element on Netscape and other non–Internet Explorer browsers, you may need to find another way to do the formatting if you want cross-browser compatibility.

One way to accomplish this is through browser sniffing. The *Request* object exposed by the *Page* class has a *Browser* property that provides information on the browser making the current request. By querying the *Browser* property (and its subproperties), you can perform a simple *if* statement that links to one style sheet if the browser is IE, and to another style sheet if it is another browser.

AdRotator

The *AdRotator* control is used to display a random selection from a collection of banner advertisements specified in an XML-based advertisement file. The advertisement file contains an *<Ad>* node for each specified advertisement. This node contains nodes that configure the path to the image to display for the ad, the URL to navigate to when the ad is clicked, the text to be displayed when/if the image is not available, the percentage of time the ad should come up in rotation, and any keyword associated with the ad. (Keywords can be used to filter ads, allowing the use of a single advertisement file with multiple *AdRotator* controls and providing each control with different content.)

note

The random selection for the *AdRotator* control will be identical for any *AdRotators* on the page that have identical attributes. You can take advantage of this by using the *AdRotator* control to display a random selection of header/footer information that you want to be the same for both header and footer.

To use this control from a Web Form, follow these steps:

1   Create a new file and save it as AdRotator.aspx.

2   Add the @ *Page* directive, standard HTML elements, and an *HtmlForm* control to the page.

```
<%@ Page Language="vb" %>
<html>
```

```
<head>
</head>
<body>
    <form runat="server">
    </form>
</body>
</html>
```

3   Add three *Label* controls and two *AdRotator* controls between the *<form>* tags, with the attributes shown in the following code:

```
<asp:label id="title" font-name="Verdana" font-size="18"
    text="AdRotator Example" runat="server"/>
<br/><br/>
 <asp:label id="Dev" font-name="Verdana" font-size="16"
   text="Ad 1" runat="server"/>
<br/>
<asp:AdRotator id="AdRotDev" target="_blank" runat="server"
    advertisementfile="Ads.xml" keywordfilter="Developers"/>
<br/><br/>
<asp:label id="User" font-name="Verdana" font-size="16"
    text="Ad 2" runat="server"/>
<br/>
<asp:AdRotator id="AdRotUsr" target="_blank" runat="server"
    advertisementfile="Ads.xml" keywordfilter="Users"/>
```

4   Save AdRotator.aspx. Then create a new text file called Ads.xml and add the following XML to the file:

```
<Advertisements>
    <Ad>
        <ImageUrl>image1.gif</ImageUrl>
        <NavigateUrl>http://www.microsoft.com</NavigateUrl>
        <AlternateText>Microsoft Main Site</AlternateText>
        <Impressions>60</Impressions>
        <Keyword>Users</Keyword>
    </Ad>
    <Ad>
        <ImageUrl>image2.gif</ImageUrl>
        <NavigateUrl>http://msdn.microsoft.com/net</NavigateUrl>
        <AlternateText>Microsoft .NET on MSDN</AlternateText>
        <Impressions>80</Impressions>
        <Keyword>Developers</Keyword>
    </Ad>
```

```
<Ad>
    <ImageUrl>image3.gif</ImageUrl>
    <NavigateUrl>http://www.microsoft.com</NavigateUrl>
    <AlternateText>Microsoft Main Site</AlternateText>
    <Impressions>40</Impressions>
    <Keyword>Users</Keyword>
</Ad>
<Ad>
    <ImageUrl>image4.gif</ImageUrl>
    <NavigateUrl>http://msdn.microsoft.com/net</NavigateUrl>
    <AlternateText>Microsoft .NET on MSDN</AlternateText>
    <Impressions>20</Impressions>
    <Keyword>Developers</Keyword>
</Ad>
</Advertisements>
```

5   Save Ads.xml in the same location and browse AdRotator.aspx. The output should look similar to the following figure.

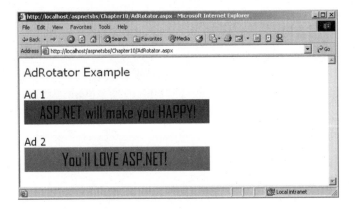

Calendar

The *Calendar* control is one of the richest and most flexible of the specialized controls, providing nearly 30 properties for controlling the appearance of the calendar. The *Calendar* control allows you to provide a calendar-based interface for choosing dates, or for viewing date-related data.

For example, you could query date data for a series of events and then use a *Calendar* control to display them by adding the dates to the calendar's *SelectedDates* collection. When a user clicks on a selected date on the calendar, you could then display additional information about the event on that date.

You could also allow users to specify one or more dates for data entry by providing a *Calendar* control for them to click. The *Calendar* control supports selection of both single dates and date ranges (by week or month). Using a *Calendar* control for date entry instead of a text box can help prevent errors in converting the date entered by the user into a *Date* data type for storage or manipulation.

To create a Web Forms page that uses a *Calendar* for data entry, complete these steps:

1 Create a new text file and save it as Calendar.aspx.

2 Add the @ *Page* directive, standard HTML elements, and an *HtmlForm* control to the page, as shown in the previous example.

3 Create the UI by adding three Label controls, two *RadioButton* controls, two text boxes, and a *Calendar* control to the *HtmlForm*. Note that the *GroupName* property is used to make the radio buttons mutually exclusive.

```
<font runat="server">
    <asp:label id="title" text="Calendar Example"
        font-name="Verdana" font-size="18" runat="server"/>
    <br/>
    <asp:calendar runat="server"/>
    <asp:radiobutton id="Start" text="Start Date"
        groupname="Chooser" runat="server"/>
    <asp:radiobutton id="End" text="End Date"
        groupname="Chooser" runat="server"/>
    <br/>
    <asp:label id="StartDateLabel" text="Start Date"
        runat="server"/>
    <asp:textbox id="StartDate" runat="server"/>
    <br/>
    <asp:label id="EndDateLabel" text="End Date"
        runat="server"/>
    <asp:textbox id="EndDate" runat="server"/>
</font>
```

4   Save and browse the page. The output should look similar to the
following figure.

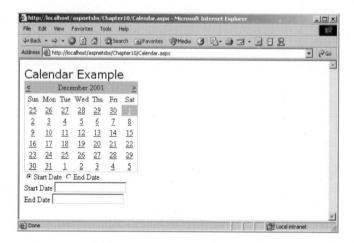

5   Looks good so far, but now you need to relate clicking on a date on the calendar
to setting the text in the text boxes. First, add the *OnSelectionChange* attribute
to the *<asp:calendar>* tag to map the event to the event handler.

```
<asp:calendar onselectionchange="Set_DateText" runat="server"/>
```

6   Next add the following *<script>* block to the *<head>* section of the page. The
Page_Load event handler simply ensures that the Start radio button is checked
the first time the page is loaded, while the *Set_DateText* event handler takes care
of setting the dates.

```
<script runat="server">
    Sub Page_Load
        If Not Page.IsPostBack Then
            Start.Checked =True
            Calendar1.SelectedDate = Now()
            StartDate.Text = Calendar1.SelectedDate
            Calendar1.TodaysDate =Calendar1.SelectedDate
        End If
    End Sub
    Sub Set_DateText(Sender As Object,e As EventArgs)
        If Start.Checked =True Then
            StartDsate.Text =Calendar1.SelectedDate
        Else 'End must be checked
            EndDate.Text ='Calendar1.SelectedDate
        End If
```

```
        End Sub
    </script>
```

7 Save and browse the page. At this point, you should be able to use the calendar to set the value of both text boxes. Which text box is set depends on which radio button is checked.

8 At this point the calendar is fairly plain, so let's use some of the available properties to liven it up a bit. Modify the *<asp:calendar>* tag to match the following code. Notice that there's a closing *</asp:calendar>* tag so that you can use the child *<titlestyle>* tag to set attributes of the calendar's *TitleStyle* property.

```
<asp:calendar id="Calendar1"
    onselectionchanged="Set_DateText"
    backcolor="lightgray"
    borderstyle="groove"
    borderwidth="5"
    bordercolor="blue"
    runat="server">

    <titlestyle backcolor="blue" forecolor="silver"
        font-bold="true"/>

</asp:calendar>
```

9 Save and browse the file again. The output should look similar to the following figure.

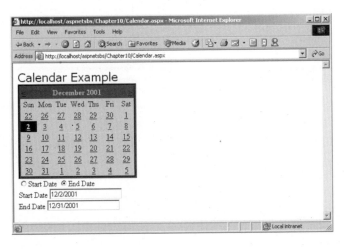

10 Save this file. You'll be coming back to it later in this chapter.

Xml

The *Xml* control is a specialty control that lets you display XML code in Web Forms pages. This is important because raw XML within an ASP.NET Web Form will not be displayed predictably. The *Xml* control can read XML from a string, from a provided URL, or from an object of type *System.Xml.XmlDocument*.

In addition to simply displaying XML from a given source, the *Xml* control can also apply an XSL *Transform* document to the XML to perform formatting on the document. The XSL Transform can come from a URL, or it can be provided by an object of type *System.Xml.Xsl.XslTransform*.

Validation Controls

Another specialized set of controls that reside in the *System.Web.UI.WebControls* namespace are the *Validation* controls, which perform various kinds of validation on other controls.

You can use *Validation* controls to do the following:

- Ensure that required fields are filled out
- Ensure that data entered by the user falls within a given range
- Ensure that data entered by the user matches a specific pattern
- Compare the values of two controls for a given condition (equality, greater than, etc.) or compare the value of a control to a specified value
- Ensure that all controls on a page are valid before submitting the page

Shared Members

There are a number of important properties and methods that all *Validation* controls share. These properties and methods are inherited from the *BaseValidator* class and include the following:

- *ControlToValidate*   This property sets or retrieves a value of type *String* that specifies the input control to validate.
- *Display*   This property sets or retrieves a value that determines how the error message for a *Validation* control will be displayed. The value must be one of the values specified by the *ValidatorDisplay* enumeration. The default is *Static*.
- *EnableClientScript*   This property sets or retrieves a boolean value that determines whether client-side validation will be performed. Server-side validation is always performed with the *Validation* controls, regardless of this setting. The default is *true*.

■ *Enabled*   This property sets or retrieves a boolean value that determines whether the control is enabled. The default is *true*.

■ *ErrorMessage*   This property sets or retrieves a value of type *String* that specifies the error message to be displayed if the input from the user is not valid.

■ *ForeColor*   This property sets or retrieves a value of type *Color* that represents the color of the error message specified in the *ErrorMessage* property. The default is *Color.Red*.

■ *IsValid*   This property sets or retrieves a boolean value that signifies whether the control specified by the *ControlToValidate* property passes validation.

■ *Validate*   This method causes the control on which it is called to perform validation, and it updates the *IsValid* property with the result.

The following table lists the *Validation* controls available in ASP.NET.

Validation Controls

Control Type	Purpose	Important Members
CompareValidator	Performs validation of a user-entered field with either a constant or another user-entered field. The *ControlToCompare* and *ValueToCompare* properties are mutually exclusive. If both are set, the *ControlToCompare* property takes precedence.	*ControlToCompare* This property sets or retrieves a value of type *String* containing the name of the control whose value will be compared to the value of the control specified by the *ControlToValidate* property. *Operator* This property sets or retrieves a value that represents the type of comparison to be performed. The value must be one of the values specified by the *ValidationCompareOperator* enumeration. The default is *Equal*. *ValueToCompare* This property sets or retrieves a value of type *String* containing a constant value to which the value of the control specified by the *ControlToValidate* property will be compared.

(continued)

Validation Controls *(continued)*		
Control Type	**Purpose**	**Important Members**
CustomValidator	Performs customized validation based on developer-specified logic.	*ServerValidate* This event is raised when server-side validation is to be performed. Map the *OnServerValidate* method in the *Validation* control tag to the desired server-side event handler to perform custom validation. *ClientValidationFunction* This property sets or retrieves a value of type *String* containing the name of a client-side function with which to perform client-side validation, if desired.
RangeValidator	Performs validation of a user-entered field to ensure that the value entered is within a specified range.	*MaximumValue* This property sets or retrieves a value of type *String* containing the maximum value of the range to validate against. *MinimumValue* This property sets or retrieves a value of type *String* containing the minimum value of the range to validate against.
RegularExpressionValidator	Performs validation of a user-entered field to ensure that the value entered matches a specified pattern.	*ValidationExpression* This property sets or retrieves a value of type *String* containing the regular expression to validate against.
RequiredFieldValidator	Performs validation of a user-entered field to ensure that a value is entered for the specified field.	*InitialValue* This property sets or retrieves a value of type *String* containing the initial value of the range to validate against. The default is an empty string. If this property is set to a string value, validation will fail for the control only if the user-entered value matches the value of this property.

Validation Controls *(continued)*

Control Type	Purpose	Important Members
ValidationSummary	Provides a summary of validation errors in a given Web Form, either in the Web Form page, a message box, or both.	*DisplayMode* This property sets or retrieves a value that determines the way the control will be displayed. The value must be one of the values specified by the *ValidationSummaryDisplayMode* enumeration. The default is *BulletList*. *HeaderText* This property sets or retrieves a value of type *String* containing the header text to be displayed for the validation summary. *ShowMessageBox* This property sets or retrieves a boolean value that determines whether the validation summary is displayed in a client-side message box. The default is *false*. This property has no effect if the *EnableClientScript* property is set to *false*. *ShowSummary* This property sets or retrieves a boolean value that determines whether the validation summary is displayed in the Web Form page. The default is *true*.

Validating Required Fields

To see how the *Validation* controls operate, let's return to one of the earlier examples, the Web Form named SmtpEmail.aspx. One of the problems that you had with the page was that if it was submitted without a To, CC, or BCC address, it would throw an exception. You can prevent this problem by requiring at least one To address. Follow these steps:

1   Open SmtpEmail.aspx in your favorite text editor.

2   Add a *RequiredFieldValidatorControl* to the same table cell as the *ToText* textbox control:

```
<td>
    <asp:textbox id="ToText" runat="server"/>
    <asp:requiredfieldvalidator
        id="ToTextValidator"
```

```
            controltovalidate="ToText"
            display="dynamic"
            errormessage="Required"
            runat="server"/>
</td>
```

3   Save and browse the page. Now, if you do not enter a To address, the output will look something like the following figure, and you will not be able to submit the page.

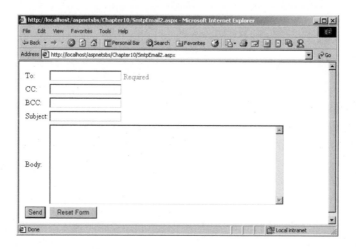

4   One problem with this set-up is that once you add a To address and submit the page, you'll get a JavaScript error. This is because the newly added *Validation* control is looking for the text box on the client, but since you hid the control in the event handler by setting its *Visible* property to *False*, the control no longer exists on the client. You can solve this by making some modifications to how you hide the elements on the page. First you need to add a new *Label* control for your status message. (In the original page, the first label in the table was used for this purpose.) This control should go just before the HTML *<table>* element.

```
<asp:label id="Status" text="" runat="server"/>
```

5   Now you need to turn the HTML *<table>* element into an *HtmlTable* control by adding an *id* attribute and the *runat="server"* attribute.

```
<table id="MailTable" runat="server">
```

6   Next you need to take out the line of code in the *Send_Click* event handler that sets the status message and replace it with the following code:

```
'Use the first label to display status
Status.Text = "Mail Sent"
```

7   Finally you need to replace the lines of code in the *Send_Click* event handler that set the *Visible* property of the controls to *False* with the following lines:

```
'Hide the table
MailTable.Visible = False
```

8   Save the page, browse it, and submit an e-mail. You should no longer get the JavaScript error (and your code's a lot cleaner to boot).

In addition to using the *RequiredFieldValidator* to ensure that an e-mail address is entered, you could also add a *RegularExpressionValidator* to each of the address fields to ensure that the data entered by the user matches the pattern for a valid e-mail address. This prevents delivery errors due to malformed e-mail addresses and helps prevent the mail server's resources from being wasted attempting to deliver such mail.

Validating by Comparison

Another one of the previous examples with the potential for trouble is the *Calendar* control example. As coded in the example, the *Calendar* control can be used to set a start date that is later than the end date. Clearly, if you're storing these dates or using them to drive some programmatic logic, this is not something you want to allow. Fortunately, the *CompareValidator* control can help prevent this problem, as illustrated by the following example:

1   Open Calendar.aspx.

2   Add a *CompareValidator* control below the *EndDate TextBox* control:

```
<br/>
<asp:comparevalidator
    id="DateValidator"
    controltovalidate="StartDate"
    controltocompare="EndDate"
    type="Date"
    operator="lessthan"
    display="dynamic"
    errormessage="Start Date must be before End Date!"
    srunat="server"/>
```

3   Add a line of code to the *Set_DateText* event handler to cause the *Validation* control to validate each time the event handler is fired. The *Page.Validate* call should go between the *End If* and *End Sub* statements.

```
Page.Validate
```

4   Save and browse the file. Set the end date to a date earlier than the start date. The validation error message will appear, as shown in the following figure. Additionally, the *IsValid* property of the page will be set to *False*. You can test this property before saving the date values to ensure that they are valid.

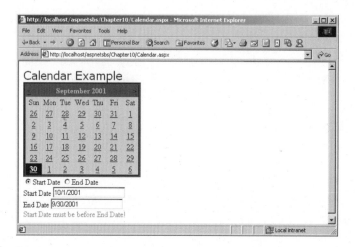

Validation controls can also improve the security of your application. For example, you can use the *RegularExpressionValidator* control to ensure that passwords entered by users (such as when establishing account information) meet minimum length and complexity requirements. This can make it more difficult for the bad guys to crack your application.

Data-Bound Controls

One of the most significant advances in ASP.NET is in the area of data binding. The *System.Web.UI.WebControls* namespace contains a set of data-bound controls that offer substantial functionality and flexibility, without the necessity of tying front-end UI logic into back-end database logic, as was the case with the data-bound Design-Time Controls available in classic ASP through the Visual InterDev 6.0 development environment. The data-bound controls also allow you to provide data binding regardless of the browser that your clients are using. This is because the controls run on the server and return plain HTML to the client, unlike some of the data-binding techniques that were possible with Internet Explorer versions 4.0 and later.

Another major improvement is that the data-bound controls can use a variety of sources, not just data from a database. Data-bound controls in ASP.NET can be bound to data from an array, an ADO.NET DataSet, a DataView, or any data source that implements the ICollection or IList interfaces. The data-bound controls include the *DataGrid*, *DataList*, and *Repeater* controls. Chapter 11 will discuss these controls in detail.

Other Controls

In addition to the HTML controls and Web controls that come with the .NET Framework, there are also some additional controls that are currently available as separate downloads. These are the ASP.NET Mobile controls and the Internet Explorer Web controls.

ASP.NET Mobile Controls

The ASP.NET Mobile controls are currently available as the .NET Mobile Internet Toolkit. These controls are designed to tailor their output to handheld devices, such as cell phones, PocketPCs, and other mobile devices. The Mobile Internet Toolkit is currently available at *http://download.microsoft.com/ download/VisualStudioNET/Install/1.0/NT45XP/EN-US/MobileIT.exe*. More information about the Mobile Web Toolkit can be found at *http://msdn.microsoft.com/vstudio/nextgen/technology/mobilewebforms.asp*. At the time of this writing, it's unclear whether these controls will ship with the .NET Framework in the future or will continue to be a separate download.

Internet Explorer Web Controls

The Internet Explorer Web controls are a set of ASP.NET server controls that take advantage of advanced features of Internet Explorer 5.5 or later, while still providing cross-browser compatibility by rendering HTML 3.2 output for down-level browsers. The controls include the following:

- *MultiPage*   Used with the *TabStrip* control to provide sophisticated tabbed interfaces in ASP.NET.
- *TabStrip*   Provides a tabbed interface for navigation.
- *Toolbar*   Provides toolbar functionality for ASP.NET Web Forms pages.
- *TreeView*   Provides the ability to display and navigate hierarchical structures or data. It can be used for site navigation, or to provide a Web-based Explorer-style interface.

The Internet Explorer Web controls can be downloaded from *http://msdn.microsoft.com/downloads/samples/internet/ ASP_DOT_NET_ServerControls/WebControls/default.asp*. You can read more about the Internet Explorer Web controls and their use at *http://msdn.microsoft.com/workshop/webcontrols/overview/overview.asp*.

At the time of this writing, it's unclear whether these controls will ship with the .NET Framework in the future or will continue to be a separate download.

Chapter 10 Quick Reference

To	Do This
Create a control that can handle both client- and server-side events	Use an HTML control by adding an *id* attribute and the *runat="server"* attribute to the desired HTML element (note that the element must support the desired client-side event) and add attributes to map the events to the appropriate client- and server-side event handlers.
Show or hide an ASP.NET server control	Modify the *Visible* property of the control.
Add or modify an HTML attribute to an HTML control or Web control that is not exposed as a property of the control	Add or modify the attribute by its name using the *Attributes* collection of the control: *MyControl.Attributes("Attribute")*. Note that all attributes, including those exposed as properties on a control, are available via the *Attributes* collection.
Apply styles to a control	Set the *Style* or *CssClass* (Web controls only) of the control to the desired CSS style or class string.
Validate user input	Add a *Validator* server control to the page, and set its *ControlToValidate* property to the ID of the control the user will use to enter input. The type of control to use depends on what you want to validate.

11

Accessing and Binding Data

In this chapter, you will learn about

✔ *Namespaces and classes that make up ADO.NET*

✔ *ASP.NET data-bound controls*

✔ *Data-binding against properties, arrays, or ADO.NET data*

In the previous two chapters, you learned about creating Web Forms and taking advantage of ASP.NET server controls in your Web Forms applications. With that overview of these two important technologies under your belt, let's look at data access. The ability to store and access data is central to most Web applications, and this is an area that classic ASP made very simple for developers through the ActiveX Data Objects (ADO) COM components. The .NET platform provides a set of classes called ADO.NET that is the logical successor to ADO, although the underlying object model has undergone significant changes. ASP.NET, meanwhile, exposes a set of data-bound controls (which were touched on briefly in Chapter 10) that integrate seamlessly with ADO.NET to provide data-binding services.

important

ADO.NET is a large enough topic to merit a book of its own, so at best this chapter will provide an overview. You're strongly encouraged to use the available resources, such as the ASP.NET and HowTo QuickStart tutorials (installed with the .NET Framework SDK samples), which have numerous ADO.NET examples. Other resources include the .NET Framework SDK and Visual Studio .NET documentation, and of course other books, such as the forthcoming Microsoft Press title *Building Web Solutions with ASP.NET and ADO.NET* by Dino Esposito, a noted expert on ADO and ADO.NET.

Understanding ADO.NET

In classic ASP, the most common way to access data was through ADO. Developers used ADO *Connection* objects to connect to a database, and then used ADO *Command* and *Recordset* objects to retrieve, manipulate, and update data. When designing applications, particularly those with high scalability requirements or those whose back-end datasource might change at some point, developers needed to be careful not to tie in their front-end presentation code with their back-end database. Otherwise, they'd end up having to rewrite everything if there was a change in the back-end database.

The ADO.NET class architecture is factored somewhat differently from classic ADO. ADO.NET classes are separated into two major categories: datasource-specific and non-datasource-specific.

Understanding .NET Data Providers

Classes that are specific to a particular datasource are said to work with a specific *.NET Data Provider*. A .NET Data Provider is a set of classes that allow managed code to interact with a specific datasource to retrieve, update, and manipulate data. ADO.NET comes with two .NET Data Providers: the SQL Server .NET Data Provider, which provides optimized access to SQL Server databases, and the OLE DB .NET Data Provider, which lets you connect to any datasource for which you have an OLE DB provider installed.

important

The OLE DB .NET Data Provider does not support the OLE DB 2.5 interfaces. This means that the Microsoft OLE DB Provider for Exchange and the Microsoft OLE DB Provider for Internet Publishing cannot be used with the OLE DB .NET Data Provider. Additionally, the OLE DB .NET Data Provider is incompatible with the OLE DB Provider for ODBC. At the time of this writing, Microsoft was providing a downloadable .NET Data Provider for ODBC at *http:// msdn.microsoft.com/downloads/sample.asp?url=/msdn-files/027/001/668/ msdncompositedoc.xml*. It is unclear whether this data provider will be a part of the released product.

The following figure shows the major classes of the SQL Server .NET Data Provider and how they relate to one another.

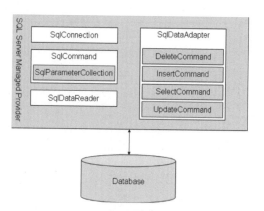

The *SqlConnection* class is used to establish a connection to a SQL Server database. Unlike the ADO *Connection* object, the *SqlConnection* class (or its OLE DB equivalent, the *OleDbConnection* class) cannot be used to execute SQL statements against a datasource. The *SqlConnection* class is used solely for opening connections, setting or retrieving properties of a connection, or handling connection-related events. You'll learn how to use the *SqlConnection* class to connect to a database later in this chapter.

The *SqlCommand* class is used to execute SQL statements or stored procedures against a SQL Server database. The *SqlCommand* class (and its OLE DB equivalent, the *OleDbCommand* class) can execute statements or stored procedures that do not return values, or that return single values, XML, or datareaders.

The *SqlDataReader* class provides forward-only, read-only access to a set of rows returned from a SQL Server database. Datareaders (including both the *SqlDataReader* and *OleDbDataReader*) provide lightweight, high-performance access to read-only data and are the best choice for accessing data to be displayed in ASP.NET.

The *SqlDataAdapter* class is used as a bridge between the *DataSet* class and SQL Server. The *SqlDataAdapter* class can be used to create a dataset from a given SQL statement or stored procedure represented by a *SqlCommand* instance, update the back-end SQL Server database based on the contents of a dataset, or insert rows into or delete rows from a SQL Server database. The *OleDbAdapter* class performs the same tasks for OLE DB datasources.

important

You may have noticed that in the discussion of the classes that make up the SQL Server .NET Data Provider, the names of the classes start with *Sql* rather than *SQL*. This is because the names of the classes in the .NET Framework use *Pascal casing* (after the style of the Pascal language), in which the first character of each distinct word in a given class is capitalized.

This is important because class and namespace names are case sensitive in a language such as C#. Using the incorrect case name (for example, *SQLConnection* instead of *SqlConnection*) will result in a compiler error. So if you get an error complaining that the type isn't defined or the namespace doesn't exist, there's a pretty good chance that you're dealing with a capitalization problem.

Understanding Datasets

The main class not specific to a datasource is the *DataSet* class. This is essentially an in-memory representation of one or more tables of data. This data may be read from an XML file or stream, or may be the result of a query against a datasource.

One important thing about the *DataSet* class is that it doesn't know anything about the datasource from which it receives its data, other than what that data is and sometimes the types of the data columns. (See the section on typed datasets later in this chapter.) The following figure shows the major classes associated with the *DataSet* class and how they relate to one another. Note that the *Rows*, *Columns*, and *Constraints* objects are properties of the *DataTable* class.

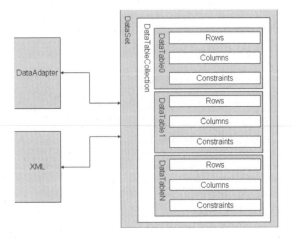

The fact that a dataset knows nothing about the source of its data means that it's *abstracted* from the back-end datasource. This is important because it means that if you pass a dataset from a component used for data retrieval to your Web Forms page to be used for data-binding, your Web Forms page neither knows nor cares where the data comes from, as long as the dataset structure remains the same. The back-end database can be changed without necessitating any changes in the Web Forms page. This makes it much easier to maintain a Web application.

Datasets contain a collection of tables, each of which contains a collection of rows, a collection of columns, and a collection of constraints. You can use these collections to get information on the objects contained within them, as well as to access and update individual data values. The dataset can also contain a collection of relationships between the tables it contains, allowing hierarchical data to be represented. You'll learn about the *DataSet* class and related classes in detail later in this chapter.

XML in ADO.NET

Unlike classic ADO, in which XML support was added after the initial object model had been created, XML support has been designed into the ADO.NET model from the ground up. Classes such as *SqlCommand*, *OleDbCommand*, and *DataSet* have built-in support for reading and writing XML data. Datasets in particular can be built from or saved as XML, making them ideal for transporting data between tiers in a multitier application, or for temporarily storing data to disk for later retrieval.

Creating and Opening Connections

The first step in accessing data from a database is, of course, creating the connection. ADO.NET provides two classes for creating connections to a database: *SqlConnection* and *OleDbConnection*. Which one you use depends on the type of database you will be connecting to and the needs of your application.

SqlConnection

For applications that use SQL Server as the back-end database and are unlikely to change to a different database in the future, the *SqlConnection* class is the appropriate choice. This class is optimized for the best performance when connecting to a SQL Server database. The *SqlConnection* class will also provide superior performance when accessing data in an MSDE database, since MSDE uses the same database engine and protocols as SQL Server.

Creating a *SqlConnection* class is simple and can be done in one line of code.

```
Dim mySqlConn as New SqlConnection(ConnectionString)
```

This creates a connection called *mySqlConn* to the SQL Server specified by the *ConnectionString* passed to the constructor of the *SqlConnection* class. Opening the connection is as simple as calling the following:

```
mySqlConn.Open
```

Closing the connection is just as easy.

```
mySqlConn.Close
```

important

As with classic ADO, it is very important that you close any connection you open when you are finished with it. Connections are not closed automatically when they go out of scope. Open connections are not returned to the connection pool, where they would be available to other clients. This can prevent your application from effectively handling larger numbers of users without unacceptable performance degradation.

In addition to setting the connection string by passing it to the constructor of the *SqlConnection* instance, you can also create the *SqlConnection* instance with no constructor argument and set the connection string later through the *ConnectionString* property.

The connection string for *SqlConnection* consists of key/value pairs separated by semicolons. Values may be delimited by either single or double quotes, but both may not be used for the same value (for example, *key='value's'* should be *key="value's"*). All spaces, except those appearing in quotes, are ignored.

important

When you're creating connection strings dynamically based on user input, make sure to validate user input so that additional keys are not intentionally added to the connection string by the user. For example, a user could add the database key to his password in an attempt to connect to a different database. Since the last key with the same name will be used to set the value for a connection string, failure to validate input may result in inappropriate access.

The following table lists the valid keys for a *SqlConnection* connection string.

SqlConnection Connection String Keys	
Key	**Description**
Application Name	The name of the application from which the connection is being made.
AttachDBFilename	The file name and full path to the primary file of an attachable database. This key requires the *Database* key to specify the database name.
Connect Timeout or *Connection Timeout*	The number of seconds before an attempted connection is aborted and an error is raised. The default is *15*.
Connection Lifetime	The time, in seconds, that a pooled connection should remain alive. When a connection is returned to the connection pool, it is destroyed if the current time is more than this many seconds past its creation time. The default is *0*, meaning that the connection will not be destroyed.
Connection Reset	A Boolean value that determines whether the connection state is reset when a connection is retrieved from the pool. If set to *false*, the connection state will not be reset, which saves a trip to the server. But the programmer must then manually take any steps necessary to ensure that the connection state is appropriate for the application's use. The default is *true*.
Current Language	The SQL Server language name.
Data Source or *Server* or *Address* or *Addr* or *Network Address*	The server name or network address of the SQL Server instance to connect to.
Enlist	Determines whether the connection is automatically enlisted in the creator's current transaction context. The default is *true*.
Initial Catalog or *Database*	The name of the database to connect to.

(continued)

SqlConnection Connection String Keys *(continued)*

Key	Description
Integrated Security or *Trusted Connection*	Determines whether the connection uses the Windows authentication credentials of the caller to authenticate against SQL Server. Setting this to *true* alleviates the need for authenticating a user ID and password, which means that you don't need to worry about storing these values. The default is *false*.
Max Pool Size	Determines the maximum number of connections to be pooled. The default is *100*.
Min Pool Size	Determines the minimum number of connections that should be in the pool. The default is *0*.
Network Library or *Net*	Specifies the network library to use when connecting to the specified SQL Server. The default is *dbmssocn*, which specifies the TCP/IP sockets library. Other valid values are *dbnmpntw* Named pipes *dbmsrpcn* Multiprotocol *dbmsadsn* Apple Talk *dbmsgnet* VIA *dbmsipcn* Shared memory *dbmsspxn* IPX/SPX The server must have the appropriate DLL for the specified network library.
Packet Size	Specifies the number of bytes per network packet to use in communicating with SQL Server. The default is *8192*.
Password or *Pwd*	Specifies the password to use to log into the SQL Server database.
Persist Security Info	If set to *false*, this key prevents sensitive information, such as passwords, from being returned as a part of the connection if the connection is open. The default is *false*.
Pooling	Determines whether pooling is enabled for this connection. When *true*, a requested connection will be pulled from the appropriate pool. If no connections are available from the pool, the requested connection is created and then returned to the pool when closed. The default is *true*.
User ID	The name of the SQL Server user account with which to log into the server.
Workstation ID	The name of the machine connecting to SQL Server. The default is the local machine name.

OleDbConnection

For applications that need to be able to query databases other than SQL Server, such as Access or Oracle, the *OleDbConnection* class is the appropriate choice. This class uses a standard OLE DB *Provider* string to connect to any OLE DB datasource through the OLE DB provider for that datasource.

Creating an *OleDbConnection* is simple and can be done in one line of code.

```
Dim myOleDbConn as New OleDbConnection(ConnectionString)
```

This creates a connection called *myOleDbConn* to the database specified by the *ConnectionString* passed to the constructor of the *OleDbConnection* class. The *ConnectionString* argument is a standard OLE DB provider string. The following, from the MSDN .NET Framework Class Library Reference, shows some examples of OLE DB *Provider* strings for connecting to Oracle, MS Access, and SQL Server datasources, respectively:

```
Provider=MSDAORA; Data Source=ORACLE8i7; User ID=OLEDB;
    Password=OLEDB;


Provider=Microsoft.Jet.OLEDB.4.0;
    Data Source=c:\bin\LocalAccess40.mdb;


Provider=SQLOLEDB;Data Source=MySQLServer;Integrated Security=SSPI;
```

The *Provider=* clause is required. You can also use other clauses supported by the particular OLE DB provider to set other properties for the provider. For example, the *Initial Catalog=* clause is used by the SQL Server OLE DB Provider to indicate the database against which queries will be run.

You open the connection by calling the following:

```
myOleDbConn.Open
```

And you close it by calling the following:

```
myOleDbConn.Close
```

note

You cannot use the OLE DB Provider for ODBC with the OLE DB .NET Data Provider. You can download a separate .NET Data Provider for ODBC from *http://msdn.microsoft.com/downloads/*.

Later in this chapter, you'll see examples of using connections to perform data access.

Using Trusted Connections

As mentioned in Chapter 8, ASP.NET is configured by default to use the unprivileged ASPNET account to run ASP.NET worker processes. This means that unlike in beta versions of ASP.NET, you must now use either of the following two techniques to use a trusted connection.

■ Use Windows authentication and impersonation to connect to the database using the credentials of the logged-in user

or

■ Set up the ASPNET account as a SQL Server login

In this section you'll learn how to use the latter technique to enable the use of trusted connections without the need for Windows authentication.

important

Setting up the ASPNET account in SQL Server will allow any ASP.NET application on the Web server to access the database with whatever privileges have been granted to the ASPNET account. For this reason, this technique should be used only on development systems or production systems on which you are in control of all ASP.NET applications. This technique should generally not be considered for shared server applications.

To set up the ASPNET account to access the Pubs SQL Server sample database using SQL Enterprise Manager, follow these steps.

1   Open SQL Enterprise Manager by clicking Start, Programs, Microsoft SQL Server, Enterprise Manager.

2   Expand the tree and locate the desired SQL Server or MSDE instance. Expand this instance and locate the Security node.

3   Expand the Security node, right-click the Logins node, and then select New Login.

4   On the General tab, select the desired domain (or local machine name) from the Domain drop-down list, then click the elipsis (...) button next to the Name textbox.

5   Locate and select the account named ASPNET (aspnet_wp account), click Add, and then click OK.

6   Also on the General tab, change the Database default to pubs. Click the Database Access tab.

7 On the Database Access tab, scroll to the pubs database, check the Permit checkbox, and then add the db_datareader and db_datawriter roles to the ASPNET login account by checking the checkboxes for these roles.

8 Click OK. You can now use a trusted connection to read from and write to the pubs sample database.

To set up the ASPNET account to access the Pubs sample database in the NetSDK MSDE database using the oSql command-line tool, follow these steps.

1 Start the oSql command-line utility by entering the following at a command prompt. (If using a SQL Server database other than a local version of the NetSDK MSDE instance, enter that server or instance name as the *-S* parameter.)

```
oSql -S(local)\NetSDK -Usa
```

2 When prompted, enter the *sa* password for the instance indicated by the *-S* parameter. You should see a *1>* prompt.

3 Call the sp_grantlogin system stored procedure to grant login access to the ASPNET account. The syntax should look like the following, with *<domain>* replaced by your domain or local machine name. The *go* command entered at the *2>* prompt tells oSql to execute the stored procedure.

```
1> sp_grantlogin '<domain>\ASPNET'
2> go
```

4 Call the sp_defaultdb system stored procedure to change the default database for the ASPNET account to pubs. The syntax should look like the following, with *<domain>* replaced by your domain or local machine name.

```
1> sp_defaultdb '<domain>\ASPNET', 'pubs'
2> go
```

5 Call the sp_adduser system stored procedure to add the ASPNET login account to the pubs database, passing the *db_datareader* argument to add the account to the db_datareader role. The syntax should look like the following, with *<domain>* replaced by your domain or local machine name.

```
1> sp_adduser '<domain>\ASPNET', 'ASPNET', 'db_datareader'
2> go
```

6 If desired, call the sp_addrolemember system stored procedure to add the ASPNET account to the db_datawriter role. In this step, ASPNET is the username added to the pubs database in the previous step. The syntax should look like the following, with *<domain>* replaced by your domain or local machine name.

```
1> sp_addrolemember 'db_datawriter', 'ASPNET'
2> go </code>
```

7 Type *exit* and press the Enter key to exit the oSql utility.

Once you've set up the ASPNET account as described above, you should be able to access the desired database using a trusted connection, as shown in the connection strings used in the samples later in this chapter.

Reading and Updating Data with Commands

The *Command* classes, *SqlCommand* and *OleDbCommand*, are the ADO.NET equivalents of the ADO *Command* object. These classes can be used to retrieve read-only data through a datareader (you'll see examples of this later in this chapter), execute *Insert*, *Update*, *Delete*, and other statements that don't return records, retrieve aggregate results, or retrieve an XML representation of data. *SqlCommands* and *OleDbCommands* can also be used in conjunction with a related datareader to populate a dataset with data, or to update a back-end database with updated data from a dataset. The *SqlCommand* and the *OleDbCommand* classes can work with either SQL statements or stored procedures (for datasources that support them).

SqlCommand

The *SqlCommand* class is the appropriate class to use when you want to run commands against a SQL Server. Here are the steps to follow when using a *SqlCommand* object. Each step outlines one or more ways to initialize or use the *SqlCommand* class.

1   Create the *SqlCommand* object. Note that the constructor of the *SqlCommand* is overloaded, so you can save steps by passing arguments (such as the query for the *Command* and/or the *SqlConnection* object to use for the command) to its constructor, rather than setting the properties after the object is created.

```
'Default constructor
Dim mySqlCmd As New SqlCommand()

'Passing in a query
Dim SQL As String = "SELECT au_id FROM authors"
Dim mySqlCmd2 as New SqlCommand(SQL)

'Passing in a query and a connection
Dim mySqlConn As New _
SqlConnection("datasource=localhost\
NetSDK;database=pubs;integratedsecurity=true")
Dim SQL As String = "SELECT au_id FROM authors"
Dim mySqlCmd3 as New SqlCommand(SQL, mySqlConn)
```

```
'Passing in a query, a connection, and a transaction
Dim mySqlConn As New _
SqlConnection("datasource=localhost\
NetSDK;database=pubs;integratedsecurity=true")
Dim mySqlTrans As SqlTransaction = mySqlConn.BeginTransaction()
Dim SQL As String = "SELECT au_id FROM authors"
Dim mySqlCmd4 as New SqlCommand(SQL, mySqlConn, mySqlTrans)
```

2   If you haven't set them in the constructor, set the *CommandText* property to the desired SQL query or stored procedure name and the *Connection* property to an open *SqlConnection* object.

```
mySqlCommand.CommandText = "SELECT au_id FROM authors"
'Assumes that mySqlConn has already been created and opened
mySqlCommand.Connection = mySqlConn
```

3   Call one of the following four methods that execute the command:

```
'Use ExecuteNonQuery to execute an INSERT, UPDATE or
'DELETE query where that query type has been set using the
'CommandText property
mySqlCmd.ExecuteNonQuery()
```

```
'Use ExecuteReader to execute a SELECT command and
'return a datareader
Dim mySqlReader As SqlDataReader = mySqlCmd.ExecuteReader
```

```
'Use ExecuteScalar to execute a command and return the value of
'the first column of the first row. Any additional results
'are ignored.
Dim Result As Object
Result = mySqlCmd.ExecuteScalar
```

```
'Use ExecuteXmlReader to execute a SELECT command and
'fill a DataSet using the returned XmlReader
Dim SQL As String = "SELECT * FROM authors FOR XML AUTO, XMLDATA"
Dim mySqlCmd as New SqlCommand(SQL, mySqlConn)
Dim myDS As New DataSet()
MyDS.ReadXml(mySqlCmd.ExecuteXmlReader(), XmlReadMode.Fragment)
```

4   Make sure to close the connection when you're finished with it.

The following listing shows the code necessary to retrieve the contents of the Authors table of the Pubs sample SQL Server database as XML, and to display that data in a Web Forms page.

11

Data Binding

> **note**
>
> The data access samples in this book are written to run against the MSDE sample database installed by the .NET Framework SDK. If you want to run the data access samples against a SQL Server database other than the NetSDK MSDE database, or if you are unable to use a trusted connection to SQL Server or MSDE, you must modify the connection string in the examples to match the appropriate server name and logon credentials.

ExecuteXmlReader.aspx

```
<%@ Page Language="vb" %>
<%@ Import Namespace="System.Data" %>
<%@ Import Namespace="System.Data.SqlClient" %>
<%@ Import Namespace="System.Xml" %>
<html>
  <script runat="server">
  Sub Page_Load(sender As Object, e As EventArgs)
   Dim ConnStr As String
   ConnStr = "data source=(local)\NetSDK;"
   ConnStr &= "database=pubs;integrated security=true"
   Dim mySqlConn As New SqlConnection(ConnStr)
   mySqlConn.Open
   Dim SQL As String = "SELECT * FROM authors FOR XML AUTO, XMLDATA"
   Dim mySqlCmd as New SqlCommand(SQL, mySqlConn)
   Dim myDS As New DataSet()
   myDS.ReadXml(mySqlCmd.ExecuteXmlReader(), XmlReadMode.Fragment)
   XmlDisplay.DocumentContent = MyDS.GetXml
  End Sub
</script>
<body>
   <asp:xml id="XmlDisplay" transformsource="authors.xsl"
      runat="server"></asp:xml>
</body>
</html>
```

This listing creates and opens a *SqlConnection* to the Pubs database, creates a SQL query string to retrieve the contents of the Authors table as XML, and creates a new *SqlCommand*, passing in the SQL query and the *SqlConnection*. Then it creates a dataset and uses the *ExecuteXmlReader* method of the *SqlCommand* to pass an *XmlReader* to the dataset's *ReadXml* method, which allows the dataset to populate itself from the *XmlReader*. Finally the code sets the *DocumentContent* property of the declared *Xml* server control to the result of the *GetXml* method of the dataset. The *Xml* control uses the XSL Transformation document authors.xsl to format the *Xml* content displayed by the *Xml* control. The following listing shows the content of authors.xsl.

Authors.xsl

```
<xsl:stylesheet version='1.0'
   xmlns:xsl='http://www.w3.org/1999/XSL/Transform'>
   <xsl:template match="/">
   <style>
      .header{font-weight:bold;color:white;background-color:black;}
      .value{font-family:arial;font-size:.7em;background-
color:silver}
   </style>
   <table border="1" cellspacing="0" cellpadding="1"
      bordercolor="black">
      <tr class="header">
         <th>Author ID</th>
         <th>Last Name</th>
         <th>First Name</th>
         <th>Phone</th>
         <th>Address</th>
         <th>City</th>
         <th>State</th>
         <th>Zip</th>
         <th>Contract</th>
      </tr>
   <xsl:for-each select='Schema1/authors'>
      <tr>
         <td nowrap="true" class="value">
            <b>
               <xsl:value-of select='@au_id' />
            </b>
         </td>
         <td nowrap="true" class="value">
            <xsl:value-of select='@au_lname' />
         </td>
         <td nowrap="true" class="value">
            <xsl:value-of select='@au_fname' />
         </td>
```

Data Binding

11

```
        <td nowrap="true" class="value">
          <xsl:value-of select='@phone' />
        </td>
        <td nowrap="true" class="value">
          <xsl:value-of select='@address' />
        </td>
        <td nowrap="true" class="value">
          <xsl:value-of select='@city' />
        </td>
        <td nowrap="true" class="value">
          <xsl:value-of select='@state' />
        </td>
        <td nowrap="true" class="value">
          <xsl:value-of select='@zip' />
        </td>
        <td nowrap="true" class="value">
          <xsl:value-of select='@contract' />
        </td>
      </tr>
    </xsl:for-each>
    </table>
    </xsl:template>
</xsl:stylesheet>
```

The output of ExecuteXmlReader.aspx is shown in the following figure.

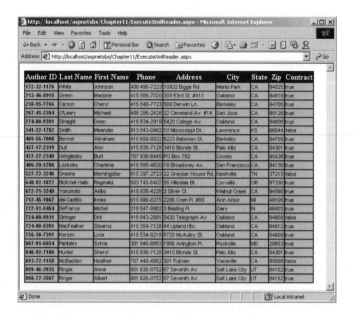

OleDbCommand

For most purposes, using the *OleDbCommand* class is effectively the same as using the *SqlCommand* class. Instead of connecting with the *SqlConnection* class, you can just use the *OleDbConnection* class. One significant difference, however, is that the *OleDbCommand* class does not have an *ExecuteXmlReader* method.

Here's how to use an *OleDbCommand* to execute an aggregate query against the Northwind Microsoft Access sample database and return a result (this example assumes that you have the Northwind.mdb database installed locally):

1. Create and open an *OleDbCommand* with the appropriate connection string for connecting to the Northwind database, where *<filepath>* is the path to Northwind.mdb on your machine.

```
Dim ConnStr As String
ConnStr = "Provider=Microsoft.Jet.OLEDB.4.0;"
ConnStr &= "Data Source=<filepath>\northwind.mdb;"
Dim myOleDbConn As New OleDbConnection(ConnStr)
myOleDbConn.Open
```

2. Create a variable to contain the SQL query (note that the query can also be passed as a literal string to the constructor of the *OleDbCommand* class).

```
Dim SQL As String = "SELECT Count(*) FROM products"
```

3. Create an *OleDbCommand* object, passing the SQL query and the connection object to the constructor.

```
Dim myOleDbCmd as New OleDbCommand(SQL, myOleDbConn)
```

4. Create a variable to receive the return value from the command. This variable is declared as type *Object* because that is the return type of the *ExecuteScalar* method of the *OleDbCommand* object.

```
Dim Result As Object
```

5. Finally call the *ExecuteScalar* method of the *OleDbCommand* object, and use the returned value. Note that the value must be cast to the correct type before using it because the returned type is *Object*. This is especially important if you need to use methods of a particular type that are not implemented by *Object*.

```
Result = myOleDbCmd.ExecuteScalar()
Value.Text &= CType(Result, String)
```

The following listing shows how you would use this example to display the returned result in a Web Forms page.

ExecuteScalar.aspx

```
<%@ Page Language="vb" %>
<%@ Import Namespace="System.Data" %>
<%@ Import Namespace="System.Data.OleDb" %>
<html>
    <script runat="server">
    Sub Page_Load(sender As Object, e As EventArgs)
        Dim ConnStr As String
        ConnStr = "Provider=Microsoft.Jet.OLEDB.4.0;"
        ConnStr &= "Data Source=<filepath>\northwind.mdb;"
        Dim myOleDbConn As New OleDbConnection(ConnStr)
        myOleDbConn.Open
        Dim SQL As String = "SELECT Count(*) FROM products"
        Dim myOleDbCmd as New OleDbCommand(SQL, myOleDbConn)
        Dim Result As Object
        Result = myOleDbCmd.ExecuteScalar()
        Value.Text &= CType(Result, String)
    End Sub
    </script>
<body>
    <form runat=server>
        <asp:label id="Value" runat="server">The count is:
            </asp:label>
    </form>
</body>
</html>
```

The following figure shows the output of ExecuteScalar.aspx.

Using Stored Procedures

In addition to using SQL text queries, you can also use stored procedures as the basis of a *SqlCommand* or *OleDbCommand* object. This is as simple as setting

> **note**
>
> Although the previous example uses Microsoft Access to demonstrate the ability of the *OleDbCommand* object to connect to non–SQL Server databases, you shouldn't use Access for ASP.NET applications. For initial prototyping and development, or for applications with minimal scalability requirements (5–10 concurrent users or fewer), MSDE is the better choice.
>
> MSDE is a SQL Server–compatible database that is available with a number of Microsoft products, including SQL Server, Microsoft Office, and Visual Studio. A version of MSDE also comes with the .NET Framework SDK, and it's installed with and used to run the SDK samples, if you choose to install them. (Please refer to Chapter 8 for important guidance about installing sample applications.) MSDE is built on the same database engine as SQL Server, but it's tuned for approximately five concurrent users.
>
> The advantage of using MSDE is that all of your development tasks are then identical to developing against SQL Server, without the licensing expense of a full-blown SQL Server. (The license to use and distribute MSDE is included in the aforementioned products. Check the end-user license agreement to ensure that your use is within the terms of the agreement.) And if your application's scalability needs to grow, you can simply move your database to SQL Server for increased performance and scalability, with no code or data changes required.

the *CommandText* property of the object to the name of the stored procedure that you want to execute, and setting the *CommandType* to *CommandType.StoredProcedure*. If you're familiar with the execution of stored procedures under classic ADO, this isn't so different from what you would have done with the ADO *Command* object.

Calling Stored Procedures with Parameters

Calling stored procedures with input or output parameters is a little more involved, but it's still pretty straightforward. You simply create parameters (either *SqlParameter* or *OleDbParameter* objects); set the appropriate properties, such as *ParameterName*, *Direction*, type (*SqlType* or *OleDbType*), and *Value*; and then add the parameter object to the *Parameters* collection of the *Command* object. The following listing shows the code required to execute the *byroyalty* stored procedure in the Pubs sample SQL Server database, and it returns a *SqlDataReader*, which is then bound to an ASP.NET *DataGrid* control. (You'll learn more about data-binding later in this chapter.)

ExecuteReader_SP.aspx

```
<%@ Page Language="vb" %>
<%@ Import Namespace="System.Data" %>
<%@ Import Namespace="System.Data.SqlClient" %>
<html>
 <script runat="server">
 Sub Page_Load(sender As Object, e As EventArgs)
    Dim ConnStr As String
    ConnStr = "Data Source=(local)\NetSDK;"
    ConnStr &= "database=pubs;integrated security=true"
    Dim mySqlConn As New SqlConnection(ConnStr)
    mySqlConn.Open
    Dim SQL As String = "byroyalty"
    Dim mySqlCmd as New SqlCommand(SQL, mySqlConn)
    mySqlCmd.CommandType = CommandType.StoredProcedure
    Dim mySqlParam As New SqlParameter("@percentage", SqlDbType.Int)
    mySqlParam.Value = 40
    mySqlCmd.Parameters.Add(mySqlParam)
    Dim Reader As SqlDataReader
    Reader = mySqlCmd.ExecuteReader()
    MyGrid.DataSource = Reader
    MyGrid.DataBind()
    Reader.Close()
 End Sub
 </script>
<body>
 <form runat=server>
    <asp:datagrid id="MyGrid" runat="server"></asp:datagrid>
 </form>
</body>
</html>
```

The following figure shows the output of ExecuteReader_SP.aspx.

The previous listing creates and opens a connection to the Pubs database, creates a *SqlCommand* and sets its *CommandType* to *CommandType.StoredProcedure*, and then creates a *SqlParameter*, passing the parameter name and datatype to the parameter's constructor. The code then sets the value of the parameter, adds it to the *Parameters* collection of the *SqlCommand*, and executes the command. The resulting *SqlDataReader* is then bound to a *DataGrid* control, which displays the results.

Using Datasets

Datasets are one of the two main ways of working with data in ADO.NET. (The other one is datareaders, which you've been using and will learn about in more detail later in this chapter.) Datasets provide a database-independent in-memory representation of data. This data can be used for display or to update a back-end database through the appropriate *DataAdapter*. A dataset can also read data from and write data to an XML file or a *Stream* object.

Datasets can be constructed and manipulated programmatically by adding, modifying, or deleting *DataTables*, *DataColumns*, and *DataRows* in the dataset. You can also use such datasets to update a back-end database (assuming that the schema of the tables you've constructed is compatible) by calling the *Update* method of the dataset.

You can work with typed datasets to make your code easier to read and your ADO.NET code less error-prone. Also, you can use a *DataView* to filter the contents of a dataset for use in display (such as for data-binding) or calculations.

Using DataAdapters

DataAdapters allow you to get data from a back-end database into a dataset, and to update a back-end database from a dataset. There are two *DataAdapters* that are installed with the .NET Framework, the *SqlDataAdapter* and the *OleDbDataAdapter*. Each of these *DataAdapters* uses the appropriate *Connection* class and *Command* classes to either retrieve or update data.

The *Fill* method of the *SqlDataAdapter* and *OleDbAdapter* classes can be used to populate a dataset with results from a back-end database, using the *Command* object specified by the *SelectCommand* property of the *DataAdapter*. The following code creates and opens a connection to the database specified by the *ConnStr* argument. Then it creates a new *SqlDataAdapter* and sets its *SelectCommand* property to a newly created *SqlCommand* object that uses the query specified by the SQL argument. Finally the code creates a new dataset, populates it using the *Fill* method of the *SqlDataAdapter*, and closes the connection.

```
Dim mySqlConn As New SqlConnection(ConnStr)
mySqlConn.Open()
Dim mySqlAdapter As New SqlDataAdapter()
mySqlAdapter.SelectCommand = New SqlCommand(SQL, mySqlConn)
Dim myDS As New DataSet
mySqlAdapter.Fill(myDS)
mySqlConn.Close()
```

At this point, the data in the dataset can be updated or deleted, new rows can be added, or the entire dataset can be passed to another component because it no longer has a connection to the back-end database.

Reading XML Data

In addition to populating a dataset from a database using a *DataAdapter*, you can also read the data for a dataset from an XML file or stream using the *ReadXml* method of the dataset. Since you can also save a dataset as XML using the *WriteXml* method, the two techniques together can be a convenient way of serializing and deserializing the data in a dataset. The ExecuteXmlReader.aspx listing on page 310 shows an example of using the ReadXml method to populate a dataset with XML data retrieved from SQL Server using the *FOR XML AUTO* query syntax.

Using DataTables, DataColumns, and DataRows

Another way of populating a dataset is to create its tables, columns, and rows programmatically. This allows you to create a dataset without connecting to a back-end database. Assuming that the schema of the created table(s) matches your database (which is handled in the following code by reading in an XSD schema file, shown on page 327, created from the Pubs Titles table), you can then connect to the database and update it based on the row(s) you've added to the dataset programmatically.

The following listing shows the code for adding a new row to the Titles table of the Pubs sample SQL Server database. Note that the *SelectCommand* property of the *SqlDataAdapter* is set by passing the *SQLSelect* string variable to the constructor of the *SqlDataAdapter*. This is necessary to allow the *UpdateCommand* (the command that is called when the *Update* method of the *SqlDataAdapter* is called) to be built automatically, using the *SqlCommandBuilder* object.

important

Depending on which version of the .NET Framework you've installed, you may need to add the path to the folder containing the Visual Basic .NET compiler to your PATH environment variable in order for the preceding command to work. The procedure for locating and adding this path to the PATH environment variable is detailed on page xv of the "Installing the Sample Files" section at the beginning of this book.

AddTitle.aspx

```vb
<%@ Page Language="vb" %>
<%@ Import Namespace="System.Data" %>
<%@ Import Namespace="System.Data.SqlClient" %>
<html>
   <head>
   <script language="VB" runat="server">
      Sub Page_Load
          Dim myDS As New DataSet()
          Dim TitleTable As DataTable
          Dim TitleRow As DataRow
          Dim ConnStr As String
          ConnStr = "server=(local)\NetSDK;database=pubs;"
          ConnStr &= "Trusted_Connection=yes"
          Dim SQLSelect As String
          SQLSelect = "SELECT * FROM Titles"
          Dim mySqlConn As New SqlConnection(ConnStr)
          Dim mySqlDA As New SqlDataAdapter(SQLSelect, ConnStr)
          Dim mySqlCB As New SqlCommandBuilder(mySqlDA)

          myDS.ReadXmlSchema(Server.MapPath("AddTitle.xsd"))

          If IsPostBack Then
             TitleTable = myDS.Tables(0)
             TitleRow = TitleTable.NewRow()

             TitleRow("title_id") = title_id.Text
             TitleRow("title") = title.Text
             TitleRow("type") = type.Text
             TitleRow("pub_id") = pub_id.Text
             TitleRow("price") = CDbl(price.Text)
```

```
                        TitleRow("advance") = CDbl(advance.Text)
                        TitleRow("royalty") = CInt(royalty.Text)
                        TitleRow("ytd_sales") = CInt(ytd_sales.Text)
                        TitleRow("notes") = notes.Text
                        TitleRow("pubdate") = CDate(pubdate.Text)
                        TitleTable.Rows.Add(TitleRow)

                        mySqlDA.Update(myDS)

                        titlegrid.DataSource = myDS.Tables(0).DefaultView
                        titlegrid.Databind()
                    End If
                End Sub
            </script>
        <body>
            <form runat="server">
                <h3>Inserting a Title</h3>
                <table width="300">
                    <tr>
                        <td colspan="2" bgcolor="silver">Add a New Title:</td>
                    </tr>
                    <tr>
                        <td nowrap>Title ID: </td>
                        <td>
                        <asp:textbox id="title_id" text="XX0000" runat="server"/>
                        </td>
                    </tr>
                    <tr>
                        <td nowrap>Title: </td>
                        <td>
                            <asp:textbox id="title" text="The Tao of ASP.NET"
                                runat="server"/>
                        </td>
                    </tr>
                    <tr nowrap>
                        <td>Type: </td>
                        <td>
                            <asp:textbox id="type" text="popular_comp"
                                runat="server"/>
                        </td>
                    </tr>
```

```
<tr>
  <td>Publisher ID: </td>
  <td>
    <asp:textbox id="pub_id" text="1389" runat="server"/>
  </td>
</tr>
<tr>
   <td>Price: </td>
   <td>
     <asp:textbox id="price" text="39.99" runat="server"/>
   </td>
</tr>
<tr>
   <td>Advance: </td>
   <td>
     <asp:textbox id="advance" text="2000" runat="server"/>
   </td>
</tr>
<tr>
   <td>Royalty: </td>
   <td>
     <asp:textbox id="royalty" text="5" runat="server"/>
   </td>
</tr>
<tr>
   <td nowrap>Year-to-Date Sales: </td>
   <td>
     <asp:textbox id="ytd_sales" text="0" runat="server"/>
   </td>
</tr>
<tr>
   <td>Notes: </td>
   <td>
     <asp:textbox id="notes" textmode="multiline"
        text="Philosophy and Code...a perfect mix."
        rows="3" columns="30" runat="server"/>
   </td>
</tr>
<tr>
   <td nowrap>Publication Date: </td>
   <td>
```

```
                    <asp:textbox id="pubdate" text="12/01/01"
                        runat="server"/>
                </td>
            </tr>
            <tr>
                <td></td>
                <td style="padding-top:15">
                    <asp:button text="Add Title" runat="server"/>
                </td>
            </tr>
            <tr>
                <td colspan="2">
                    <asp:datagrid id="titlegrid" runat="server"/>
                </td>
            </tr>
        </table>
    </form>
</body>
</html>
```

Setting Up Relationships

Since datasets can contain multiple tables of data, it only makes sense that you might want the dataset to contain information about the relationships between these tables. This would allow you to treat them as true relational data, as well as to maintain any hierarchy and foreign key relationships inherent in the data. The *DataSet* class fulfills this need with its *Relations* collection, which contains a collection of *DataRelation* objects, each of which describes a parent/child relationship between two matching columns in different tables in the dataset.

DataRelation objects can be added to a dataset programmatically, or can be inferred from a supplied XSD schema.

Accessing Values

Values in a dataset are accessed by referring to the *DataTables* and *DataRows* containing the data. The *DataTables* are available via the *Tables* collection of the dataset, and you can reference a particular table either by index (zero-based) or by table name (key) as follows:

```
Dim myTable As DataTable = myDS.Tables(0)
Dim myTable As DataTable = myDS.Tables("tablename")
```

You can also iterate over the *DataTableCollection* (returned by the *Tables* property of the dataset), *DataRowCollection* (returned by the *Rows* property of a

DataTable), or the *DataColumnCollection* (returned by the *Columns* property of
a *DataTable*). The code in the following listing iterates over all of the tables in a
dataset and all of the rows in each table. Then it displays the value of each column in the row, using an ASP.NET *Literal* control as a placeholder for the text.

DisplayDataSetItems.aspx

```
<%@ Page Language="vb" %>
<%@ Import Namespace="System.Data" %>
<%@ Import Namespace="System.Data.SqlClient" %>
<html>
   <head>
   <script language="VB" runat="server">
      Sub Page_Load
         Dim myDS As New DataSet()
         Dim ConnStr As String
         ConnStr = "server=(local)\NetSDK;database=pubs;"
         ConnStr &= "Trusted_Connection=yes"
         Dim SQLSelect As String
         SQLSelect = "SELECT * FROM Titles "
         SQLSelect &= "SELECT * FROM Publishers"
         Dim mySqlConn As New SqlConnection(ConnStr)
         Dim mySqlDA As New SqlDataAdapter(SQLSelect, ConnStr)

         mySqlDA.Fill(myDS)

         'Get each DataTable in the DataTableCollection
         '  and display each row value by appending it to
         '  the Text property of the Literal control.
         Dim CurrentTable As DataTable
         Dim CurrentRow As DataRow
         Dim CurrentColumn As DataColumn
         For Each CurrentTable In myDS.Tables
          value.Text &= "Table: " & CurrentTable.TableName & "<br/>"
          value.Text &= "--------------------------------<br/>"
            For Each CurrentRow In CurrentTable.Rows
               value.Text &= "<br/>   "
               For Each CurrentColumn in CurrentTable.Columns
                  If Not (CurrentRow(CurrentColumn) Is Nothing) Then
                     If Not IsDbNull(CurrentRow(CurrentColumn)) Then
                        value.Text &= CStr(CurrentRow(CurrentColumn))
                     Else
```

```
                        value.Text &= "NULL"
                    End If
                    value.Text &= "<br/>   "
                End If
            Next
        Next
        value.Text &= "--------------------------------<br/>"
        value.Text &= "<br/><br/>"
    Next
    End Sub
  </script>
<body>
  <asp:literal id="value" runat="server"/>
</body>
</html>
```

The output of DisplayDataSetItems.aspx is shown in the following figure.

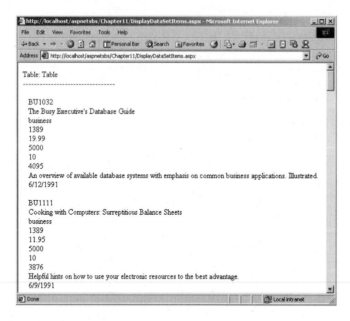

Updating Datasets

Once you've populated a dataset with data, either by using a *DataAdapter* or by calling the *ReadXml* method of the dataset, you may want to update that data. You can edit an individual value by specifying the table, row, and column of the item you want to edit and supplying a new value.

```
myDS.Tables(0).Rows(0).Columns(2) = "popular_comp"
```

But what if you edit several values, and then you realize that you want to roll back one or more of the changes? Fortunately, the dataset provides robust support for accepting and rejecting changes in the its data by maintaining multiple versions of the data for each row. Each row contains the following versions.

- *Original*   This contains the data originally loaded into the row.
- *Default*   This contains the default values for the row (specified by the *DefaultValue* property of the row's columns). If no defaults have been specified, this contains the same data as *Original*.
- *Current*   This contains updated data for any columns that have been updated, and the same data as *Original* for columns that have not been updated.
- *Proposed*   After calling *BeginEdit* on a row and before calling the *EndEdit* or *CancelEdit* methods of the *DataRow*, the *Proposed* version contains changes to data that have not yet been applied to the *Current* version. If *CancelEdit* is called, the *Proposed* version is deleted. If *EndEdit* is called, the changes in the *Proposed* version are applied to the *Current* version.

You can determine whether or not changes have been made to an item in a row by comparing the item's *Original* or *Default* version with the *Current* version.

```
If CurrentRow(1, DataRowVersion.Current) Is _
   CurrentRow(1, DataRowversion.Proposed) Then
   'Take appropriate action
End If
```

You can accept or reject changes to data on a row-by-row basis.

```
If CurrentRow(0, DataRowVersion.Current) = "" Then
   'Blank field not allowed
   CurrentRow.RejectChanges()
Else
   CurrentRow.AcceptChanges
End If
```

Finally you can check the current state of a row by checking the row's *RowState* property.

```
Dim CurrentState As String
CurrentState = CurrentRow.RowState
If CurrentState = DataRowState.Modified Then
   'Take appropriate action
End If
```

There are five possible row states.

- **Added**   This represents a row that has been added to the table prior to *AcceptChanges* being called. Once *AcceptChanges* is called, this row's *RowState* will be set to *Unchanged*.
- **Deleted**   This represents a row whose *Delete* method has been called.
- **Detached**   This represents a newly created row that has not yet been added to a *DataRowCollection*, or a row that has been removed from a *DataRowCollection* but not destroyed.
- **Modified**   This represents a row whose data has changed, but whose *AcceptChanges* method has not been called.
- **Unchanged**   This represents a row whose data has not changed since the last call to *AcceptChanges*.

Once you've called *AcceptChanges* on the dataset, you would call the *Update* method of the *DataAdapter* used to load data into the dataset to update the underlying database with the new values. See the the AddTitle_TypedDS.aspx listing on page 328 for an example of using the *Update* method.

Typed Datasets

One of the coolest new features of ADO.NET is the ability to create strongly typed datasets. Typed datasets are special classes, generated by the xsd.exe command-line utility, that inherit from the *DataSet* class. They use an XSD schema to create additional public properties and methods that allow you to access the columns of the dataset's tables directly by name, rather than having to use either an index or a late-bound key. This can improve runtime performance and reduce the likelihood of errors in coding against the dataset. Creating a typed dataset for the *AddTitles* example that was shown earlier requires just a few steps. The following example assumes that you've already created an XSD schema for the table or tables in the dataset, which you can do with the *WriteXmlSchema* method of a dataset that's been loaded with data from the table or tables:

1   Open a command prompt at the location of the XSD schema file.

2   Create the class for the typed dataset, using the xsd.exe utility. The */d* option specifies that we want to create a dataset, the */l* option sets the language as VB, and the */n* option specifies that the class should use the namespace *AddTitle*. AddTitle.xsd is the name of your XSD schema file, which is shown in the AddTitle.xsd listing.

```
xsd.exe /d /l:vb AddTitle.xsd /n:AddTitle
```

3   Compile the class, using the vbc.exe command-line compiler. The */t* option specifies that you want to compile as a library component (DLL), the */r* options specify assemblies that you need to reference, and the */out* option directs the compiler to save the compiled assembly in the bin subdirectory of the current directory.

```
vbc.exe /t:library AddTitle.vb /r:System.dll
/r:System.Data.Dll /r:System.Xml.Dll
/out:bin/AddTitle.dll
```

AddTitle.xsd

```xml
<?xml version="1.0" standalone="yes"?>
<xsd:schema id="TitleDataSet" targetNamespace="http://
www.aspnetb.com.ns" xmlns="" xmlns:xsd="http://www.w3.org/2001/
XMLSchema" xmlns:msdata="urn:schemas-microsoft-com:xml-msdata">
 <xsd:element name="TitleDataSet" msdata:IsDataSet="true">
  <xsd:complexType>
   <xsd:choice maxOccurs="unbounded">
    <xsd:element name="Titles">
    <xsd:complexType>
    <xsd:sequence>
    <xsd:element name="title_id" type="xsd:string" minOccurs="0" />
    <xsd:element name="title" type="xsd:string" minOccurs="0" />
    <xsd:element name="type" type="xsd:string" minOccurs="0" />
    <xsd:element name="pub_id" type="xsd:string" minOccurs="0" />
    <xsd:element name="price" type="xsd:decimal" minOccurs="0" />
    <xsd:element name="advance" type="xsd:decimal" minOccurs="0" />
    <xsd:element name="royalty" type="xsd:int" minOccurs="0" />
    <xsd:element name="ytd_sales" type="xsd:int" minOccurs="0" />
    <xsd:element name="notes" type="xsd:string" minOccurs="0" />
    <xsd:element name="pubdate" type="xsd:dateTime" minOccurs="0" />
    </xsd:sequence>
    </xsd:complexType>
    </xsd:element>
   </xsd:choice>
  </xsd:complexType>
 </xsd:element>
</xsd:schema>
```

The following listing shows how you would write the AddTitle.aspx example to work with the typed dataset.

AddTitle_TypedDS.aspx

```vb
<%@ Page Language="vb" %>
<%@ Import Namespace="System.Data" %>
<%@ Import Namespace="System.Data.SqlClient" %>
<%@ Import Namespace="AddTitle" %>
<html>
    <head>
    <script language="VB" runat="server">
        Sub Page_Load
            Dim myTDS As New TitleDataSet()
            Dim myTitleTable As TitleDataSet.TitlesDataTable
            Dim myTitleRow As TitleDataSet.TitlesRow
            Dim ConnStr As String
            ConnStr = "server=(local)\NetSDK;database=pubs;"
            ConnStr &= "Trusted_Connection=yes"
            Dim SQLSelect As String
            SQLSelect = "SELECT * FROM Titles"
            Dim mySqlConn As New SqlConnection(ConnStr)
            Dim mySqlDA As New SqlDataAdapter(SQLSelect, ConnStr)
            Dim mySqlCB As New SqlCommandBuilder(mySqlDA)

            mySqlConn.Open()
            mySqlDA.Fill(myTDS, "Titles")
            mySqlConn.Close()

            If IsPostBack Then
                myTitleTable = myTDS.Titles
                myTitleRow = myTitleTable.NewTitlesRow()

                myTitleRow.title_id = title_id.Text
                myTitleRow.title = title.Text
                myTitleRow.type = type.Text
                myTitleRow.pub_id = pub_id.Text
                myTitleRow.price = CDbl(price.Text)
                myTitleRow.advance = CDbl(advance.Text)
                myTitleRow.royalty = CInt(royalty.Text)
                myTitleRow.ytd_sales = CInt(ytd_sales.Text)
                myTitleRow.notes = notes.Text
                myTitleRow.pubdate = CDate(pubdate.Text)
                myTitleTable.Rows.Add(myTitleRow)

                mySqlDA.Update(myTDS, "Titles")
```

```
                    titlegrid.DataSource = myTitleTable.DefaultView
                    titlegrid.Databind()
                End If
            End Sub
        </script>
<body>
        <!-- This code is identical to AddTitle.aspx -->
</body>
</html>
```

Note that you add the *AddTitle* namespace using the @ *Import* directive. This lets you use its types directly. Because the assembly was placed in the bin subdirectory by the compiler, it will be loaded automatically by your Web application.

Now when you create the dataset, you create an instance of *TitleDataSet* instead of *DataSet*. Similarly, you use strong types for the table and row. To successfully load data from and update the underlying database table, you also need to pass the name of the table to the *Fill* and *Update* methods of the *DataAdapter*. Once you've created the table and row objects, you can access the column values via early-bound properties instead of through an index.

Another useful thing about typed datasets is that when you use them with Visual Studio .NET, you automatically get IntelliSense code completion for all the members of the *TitleDataSet*. This makes coding against a typed dataset much easier and considerably less error-prone.

Using DataViews

The *DataView* class provides a means for sorting, searching, editing, filtering, and navigating *DataTables*. Dataviews can also be data-bound, as you'll see in later examples. Data-binding allows ASP.NET server controls to display bound data automatically, even when multiple rows or columns of data are contained in the datasource. This greatly simplifies the display of data in ASP.NET. You can access an unfiltered view of the data in a table in a dataset as follows:

```
Dim myDV As DataView
myDV = myDS.Tables(0).DefaultView
```

Once you have a reference to the *DataView*, you can filter it by adding an expression to the *RowFilter* property.

```
myDV.RowFilter = "type='business'"
```

Search the *DataView* using the *Find* method.

```
Dim RowNum As Integer = myDV.Find("BU1032")
```

Sort the *DataView* by adding an expression to the *Sort* property.

```
myDV.Sort = "type, title_id DESC"
```

You've already seen some basic examples of binding to a *DataView*. You'll look at data-binding in more detail later in this chapter.

Reading Data with Datareaders

Datasets are great when you need really rich control over your data—updates, rollbacks, reading and writing schemas, etc. But when all you need to do is display some data quickly and efficiently, the dataset (and the *DataAdapter* used to fill it) has a fair amount of overhead that you may not want to incur. Enter the datareader.

A datareader provides the equivalent of a forward-only, read-only cursor on your data. It is both faster and more lightweight than a dataset, making it ideal when you need to retrieve a set of rows and iterate over them just once (to display them, for example). Unlike datasets, you can also data-bind directly to datareaders, without the need for a *DataView*.

SqlDataReader

SqlDataReader is the class to use when accessing data from a SQL Server database. You create this class by calling the *ExecuteReader* method on a *SqlCommand* object.

```
Dim mySqlDR As SqlDataReader = mySqlCmd.ExecuteReader()
```

To access the rows in a *SqlDataReader* instance, you call the *Read* method of the instance, usually in a loop.

```
While mySqlDR.Read()
    Response.Write(mySqlDR.Item(0))
End While
```

Once you're finished with the *SqlDataReader*, you should always call its *Close* method, as well as calling the *Close* method on the associated *Connection* object.

```
mySqlDR.Close()
```

OleDbDataReader

Creating and using an *OleDbDataReader* is essentially the same as for the *SqlDataReader*, with one notable exception. The *OleDbDataReader* can handle hierarchical recordsets retrieved using the *MSDataShape* OLE DB Provider. When

> **note**
>
> To avoid having to explicitly close the connection associated with the command used to create either a *SqlDataReader* or an *OleDbDataReader,* pass the *CommandBehavior.CloseConnection* argument to the *ExecuteReader* method of the connection.
>
> *mySqlDR = mySqlCmd.ExecuteReader(CommandBehavior.CloseConnection)*
>
> The associated connection will be closed automatically when the *Close* method of the datareader is called. This makes it all the more important to always remember to call *Close* on your datareaders!

an *OleDbDataReader* is created based on an *OleDbCommand* that returns a hierarchical recordset, the OLE DB chapter is returned as a column in the *OleDbDataReader.* The value of the column is an *OleDbDataReader* representing the child records.

Data-Binding

One exciting advance in the move from classic ASP to ASP.NET is the availability of server-side data-binding. Data-binding is the process of declaratively tying elements of the UI for a page (such as controls) to data in an underlying datastore. Data-binding on the client has been available in Internet Explorer for a number of years, but it requires all of your users to use the same browser, or else you need to do a massive amount of testing to ensure compatibility with different browser versions. Server-side data-binding solves this problem by binding and rendering data on the server and returning cross-browser-compatible HTML.

ASP.NET allows you to bind against a variety of sources, including properties and method call results, arrays and collections, and datareaders and dataviews. Typically, binding is done either declaratively, using the <%#*expression*%> syntax, or by programmatically setting the *DataSource* property of a control to the desired datasource. The data is bound by calling the *DataBind* method, either at the *Page* level (which binds all controls on the page) or on the control being bound (which binds the control and any child controls). The *DataBind* method causes the control and its children to evaluate any data-binding expression(s) associated with the control and assign the resulting values to the appropriate control attribute. Data-binding allows controls like the *DataGrid* control, which can handle multiple rows and columns, to iterate over and format the data specified by their *DataSource* property for display.

Simple Data-Binding

The simplest type of data-binding uses the <%#*expression*%> syntax to replace
the <%#*expression*%> construct with the value represented by the expression.
For example, the following listing shows a simple page that binds to a page-level
property.

SimpleDataBinding.aspx

```
<%@ Page Language="vb" %>
<html>
   <head>
      <script runat="server">
         Dim Name As String
         Sub btnSubmit_Click(sender As Object, e As EventArgs)
            Name = txtHello.Text
            lblHello.Visible = True
            DataBind()
         End Sub
      </script>
   </head>
   <body>
      <asp:label id="lblHello" visible="false" runat="server">
         Hello, <%# Name %>!
      </asp:label>
      <form runat="server">
         <asp:textbox text="" id="txtHello" runat="server"/>
         <br>
         <asp:button text="Submit" id="btnSubmit"
            OnClick="btnSubmit_Click" runat="server" />
      </form>
   </body>
</html>
```

The output of this listing after entering a value and clicking the button is shown
in the following figure.

Binding to Controls

The same syntax can be used to bind to controls. For example, you can bind the selected item of a *DropDownList* control to the *Text* property of an ASP.NET *Label* control using the code shown in the following listing.

ControlBinding.aspx

```
<%@ Page Language="vb" %>
<html>
   <head>
      <script runat="server">
         Dim myArrayList As New ArrayList
         Sub Page_Load(sender As Object, e As EventArgs)
            If Not IsPostBack Then
               myArrayList.Add("Chocolate")
               myArrayList.Add("Vanilla")
               myArrayList.Add("Strawberry")
               myList.DataSource = myArrayList
               myList.DataBind()
            End If
            Page.DataBind()
         End Sub
      </script>
   </head>
   <body>
      <form runat="server">
         <asp:dropdownlist id="myList" runat="server"/>
         <asp:button Text="Submit" runat=server/>
         <br/>
         Favorite Ice Cream:
         <asp:label text="<%# myList.SelectedItem.Text %>"
            runat=server/>
      </form>
   </body>
</html>
```

Using DataBinder.Eval

DataBinder.Eval is a static method that is used to evaluate a data-binding expression at runtime. This can simplify the process of casting various datatypes to be displayed as text. The basic syntax of *DataBinder.Eval* is

```
<%# DataBinder.Eval(Container, EvalExpression, FormatExpression) %>
```

Container is the object that contains the expression to be evaluated (for *DataGrid*, *DataList*, or *Repeater* controls, this is always *Container.DataItem*), *EvalExpression* is the full name of the property or item to be evaluated, and *FormatExpression* is a string formatting expression (such as *{0:c}*) to be used to format the string result. Note that if no format expression argument is passed, *DataBinder.Eval* will return an object instead of a string.

important

Because *DataBinder.Eval* uses late binding and reflection (which allows managed code to interrogate other managed code at runtime), it may be significantly slower than the other data-binding techniques. For this reason, you should only use *DataBinder.Eval* when you need to, such as for performing string formatting on numeric data.

Using the Data-Bound Controls

Chapter 10 looked at the ASP.NET server controls and mentioned briefly one very important group of controls. The *DataBound* controls, which include the *DataGrid* control (and its constituent controls), the *DataList* control, and the *Repeater* control, allow you to set a datasource programmatically. Then they iterate over that datasource and display the data based on formatting that you define, either through properties of the control or by adding template definitions. The neat thing about this is that you define the formatting for a single row, and the data-bound controls take care of applying that formatting to all rows of data.

Choosing which control to use rests largely on the format you want your data in and how much control you want over the formatting of the data. The *DataGrid* control is the simplest to use and displays data in a table format. The *DataList* control is a little more involved in terms of implementation, but it provides a greater degree of control over formatting through the use of templates. Finally, for the control freak in all of us, the *Repeater* control, which has no built-in formatting of its own, provides ultimate control over formatting through templates.

Using DataGrids

The *DataGrid* control presents bound data in a tabular format and provides a number of properties that you can use to format the data. This control can automatically generate all columns in the table from the datasource, or you can use specialized column controls to provide additional functionality or formatting for a given column or columns.

At its simplest, there are three basic steps to using a *DataGrid* control.

1   Add the *DataGrid* to the page.

2   Set the *DataSource* property of the *DataGrid* to an appropriate datasource. This datasource can be defined in the page, or you can call a method in an external object to supply the data.

3   Call the *DataBind* method of the control to automatically bind the data to the control. You can also call the *DataBind* method of the *Page* object, which will bind (or rebind) all of the data-bound controls on the page by calling *DataBind* on each control in turn.

Let's look at an example. In "HTML Controls" in Chapter 10, there is an example that used a drop-down listbox to list flavors of ice cream for a user to choose from. Suppose that you want to show similar information in a table format. The problem with this approach is that the data is explicitly added to the control in the code (or declaratively by adding items to the control in its tag declaration). Thus, anytime the data changes, you have to explicitly change the code that creates the control. Additionally, because the creation of the data and the creation of the control are tightly coupled, it's not possible to reuse this data, either elsewhere on the page or elsewhere in the application.

So in this first example, you'll create the data that you want to use in a custom procedure in a *<script>* block, and then call that procedure in order to populate the datasource of your *DataGrid* control. Start with a very simple *DataGrid* that has no formatting whatsoever.

1   Create a new file and save it as DataGrid.aspx.

2   Add the @ *Page* directive, standard HTML elements, and an *HtmlForm* control to the page, as in earlier examples.

3   Add a *Label* control and a *DataGrid* control to the *HtmlForm* control, with the following attributes:

```
<form runat="server">
   <asp:label id="title" text="DataGrid Example"
      font-name="Verdana" font-size="18" runat="server"/>
   <asp:datagrid
      id="MyGrid"
      autogeneratecolumns="true"
      runat="server"/>
</form>
```

4   Add a *<script>* block with a function called *CreateData* to create the data that you'll bind to the grid. Remember that the *<script>* block goes between the *<head>* and *</head>* tags.

```
<script language="vb" runat="server">
```

11

Data Binding

```
Function CreateData() As ICollection
    Dim DataArray As New ArrayList()

    DataArray.Add("Chocolate")
    DataArray.Add("Vanilla")
    DataArray.Add("Strawberry")
    DataArray.Add("Pistachio")
    DataArray.Add("Rocky Road")

    Return DataArray
End Function
</script>
```

5   Finally add a *Page_Load* event handler and use it to set the *DataSource* property of the grid (which can only be set at runtime) and call the *DataBind* method of the *DataGrid*.

```
Sub Page_Load()
    MyGrid.DataSource = CreateData()
    MyGrid.DataBind()
End Sub
```

6   Save and browse the page. The output should look something like the following figure.

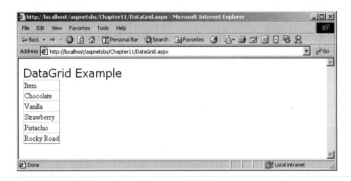

Although this is a very simple example, you used two lines of code (setting the *DataSource* and calling *DataBind*) to accomplish what would have taken considerably more code in classic ASP. Now let's jazz things up a bit.

1   Before making any changes, save the current file as DataGrid2.aspx.

2   Start by making the data a little richer, substituting an ADO.NET *DataTable* for the *ArrayList*. To make this easier, add an @ *Import* directive to import the

System.Data namespace, which contains the *DataTable* class. This directive should go directly below the @ *Page* directive.

```
<%@ Import Namespace="System.Data" %>
```

3   Next delete all of the code in the *CreateData* function and add the following code. It creates a new *DataTable*, adds three columns to it (using the constructor for the *DataTable* class), and then adds five rows to it. Finally, since you can't bind directly to a *DataTable*, create an instance of the *DataView* class based on the *DataTable* and return that as the datasource for your *DataGrid*.

```
Dim dt As New DataTable()
Dim dr As DataRow

dt.Columns.Add(New DataColumn("IceCreamID", GetType(Int32)))
dt.Columns.Add(New DataColumn("Flavor", GetType(String)))
dt.Columns.Add(New DataColumn("Price", GetType(Double)))

'Add row 1
dr = dt.NewRow()
dr(0) = 1
dr(1) = "Chocolate"
dr(2) = 2.00 'Chocolate is popular, so it costs more
dt.Rows.Add(dr)

'Add row 2
dr = dt.NewRow()
dr(0) = 2
dr(1) = "Vanilla"
dr(2) = 1.50
dt.Rows.Add(dr)

'Add row 3
dr = dt.NewRow()
dr(0) = 3
dr(1) = "Strawberry"
dr(2) = 1.00
dt.Rows.Add(dr)

'Add row 4
dr = dt.NewRow()
dr(0) = 4
dr(1) = "Pistachio"
```

11

Data Binding

```
dr(2) = 1.75
dt.Rows.Add(dr)

'Add row 5
dr = dt.NewRow()
dr(0) = 5
dr(1) = "Rocky Road"
dr(2) = 1.25
dt.Rows.Add(dr)

Dim dv As New DataView(dt)
Return dv
```

4   Save and browse the page. The output should look something like the following figure.

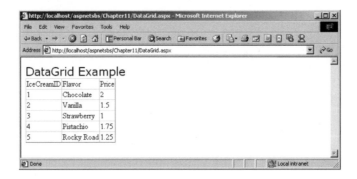

5   Now that you have more interesting data, let's work on the formatting. First add the following attributes to the *DataGrid* tag declaration:

```
<asp:datagrid
    id="MyGrid"
    autogeneratecolumns="true"
    bordercolor="black"
    borderwidth="2"
    cellpadding="3"
    runat="server"/>
```

6   Next, add child tags to the *DataGrid* to provide row formatting. In order to do this, you need to remove the / character that closes the single *DataGrid* tag, and add a closing *DataGrid* tag.

```
<asp:datagrid
    id="MyGrid"
```

```
            autogeneratecolumns="true"
            bordercolor="black"
            borderwidth="2"
            cellpadding="3"
            runat="server">
            <headerstyle backcolor="silver" font-bold="true"/>
            <itemstyle backcolor="black" forecolor="white"/>
            <alternatingitemstyle backcolor="white" forecolor="black"/>
</asp:datagrid>
```

7   Save and browse the page. The output should look something like the following figure.

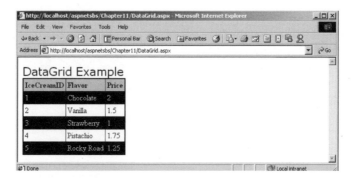

But wait! There's more. In addition to autogenerating columns from the bound data, *DataGrids* also support creating columns declaratively. This gives you greater control over both the formatting and the behavior of individual columns. For example, you can use a *BoundColumn* control to provide customized header text for a column, or to apply special formatting to the bound text in each row. You can also use a *ButtonColumn* control to display a command button in each row of a column, an *EditButtonColumn* to provide in-place editing for a row, or a *HyperlinkColumn* control to provide a hyperlink for each row of the grid, with the text caption, the URL, or both being data-bound. Finally, you use a *TemplateColumn* control to apply complex formatting to each row of a specific column. Let's see what this example will look like using *EditColumn* and *BoundColumn* controls.

1   Before making any changes, save the current file as DataGrid3.aspx. Then change the *autogeneratecolumns* attribute of the *DataGrid* tag declaration to *false*.

2   Next add a pair of *<columns>* tags to the *Datagrid* tag to contain the column definitions.

```
<asp:datagrid
    id="MyGrid"
    autogeneratecolumns="false"
    bordercolor="black"
    borderwidth="2"
    cellpadding="3"
    runat="server">
    <headerstyle backcolor="silver" font-bold="true"/>
    <itemstyle backcolor="black" forecolor="white"/>
    <alternatingitemstyle backcolor="white" forecolor="black"/>
    <columns>
    </columns>
</asp:datagrid>
```

3   Next add the column definitions. The *EditCommandColumn* isn't data-bound, so
set its properties explicitly. For the ID column, set the *ReadOnly* property to *true*
to prevent the column from being edited when the Edit link is clicked. Set the
DataField property for the bound columns to the desired fields and use the *{0:c}*
format string to format the Price column as currency.

```
<columns>
    <asp:editcommandcolumn
        canceltext="Cancel"
        edittext="Edit"
        updatetext="Update"
        headertext="Edit?"/>
    <asp:boundcolumn
        headertext="Ice Cream ID"
        readonly="true"
        datafield="IceCreamID"/>
    <asp:boundcolumn
        headertext="Flavor"
        datafield="Flavor"/>
    <asp:boundcolumn
        headertext="Price"
        datafield="Price"
        dataformatstring="{0:c}"/>
</columns>
```

4   Now you need to create event handlers for when the Edit links are clicked. For
this example, since you're dealing with local data, skip the Update command.
Add the following code to the *<script>* block, just after the *CreateData* function.
In the *Grid_Edit* handler, use the argument *e*, which contains information about

the *DataGrid* command that occurred, to determine which row to edit. Then rebind the grid.

```
Sub Grid_Edit(Sender As Object, e As DataGridCommandEventArgs)
    MyGrid.EditItemIndex = e.Item.ItemIndex
    MyGrid.DataBind
End Sub
Sub Grid_CancelEdit(Sender As Object, e As DataGridCommandEvent
Args)
    MyGrid.EditItemIndex = -1
    MyGrid.DataBind
End Sub
```

5   Next you need to map the *OnEditCommand* and *OnCancelCommand* events to the event handlers you just created by adding the appropriate attributes to the *DataGrid* tag.

```
<asp:datagrid
    id="MyGrid"
    autogeneratecolumns="false"
    bordercolor="black"
    borderwidth="2"
    cellpadding="3"
    oneditcommand="Grid_Edit"
    oncancelcommand="Grid_CancelEdit"
    runat="server">
```

6   Save and browse the page. When you click the Edit link for a row, the output should look similar to the following figure. Clicking Cancel will cancel Edit mode.

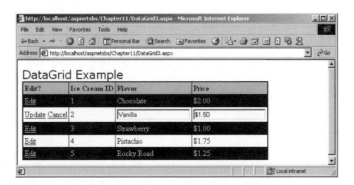

In addition to the features demonstrated in the preceding examples, the *DataGrid* control also supports the sorting and paging of bound data. Follow these steps to enable sorting:

1   Set the *AllowSorting* property of the *DataGrid* control to *true*.

```
<asp:DataGrid id="ItemsGrid"
    BorderColor="black"
    BorderWidth="1"
    CellPadding="3"
    AllowSorting="true"
    OnSortCommand="Sort_Grid"
    AutoGenerateColumns="false"
    runat="server">
```

2   If you have not defined bound columns, set the *AutoGenerateColumns* property of the *DataGrid* control to *true*.

3   Add an event handler to handle the *OnSortCommand* event and map the event to the handler (similar to the preceding example for editing).

```
<asp:DataGrid id="ItemsGrid"
    BorderColor="black"
    BorderWidth="1"
    CellPadding="3"
    AllowSorting="true"
    OnSortCommand="Sort_Grid"
    AutoGenerateColumns="false"
    runat="server">
```

4   Use the *SortExpression* passed as part of the *DataGridCommandEventArgs* argument to sort the source data.

```
Sub Sort_Grid(sender As Object,
        e As DataGridSortCommandEventArgs)
    SortExpression = e.SortExpression.ToString()
    ItemsGrid.DataSource = CreateDataSource()
    ItemsGrid.DataBind()
End Sub
```

5   Rebind the grid. See the BoundColumn_Sort.aspx sample file on this book's CD for the full implementation of sorting in a *DataGrid*.

When sorting is enabled, links are provided automatically in the header of each column to sort by that field. Note that if you are using *BoundColumn* controls, you can skip step 2, but you must explicitly set the *SortExpression* property of the controls. The value of the property should be the same as the *DataField* property (that is, the name of the column in the datasource to which the column in the *DataGrid* is bound).

Enabling paging is even simpler.

1   Set the *AllowPaging* property of the *DataGrid* control to *true*.

```
<asp:DataGrid id="ItemsGrid" runat="server"
   BorderColor="black"
   BorderWidth="1"
   CellPadding="3"
   AllowPaging="true"
   AutoGenerateColumns="false"
   OnPageIndexChanged="Grid_Change">
```

2   Add an event handler to handle the *OnPageIndexChanged* event and map the event to the handler (similar to the preceding example for sorting).

```
<asp:DataGrid id="ItemsGrid" runat="server"
   BorderColor="black"
   BorderWidth="1"
   CellPadding="3"
   AllowPaging="true"
   AutoGenerateColumns="false"
   OnPageIndexChanged="Grid_Change">
```

3   In the event handler, use the *NewPageIndex* property passed as part of the *DataGridPageChangedEventArgs* argument to set the *CurrentPageIndex* property of the *DataGrid* to the new page.

```
Sub Grid_Change(sender As Object,
      e As DataGridPageChangedEventArgs)
   ' Set CurrentPageIndex to the page the user clicked.
   ItemsGrid.CurrentPageIndex = e.NewPageIndex
   ' Rebind the data.
   ItemsGrid.DataSource = CreateDataSource()
   ItemsGrid.DataBind()
End Sub
```

4   Rebind the grid.

```
Sub Grid_Change(sender As Object,
      e As DataGridPageChangedEventArgs)
   ' Set CurrentPageIndex to the page the user clicked.
   ItemsGrid.CurrentPageIndex = e.NewPageIndex
   ' Rebind the data.
   ItemsGrid.DataSource = CreateDataSource()
   ItemsGrid.DataBind()
End Sub
```

Using DataLists

DataLists provide an excellent mix of built-in functionality and control over display formatting. Unlike the *DataGrid* control, in which the rows are displayed one after the other in a table format, the *DataList* can display its items in multiple columns and can display rows horizontally or vertically.

Follow these steps to display information from the Titles table of the Pubs SQL Server sample database:

1 Create a new text file and save it as TitlesDataList1.aspx.

2 Add the @ *Page* directive, standard HTML elements, and an *HtmlForm* control to the page, as in earlier examples. You should also add the necessary @ *Import* statements to import the *System.Data* and *System.Data.SqlClient* namespaces.

3 Add the following code to the *<form>* section of the page to declare the *DataList* control, and to set up some simple formatting.

```
<h3>Binding to a DataList Control</h3>
<asp:datalist id="titlelist" repeatcolumns="3"
    gridlines="both" cellpadding="5" runat="server">
    <ItemTemplate>
        <h5>
            <%# DataBinder.Eval(Container.DataItem, "title")%>
            <br/>
        </h5>
    </ItemTemplate>

</asp:datalist>
```

4 Add the following code to a server-side *<script>* block in the *<head>* section of the page. This code creates and fills a dataset with data from the Titles table, and then it binds the *DataList* to the *DefaultView* of the dataset.

```
<script runat="server">
    Sub Page_Load
        Dim myDS As New DataSet()
        Dim ConnStr As String
        ConnStr = "server=(local)\NetSDK;database=pubs;"
        ConnStr &= "Trusted_Connection=yes"
        Dim SQLSelect As String
        SQLSelect = "SELECT * FROM Titles"
        Dim mySqlConn As New SqlConnection(ConnStr)
        Dim mySqlDA As New SqlDataAdapter(SQLSelect, ConnStr)

        mySqlDA.Fill(myDS)
```

```
        titlelist.DataSource = myDS.Tables(0).DefaultView
        titlelist.Databind()
    End Sub
</script>
```

5   Save and browse the page. The output should look something like the following figure.

Clearly, this layout isn't too pleasing visually, so let's spice it up a bit:

1   Before making changes, save a copy of the file as TitlesDataList2.aspx.

2   Replace the entire contents of the *<ItemTemplate>* section with the following (note that the first table row uses a format string containing the path to an image file, with a placeholder for the *title_id*, to bind the *title_id* for each item to its graphic).

```
<table>
 <tr>
  <td rowspan="4">
  <img align="top"
      src='<%# DataBinder.Eval(Container.DataItem, "title_id", _
          "/quickstart/aspplus/images/title-{0}.gif") %>' >
  </td>
  </tr>
  <tr>
    <td>
        <em>Title: </em>
```

Data Binding

11

```
         </td>
         <td nowrap>
            <%# DataBinder.Eval(Container.DataItem, "title")%>
            <br/>
         </td>
      </tr>
      <tr>
         <td>
            <em>Price: </em>
         </td>
         <td nowrap>
       <%# DataBinder.Eval(Container.DataItem, "price", "{0:c}")%>
            <br/>
         </td>
      </tr>
      <tr>
         <td>
            <em>Category: </em>
         </td>
         <td nowrap>
            <%# DataBinder.Eval(Container.DataItem, "type")%>
            <br/>
         </td>
      </tr>
   </table>
```

3   Save and browse the page. The output should look similar to the following figure. Note that for the images to be displayed, the ASP.NET QuickStart samples must be installed.

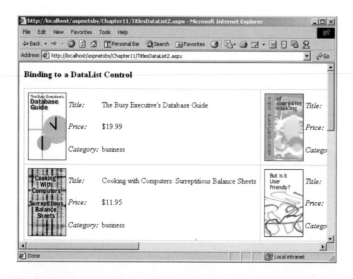

The *<ItemTemplate>* is but one of the templates that can be used with the *DataList* control, but they all work similarly. Other templates that you can define include the following:

- *AlternatingItemTemplate* Sets the formatting for alternating items.
- *EditItemTemplate* Formats the fields used when an item in the *DataList* is switched to *Edit* mode.
- *FooterTemplate* Sets formatting for the footer of the *DataList*.
- *HeaderTemplate* Sets formatting for the header of the *DataList*.
- *SelectedItemTemplate* Sets the formatting for the item in the *DataList* that has been selected by the user.
- *SeparatorTemplate* Sets the format of the divider between items in the *DataList*.

Like a *DataGrid*, a *DataList* can be set up for in-place editing of values. This requires adding a *LinkButton* or *Button* control to the *ItemTemplate* with the *CommandName* set to *"edit"*; implementing an *EditItemTemplate*; setting up the event handlers for the *EditCommand*, *DeleteCommand*, *CancelCommand*, and *UpdateCommand* events; and mapping the event handlers to the events. When the Edit button for an item is clicked, the event handler should set the *EditItemIndex* to the number of the item that was clicked, which can be retrieved from the *DataListCommandEventArgs* passed to the event handler. The *EditItemTemplate* should include *LinkButton* or *Button* controls for the *DeleteCommand*, *CancelCommand*, and *UpdateCommand*, and event handlers should be added for each.

Using Repeaters

The *Repeater* control lets you go "hog-wild" with templates. If you can write it in HTML and/or server controls, you can put it into a template. The following listing shows how the previous example can be updated to work with a *Repeater* instead of a *DataList*. It adds a *HeaderTemplate* and a *SeparatorTemplate* to further improve the look of the page.

TitlesRepeater.aspx

```
<%@ Page Language="vb" %>
<%@ Import Namespace="System.Data" %>
<%@ Import Namespace="System.Data.SqlClient" %>
<html>
   <head>
   <script runat="server">
```

```
        Sub Page_Load
            Dim myDS As New DataSet()
            Dim ConnStr As String
            ConnStr = "server=(local)\NetSDK;database=pubs;"
            ConnStr &= "Trusted_Connection=yes"
            Dim SQLSelect As String
            SQLSelect = "SELECT * FROM Titles"
            Dim mySqlConn As New SqlConnection(ConnStr)
            Dim mySqlDA As New SqlDataAdapter(SQLSelect, ConnStr)

            mySqlDA.Fill(myDS)

            titlerepeater.DataSource = myDS.Tables(0).DefaultView
            titlerepeater.Databind()
        End Sub
    </script>
    </head>
<body>
    <form runat="server">
        <h3>Binding to a DataList Control</h3>
        <asp:repeater id="titlerepeater" runat="server">
            <ItemTemplate>
                <table>
                    <tr>
                        <td rowspan="4">
                            <img align="top"
                            src='<%# DataBinder.Eval(Container.DataItem, _
        "title_id", "/quickstart/aspplus/images/title-{0}.gif") %>' >
                        </td>
                    </tr>
                    <tr>
                        <td>
                            <em>Title: </em>
                        </td>
                        <td nowrap>
                        <%# DataBinder.Eval(Container.DataItem, "title")%>
                            <br/>
                        </td>
                    </tr>
```

```
            <tr>
                <td>
                    <em>Price: </em>
                </td>
                <td nowrap>
                <%# DataBinder.Eval(Container.DataItem, "price", _
                        "{0:c}")%>
                    <br/>
                </td>
            </tr>
            <tr>
                <td>
                    <em>Category: </em>
                </td>
                <td nowrap>
                 <%# DataBinder.Eval(Container.DataItem, "type")%>
                    <br/>
                </td>
            </tr>
        </table>
    </ItemTemplate>
    <HeaderTemplate>
        <h4 style="background-color:silver;">Titles</h4>
    </HeaderTemplate>
    <SeparatorTemplate>
        <hr>
    </SeparatorTemplate>
    </asp:repeater>
  </form>
</body>
</html>
```

The output of TitlesRepeater.aspx is shown in the following figure. Remember that for the images to be displayed, the ASP.NET QuickStart samples must be installed.

All templates available to the *DataList* control can be used with the *Repeater* control, and editing is handled the same with a *Repeater* as with a *DataList*.

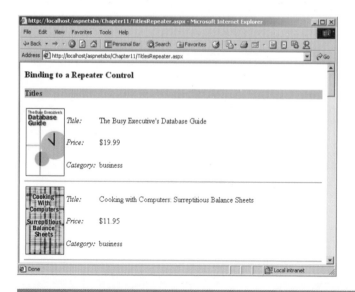

Chapter 11 Quick Reference

To	Do This
Connect to a SQL Server database	Create and open an instance of the *SqlConnection* class from the *System.Data.SqlClient* namespace.
Connect to an OLE DB datasource	Create and open an instance of the *OleDbConnection* class from the *System.Data.OleDb* namespace.
Execute *SELECT, UPDATE, INSERT,* or *DELETE* statements against a database	Create an instance of the *SqlCommand* or *OleDbCommand* class and call one of its *Execute* methods.
Use an in-memory cache of hierarchical data	Create an instance of the *DataSet* class from the *System.Data* namespace. Populate the dataset by calling the *Fill* method of the *SqlDataAdapter* or *OleDbDataAdapter* class.
Display read-only data in a bound control	Bind the control to a *SqlDataReader* or an *OleDbDataReader*. Be sure to pass the *CommandBehavior.CloseConnection* argument to the *ExecuteReader* method when creating the datareader. This ensures that the underlying connection is closed when the datareader is closed.
Bind data to a control	Set the *DataSource* property of the control to the datareader, *DataView*, or other datasource, and then call the *DataBind* method of the control (or call the page's *DataBind* method).

12

Creating Custom
Server Controls

In this chapter, you will learn about

✔ *Choosing a base class for your control*

✔ *Creating a namespace for your control(s)*

✔ *Registering and using your control in a page*

✔ *Extending and aggregating existing controls*

✔ *Maintaining state in custom server controls*

✔ *Handling postbacks*

✔ *Providing "lookless" UI with templated controls*

Having spent the last two chapters studying ASP.NET server controls, ADO.NET, and data-binding, by now you're probably thinking, "These server controls sure are cool, but I wish I could create my own." Well, wish no longer! In this chapter, you'll learn how to create custom ASP.NET server controls.

There are as many reasons for developing custom server controls as there are developers, but generally they fall into three main categories: reuse, specialization, and maintenance.

Creating custom server controls makes reuse easy. You can wrap up a bunch of related functionality and UI elements into a control, and then reuse that control where you need that functionality. For example, you could create a server control that encapsulates all of the fields and validation controls necessary for user registration. Then, instead of rewriting that code anytime you need a user registration screen, you simply add your control to the page instead.

Specialization refers to taking an existing functionality, such as a server control, and adding your own customized functionality to it. Specialization in ASP.NET server controls is done through either inheritance or composition. You specialize in inheritance by inheriting from a class that provides most of the functionality you want, and then adding additional functions or overriding existing ones and adding your own implementation of those functions. Composition allows you to combine the functionality of two or more existing controls into a reusable control, adding additional functionality as desired.

Finally, custom ASP.NET server controls simplify the maintenance of your applications. Once a server control has been developed and tested, it can be reused reliably in many places. If you find a bug in your control, it can be fixed in a single place (the source class for your control), and all you need to do to distribute the fix is replace the assembly containing the fixed control. This is a major improvement over reuse through include files, or having no reuse at all.

Creating Your First Control

Creating custom server controls with ASP.NET is fairly straightforward. A custom ASP.NET server control is any class that inherits from the *Control* class of the *System.Web.UI* namespace, or one that inherits from any of the controls derived from *Control*. Choosing the control from which to derive your custom control is largely a matter of how much functionality you want to build into your control. You'll learn how to choose a control to inherit from later in this section.

All server controls that send output directly to the browser do so by overriding the *Render* method of the control from which they're derived. Controls that are derived from a control with its own UI rendering (such as the *TextBox* server control) should also call the *Render* method on the base class in order to have the base control render its own output. Note that the location in your code at which you call the *Render* method of the base class is important. That's where the rendered output of the base control will appear. The *Render* method of the sample file TextBoxPlus.vb on this book's CD demonstrates this concept.

In addition to sending output to the browser directly through the *Render* method, some custom controls (in particular, compositional controls) send output to the browser indirectly by overriding the *CreateChildControls* method of the base *Control* class, which is used to add controls to a custom control at runtime. Some also call the *RenderChildren* method, which causes all of the child controls of a given control to execute their *Render* methods.

Creating a Namespace

Each custom control must belong to a namespace because the @ *Register* directive, which makes custom controls available for use in a page, has a *Namespace* attribute that is used to locate the control class to instantiate at runtime.

You create a namespace using the *namespace* keyword. In Visual Basic .NET, you use both the *Namespace* keyword and a closing *End Namespace* keyword to define the scope of the namespace.

```
Namespace myNS
    'Class definitions, etc. go inside the namespace
End Namespace
```

In C#, you use the *namespace* keyword and a pair of curly braces that define the scope of the namespace.

```
namespace myNS
{
    //Class definitions, etc.
}
```

Note that if you are creating your custom control using Visual Studio .NET, the IDE will create the namespace for you automatically.

important

Although Visual Studio .NET creates a namespace for each new project automatically, this is implemented differently depending on the language you choose. For example, in a Visual Basic .NET Web application, the namespace for the project is defined by the *Root Namespace* option set in the Project Properties dialog for the project. This means that although you will not actually see the *Namespace* keyword in your class files, a namespace will be created when the class is compiled.

In a Visual C# project, the *namespace* keyword is added to class files and code-behind files automatically.

In both languages, the default name for the namespace is the name of the project.

Creating a Class

Each custom server control is defined in a class. You can have more than one class defined in a single namespace within a file, but the class is what defines the boundary of the control. You may put multiple controls within a single file, if you want. When you compile this file, all of the classes (and the controls they represent) are compiled into a single assembly. When you have multiple related controls, this can make deploying your controls simpler.

You define classes in Visual Basic .NET and C# with the *class* keyword. As with namespaces, classes in Visual Basic .NET are defined with a *Class* keyword and an *End Class* keyword that together define the scope of the class.

```
Class myControl
    'Variables, procedures, etc.
End Class
```

C# uses the *class* keyword with a pair of curly braces to define the scope of the class.

```
class myControl
{
    //Variables, procedures, etc.
}
```

Inheriting from a Base Class

One of the most important steps in creating a custom server control is choosing the class from which your control will inherit. This can be a more difficult decision than you might think, because there are so many choices.

You need to consider both how the control will be used and who will use it. Since one of the reasons for creating custom controls in the first place is to reuse controls that have most (but not quite all) of the functionality you need, you may be tempted to simply jump right into inheriting a very rich control and get the most bang for your buck. But you should keep in mind that any public property, method, or event exposed by the base control will be exposed by a derived control automatically. If you don't plan for this, your control may do something unexpected, or you may unwittingly introduce bugs when someone uses the control in a way that you didn't anticipate.

This may not be a problem if you are creating the control for your own use. If you plan to share it with others, however, just remember that people can be very creative in finding ways to break software, and developers are more creative than most. By making available a lot of public methods that you didn't write, you increase the chances that another developer will break your code. To avoid this problem, generally you should inherit from the class that provides the fewest public members while still providing the desired functionality.

For example, let's say you want basic UI plumbing code but don't want the additional functionality of a *TextBox* or *Label* control. You can inherit from the *WebControl* class, which implements such basic UI features as the *BackColor* and *ForeColor* properties, and the *ApplyStyle* method. If you don't even need the UI plumbing, you can inherit from the *Control* class, which has no UI-related members. Of course, this means that you have to implement UI-related code yourself.

For this first example, you'll inherit from the *Control* class. In Visual Basic .NET, this looks like the following:

```
Namespace myNS
    Public Class myControl
        Inherits System.Web.UI.Control
        'Variables, procedures, etc.
    End Class
End Namespace
```

Of course, if you wanted to avoid typing the *System.Web.UI*, you could add an *Imports* statement to import the namespace as follows:

```
Imports System.Web.UI
```

In C#, the code would look like the following:

```
namespace myNS
{
    public class myControl : System.Web.UI.Control
    {
        //Variables, procedures, etc.
    }
}
```

Rendering Output from a Control

The final step in the implementation of a control is rendering its output. To do this, you override the *Render* method of the base class.

```
Protected Overrides Sub Render(writer As HtmlTextWriter)
    'custom rendering code
End Sub
```

As mentioned earlier, you can also call the *Render* method of the base class in order to send its rendered output to the browser as well. Note that the call to the *Render* method of the base class can appear anywhere within the *Render* method of the derived control, allowing you to determine where in your custom control the rendered output of the base class will appear.

```
Protected Overrides Sub Render(writer As HtmlTextWriter)
    'custom rendering code
    MyBase.Render(writer)
    'addition custom rendering code, if desired
End Sub
```

Note that since ASP.NET calls the overridden *Render* method automatically at runtime, passing in the necessary *HtmlTextWriter* instance, you can simply pass that instance as the argument to the *Render* method in the base class.

Compiling Your Control

In order for clients to be able to use your custom server control, you need to compile it into a managed assembly, usually in the form of a library or DLL. You do this with the appropriate command-line compiler for the language with which you're creating your control, or, if you're using Visual Studio .NET, by issuing the *Build* command (clicking Build on the Build menu).

The command for compiling a custom control written in Visual Basic .NET looks like the following:

```
vbc /t:library <sourcefile> /r:System.Web.dll /r:System.dll
```

Note that *sourcefile* is the name of the file (with a .vb extension) containing the definition of your control class. The */t* parameter specifies that the compiler should create a library (DLL) assembly. The */r* parameter (of which there may be more than one) specifies assemblies that should be referenced when compiling your control class. Each assembly whose types are used within your class must be referenced using a separate */r* parameter that points to the physical name of the assembly. You can also add the */out* parameter, which specifies the path and file name to use for the compiled assembly. One use for this is to direct the compiled output to be placed directly in the bin directory of the application that will use the control, which saves the step of having to copy the assembly there later.

The command for compiling a control written in C# looks like the following:

```
csc /t:library <sourcefile> /r:System.Web.dll /r:System.dll
```

important

Depending on which version of the .NET Framework you've installed, you may need to add the path to the folder containing the Visual Basic .NET compiler to your PATH environment variable in order for the preceding command to work. The procedure for locating and adding this path to the PATH environment variable is detailed on page xv of the "Installing the Sample Files" section at the beginning of this book.

The only things that are different are the name of the compiler (csc.exe instead of vbc.exe) and the extension of *sourcefile*, which for C# will be .cs. This highlights one of the advantages of the .NET platform, which is improved consistency of operations from language to language. This consistency can make it easier for developers to work in multiple languages without facing a steep learning curve.

note

When you're developing controls using Visual Studio .NET, many of the most commonly used assemblies are referenced for you automatically by the IDE. This means that when you issue a *Build* command, you do not need to explicitly tell the compiler to reference those assemblies. The IDE has taken care of it already. The assemblies automatically referenced for a Web Control Library project are System, System.Data, System.Drawing, System.Management, System.Web, and System.Xml.

If you use types from other assemblies, you will need to add a reference to the assemblies. You can do this either by right-clicking the References folder in the Solution Explorer and clicking Add Reference, or by selecting Add Reference from the Project menu. Either one opens the Add Reference dialog, which allows you to select .NET or COM components or projects to reference and browse to find assemblies or components not listed. (Only .NET assemblies that have been placed in the Global Assembly Cache and COM components that have been registered are listed.)

Note that if you add a reference to a COM component, Visual Studio .NET will create a Runtime Callable Wrapper (RCW) for the component automatically.

Putting It All Together: Creating a New Control

Now that you've looked at all of the pieces that go into creating a custom ASP.NET server control, let's put it all together in a simple working control.

1   Create a new file in your preferred editor and save it as HelloControl.vb.

2   Add an *Imports* statement to import the *System.Web.UI* namespace.

```
Imports System.Web.UI
```

3   Add the *Namespace* and *End Namespace* keywords to define the namespace *ASPNETSBS*.

```
Namespace ASPNETSBS

End Namespace
```

4   Within the namespace you just created, add a class named *HelloControl*. Use the *Public* modifier to make the class accessible to clients.

```
Public Class HelloControl

End Class
```

5   On the first line within the class, add an *Inherits* statement to inherit the *Control* class. Since you imported the *System.Web.UI* namespace, you can just use the class name.

```
Inherits Control
```

6   Finally, override the *Render* method of the base *Control* class to send a message to the browser.

```
Protected Overrides Sub Render(writer As HtmlTextWriter)
    writer.Write("Hello, World!</br>")
End Sub
```

7   Open a command prompt window, navigate to the directory containing HelloControl.vb, and compile the control using the syntax shown earlier.

```
vbc /t:library HelloControl.vb /r:System.Web.dll /r:System.dll
```

Your control is now compiled and ready to use. Remember that you will need to copy the assembly (in the case of the preceding command, the assembly name will be HelloControl.dll) to the bin directory of the application from which you want to use your control. That is, unless you used the *out* parameter to direct the compiler to put the assembly there for you.

Private vs. Shared Assemblies

By default, all custom assemblies that you create are private and are made available to a Web application by placing them in the bin directory of the application, where they are loaded by ASP.NET automatically. Assemblies may also be shared across all clients on a machine by placing them in the GAC. Barring any security configuration in the assembly that prevents it, assemblies in the GAC may be used by any managed application on that machine.

Private assemblies allow you to limit the use of an assembly to the application in whose bin subdirectory the assembly resides. Shared assemblies allow you to reuse your assemblies in multiple applications without needing to maintain a copy of an assembly for each application that uses it.

To install an assembly into the GAC, you need to give the assembly a strong name (signing it with a public key, which you can generate with the sn.exe .NET Framework utility). Then add it to the GAC either by using the gacutil.exe .NET Framework utility or by dragging and dropping the assembly into the %windir%\assembly folder, which will add the assembly to the GAC automatically.

The GAC supports versioning of assemblies, so you can install multiple versions of the same assembly by setting its *AssemblyVersionAttribute* attribute. Clients can then specify which version of an assembly to load at runtime.

Registering Your Control

No, it's not *that* kind of registering. Unlike COM components, .NET assemblies don't have to be registered in the system registry in order to be used. Rather, you need to use the @ *Register* directive to tell ASP.NET which tag you're going to use for the custom control. The basic syntax for the @ *Register* directive, which was discussed in Chapter 9, looks like the following:

```
<%@ Register TagPrefix=<tag prefix> Namespace=<namespace name>
  Assembly=<assembly name> %>
```

Here, *tag prefix* is the text that you will use in the tag for your control to associate it with your assembly, *namespace name* is the name of the namespace defined in the assembly, and *assembly name* is the name of the compiled assembly (without the .dll extension). Once your control is registered in the page, you can declare the control using a combination of the tag prefix you defined and the class name of the control, as you'll see in the next section.

Using Your Control in a Page

Once you've registered the control, you can use it in a Web Forms page by adding the appropriate tag to the page. The syntax for the tag for a custom control is

```
<tagprefix:classname id="identifier" runat="server">
```

Here, *tagprefix* is the tag prefix specified in the @ *Register* directive, *classname* is the name of the class that contains the control, and *identifier* is a unique (to the page) ID that you will use to refer to the control in server-side code.

Adding Controls Programmatically

In addition to adding the control to the page declaratively as shown earlier, you can add custom controls to the page programmatically, just as you can with the standard ASP.NET server controls. Adding controls programmatically does not require the @ *Register* directive. You may want to add an @ *Import* directive, however, to avoid the need to use the fully qualified name to refer to the controls in your assembly.

Adding a custom control to the page programmatically is essentially the same as adding a standard ASP.NET server control to the page programmatically, and uses the following syntax:

```
<%@ Import Namespace=<namespace name> %>
<script runat="server">
    Sub Page_Load
        Dim myControl As New ControlClassName()
        me.Controls.Add(myControl)
    End Sub
</script>
```

Here, *namespace name* is the name of the namespace containing the control, and *ControlClassName* is the name of the control's class. In the preceding example, the *New* keyword is used to create an instance of the control class, which is then added to the *Controls* collection of the page (referenced by the *me* keyword). Once the control has been added to the *Controls* collection, ASP.NET will take care of rendering it for you.

You'll see examples of both declarative and programmatic use of a custom control in the next section.

Putting It All Together: Using a Custom Control

Let's put your simple control to work. First practice implementing the control declaratively, as follows:

1 Create a new file in your preferred editor and save it as HelloControl_Client.aspx. This file should be saved to an IIS application directory, which also contains a bin directory to which the compiled assembly containing the custom control has been copied.

2 Add the @ *Page* directive and standard HTML tags to the file.

```
<%@ Page Language="VB" %>
<html>
<body>
</body>
</html>
```

3 Next add an @ *Register* tag with the appropriate attributes for the control.

```
<%@ Register TagPrefix="ASPNETSBS" Namespace="ASPNETSBS"
    Assembly="HelloControl" %>
```

4 Finally add the tag to declare the control. This tag should go in the *<body>* section of the page.

```
<ASPNETSBS:HelloControl id="hello" runat="server"/>
```

5 Save and browse the page. The output from the page should look like the following figure.

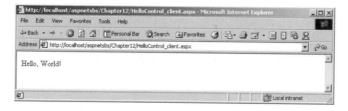

Here's the full code for the page that uses the *HelloControl* control:

```
<%@ Page Language="VB" %>
<%@ Register TagPrefix="ASPNETSBS" Namespace="ASPNETSBS"
    Assembly="HelloControl" %>
<html>
<body>
    <ASPNETSBS:HelloControl id="hello" runat="server"/>
</body>
</html>
```

That's right; just seven lines of code to use the control you created. Just imagine how much time you're going to save by encapsulating frequently used code into a custom control!

Now that you've conquered declarative use of your custom control, let's implement the control programmatically, as follows:

1   Create a new file in your preferred editor and save it as HelloControl_Client_Programmatic.aspx.
This file should be saved to the same location as in the previous example.

2   Add the @ *Page* directive and standard HTML tags.

3   Add the following code to the *<head>* section of the page:

```
<script runat="server">
    Sub Page_Load
        Dim myControl As New HelloControl()
        me.Controls.Add(myControl)
    End Sub
</script>
```

4   Save the page and browse it. The output should look the same as the preceding figure.

While the output of both HelloControl_Client.aspx and HelloControl_Client_Programmatic.aspx *look* the same, there is one significant difference: the text Hello, World! in the second example appears *after* the closing *</html>* tag. This is because when you add a control to the page's *Controls* collection using the *Add* method, it is added at the end of the collection.

There are two ways to fix this: use the *AddAt* method instead of *Add*, or use an ASP.NET *PlaceHolder* control. The *AddAt* method takes both the name of a control and an integer representing the location in the collection where the control should be inserted. The usefulness of this method is limited because you must know by number where you want your control to be located, and static HTML content is dynamically converted at runtime into ASP.NET *Literal* controls. The easiest method of precisely placing a programmatically created control on the page is with a *PlaceHolder* control. Add a *PlaceHolder* control at the desired location in the page, making sure to provide an *id* attribute for the control.

```
<asp:placeholder id="ph1" runat="server"/>
```

Then, when you create your control, add it to the *Controls* collection of the *PlaceHolder*, rather than the page's *Controls* collection.

```
ph1.Controls.Add(myControl)
```

Adding Functionality

As cool as it may be to create and consume a custom server control in a grand total of 16 lines of code (including both the control and the Web Forms page that consumes it), it provides minimal functionality. Clearly, to be truly useful, you need to add to the control.

The next several sections will look at how to add properties and methods to a control, create raise and handle events, handle postbacks, maintain state in a control, and create templated controls. By the end of this section, you'll be able to add a great deal of functionality to what is now a very simple control.

Adding Properties and Methods

To make the control more functional, you're going to provide the ability to change the greeting from Hello, World! to Hello, <somename>! with somename being supplied by a property you'll define in the control. You'll also define a method to emit HTML and script to the browser to show a popup message box.

Adding a Property

Let's start with adding a property by following these steps:

1 Open HelloControl.vb.

2 Copy the *HelloControl* class and paste a copy below the original. Modify the class name to *HelloControlProp*. The following code added to the class creates a private string variable and a public *Property* procedure to provide access to the private member variable. It also modifies the *Render* method to use the value of the local variable.

```
Public Class HelloControlProp
    Inherits Control
    Dim _name As String = "World"
    Public Property Name As String
      Get
         Name = _name
      End Get
      Set(ByVal Value As String)
         _name = Value
      End Set
    End Property
    Protected Overrides Sub Render(writer As HtmlTextWriter)
       writer.Write("Hello, " & _name & "!</br>")
    End Sub
End Class
```

3   Save and recompile the class file. You can save yourself time by creating a batch file (saved with a .bat extension) in the same directory as the class file containing the following commands:

```
vbc /t:library HelloControl.vb /r:System.Web.dll /r:System.dll
pause
```

4   Copy the compiled assembly to the bin directory of the Web application that uses the control.

5   Open HelloControl_Client.aspx and add the following tag:

```
<ASPNETSBS:HelloControlProp id="helloprop" runat="server"/>
```

6   Save and browse HelloControl_Client.aspx. The output should look like the following figure.

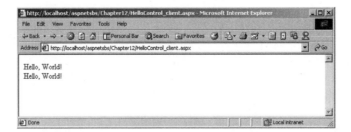

Note that the output in this figure uses the default value of the _name private variable, which you set to *World*. This way, if the person using the control does not explicitly set the property, you still get valid output. You could also have added code to the *Get* portion of the *Property* procedure to check the value of _name, and substitute a default value if it is blank.

To check that your property works correctly, change the tag definition by adding a name attribute, with your name for the value. By default, properties defined on custom controls are available as attributes on the tag used to declare the control, without any additional coding on your part. The updated tag would look like the following:

```
<ASPNETSBS:HelloControlProp id="helloprop" name="Andrew"
    runat="server"/>
```

The output with the modified tag should look like the following figure.

Adding a Method

Now let's look at adding a method.

1 Open HelloControl.vb.

2 Copy the *HelloControlProp* class and paste a copy below the original. Modify the class name to *HelloControlPropMeth*. The following code added to the class creates another private string variable to hold the rest of the message you're outputting, a private boolean variable to flag whether the *Sub* has been called, and a public *Sub* procedure that formats the variable to show a client-side message box. Added to the *Render* method is an *If* statement, which checks the boolean variable to determine whether to pop up a client-side message box or simply render the text message.

```vb
Public Class HelloControlPropMeth
    Inherits Control
    Dim _name As String = "World!"
    Dim _messageText As String = "Hello, "
    Dim _clientMessage As Boolean = False
    Public Property Name As String
        Get
            Name = _name
        End Get
        Set(ByVal Value As String)
            _name = Value
        End Set
    End Property
    Public Sub FormatClientMessage()
    _messageText = "<script>alert('" & _messageText & _name & _
        "!');</script>"
        _clientMessage = True
```

```
        End Sub
        Protected Overrides Sub Render(writer As HtmlTextWriter)
            If _clientMessage = True Then
                writer.Write(_messageText)
            Else
                writer.Write(_messageText & _name & "</br>")
            End If
        End Sub
    End Class
```

3   Save and recompile the class file.

4   Copy the compiled assembly to the bin directory of the Web application that uses the control.

5   Open HelloControl_Client.aspx and add the following tag:

```
<ASPNETSBS:HelloControlPropMeth id="hellopropmeth"
runat="server"/>
```

6   Add a *<head>* section to the page containing the following code:

```
<script runat="server">
    Sub Page_Load
        hellopropmeth.FormatClientMessage()
    End Sub
</script>
```

The completed page should look like the following listing.

HelloControl_Client.aspx

```
<%@ Page Language="VB" %>
<%@ Register TagPrefix="ASPNETSBS" Namespace="ASPNETSBS"
    Assembly="HelloControl" %>
<html>
<head>
<script runat="server">
    Sub Page_Load
        hellopropmeth.FormatClientMessage()
    End Sub
</script>
</head>
<body>
    <ASPNETSBS:HelloControl id="hello" runat="server"/>
    <ASPNETSBS:HelloControlProp id="helloprop" name="Andrew"
        runat="server"/>
```

```
<ASPNETSBS:HelloControlPropMeth id="hellopropmeth" name="Andrew"
    runat="server"/>
</body>
</html>
```

7   Save and browse HelloControl_Client.aspx. The output should look like the
following figure.

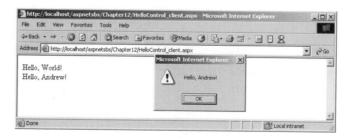

Note that even though you've created three separate controls, they're all in the
same assembly and use the same namespace, so you only need one @ *Register*
directive to use all three.

Try commenting out the line in the *Page_Load* event handler that calls the
FormatClientMessage method by adding a single quote (') to the beginning of the
line, and see what that does to the output.

Creating, Raising, and Handling Events

Another important aspect of creating a custom server control is dealing with
events. While the event model in ASP.NET is designed to closely emulate event
handling in a desktop application, such as a Visual Basic forms application, there
are some significant differences in the models.

The most significant difference is that control events are raised and handled only
on the server. Only after a Web Forms page has been posted back to the server can
the state of each control be examined and appropriate events raised and handled.

Another difference is that custom ASP.NET server controls do not handle client
events, such as clicks, mouseovers, and key presses, because these events occur on
the client. In order to communicate a client event to the server, the control must
initiate a postback. ASP.NET supplies a relatively simple method for allowing a
control to initiate a postback, which is described in "Handling Postbacks" on
page 371.

There are three parts to dealing with events in a custom control: creating the
event, raising the event, and handling the event. (Handling the event is typically
done outside the control, but the plumbing for making it work is set up in
the control.)

Creating and Raising Events

Events in ASP.NET use two classes exposed by the *System.ComponentModel* namespace: *EventHandler* and *EventArgs*. The *EventHandler* class is used as the basis for creating a new event, while the *EventArgs* class is used to pass data with an event, or to signify that no event data was passed.

You create events using the *Events* keyword as follows:

```
Public Event EventName As EventHandler
```

EventName is the name of the event being created. Notice that the event is declared as type *EventHandler*. Next, you call the event (based on whatever criteria you set up within your control to determine if the event should be called) using the *RaiseEvents* keyword as follows:

```
Public Overridable Sub RaisePostBackEvent(eventArgument As String) _
    Implements IPostBackEventHandler.RaisePostBackEvent

    If SomeExpression = True Then
        RaiseEvent EventName(Me, EventArgs.Empty)
    End If
End Sub
```

This code is executed when the *RaisePostBackEvent* method is called during page execution. It tests whether *SomeExpression* is *True*, and if it is, it raises the *EventName* event, which is typically handled outside of the control. You'll learn about *RaisePostBackEvent* in more detail in "Handling Postbacks" on page 371.

Handling Custom Events

Once you've created the event and the code to raise the event, you (or the developer consuming the event) will need to write code to handle the event. This consists of two steps: creating an event handler and wiring the event to it.

An event handler is a page-level procedure that accepts two arguments: the source of the event and an *EventArgs* instance representing any data passed with the event. An event handler for the *EventName* event would look like the following:

```
Sub ControlName_EventName(Source As Object, e As EventArgs)
    'Event handling code
End Sub
```

In this code, *ControlName* represents the name of the control in which the event is defined, and *EventName* represents the name of the event. This syntax is not required, but it's the naming convention typically followed for event handlers. You can call your event handlers whatever you want, but following the naming standard will make your code easier to read and maintain.

To wire the event handler to your control, add an *OnEventName* attribute to the tag in which you declare the control, with the value set to the name of the event handler.

```
<ASPNETSBS:MyControl id="MC1" OnEventName="MC1_EventName"
   runat="server">
```

You'll see a full implementation of these principles after the discussion of handling postbacks.

Overriding Inherited Events

You can override events that are defined on the base control from which your control is derived. The standard events that are defined by the control class are as follows:

- *Init*   Initialize settings for the current request
- *Load*   Perform actions that need to be performed for each request once child controls have been created and initialized
- *DataBinding*   Perform actions needed to evaluate data-binding expressions associated with a control
- *PreRender*   Perform any modifications to the control or data necessary before rendering the control
- *UnLoad*   Perform clean-up tasks before the control is removed from memory

To override an event exposed by an inherited class, you override its associated *OnEventName* method. For example, to override the *PreRender* event, you would use the following code in your control:

```
Protected Overrides Sub OnPreRender(Source As Object, e As EventArgs)
   'Event handling code
   MyBase.OnPreRender(Source, e)
End Sub
```

Control Execution Order

When you're handling events, it's important to understand that the standard control events and methods occur in a consistent order, including events and methods related to postbacks. This is important because if you write code in an event handler that occurs before the objects manipulated by that code have been created and initialized, the results will be unpredictable at best. The following is the order of the standard events and methods for controls.

- *Initialize*   During this phase, the *Init* event is raised.

- *LoadViewState*   During this phase, controls that use *ViewState* are populated with data from the hidden __VIEWSTATE field submitted with the request. The *LoadViewState* method can be overridden to customize this process.

- *LoadPostData*   During this phase, data posted back with the request is evaluated and appropriate action is taken. Override the *LoadPostData* method to write code for this phase.

- *Load*   During this phase, the *Load* event is raised.

- *RaisePostDataChangedEvent*   During this phase, change events are raised in response to differences between the current state of a control's members and the values submitted with the request. Override the *RaisePostDataChangedEvent* method to write code for this phase.

- *RaisePostBackEvent*   During this phase, event handlers for server-side events are called. Override the *RaisePostBackEvent* method to write code for this phase.

- *PreRender*   During this phase, any modifications necessary before rendering are made. Changes made after this phase will not be saved to *ViewState*.

- *SaveViewState*   During this phase, controls that use *ViewState* save their data to the hidden __VIEWSTATE field. The *ViewState* method can be overridden to customize this process.

- *Render*   During this phase, the control and its children are rendered to the browser.

- *Dispose*   During this phase, any clean-up of expensive resources such as file handles, database connections, etc., is performed. Override the *Dispose* method to write code for this phase.

Control Execution Order

When overriding methods for inherited events (*Init*, *Load*, *PreRender*, etc.), it's usually a good idea to call the base implementation of the event's method from within your overridden version. This ensures that any handlers associated with those events are called. The syntax for calling the base handler is as follows:

```
Protected Overrides Sub OnLoad(e As EventArgs)
    'Event handling code
    MyBase.OnLoad(e)
End Sub
```

Handling Postbacks

As discussed previously, a postback is the process by which a Web Forms page submits an HTTP *POST* request to itself in response to some user action, such as clicking a button. At some point, it is likely that you will want to develop a control that handles postback data and/or events. In this section, you'll learn how to handle both.

There are three phases in the execution of an ASP.NET Web Forms page during which you have the opportunity to work with postback information: the *LoadPostData* phase, the *RaisePostDataChangedEvent* phase, and the *RaisePostBackEvent* phase. To work with the associated data or events, you override the associated method for the desired phase. To override the methods, you need to implement the *IPostBackDataHandler* interface, the *IPostBackEventHandler* interface, or both. *IPostBackDataHandler* defines the *LoadPostData* method and the *RaisePostDataChangedEvent* method. *IPostBackEventHandler* defines the *RaisePostBackEvent* method.

You implement interfaces in the fashion specified by the language you're using. For Visual Basic .NET, interfaces are implemented using the *Implements* keyword, and you can implement as many interfaces as you'd like. The *Implements* statement should directly follow the *Inherits* statement for your control. Separate each interface name with a comma, as follows:

```
Inherits Control
Implements IPostBackDataHandler, IPostBackEventHandler
```

In C#, both the class from which the control is derived and any interfaces it implements are named on the same line as the class definition.

```
public class classname : Control, IPostBackDataHandler,
    IPostBackEventHandler
```

Note that the class from which the control is derived must come first in the list, because a control can only inherit from a single class. All items in the list after the first one are assumed to be interfaces, and a compiler error will result if the items are not in the correct order.

A Login Control

To demonstrate event handling and postback handling, you're going to leave the *HelloControl* example behind and build a control that can handle user logins. Your control will render two text boxes, one for the username and another for the password, and a Submit button. The control will expose two events, *AuthenticateSuccess* and *AuthenticateFailure*, that the client can use to determine whether the user entered the correct credentials. To raise these events, you'll use some of the postback methods that were described earlier. Let's get started.

1   Create a new file called LoginControl.vb.

2   Add the following *Imports* statements to the file.

```
Imports System
Imports System.Web
Imports System.Web.UI
Imports System.Collections.Specialized
```

3   Add a namespace with the name *ASPNETSBS*, and a class within the namespace named *LoginControl_VB*.

```
Namespace ASPNETSBS
    Public Class LoginControl_VB

    End Class
End Namespace
```

4   Directly below the class definition, add an *Inherits* statement to inherit the *Control* class.

```
Public Class LoginControl_VB
    Inherits Control
```

5   Directly below the *Inherits* statement, add an *Implements* statement to implement the *IPostBackDataHandler* and *IPostBackEventHandler* interfaces.

```
    Inherits Control
    Implements IPostBackDataHandler, IPostBackEventHandler
```

6   Within the class, add private variables and public property procedures for the username and password.

```
Private _UserName As String = ""
Private _Password As String  = ""

Public Property UserName As String
    Get
        Return _UserName
    End Get
    Set(ByVal Value As String)
      _UserName = Value
    End Set
End Property

Public Property Password As String
    Get
        Return _Password
    End Get
    Set(ByVal Value As String)
      _Password = Value
    End Set
End Property
```

7   Override the *Render* method of the *Control* class, and display the desired controls. The *Me.UniqueID* property is used to associate the client controls being rendered with the custom control containing them. Note that while you set the value of the first text box to the *UserName* property to allow it to be pre-populated on a postback, you don't do the same with the password, for security reasons.

```
Protected Overrides Sub Render(writer As HtmlTextWriter)
    writer.Write("<h3>User Name: <input name=" & _
        Me.UniqueID & _
        " id = UserNameKey" & _
        " type=text value=" & _
        Me.UserName & _
        "> </h3>")
    writer.Write("<h3>Password: <input name=" & _
        Me.UniqueID & _
        " id = Password" & _
        " type=password > </h3>")
    writer.Write("<input type=button " & _
```

```
            "value=Submit OnClick=""jscript:" & _
            Page.GetPostBackEventReference(Me) & _
            """>    ")
    writer.WriteLine("")
    writer.WriteLine("<br>")
    writer.WriteLine("<br>")
End Sub
```

8   Define events for authentication success and failure.

```
Public Event AuthSuccess As EventHandler
Public Event AuthFailure As EventHandler
```

9   Override the *LoadPostData* method defined in the *IPostBackDataHandler* interface to load the posted values into the local variables. The *Implements* statement declares that this event handler provides the necessary implementation of *LoadPostData*. The return value of this function determines whether the *RaisePostDataChangedEvent* method is called on this control.

```
Public Overridable Function LoadPostData(postDataKey As String, _
    values As NameValueCollection) As Boolean _
    Implements IPostBackDataHandler.LoadPostData

    Dim newValues As String = values(postDataKey)
    Dim Index As Integer = newValues.IndexOf(",")
    Dim newUserName As String = ""
    Dim newPassword As String = ""

    'get the UserName
    newUserName = (newValues.Substring(0, Index))
    ' get the Password
    newPassword = (newValues.Substring(Index + 1, _
        newValues.Length - Index - 1))

    If((Not newUserName = UserName) Or _
        (Not newPassword = _Password)) Then
        _UserName = newUserName
        _Password = newPassword
        Return True
    Else
        Return False
    End If
End Function
```

10 Override the *RaisePostDataChangedEvent* method. In your control, you do not take any action with this method, but you are still required to implement it because it is defined on one of the interfaces you're implementing.

```
Public Overridable Sub RaisePostDataChangedEvent() _
    Implements IPostBackDataHandler.RaisePostDataChangedEvent
    ' Respond to changes in posted data
End Sub
```

11 Finally override the *RaisePostBackEvent* method. In the following code, you check the *_UserName* and *_Password* local variables (populated with the posted values in *LoadPostData*) against static text values. If they both match, you raise the *AuthSuccess* event with the *RaiseEvent* keyword. If not, you raise the *AuthFailure* event. In a real authentication control, you would use information from a database, or from the Microsoft Active Directory service, to determine if the entered values were valid.

```
Public Overridable Sub RaisePostBackEvent(eventArgument As
String) _
    Implements IPostBackEventHandler.RaisePostBackEvent
    If Me._UserName = "SomeUser" _
        And Me._Password = "password" Then
        RaiseEvent AuthSuccess(Me, EventArgs.Empty)
    Else
        RaiseEvent AuthFailure(Me, EventArgs.Empty)
    End If
End Sub
```

12 Save the class file.

13 Compile the control, using the following command line. If you plan to make changes to the control, you may want to put this command into a batch file in the same directory as the class file, allowing you to recompile by double-clicking the batch file. Note that the command should all go on a single line.

```
vbc /t:library /r:System.Web.dll /r:System.dll
    /out:LoginControl_VB.dll LoginControl.vb
```

14 Copy the compiled assembly to the bin directory of the Web application that will use the control.

To use the control, you'll need to create a new Web Forms page, create the control (either declaratively or programmatically), and set up handlers for its exposed events.

1   Create a new file in the Web application where you copied the control. Name the file LoginControl_Client_VB.aspx.

2   Add the @ *Page* directive and standard HTML tags to the file.

```
<%@ Page Language="vb" %>
<html>
   <head>
   </head>
   <body>
      <form runat="server">
      </form>
   </body>
</html>
```

3   Add a @ *Register* directive to the page to register the custom control.

```
<%@ Register TagPrefix="ASPNETSBS" Namespace="ASPNETSBS"
   Assembly="LoginControl_VB" %>
```

4   Declare the control within the *<body>* of the page, using the tag prefix defined in the @ *Register* directive and the class name defined for the control.

```
<ASPNETSBS:LoginControl_VB id="Login" runat=server/>
```

5   Directly after the login control, add an ASP.NET *Label* control to display authentication messages.

```
<asp:label id="Message" Font-Bold="True" ForeColor="Red"
   runat="server"/>
```

6   Add a *<script>* block containing event handlers for the *AuthSuccess* and *AuthFailure* events to the *<head>* section of the page.

```
<script runat="server">
   Sub Login_AuthSuccess(Source As Object, e As EventArgs)
      Message.Text = "Authenticated!"
   End Sub
   Sub Login_AuthFailure(Source As Object, e As EventArgs)
      Message.Text = "Authentication Failed!"
   End Sub
</script>
```

7   Finally wire the events to the event handlers by adding the appropriate attributes to the control's tag.

```
<ASPNETSBS:LoginControl_VB id="Login"
   OnAuthSuccess="Login_AuthSuccess"
   OnAuthFailure="Login_AuthFailure"
   runat=server/>
```

8   Save and browse the page. The output should look similar to the following figure.

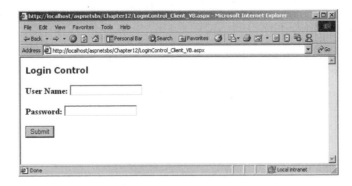

If you enter *"SomeUser"* for the username and *"password"* for the password, the output should look similar to this figure.

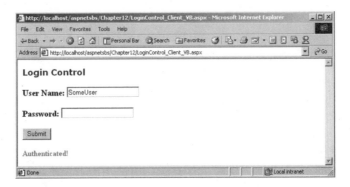

If you enter any other values, the output should look similar to the following figure.

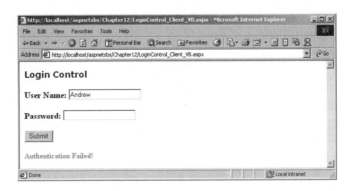

The full code for the control is shown in the following listing.

LoginControl_Client_VB.aspx

```vb
Imports System
Imports System.Web
Imports System.Web.UI
Imports System.Collections.Specialized

Namespace ASPNETSBS

    Public Class LoginControl_VB
    Inherits Control
    Implements IPostBackDataHandler, IPostBackEventHandler

    Private _UserName As String = ""
    Private _Password As String  = ""
    Public Property UserName As String
        Get
            Return _UserName
        End Get
        Set(ByVal Value As String)
          _UserName = Value
        End Set
    End Property
    Public Property Password As String
        Get
            Return _Password
        End Get
        Set(ByVal Value As String)
          _Password = Value
        End Set
    End Property

    Public Event AuthSuccess As EventHandler
    Public Event AuthFailure As EventHandler

    Public Overridable Function LoadPostData(postDataKey As String, _
        values As NameValueCollection) As Boolean _
        Implements IPostBackDataHandler.LoadPostData

        Dim newValues As String = values(postDataKey)
```

```vb
    Dim Index As Integer = newValues.IndexOf(",")
    Dim newUserName As String = ""
    Dim newPassword As String = ""

    'get the UserName
    newUserName = (newValues.Substring(0, Index))
    ' get the Password
    newPassword = (newValues.Substring(Index + 1, _
        newValues.Length - Index - 1))

    If((Not newUserName = UserName) Or _
       (Not newPassword = _Password)) Then
        _UserName = newUserName
        _Password = newPassword
        Return True
    Else
        Return False
    End If
End Function

Public Overridable Sub RaisePostDataChangedEvent() _
    Implements IPostBackDataHandler.RaisePostDataChangedEvent
    ' Respond to changes in posted data
End Sub

Public Overridable Sub RaisePostBackEvent(eventArgument _
As String) Implements IPostBackEventHandler.RaisePostBackEvent
    If Me._UserName = "SomeUser" And _
       Me._Password = "password" Then
        RaiseEvent AuthSuccess(Me, EventArgs.Empty)
    Else
        RaiseEvent AuthFailure(Me, EventArgs.Empty)
    End If
End Sub

Protected Overrides Sub Render(writer As HtmlTextWriter)
    writer.Write("<h3>User Name: <input name=" & _
        Me.UniqueID & _
        " id = UserNameKey" & _
        " type=text value=" & _
        Me.UserName & _
        "> </h3>")
```

```
        writer.Write("<h3>Password: <input name=" & _
            Me.UniqueID & _
            " id = Password" & _
            " type=password > </h3>")
        writer.Write("<input type=button " & _
            "value=Submit OnClick=""jscript:" & _
            Page.GetPostBackEventReference(Me) & _
            """>   ")
        writer.WriteLine("")
        writer.WriteLine("<br>")
        writer.WriteLine("<br>")
    End Sub
  End Class
End Namespace
```

important

There are significant differences in how events are handled in different languages used in ASP.NET. The code shown in the previous example demonstrates how to create, raise, and handle events in Visual Basic .NET. To see how the same control would be implemented in C#, see the sample files LoginControl.cs and LoginControl_Client_CS.aspx on the CD that accompanies this book.

Maintaining State

In the previous examples, data used by the controls has been stored in local variables. For many controls, this may work just fine. But unless you explicitly retrieve submitted values and repopulate the member controls with these values, as you did in the *LoadPostData* method of the previous example, the member controls will be blank when the page is posted back to the server and the results are returned. In many cases, you may want to maintain the state of the constituent controls of your custom server control, without explicitly having to write code to test for new values and repopulate the member controls with each postback.

To solve this problem, ASP.NET provides a state-management facility called *ViewState*. This is provided by an instance of the *StateBag* class of the *System.Web.UI* namespace. You store data in *ViewState* as key/value pairs, which makes working with it quite similar to working with session state. To add a value to *ViewState* or modify an existing value, you can simply specify the item's key and assign a value as follows:

```
' Visual Basic .NET
ViewState("MyKey") = MyValue
```

```
// C#
ViewState["MyKey"] = MyValue;
```

> **important**
>
> In order to use *ViewState*, controls must be contained within a *<form>* block with the *runat="server"* attribute set.

Note that in C#, you use square brackets around the key rather than parentheses. You can also add items to *ViewState* using the *Add* method of the *StateBag* class, and remove them using the *Remove* method. You can clear all *ViewState* values with the *Clear* method.

Retrieving values from *ViewState* is a bit more involved. Since the *Item* property of the *StateBag* class returns an object, you will need to cast the object to the proper type before performing any type-specific actions on it or passing it to another procedure that expects a particular type. The syntax for retrieving a string value is as follows:

```
' Visual Basic .NET
Dim MyString As String
MyString = CType(ViewState("MyKey"), String)
```

```
// C#
string MyString;
MyString = (string)ViewState["MyKey"];
```

The simplest way to automate the process of saving control state to *ViewState* is to substitute *ViewState* items for the local member variables for storing the values of properties of the control.

> **important**
>
> Using *ViewState* has both performance and security implications, because all of the information stored in *ViewState* is round-tripped to the client as a base64 encoded string. The size of the *ViewState* hidden field can become quite large with controls that contain a lot of data, which can have a negative impact on performance. You may want to disable *ViewState* for these controls by setting their *EnableViewState* property to *False*.
>
> Because the *ViewState* field is sent as a text string, you should never use *ViewState* to store information such as connection strings, server file paths, credit card information, or other sensitive data. Remember that once the *ViewState* has been sent to the client, it would be fairly simple for a hacker to decode the string and retrieve any data contained within. Don't count on base64 encoding to protect sensitive data sent to the client.
>
> Finally, the *ViewState* of controls is saved between the firing of the *PreRender* and *Render* events, so any changes to control state that you want to save in *ViewState* must be made during the *PreRender* event. Changes made to control state after the *PreRender* event will not be saved to *ViewState*.

For the previous example, you would make the following modifications to the *UserName* and *Password* property procedures (in addition to eliminating the *_UserName* and *_Password* local variables):

```
Public Property UserName As String
    Get
        Return CType(ViewState("UserName"), String)
    End Get
    Set(ByVal Value As String)
        ViewState("UserName") = Value
    End Set
End Property
Public Property Password As String
    Get
        Return CType(ViewState("Password"), String)
    End Get
    Set(ByVal Value As String)
        ViewState("Password") = Value
    End Set
End Property
```

Creating Custom Controls Through Composition

Both of the previous examples in this chapter overrode the *Render* method of the *Control* class to render their custom output. This method works fine, but it's not easy to take advantage of preexisting controls unless you inherit from them and call the *Render* method of the base class. (See "Extending Existing Controls" on page 390 for more information on this technique.)

Compositional controls use another technique to compose a custom control out of a number of preexisting or custom controls. These controls override the *CreateChildControls* method exposed by the *Control* class, and in that method, they programmatically instantiate and set properties of the constituent controls that make up the custom server control. Compositional controls should also implement the *INamingContainer* interface, which provides a new naming scope for the constituent controls, to ensure that their names are unique within the page.

Overriding CreateChildControls

The *CreateChildControls* method is substituted for the *Render* method in compositional controls. A sample *CreateChildControls* method is as follows:

```
Protected Overrides Sub CreateChildControls()
    Dim MyLabel As New Label()
    MyLabel.Text = "Label: "
    Me.Controls.Add(MyLabel)
    Dim MyText As New TextBox()
    Me.Controls.Add(MyText)
    Dim MyButton As New Button()
    Me.Controls.Add(MyButton)
End Sub
```

It is not necessary in a compositional server control to call the *Render* method, because all of the individual controls added to the *Controls* collection will take care of rendering themselves during the *Render* stage of page processing.

If you want to manipulate controls after they've been added to the *Controls* collection, you can access them either by their numeric index, as shown here, or by calling the *FindControl* method of the *Control* class and passing in the ID of the control you want to manipulate.

```
Dim MyText As TextBox = Controls(1)
```

Implementing INamingContainer

Compositional controls should always implement the *INamingContainer* interface. This interface does not contain any property or method declarations. It simply creates a new naming scope for the current control to ensure that the names of child controls are unique within the page.

In the next section, you'll see examples of both overriding the *CreateChild-Controls* method and implementing *INamingContainer*.

Creating Templated Controls

Another innovative feature of ASP.NET server controls allows you to separate the UI from the implementation of a control through inline templates. Templated controls contain no formatting code themselves. Instead, they rely on the consumer of the control to add templates that provide the necessary formatting of the control's output.

To demonstrate templated controls, let's walk through the process of turning your *HelloControl* example into a templated control:

1   Open the file HelloControl.vb, and save a copy as HelloControlTemplated.vb.

2   Remove the *HelloControl* and *HelloControlPropMeth* classes from the file, and rename the *HelloControlProp* class to *HelloControlTemplateItem*.

3   Add an *Implements* statement on the line following the *Inherits* statement to implement the *INamingContainer* interface. This sets up a separate naming scope for the controls that are a part of your custom control.

```
Inherits Control
Implements INamingContainer
```

4   Remove the overridden *Render* method from the class.

5   Add a *New* method to allow the *Name* property to be passed to the *HelloControlTemplateItem* class when it is created.

```
Public Sub New(Name As String)
    _name = Name
End Sub
```

6   Set the default value for the *_name* variable to "". The completed class should look like the following:

```
Public Class HelloControlTemplated
    Inherits Control
    Implements INamingContainer
```

```
Dim _name As String = ""

Public Sub New(Name As String)
    _name = Name
End Sub

Public Property Name As String
  Get
      Name = _name
  End Get
  Set(ByVal Value As String)
      _name = Value
  End Set
End Property
End Class
```

7   Copy the *HelloControlTemplateItem* class and paste a copy below the original. Rename the copy to *HelloTemplate*.

8   Add the *ParseChildren* attribute to the class. In Visual Basic .NET, the attribute definition for a class appears on the same line as the class declaration, right before the declaration. (For readability, the Visual Basic line continuation character is used to place these on separate lines.) The *ParseChildren* attribute tells ASP.NET how to interpret child elements within the control declaration.

```
<ParseChildren(true)> _
Public Class HelloTemplate
```

9   Add a local member variable just below the definition of the *_name* property for the template. The type of the variable should be *ITemplate*.

```
Private _name As String = ""
Private _nameTemplate As ITemplate = Nothing
```

10   Add a public property procedure to set and retrieve the *NameTemplate* property. The definition of the property needs to include the *TemplateContainer* attribute, which tells ASP.NET the container in which the template should be created. Like the *ParseChildren* attribute, this attribute goes on the same line as the *Property* declaration (again, in the interest of readability, this is separated into two lines using the Visual Basic .NET line-continuation character).

```
<TemplateContainer(GetType(HelloControlTemplateItem))> _
Public Property NameTemplate As ITemplate
  Get
      Return _nameTemplate
  End Get
```

Custom Server Controls

12

```
   Set
      _nameTemplate = Value
   End Set
End Property
```

11 Override the *DataBind* method, calling the *EnsureChildControls* method of the *Control* class. This makes sure that all child controls are created before data-binding occurs. Call the *DataBind* method of the base class to perform data-binding.

```
Public Overrides Sub DataBind()
   EnsureChildControls()
   MyBase.DataBind()
End Sub
```

12 Override the *CreateChildControls* method to create an instance of the *HelloControlTemplateItem*, passing it the *Name* property of the *HelloTemplate* class (which is what you'll instantiate declaratively in the Web Form code). Then add the control to the *Controls* collection of the *HelloTemplate* control. If no *NameTemplate* tags are defined in the Web Forms page, the following code will simply create a *LiteralControl* with the value of the *Name* property.

```
Protected Overrides Sub CreateChildControls()
   If Not (NameTemplate Is Nothing)
      Controls.Clear()
      Dim HelloTemplateCtl As New _
         HelloControlTemplateItem(Me.Name)
      NameTemplate.InstantiateIn(HelloTemplateCtl)
      Controls.Add(HelloTemplateCtl)
   Else
      Me.Controls.Add(New LiteralControl(Me.Name))
   End If
End Sub
```

13 Compile the class using the following command line, and copy the compiled assembly to the bin directory of the Web application from which the control will be used.

```
vbc /t:library /r:System.Web.dll
/r:System.dll HelloControlTemplated.vb
```

You can create a batch file to make the compilation process quicker.

Using the control from a Web Forms page requires the standard steps of registering the control with the @ *Register* directive and adding a tag to instantiate the control declaratively.

1   Create a new file called HelloControlTemplated_Client.aspx, add the @ *Page* directive and standard HTML controls, and save the file.

2   Add an @ *Register* directive for your new control, which should look like the following:

```
<%@ Register TagPrefix="ASPNETSBS" Namespace="ASPNETSBS"
    Assembly="HelloControlTemplated" %>
```

3   Add the tags to instantiate the control. This time, instead of using a single tag with the closing / at the end to instantiate the control, you'll use a tag pair, since you need two tags to contain the *NameTemplate* tags. Notice that you set the *Name* property to *World*.

```
<ASPNETSBS:HelloTemplate id="hello" Name="World" runat="server">
    <%--Template tags and formatting tags go here --%>
</ASPNETSBS:HelloTemplate>
```

4   Add the *NameTemplate* tags to the *HelloTemplate* control. The *NameTemplate* tags contain HTML formatting to be applied to the templated item. In addition to the HTML formatting tags, you also add literal content to round out your message.

```
<ASPNETSBS:HelloTemplate id="hello" Name="World" runat="server">
    <NameTemplate>
        <h3><font color="Blue">
            <em>Hello, <%# Container.Name%>!</em>
        </font></h3>
    </NameTemplate>
</ASPNETSBS:HelloTemplate>
```

5   Add another declarative instance of *HelloTemplate*, this time using the single-tag syntax. This allows you to test the output of the control without templates.

```
<ASPNETSBS:HelloTemplate id="hello2" Name="Hello, World!"
    runat="server"/>
```

6   Finally add a *<script>* block with a *Page_Load* handler that calls the *DataBind* method to evaluate the *Container.Name* data-binding expression.

```
<script runat="server">
    Sub Page_Load()
        DataBind()
    End Sub
</script>
```

7   Save and browse the page. The output should look similar to the following figure.

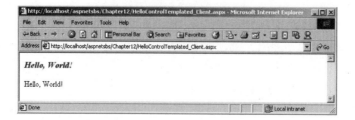

The following listing, HelloControlTemplated.vb, shows all of the control code.

HelloControlTemplated.vb

```vb
Imports System.Web.UI
Namespace ASPNETSBS
    Public Class HelloControlTemplateItem
        Inherits Control
        Implements INamingContainer

        Public Sub New(Name As String)
            _name = Name
        End Sub

        Dim _name As String = ""
        Public Property Name As String
            Get
                Name = _name
            End Get
            Set(ByVal Value As String)
                _name = Value
            End Set
        End Property
    End Class
    <ParseChildren(true)> _
    Public Class HelloTemplate
        Inherits Control
        Implements INamingContainer

        Private _name As String = ""
        Private _nameTemplate As ITemplate = Nothing

        Public Property Name As String
            Get
                Return _name
```

```
        End Get
        Set(ByVal Value As String)
            _name = Value
        End Set
    End Property


    <TemplateContainer(GetType(HelloControlTemplateItem))> _
    Public Property NameTemplate As ITemplate
        Get
            Return _nameTemplate
        End Get
        Set
            _nameTemplate = Value
        End Set
    End Property

    Public Overrides Sub DataBind()
        EnsureChildControls()
        MyBase.DataBind()
    End Sub

    Protected Overrides Sub CreateChildControls()
        If Not (NameTemplate Is Nothing)
            Controls.Clear()
            Dim HelloTemplateCtl As New _
                HelloControlTemplateItem(Me.Name)
            NameTemplate.InstantiateIn(HelloTemplateCtl)
            Controls.Add(HelloTemplateCtl)
        Else
            Me.Controls.Add(New LiteralControl(Me.Name))
        End If
    End Sub
    End Class
End Namespace
```

The following listing, HelloControlTemplated_Client.aspx, shows all of the Web Forms page code.

HelloControlTemplated_Client.aspx

```
<%@ Page Language="VB" %>
<%@ Register TagPrefix="ASPNETSBS" Namespace="ASPNETSBS"
    Assembly="HelloControlTemplated" %>
```

```
<html>
<head>
<script runat="server">
   Sub Page_Load()
       DataBind()
   End Sub
</script>
</head>
<body>
   <form runat="server">
   <ASPNETSBS:HelloTemplate id="hello" Name="World" runat="server">
       <NameTemplate>
           <h3><font color="Blue">
               <em>Hello, <%# Container.Name%>!</em>
           </font></h3>
       </NameTemplate>
   </ASPNETSBS:HelloTemplate>
   <ASPNETSBS:HelloTemplate id="hello2" Name="Hello, World!"
       runat="server"/>
   </form>
</body>
</html>
```

Extending Existing Controls

A relatively simple way of creating a custom server control is to find an existing control that does most of what you want and extend that control by inheriting from the class that defines it, instead of inheriting from *Control*, *HtmlControl*, or *WebControl*. Then you can add properties and methods that provide additional functionality, and you can override the control's *Render* method to render additional UI elements. Then, by calling the base control's *Render* method, you can take advantage of the built-in rendering capability of the base control.

The following listing, TextBoxPlus.vb, shows the code for a control that extends the *TextBox* control, adds a *Label* property, a *LabelFontColor* property, a *LabelFontSize* property, and a *LabelLocation* property, and renders a text label to go with a *TextBox* based on these properties.

TextBoxPlus.vb

```
Imports System.ComponentModel
Imports System.Drawing
Imports System.Web.UI
```

```vb
Imports Microsoft.VisualBasic
Imports Microsoft.VisualBasic.Compatibility

Namespace ASPNETSBS
    Public Enum LabelLocations
        PreviousLine
        SameLineBefore
        SameLineAfter
    End Enum

    Public Class TextBoxPlus
        Inherits System.Web.UI.WebControls.TextBox

        Dim _label As String = "TextBoxPlusLabel"
        Dim _labelFontSize As Integer = 3
        Dim _labelFontColor As Color = Color.Black
        Dim _labelLocation As LabelLocations = _
            LabelLocations.SameLineBefore

        Public Property Label() As String
            Get
                Return _label
            End Get
            Set(ByVal Value As String)
                _label = Value
            End Set
        End Property

        Public Property LabelFontColor() As Color
            Get
                Return _labelFontColor
            End Get
            Set(ByVal Value As Color)
                _labelFontColor = Value
            End Set
        End Property

        Public Property LabelFontSize() As String
            Get
                Return _labelFontSize
            End Get
```

```
            Set(ByVal Value As String)
                _labelFontSize = Value
            End Set
        End Property

        Public Property LabelLocation() As LabelLocations
            Get
                Return _labelLocation
            End Get
            Set(ByVal Value As LabelLocations)
                _labelLocation = Value
            End Set
        End Property

        Protected Overrides Sub Render(ByVal output As _
            System.Web.UI.HtmlTextWriter)
            Select Case Me.LabelLocation
                Case LabelLocations.PreviousLine
                    output.Write("<font size=""" & Me.LabelFontSize & _
                    """ color=""" & Mid(Me.LabelFontColor.ToString, 8, _
                    Len(Me.LabelFontColor.ToString) - 8) & """>" & _
                    Me.Label & "</font><br/>")
                    MyBase.Render(output)
                Case LabelLocations.SameLineAfter
                    MyBase.Render(output)
                    output.Write("<font size=""" & Me.LabelFontSize & _
                    """ color=""" & Mid(Me.LabelFontColor.ToString, 8, _
                    Len(Me.LabelFontColor.ToString) - 8) & """>" & _
                    Me.Label & "</font>")
                Case LabelLocations.SameLineBefore
                    output.Write("<font size=""" & Me.LabelFontSize & _
                    """ color=""" & Mid(Me.LabelFontColor.ToString, 8, _
                    Len(Me.LabelFontColor.ToString) - 8) & """>" & _
                    Me.Label & "</font>")
                    MyBase.Render(output)
            End Select
        End Sub
    End Class
End Namespace
```

The command line for compiling the code in the previous listing would look something like the following (the entire example should be a single command):

```
vbc /t:library /r:System.Web.dll /r:System.Drawing.dll
   /r:Microsoft.VisualBasic.dll
   /r:Microsoft.VisualBasic.Compatibility.dll /r:System.dll
   /out:bin\TextBoxPlus.dll TextBoxPlus.vb
```

The following listing, TextBoxPlus_client.aspx, shows the code necessary to instantiate the *TextBoxPlus* control and set its properties.

TextBoxPlus_client.aspx

```
<%@ Page Language="VB" %>
<%@ Register TagPrefix="ASPNETSBS" Namespace="ASPNETSBS"
   Assembly="TextBoxPlus" %>
<html>
<head>
<script runat="server">
   Sub Page_Load
      MyText.LabelLocation = LabelLocations.SameLineBefore
      MyText.LabelFontColor = System.Drawing.Color.Blue
      MyText.LabelFontSize = 6
      MyText.Label = "Name: "
   End Sub
</script>
</head>
<body>
   <ASPNETSBS:TextBoxPlus id="MyText" runat="server"/>
</body>
</html>
```

Chapter 12 Quick Reference

To	Do This
Create a namespace	Use the *Namespace* and *End Namespace* keywords (Visual Basic .NET) or the *namespace* keyword with curly braces (C#).
Inherit from a base class	In Visual Basic .NET, add the *Inherits* keyword on the line after the class definition, specifying the name of the class to inherit. In C#, add a colon after the name of the class you are creating, followed by the name of the class to be inherited.
Render output from a control	Override the *Render* method of the control class from which the custom control is derived. To take advantage of the rendered output of controls like *TextBox* and *Label*, call the *Render* method of the base class when you are finished rendering custom output.
Handle postbacks	Implement the *IPostBackDataHandler* and/or *IPostBackEventHandler* interfaces, and implement the methods defined by the interfaces.
Maintain state in a custom control	Store state in and retrieve state from the *ViewState* object in your property procedures.

PART V

ASP.NET Web Services

13

Creating and Using Web Services

In this chapter, you will learn about

✔ *What a Web service is*

✔ *How to create a Web service*

✔ *How to advertise & locate a Web service*

✔ *How to consume a Web service*

Previous chapters have focused on the creation of ASP.NET Web Forms, as well as the technologies that make ASP.NET development possible and those that make it very simple and quick to create robust, feature-rich Web applications. Another important and very useful part of ASP.NET that hasn't been discussed is XML-based Web services.

Today, Web services are not a very well-understood technology. Part of this is because of inaccurate reporting from the media, who describe Web services as everything from subscription software to a proprietary plot by Microsoft to take over the Internet. These stories may sound great in print, but they are based on misunderstandings and ignorance of this potentially revolutionary technology.

Understanding XML-Based Web Services

For many years, developers have sought ways to reuse the products of their work, or to bring together disparate systems that their organizations had already invested in to form a cohesive whole. This quest has been fraught with difficulties, ranging from disparate platforms and systems with no common standard for communication to security measures that prevented potential clients from outside a corporate network from being able to use existing functionality.

Some of the solutions for these difficulties have included creating custom Web front-ends for existing functionality, or using proprietary communications and/or packaging technologies to bridge the gap between systems. The former solution worked well in some situations, but the organization hosting the application had to create and maintain a UI for the functionality that they made available, as well as creating a front-end for any additional functionality added later. Moreover, this UI might or might not fully meet the needs of their existing and/or future clients. The use of proprietary communications or bridging software typically meant greater expense, reliance on a single vendor, and dependence on that vendor's maintenance and upgrades. XML-based Web services address both of these issues squarely, allowing programmatic functionality to be exposed without the need for a custom Web-based UI, and without the need for proprietary bridging software.

Web services are discrete units of programmatic functionality exposed to clients via standardized communication protocols and data formats, namely HTTP and XML. These protocols and formats are both well-understood and widely accepted. (While XML is still a relatively immature technology, it has rapidly gained acceptance in the industry due to its promise as a bridging technology.)

By communicating over HTTP, Web services overcome the problem of communicating across the Internet and across corporate firewalls without resorting to proprietary solutions that require additional communications ports to be opened to external access. Because Web services use XML for the formatting of requests and responses, they can be exposed from and consumed by any platform that can format and parse an XML message. This allows XML-based Web services to bring together disparate pieces of functionality, whether existing or new, whether internal or external to an organization, into a coherent whole. The following figure shows how XML-based Web services can bring together a variety of applications and platforms. Note that because XML Web services can communicate over standard protocols such as HTTP, they can work over firewalls. In addition to the interactions shown, server-to-server Web services calls are also possible.

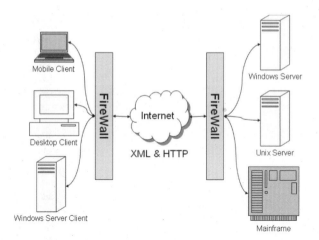

Web services are accessed by calling into a listener that is able to provide a contract to describe the Web service, and that also processes incoming requests or passes them on to other application logic and passes any responses back to the client. The following figure shows how a Web service application may be layered. It is also possible to use Web services to access legacy logic as well as new application logic, or to wrap legacy logic for access by a Web service.

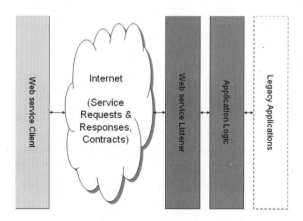

SOAP and Web Services

The SOAP protocol is a key enabler of XML-based Web services as a strategy for application integration and Internet-based software services. SOAP, which stands for Simple Object Access Protocol, is an XML-based messaging protocol that's being standardized by the World Wide Web Consortium (W3C) and has wide support from a variety of vendors. The SOAP specification provides a mandatory format for SOAP messages (referred to as *SOAP envelopes*), as well as optional standards for data encoding, request/response processing, and binding of SOAP messages to HTTP.

SOAP and XML-based Web services are too complicated to cover in a single chapter. Fortunately, one of the advantages of the ASP.NET programming model is that it abstracts the complexity of SOAP messaging from the development of Web services.

Additional Needs for Web Services

As mentioned earlier in this chapter, a Web service is nothing more than a way to provide discrete units of application functionality over standard Web protocols, using a standardized message format. To be truly useful, however, Web services also need to provide the following:

- A contract that specifies the parameters and datatypes it expects, as well as the return types (if any) that it sends to callers, and
- A facility for locating the Web service, or a means of discovering Web services offered by a given server or application, and the descriptions of those services

The next several sections will examine creating, advertising, locating, and consuming Web services from the standpoint of an ASP.NET Web developer.

Creating a Web Service

In ASP.NET, the complexities of SOAP messaging and HTTP transport are abstracted from developers, so creating XML-based Web services is actually quite simple. This abstraction is enabled through attributes that tell the common language runtime (runtime) to treat a specified class and its methods as Web services. Based on these attributes, the runtime provides all of the plumbing necessary to expose the class and methods as Web services, as well as providing a contract that clients can use to determine how to call the Web service and the return types to expect from it.

Declaring a Web Service

Web services in ASP.NET are defined in files with the .asmx file extension. The actual code for an ASP.NET Web service can reside either in the .asmx file or in a precompiled class. Either way, the Web service is declared in the .asmx file by adding the @ *WebService* directive to the file. The syntax for declaring a Web service in which the class will be defined within the .asmx files is

```
<%@ WebService Language="VB" Class="ClassName" %>
```

ClassName is the name of the class that contains the Web service methods. The syntax for declaring a Web service in which the code that defines the class and methods resides in a compiled class is

```
<%@ WebService Class="NamespaceName.ClassName,AssemblyName" %>
```

NamespaceName is the name of the namespace in which the class for the Web service resides, *ClassName* is the name of the class that contains the Web service methods, and *AssemblyName* is the name of the assembly that contains the compiled code for the Web service. This assembly should reside in the bin directory of the Web application in which the .asmx file resides. The *NamespaceName* portion of the *Class* attribute is optional if you have not specified a namespace for your class, but it is good practice to always specify a namespace for your classes. The *AssemblyName* portion of the *Class* attribute is also optional, since ASP.NET will search the bin directory for the assembly if no assembly name is provided. However, you should always provide an assembly name to avoid the performance impact of doing a search the first time the Web service is accessed.

> ## note
> Unlike using code-behind with ASP.NET Web Forms, you cannot use the *src* attribute with a Web service. This means that you must precompile the code-behind class that is to be used as the basis for the Web service, either manually using the command-line compiler or by building a Visual Studio .NET Web Service application.

Creating the Web Service Class

Each .asmx file is associated with a single class, either inline in the .asmx file or in a code-behind class. Either way, the syntax of a Web service class is as follows:

```
Imports System.Web.Services

Public Class ClassName
    Inherits WebService
    'Methods exposed by the Web service
End Class
```

ClassName is the name of the Web service class.

Inheriting from WebService

In this syntax example, there is an *Imports* statement importing the *System.Web.Services* namespace. This namespace contains the classes and attributes that provide ASP.NET's built-in support for XML-based Web services. In this case, the class we care about is *WebService*, which is inherited in this example using the *Inherits* keyword.

Inheriting from the *WebService* class is not required in order for a class to function as a Web service, but the *WebService* class provides useful plumbing for Web services. This includes access to *Application*, *Session*, and other ASP.NET objects, including the *Context* object, which provides access to information about the HTTP request that invokes the Web service.

Using the <WebService()> Attribute to Specify XML Namespace

XML-based Web services use XML namespaces to uniquely identify the endpoint or listener to which a client sends requests. By default, ASP.NET sets the XML namespace for a Web service to *<http://tempuri.org/>*. If you plan to make your Web service available publicly over the Internet, change the default namespace to avoid potential conflicts with other XML-based Web services using the same name as your Web service, and which also may use the default namespace.

You can modify the default namespace for a Web service class by adding the *WebService* metadata attribute to the class definition and setting its *Namespace* property to the desired value for the new namespace. This value can be any unique URI that you control, such as your organization's domain name.

In Visual Basic .NET, metadata attributes use the syntax *<AttributeName(PropertyName:=value)>* and are placed on the same line as the entity (class, method, etc.) that they modify. For readability's sake, you can use the Visual Basic line-continuation character to wrap the class definition onto the following line:

```
<WebService(Namespace:="http://www.aspnetsbs.com/webservices/")> _
Public Class ClassName
```

In C#, metadata attributes use the syntax *[AttributeName(PropertyName=value)]* and are placed on the line before the entity they modify.

```
[ WebService(Namespace="http://www.aspnetsbs.com/webservices/")]
public class ClassName: WebService {
```

In both Visual Basic .NET and C#, multiple properties may be set in an attribute declaration and are separated by commas.

Metadata Attributes

Prior to this chapter, the term *attributes* has referred to the key/value pairs added to HTML or ASP.NET server control tags to define specific properties of those entities or controls. This chapter introduces the concept of *Metadata* attributes.

ASP.NET and the .NET Framework make extensive use of attributes to provide programmatic plumbing for classes, as well as to add descriptive information to managed assemblies. You can also use your own attributes (by creating classes derived from *System.Attribute*) to add your own descriptive information to your classes.

Attributes in ASP.NET Web services, in addition to providing access to the XML namespace used for the Web service, are used to tell ASP.NET that a given method is to be exposed as a *WebMethod*. ASP.NET then provides all of the runtime functionality necessary for clients of the Web service to access the *WebMethod* without requiring the programmer to write additional code.

Using the <WebMethod( )> Attribute to Expose Methods

Once you've declared the class that implements the Web service, you will need to add one or more methods that provide functionality for the Web service. Each method will use the *WebMethod Metadata* attribute to declare the method as one for which ASP.NET should provide the necessary plumbing to expose it to clients.

To add the *WebMethod* attribute to a Visual Basic .NET method, use the following syntax:

```
<WebMethod()> _
Public Function MethodName() As ReturnType
    ' method code
End Function
```

MethodName is the name of the method to be exposed by the Web service, and *ReturnType* is the type of the value (if any) to be returned by the method. Even if your method does not return a value that is a result of a calculation or other action, it is usually a good idea to at least return a value that indicates the success or failure of the method.

<WebMethod()> Attribute Properties

Like the *WebService* attribute, the *WebMethod* attribute has properties that you can use to alter the behavior of the Web method. These properties are described in the following table.

WebMethod Properties	
Property	**Description**
BufferResponse	Determines whether output from the method is buffered in memory before being sent to the client. The default is *True*.
CacheDuration	Allows the output of a Web service method to be cached on the server for the specified duration, in seconds. The default is *0*, which turns off caching for the method.
Description	Sets a text description of the Web service method. This description is shown in the documentation pages auto-generated by ASP.NET, and it's included in the Web Service Description Language (WSDL) contract for the Web service.
EnableSession	Determines whether session support is enabled for the Web service method. Default is *False*. Enabling session state requires the Web service class to inherit from *WebService*. Note that enabling session state for a Web service may have a negative impact on performance.
MessageName	Allows methods to be given alias names. This can be useful when you have an overloaded method, in which the same method name has multiple implementations that accept different input parameters. In this case, you can supply a different *MessageName* for each overloaded method version, allowing you to uniquely identify each one. The default is the method name.
TransactionOption	Allows adding support for COM+ transactions in a Web service method. Allowable values are *Disabled*, *NotSupported*, *Supported*, *Required*, and *RequiresNew*. The default is *Disabled*. Note that this property requires the use of an @ *Assembly* directive to load the *System.EnterpriseServices* assembly into the Web service application.

Creating a HelloWorld Web Service

Now let's use the information you're learned thus far to put together a working Web service. This Web service will have one method, whose purpose is to return the string value Hello, World!

1   In a folder defined as an application in IIS, create a new file called HelloService.asmx.

2 Add the @ *WebService* directive to the file, specifying Visual Basic .NET as the language and "Hello" as the name of the class that implements the Web service.

```
<%@ WebService Language="VB" Class="Hello" %>
```

3 Add an *Imports* statement to import the *System.Web.Services* namespace, since you will be inheriting from the *WebService* class contained in this namespace later in this process.

```
Imports System.Web.Services
```

4 Add the class definition, including the *WebService* attribute (so that you can modify the default namespace), and the *Inherits* statement to inherit from the *WebService* class.

```
<WebService(Namespace:="http://www.aspnetsbs.com/webservices/")> _
Public Class Hello
    Inherits WebService
    ' method declaration(s)
End Class
```

5 Add a method definition for a method called *SayHello*, with a return type of *String*, that returns the string Hello, World!. Use the *WebMethod* attribute to signify to ASP.NET that this method is a Web service method.

```
<WebMethod()> _
Public Function SayHello() As String
  Return "Hello, World!"
End Function
```

6 Save the file.

7 Browse the Web service by entering the URL for the .asmx file (such as *http://localhost/appname/HelloService.asmx*). ASP.NET will generate a set of pages that describes the available Web methods and the syntax that clients can use to access those methods. The output of the initial request to the Web service is shown in the following figure.

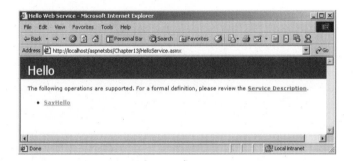

8   Click the Service Description link. ASP.NET will return the WSDL contract that describes the Web service. This contract can be used by clients to determine how to interact with the Web service. WSDL is discussed further in "Understanding WSDL Files" on page 418. A portion of the WSDL contract output is shown in the following figure. Click back in your browser after you finish looking at the WSDL contract.

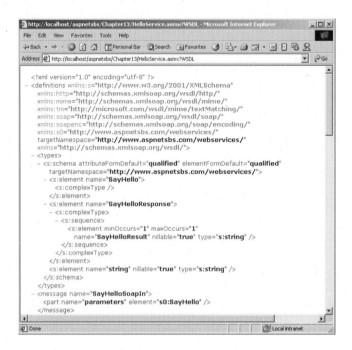

9   Click the link for the *SayHello* operation. ASP.NET will display the syntax for *SOAP*, *HTTP GET*, and *HTTP POST* requests and responses, as well as a button that allows you to invoke the *SayHello* method. A portion of this output is shown in the following figure.

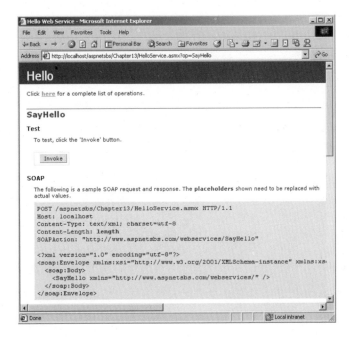

10   Click the Invoke button. A new browser window will open in which the XML result of the method invocation is returned. This output is shown in the following figure.

The preceding example shows the implementation of a Web service in which the class for the Web service is defined within the .asmx file. The following listings, HelloService_CB.asmx and listing HelloService_CB.vb, show the code for implementing the same Web service using code-behind. Remember that when using code-behind, the class that implements the Web service must be manually compiled before the Web service can be used. The following command can be used to compile the HelloService_CB.vb code-behind class (note that all three lines make up a single compilation command):

```
vbc /t:library /r:System.Web.dll /r:System.dll
/r:System.Web.Services.dll /out:bin\HelloService_CB.dll
HelloService_CB.vb
```

important

Depending on which version of the .NET Framework you've installed, you may need to add the path to the folder containing the Visual Basic .NET compiler to your PATH environment variable in order for the preceding command to work. The procedure for locating and adding this path to the PATH environment variable is detailed on page xv of the "Installing the Sample Files" section at the beginning of this book.

HelloService_CB.asmx

```
<%@ WebService Class="ASPNETSBS.Hello_(B, HelloService_CB"%>
```

HelloService_CB.vb

```
Imports System.Web.Services

Namespace ASPNETSBS
    <WebService(Namespace:="http://www.aspnetsbs.com/webservices/")> _
    Public Class Hello
        Inherits WebService

        <WebMethod()> _
        Public Function SayHello() As String
            Return "Hello, World!"
        End Function
    End Class
End Namespace
```

Note that in the code-behind implementation, a namespace has been added to wrap the *Hello* class. This is to avoid any possible naming conflicts with other assemblies that may be used in the application.

important

The example Web services in this chapter all use the XML namespace *http://www.aspnetsbs.com/webservices/*. As with the default *http://tempuri.org* namespace, if you intend to make your XML-based Web services publicly available over the Internet, you should not use *http://www.aspnetsbs.com/webservices/* as the namespace for your Web service. Instead, use a URI that you control, and one that will allow you to be sure that your Web service can be uniquely identified.

Using Primitive DataTypes

The *HelloService* example does not have any input parameters, and it returns a value of type *String*. But XML-based Web services are not limited to strings and can accept input parameters as well as returning values.

XML-based Web services in ASP.NET use the XML Schema Definition (XSD) draft specification to specify the datatypes that are supported by ASP.NET Web services. This includes primitive datatypes such as string, int, boolean, long, and so on, as well as more complex types such as classes or structs.

The definition for a Web service method that adds two numbers and returns the result would look like the following:

```
<WebMethod()> _
Public Function Add(Num1 As Integer, Num2 As Integer) As Integer
    Return (Num1 + Num2)
End Function
```

Accessing Data in a Web Service

In addition to primitive types, classes, and structs, ASP.NET Web services can also return or accept ADO.NET datasets as input parameters. This is possible because the *DataSet* class has built-in support for being serialized as XML, which can be easily sent over an HTTP connection.

To return a dataset from a Web service, follow these steps:

1   Create a new file called AuthorsService.asmx.

2   Add the @ *WebService* directive to the file, specifying Visual Basic .NET as the language and Hello as the name of the class that implements the Web service.

```
<%@ WebService Language="VB" Class="Authors" %>
```

3   Add *Imports* statements to import the *System.Data*, *System.Data.SqlClient*, and *System.Web.Services* namespaces.

```
Imports System.Data
Imports System.Data.SqlClient
Imports System.Web.Services
```

4   Add a class definition for the *Authors* class.

```
<WebService(Namespace:="http://www.aspnetsbs.com/webservices/")> _
Public Class Authors
    Inherits WebService
    ' method declaration(s)
End Class
```

5   Add a method to the class that returns the Authors table of the Pubs sample database as a dataset. Note that we have added the *Description* property of the *WebMethod* attribute to describe the purpose of the method. Refer to Chapter 11 for more information on using SQL Server trusted connections in ASP.NET.

```
<WebMethod(Description:="Returns the Pubs Authors table.")> _
Public Function GetAuthors() As DataSet
    Dim Authors As New DataSet
    Dim SqlConn As New SqlConnection
    Dim ConnStr As String
    ConnStr = "server=(local)\NetSDK;database=pubs"
    ConnStr &= ";Trusted_Connection=yes"
    SqlConn.ConnectionString = ConnStr
    Dim SqlCmd As SqlDataAdapter
    SqlCmd = New _
        SqlDataAdapter("select * from Authors", SqlConn)

    SqlCmd.Fill(Authors, "Authors")

    Return Authors
End Function
```

6   Save the file.

7   Browse the Web service by entering the URL for the .asmx file. The output of the initial request to the Web service is shown in the following figure. Note that the description added via the *Description* property of the *WebMethod* attribute is displayed as part of the output.

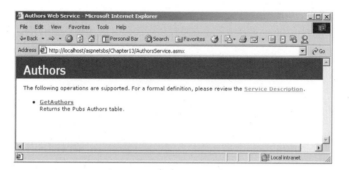

8   Click the GetAuthors link. Then click the Invoke button to see the XML returned
by the Web service, which is a serialized dataset containing both the schema and
data for the Authors table.

note

These descriptions of the datatypes supported by XML-based Web services in
ASP.NET are specific to Web services that use SOAP for requests and responses.
When using *HTTP GET* or *HTTP POST* for Web service requests, a more limited
set of datatypes is supported, all of which are represented to the client as strings.
Additionally, input parameters can only be passed by value, while parameters for
SOAP requests can be passed either by value or by reference.

Advertising a Web Service

Once you've created a Web service using the techniques in either of the previous
examples, the Web service is ready to be accessed by clients. The challenge at this
point is how to give clients the information necessary to allow them to access
your Web service.

In an intranet-based scenario, this is relatively simple. You can provide potential
internal clients with the URL to your Web service directly, either by e-mailing it to
those who need it or by creating a centrally located Web page that users within
your organization can browse to find the appropriate URL. In an Internet-based
scenario, however, you may not know who your potential clients are. This makes
it much more difficult to ensure that they can find and use your Web services.

There are two solutions to this dilemma: Web services discovery, and Web services
directories using Universal Description, Discovery, and Integration (UDDI).

Advertising Web Services Through a Discovery Document

A discovery document is an XML-based document containing references to Web services and/or other discovery documents. Through the use of discovery documents, you can easily catalog all of the available Web services on a Web server at a single location.

By publishing a discovery document to a publicly available URL, you can make it possible for clients to easily locate and consume Web services that you have made available. Clients can access the discovery document using tools such as the wsdl.exe command-line utility supplied with the .NET Framework, or with Visual Studio .NET's Add Web Reference dialog, in order to create clients for the Web service. We'll discuss this process in greater detail in "Using a Web Service" on page 415.

A discovery file uses the extension .disco and contains two types of nodes: *contractRef* nodes and/or *discoveryRef* nodes. The *contractRef* nodes refer to WSDL files that can be used to create clients for a Web service, while *discoveryRef* nodes refer to additional discovery documents. The discovery document for the two example Web services created in this chapter is shown in the following listing, Chapter13.disco. The *ref* attribute of the *contractRef* node contains the URL to the WSDL contract for the Web service, in this case generated by ASP.NET by appending the *?WSDL* argument to the URL for the .asmx file that implements the Web service. The *docRef* attribute contains the URL to the documentation for the Web service, in this case simply the URL to the .asmx file, since ASP.NET automatically generates documentation for Web services implemented in an .asmx file. The *xmlns* attributes in the *discoveryRef* and *contractRef* nodes establish the XML namespaces in which these nodes reside.

Chapter13.disco

```
<?xml version="1.0" encoding="utf-8" ?>
<discovery xmlns="http://schemas.xmlsoap.org/disco/">
    <contractRef ref="AuthorsService.asmx?wsdl"
        docRef="AuthorsService.asmx"
        xmlns="http://schemas.xmlsoap.org/disco/scl/" />
    <contractRef ref="HelloService.asmx?wsdl"
        docRef="HelloService.asmx"
        xmlns="http://schemas.xmlsoap.org/disco/scl/" />
</discovery>
```

Note that for the sake of readability, relative URLs were used in this listing. Discovery documents can contain either relative or absolute URLs. When relative URLs are used, they are assumed to be relative to the location of the URL of the discovery document.

Advertising Web Services Through UDDI

Another option for advertising Web services to potential clients is UDDI. This is a multivendor initiative, spearheaded by Ariba, IBM, and Microsoft, that is designed to provide an Internet-based business registry (or registries) in which creators of Web services may register their publicly available Web services. The UDDI specification describes how Web services may be registered in such a way as to allow clients to easily search for the type of Web service desired, or to discover all of the Web services offered by a particular partner or company.

> **note**
>
> While the UDDI initiative is based on Web standards and proposed standards such as DNS, HTTP, XML, and SOAP, UDDI itself is not a proposed standard. Rather, it's a multivendor specification, created and maintained by Ariba, IBM, and Microsoft, with input from other companies. It is the stated intent of the UDDI specification to be transitioned to a standards body eventually.

The model for UDDI is for multiple identical versions of the UDDI business registry to be hosted by multiple participants, providing redundancy and load balancing for the registry. Web service providers can register their Web services at any node and the information will be replicated to all registries daily, allowing potential clients to find these services from any registry.

Currently, both Microsoft and IBM provide online UDDI registries, and both can be reached from *http://www.uddi.org/*. You can also find a number of helpful white papers on UDDI there.

Securing a Web Service

One challenge of implementing a Web service comes when you need to limit who can access it. You may wish to limit access to only those clients who have paid a subscription fee, for example. Or, if your Web service stores and uses data that's specific to individual users, you might want to implement some sort of login process to allow clients to view and modify only data that is specific to them.

One potential issue with this is that the SOAP protocol, on which Web services are based, does not provide any specifications for securing Web services. This means that it's up to you to choose a means of securing your Web service that provides the level of security you need but that's also relatively easy to implement, both for you and your clients. The last thing you want is to make your Web service so difficult to use that potential clients go elsewhere.

Exploring Authentication Options

The first choice you must make is how to authenticate users of your Web service. There are a number of options, each with its own advantages and disadvantages.

While ASP.NET does not define any specific authentication and authorization method for Web services, you can take advantage of the authentication mechanisms that IIS offers. These mechanisms are described in detail in Chapter 8, in the section titled "Using Windows-Based Authentication."

The advantage of using one of the IIS authentication mechanisms is that the infrastructure for them already exists. You do not need to create your own credential store for user account information. One disadvantage is that each of the authentication methods offered by IIS requires the creation of NT accounts for each client of your application. This can be difficult to administer, depending on how your Web server is set up (whether it is part of an NT domain, whether it uses Active Directory, and so on). Another disadvantage is that the Integrated Windows authentication method, while secure, requires the client to belong to the same domain (or a trusted domain) as the server, making it impractical for Internet use. Basic authentication is suitable for Internet use, but it sends username and password as clear text, making it easy for them to be compromised. It can use SSL encryption to prevent this problem, but this may add an unacceptable performance overhead if user credentials must be passed with each Web service request.

Another option for authenticating users is a third-party authentication mechanism such as Microsoft Passport. Unfortunately, the developer tool support for Passport is still poor at present, and most available tools focus on allowing the use of Passport to authenticate users from Web sites, rather than Web services. While it is likely that Passport and other third-party authentication mechanisms will add support for simple implementation in Web services eventually, today these mechanisms likely will require too much effort on the part of your clients.

Finally, you can "roll your own" Web services authentication by implementing a login function in one or all of your Web services, with the login method returning a unique key (which should be hashed or encrypted) identifying the logged-in user. This key is then passed as a parameter of each Web service request, indicating that the user is an authenticated user. In order to protect the username and password, the login Web service method should be requested over an SSL connection. Subsequent requests can be made over a standard HTTP connection, however, so as to avoid the performance overhead of SSL encryption. To reduce the risk of a user being impersonated by someone who has intercepted the login key, these keys should be stored in such a way that they can be easily expired after a predetermined timeout value (in a back-end database, for example).

While this authentication method is more difficult to implement and maintain than some of the others, it's the simplest for your clients to use. Once you have given a client his account information (username and password), all he needs to do is make the request to the login Web service (over an SSL connection) and store his login key. With each subsequent request, he passes the key as one of the parameters of the Web service method he's calling. If the timeout value expires between one request and the next, the user must call the login method again to receive a new key. Therefore, the value should be set to provide a balance between security and convenience. In addition to the login method, you could also implement a logout method in your Web service to explicitly expire the login key.

important

In addition to controlling access to a Web service with authentication, you should also consider using SSL to encrypt communications if you are passing sensitive data to or from the Web service. This includes usernames and passwords sent when authenticating users.

Using a Web Service

So now that you've got a couple of nifty Web services, you'll probably want to know how to use them, beyond testing them by invoking them from a browser. While the formatting of SOAP requests and responses necessary to call a Web service can be somewhat complicated, the .NET Framework abstracts away much of this complexity.

Nonetheless, you still need to know how to locate and use a Web service, including the following:

- Locating a Web service, using either a discovery document or UDDI
- Using the WSDL.EXE utility to create a proxy class for the Web service
- Using the proxy class from an ASP.NET page or console application to access the Web service

Locating a Web Service

The first step in using an XML-based Web service is to locate it. If you're dealing with a Web service that you or someone in your organization created, you may already know the location of the Web service. If so, you can skip this step.

Locating a Web service is essentially the mirror image of advertising a Web service, so the same techniques apply here. There are two techniques for locating a Web service in ASP.NET: discovery documents and UDDI.

Locating a Web Service with a Discovery Document

In order to use a discovery document to locate Web services, you need the URL for the discovery document that describes the services in which you're interested. You might get the URL for the document from a listing on an organization's public Web site, from an e-mail promotion, or from a catalog.

Once you have the URL for a discovery document, you can use the disco.exe command-line utility to generate WSDL contracts for using the Web services described in the discovery document. The syntax for the disco.exe utility is

```
disco [options] URL
```

Here, *options* represents one or more command-line options for the utility, and *URL* represents the URL to the discovery document. The options for the disco.exe utility are shown in the following table.

disco.exe Options

Option	Description
/d:*domain* or /domain:*domain*	Sets the domain to use when connecting to a site that requires authentication.
/nosave	Prevents disco.exe from saving files for the discovered WSDL and discovery documents.
/nologo	Prevents the start-up banner from being displayed.
/o:*directory* or /out:*directory*	Provides the directory name where output should be saved.
/p:*password* or /password:*password*	Sets the password to use when connecting to a site that requires authentication.
/proxy:*url*	Sets the proxy to use for HTTP requests.
/pd:*domain* or /proxydomain:*domain*	Sets the domain to use when connecting to a proxy server that requires authentication.
/pp:*password* or /proxypassword:*password*	Sets the password to use when connecting to a proxy server that requires authentication.

disco.exe Options	
Option	**Description**
/pu:*username* or /proxyusername:*username*	Sets the username to use when connecting to a proxy server that requires authentication.
/u:*username* or /username:*username*	Sets the username to use when connecting to a site that requires authentication.
/?	Provides help for command-line options.

Locating a Web Service with UDDI

Unlike using a discovery document to locate a Web service, UDDI does not require you to know in advance the URL of a document describing the desired Web service. Any provider of a UDDI business registry usually will provide a tool for searching their instance of the registry for businesses or Web services that meet your needs. The criteria you can search on will depend on the organization hosting that instance. For example, Microsoft's UDDI registry at *http:// uddi.microsoft.com* supports searching by business name, business location, discovery URL, keyword, and a variety of other criteria. The following figure shows the list of available criteria for searching the Microsoft UDDI registry.

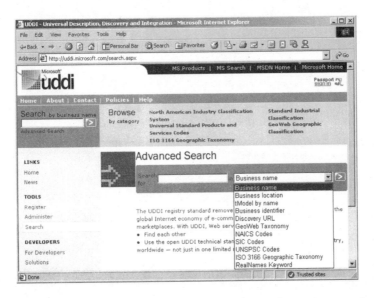

One effective technique for searching for Web services on the *http:// uddi.microsoft.com* registry is to search by discovery URL and search for URLs that contain "wsdl". These URLs are the most likely to point to live WSDL contracts that you can use to access available Web services.

Understanding WSDL Files

WSDL is an XML-based standard for documents that describe the services exposed by a Web service. You can view the WSDL contract for any of the Web services you create with ASP.NET by calling up the URL for a Web service in a browser and appending *?WSDL* to it.

WSDL contracts are similar to COM type libraries or .NET assembly metadata in that they are used to describe the public members of the Web service, including all publicly available methods, the parameters (and datatypes) those methods expect when called, and the return type of any return value. Because this information is encoded in a standard XML-based format, any client that can read XML and can understand WDSL and SOAP should be able to effectively consume the Web application that the WSDL contract describes.

important

The SOAP and WSDL specifications are still in the process of being standardized. In the short term, this means that there may be inconsistencies between different implementations of WSDL on different platforms, since these implementations may be based on different drafts of the proposed standard. Until SOAP and WSDL become settled standards (W3C Recommendations), you may need to tweak your WSDL contracts to achieve interoperability between different Web services implementations. This should become a nonissue once these specifications have received approval as W3C Recommendations. In the meantime, there is an interesting article on interoperability between various Web services implementations on the MSDN Library Web site at *http://msdn.microsoft.com/library/en-us/dn_voices_webservice/html/service08152001.asp*.

Creating a Proxy Class

Consuming a Web service via SOAP is a fairly complex affair. It involves creating and formatting a SOAP envelope, a set of SOAP headers, and a SOAP body, all with the correct elements and attributes for the Web service you're targeting. Fortunately, thanks to the built-in support for Web services in the .NET Framework, all of the plumbing necessary for accessing a Web service is provided for you. The .NET Framework provides another command-line utility, wsdl.exe, to help you by creating a .NET proxy class for a Web service described by a WSDL contract.

Using the wsdl.exe Utility

The wsdl.exe utility generates a proxy class in C#, Visual Basic .NET, or JScript .NET for a WSDL contract specified by URL or path. This proxy class can be instantiated and its methods called by any client, just like any other .NET class.

The syntax for the wsdl.exe utility is as follows:

```
wsdl [options] {URL | path}
```

Here, *options* represents one or more command-line options for the utility, and *URL* represents the URL to the WSDL contract. Alternately, a file path to the WSDL contract can be passed as the *path* argument. The options for the wsdl.exe utility are shown in the following table.

wsdl.exe Options

Option	Description
/appsettingurlkey:*key* or /urlkey:*key*	Sets the key of the configuration setting from which to read the default URL for generating code.
/appsettingbaseurl:*baseurl* or /baseurl:*baseurl*	Sets the base URL to use for calculating relative URLs when a URL fragment is specified for the *URL* argument.
/d:*domain* or /domain:*domain*	Sets the domain to use when connecting to a site that requires authentication.
/l:*language* or /language:*language*	Sets the language to use when generating the proxy class. Valid values include CS, VB, JS, or the fully qualified name of any class that implements the *System.CodeDom.Compiler.CodeDomProvider* class. Default is CS (C#).
/n:*namespace* or /namespace:*namespace*	Sets the namespace to be used when generating the proxy class.
/nologo	Prevents the start-up banner from being displayed.
/o:*filename* or /out:*filename*	Provides the file name (and path) to use for saved output.
/p:*password* or /password:*password*	Sets the password to use when connecting to a site that requires authentication.

(continued)

wsdl.exe Options *(continued)*	
Option	**Description**
/protocol:*protocol*	Sets the protocol (SOAP, HTTP-GET, or HTTP-POST) to use for requests. Default is SOAP.
/proxy:*url*	Sets the proxy to use for HTTP requests.
/pd:*domain* or /proxydomain:*domain*	Sets the domain to use when connecting to a proxy server that requires authentication.
/pp:*password* or /proxypassword:*password*	Sets the password to use when connecting to a proxy server that requires authentication.
/pu:*username* or /proxyusername:*username*	Sets the username to use when connecting to a proxy server that requires authentication.
/server	Creates an abstract base class with the same interfaces as specified in the WSDL contract.
/u:*username* or /username:*username*	Sets the username to use when connecting to a site that requires authentication.
/?	Provides help for command-line options.

Take the following steps to create proxy classes in Visual Basic .NET for the *HelloService* and *AuthorsService* example Web services created earlier in this chapter:

1   Open a command line and navigate to the directory where you would like the proxy classes to be generated. (Or, you can use the /o option to specify a path and file name for saving the proxy class.)

2   Execute the wsdl.exe utility, using the /l option to specify Visual Basic .NET as the language and passing the URL to the HelloService.asmx file, including the ?WSDL parameter, which tells ASP.NET to return the WSDL contract for the .asmx file. (Both lines below should form a single command.) The URL you specify should match the location of the .asmx file on your Web server, and it may differ from the following URL.

```
wsdl /l:vb /n:ASPNETSBS
http://localhost/aspnetsbs/Chapter13/HelloService.asmx?WSDL
```

3   Execute the wsdl.exe utility again for AuthorsService.asmx, using the same syntax as shown in step 2 but modifying the URL to point to AuthorsService.asmx.

4   Optionally, you can create a batch file (with the .bat extension) containing both of the preceding commands. If you want to see the results of the batch execution before the command window closes, add a *pause* command at the end of the batch file.

Once you've created your proxy class(es), you'll need to compile the class(es) using the command-line compiler for the language you chose to generate (in this example, Visual Basic .NET). The following listing, MakeServices.bat, shows the command-line compiler syntax to compile these classes and output the resulting assembly to the bin subdirectory of the directory from which the command is run. Note that this listing represents a single command and has been wrapped to multiple lines for readability.

MakeServices.bat

```
vbc /t:library /r:System.Web.dll /r:System.dll
/r:System.Web.Services.dll /r:System.Xml.dll /r:System.Data.dll
/out:bin\Services.dll Authors.vb Hello.vb
```

Creating a Client Web Forms Page

Once you've compiled the proxy class(es) for the Web service(s) you wish to use, you use them from a client application or Web Forms page just as you would any other .NET class. For a Web Forms page, you simply add an @ *Import* directive to the page. Then, in a page-level procedure (such as the *Page_Load* event handler), create an instance of the proxy class and call its methods.

To create a Web Forms client for the *HelloService* Web service created earlier in this chapter, follow these steps:

1   Create a new file called Hello.aspx in a directory that corresponds to an IIS application. This application should have a bin subdirectory containing the assembly created by the command in MakeServices.bat.

2   Add the standard HTML tags, the @ *Page* directive, and an ASP.NET *Label* control.

```
<%@ Page Language="VB" %>
<html>
<head>
</head>
<body>
    <asp:label id="myLabel" runat="server"/>
</body>
</html>
```

3   Add an @ *Import* directive to import the *ASPNETSBS* namespace. This directive should be on the line following the @ *Page* directive.

```
<%@ Import Namespace="ASPNETSBS" %>
```

4   Add a *<script>* block containing a *Page_Load* event handler. In the event handler, create a new instance of the *Hello* class and call its *SayHello* method, passing the result to the *Text* property of the ASP.NET *Label* control.

```
<script runat="server">
    Sub Page_Load()
        Dim Hello As New Hello()
        myLabel.Text = Hello.SayHello()
    End Sub
</script>
```

5   Save and browse the page. The output should look similar to this figure.

Creating a Client Console Application

It's important to note that Web services clients are not limited to ASP.NET Web Forms. You can just as easily consume Web services from Windows Forms applications, Console applications, or even other Web services. To demonstrate how simple it is to consume a Web service from such clients, follow these steps to create a simple Console application that uses the *AuthorsService* created earlier in this chapter.

1   Create a new class file called AuthorsConsole.vb.

2   Add the code in AuthorConsole.vb to the class file. This code creates a local dataset to receive the data from the Web service, and then iterates through each row and column and writes the data contained in the dataset to the console.

3   Compile the class using the following command. (As with MakeServices.bat, this code should be executed as a single command.) If the compiled Services.dll assembly is not in the bin directory of the application, move the resulting executable to the same directory where the assembly containing the compiled *AuthorsService* proxy class resides. If you use the batch file from the CD included with this book, this should be done automatically.

```
vbc /r:system.dll /r:system.data.dll
/r:microsoft.visualbasic.dll /r:system.xml.dll
/r:system.web.services.dll /r:bin\services.dll
/out:bin\authorsconsole.exe authorsconsole.vb
pause
```

4   Open a command line and navigate to the folder containing the assembly and execute it, using the following command.

```
AuthorsConsole
```

The following listing, AuthorConsole.vb, shows all of the code for the console application.

AuthorConsole.vb

```
Imports ASPNETSBS
Imports System
Imports System.Data
Imports System.Web.Services
Imports System.Xml
Imports Microsoft.VisualBasic


Public Class AuthorsConsole
    Public Shared Sub Main()
        Dim AuthorsDS As DataSet
        Dim thisRow As DataRow
        Dim thisColumn As DataColumn
        Dim thisTable As DataTable
        Dim AuthorsString As String
        Dim Authors As New Authors()
        AuthorsDS = Authors.GetAuthors()
        thisTable = AuthorsDS.Tables(0)
        For Each thisRow In thisTable.Rows
            AuthorsString &= "---------------------"
            For Each thisColumn in thisTable.Columns
                AuthorsString &= vbCrLf & vbTab
                If Not (thisRow(thisColumn) Is Nothing) Then
                    If Not IsDbNull(thisRow(thisColumn)) Then
                        AuthorsString &= CStr(thisRow(thisColumn))
                    Else
                        AuthorsString &= "NULL"
                    End If
```

```
                AuthorsString &= vbCrLf & vbTab
            End If
        Next
        AuthorsString &= vbCrLf
    Next
    Console.WriteLine(AuthorsString)
  End Sub
End Class
```

The following figure shows partial output of the Console application.

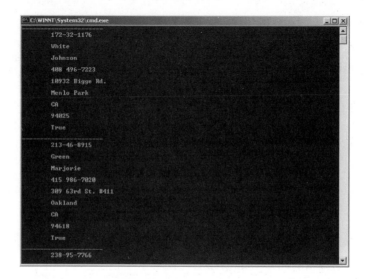

Chapter 13 Quick Reference

To	Do This
Create an XML-based Web service using ASP.NET	Create a file with the .asmx extension and add the @ *WebService* directive to the file. Create a class in the file to implement the Web service, adding the *WebMethod* attribute to each method you wish to expose from the Web service.
Test a Web service	Browse the .asmx file containing the Web service from a Web browser. ASP.NET will generate documentation pages for the Web service, as well as allowing you to invoke the Web service.
Advertise a Web service	Either create a discovery document for your Web services and publish the document to a public location, such as your organization's Web site, or register your Web services in one of the publicly available UDDI business registries, making sure to provide the URL to the WSDL contract for each Web service you register.
Consume a Web service from ASP.NET	Use the wsdl.exe utility to create a proxy class based on the WSDL contract for the Web service, compile the proxy class, and instantiate the proxy class from your client application as you would any other .NET class.

CHAPTER

14

Using Caching to Improve Performance

In this chapter, you will learn about

✔ *Taking advantage of output caching for Web Forms pages and user controls*

✔ *Taking advantage of caching for data retrieved with ADO.NET*

✔ *Using the Cache APIs to get fine-grained control over the expiration, dependencies, and other properties of cached items*

The good news about ASP.NET is that its improvements, from the use of compiled languages rather than interpreted languages to the complete rewrite of the ASP.NET execution engine, make it easy to get the performance that many applications need. Well-designed applications written in ASP.NET will almost always be faster than the equivalent applications written in classic ASP.

But there is still a class of applications for which these performance improvements alone will not be sufficient. These may be applications whose pages are computationally intensive (such as pages that use recursive procedures) or access large amounts of data, or applications that need to scale to large numbers of concurrent users.

ASP.NET offers new features for this class of applications, including a simple API for output caching and a rich and robust caching engine and API.

Understanding Caching

Caching is the process of temporarily storing expensive resources in memory. These resources may be expensive because of the amount of processor time necessary to render them, because they reside on disk, or because they reside in a back-end database on another machine.

Pages that are expensive to render can consume so much processor time that, beyond a certain number of users, the Web server becomes unable to fulfill additional requests in a timely fashion. Retrieving pages and other content from disk is much slower than serving them from memory, and this performance difference is magnified when the server needs to fulfill many requests simultaneously. Requests for large amounts of data from a back-end database often encounter both disk-based and network-based performance delays. (This makes calls from one server to another substantially more expensive than fulfilling a request on the same machine.)

For these reasons, Web applications that need high performance have long used caching to mitigate the performance costs of expensive operations. The output from recent requests, or requested data, is cached in memory. Subsequent requests are served from this in-memory cache, rather than rendering a page or querying a database again. This can substantially improve the performance and scalability of an application. Unfortunately, in the past this has come with a cost. Developers using classic ASP were limited to using the *Session* and *Application* intrinsic objects for caching, or to rolling their own caching engine.

ASP.NET now offers a rich, robust framework for caching both page output and arbitrary data that developers can access easily using both declarative and programmatic means. ASP.NET output caching allows developers to declaratively cache page and user control output to avoid wasting resources in repeatedly rendering content that does not need to change from request to request. The cache API provides a number of methods that allow developers to add items to the cache, remove items from the cache, and set properties that determine the lifetime of items stored in the cache.

Using Output Caching

Output caching allows you to cache the rendered output of any ASP.NET Web Forms page or user control, and to serve subsequent requests from the cache. This can substantially reduce the processor load on the Web server, since the processor isn't busy rendering pages whose content hasn't changed. There are two basic techniques for enabling output caching: declarative and programmatic. The declarative technique uses the @ *OutputCache* directive and its associated attributes to enable output caching, while the programmatic technique uses the *Response.Cache* property to programmatically set caching parameters.

Using the @ OutputCache Directive

The simplest method to quickly set up output caching for a given page or user control is to add the @ *OutputCache* directive. This directive and its attributes allow you to set the length of time the content should be cached, the location where it should be cached, and any parameters to be used to cache multiple versions of a page. The following table describes the available attributes for the @ *OutputCache* directive.

@ OutputCache Attributes	
Attribute	**Description**
Duration	Sets the number of seconds to cache the content. This attribute is required.
Location	Sets the location to be used to cache content. This can be one of the following values:
	Any
	Content can be cached by any cache-aware application (such as a proxy server) in the request stream, by the Web server, or by the client browser.
	Client
	Content is cached by the requesting client's browser.
	Downstream
	Content can be cached by any cache-aware application downstream of the Web server fulfilling the request.
	Server
	Content is cached on the Web server.
	None
	No caching.
	Default is *Any*.
	This attribute may be used with Web Forms pages *only*.
VaryByControl	Sets the names of properties of a user control by which to vary the caching of the user control output. Multiple properties are separated by semicolons.
	This attribute may be used with user controls *only*.

(continued)

@ OutputCache Attributes *(continued)*

Attribute	Description
VaryByCustom	Allows varying of cached content by browser user agent, browser capabilities, or custom logic. When set to any value other than *browser*, requires that the *HttpApplication.GetVaryByCustomString* be overridden in Global.asax in order to implement the custom logic.
VaryByHeader	Allows varying of cached content based on the value of one or more HTTP request headers. Multiple properties are separated by semicolons. This attribute may be used with Web Forms pages *only*.
VaryByParam	Allows varying of cached content based on the value of one or more query-string values sent with a *GET* request, or form fields sent with a *POST* request. Multiple key or field names are separated by semicolons. You can also set the value of this attribute to * to vary by all parameters, or to *None* to use the same cached page regardless of *GET/POST* parameters. This attribute is required.

Among the most important features of the @ *OutputCache* directive are the *Vary-ByX* attributes. These attributes make it possible to cache pages and user controls even when those pages are dynamically generated based on querystring values, form field values, HTTP header values, or even browser capabilities.

The *Duration* attribute lets you limit the length of time that output is cached. For pages that are updated periodically, but not as frequently as every request, the *Duration* attribute allows you to fine-tune the output caching so that you can maximize the benefit gained by caching while being reasonably sure that users will not get stale content. For example, if you had a page that, on average, was updated every two hours, you could set the *Duration* attribute of the @ *OutputCache* directive to *15*. This would cache the output of the page for 15 minutes from the last time the page was requested (subject to the *VaryBy...* attributes). This would ensure that the page would only need to be rendered once every 15 minutes, regardless of how many requests were received for the page, and that there would only be a 15-minute window in which users could get a cached page rather than updated data.

Finally, the *Location* attribute determines where the output cache is located. Setting certain values for the *Location* attribute causes ASP.NET to set the *If-Modified-Since* HTTP header to allow caching of page or control output.

Caching Web Forms Pages

To cache output for a Web Forms page, follow these steps:

1   Create a new file in a directory that is set up as an application in IIS. Name the file OutputCache.aspx.

2   Add the standard HTML tags and @ *Page* directive to the page.

```
<%@ Page Language="VB" %>
<html>
<head>
</head>
<body>
</body>
</html>
```

3   Add an ASP.NET Label control and a static text description to the *<body>* section of the page.

```
<body>
    <asp:Label id="Label1" runat="server"/>
    <p>The text above was rendered with an ASP.NET Label Server
Control, then the output was cached for 10 seconds.</p>
</body>
```

4   Add a *<script>* block to the *<head>* section of the document containing a *Page_Load* event handler. In the event handler, set the *Text* property of the *Label* control to the current time/date (using the Visual Basic *Now* property).

```
<head>
    <script runat="server">
        Sub Page_Load()
            Label1.Text = Now()
        End Sub
    </script>
</head>
```

5   Save and browse the page. The time displayed as the text of the *Label* control should change with each request.

6   Add an @ *OutputCache* directive to the page, with the *Duration* attribute set to *10* and the *VaryByParam* attribute set to *None*. This directive should appear on the line directly below the @ *Page* directive.

```
<%@ OutputCache Duration="10" VaryByParam="None" %>
```

Caching

14

7   Save and browse the page. The output should look similar to the following figure. The time displayed as the text of the *Label* control should only change once every 10 seconds.

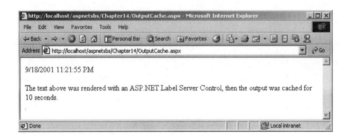

Caching User Controls

Caching the output of Web Forms pages can be very useful, but sometimes you might not be able to cache an entire page because of how frequently its content is updated. Well don't fret…you can still take advantage of output caching by moving less frequently updated portions of a page into one or more ASP.NET user controls, and then caching the output of the user controls.

Caching the output of user controls is nearly identical to caching page output. For user controls, instead of adding the @ *OutputCache* directive to the page containing the user controls, you add the directive to the user controls themselves. As noted in the table on page 429, certain @ *OutputCache* attributes, such as *Location* and *VaryByHeader*, can only be used with Web Forms pages and will cause an error if included in a user control.

To enable output caching of a user control, follow these steps:

1   In the same directory as the previous example, create two new files: FragmentCache.aspx and FragmentCache.ascx.

2   Add the following code to FragmentCache.aspx and save the file.

FragmentCache.aspx

```
<%@ Page Language="VB" %>
<%@ Register TagPrefix="ASPNETSBS" TagName="UC"
    Src="FragmentCache.ascx" %>
```

```
<html>
<head>
   <script runat="server">
     Sub Page_Load()
        Label1.Text = Now()
     End Sub
   </script>
</head>
<body>
   <asp:Label id="Label1" runat="server"></asp:Label>
   <p>The text above was rendered from the Web Forms page.</p>
   <ASPNETSBS:UC runat="server"/>
</body>
</html>
```

3   Add the following code to FragmentCache.ascx and save the file.

FragmentCache.ascx

```
<%@ Control Language="VB" %>
<%@ OutputCache Duration="10" VaryByParam="none" %>
<script runat="server">
   Sub Page_Load()
      Label1.Text = Now()
   End Sub
</script>
<asp:Label id="Label1" runat="server"></asp:Label>
<p>The text above was rendered from the User Control.</p>
```

4   Browse FragmentCache.aspx. The time displayed by the page and the user
control should be identical, as shown in the following figure.

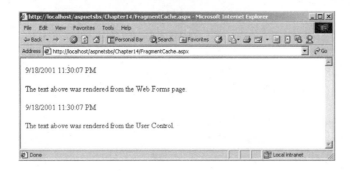

If you click the browser's Refresh button several times, you'll notice that the time displayed by the page is updated with each page request, as shown in the following figure, while the time displayed by the user control is updated only once every 10 seconds.

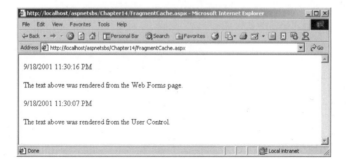

Caching Multiple Versions of Output

If your page uses either querystring values (*GET* requests) or form fields (*POST* requests) to dynamically generate content, you can still use output caching by adding the *VaryByParam* attribute to the @ *OutputCache* directive with the values set to the names of the parameters by which to vary the cache. ASP.NET will cache a copy of the output from the page for each unique combination of parameters, so any user who requests the page within the period specified by the *Duration* attribute with the same set of parameters as a previous request will have his request fulfilled from the cache.

> ## important
> Because ASP.NET will cache a copy of the output for each unique combination of parameters, you should avoid using an excessive number of parameters to vary the cache. This can result in a great deal of memory use. This caution also applies to the *VaryByHeader* and *VaryByControl* attributes as well.

To use the *VaryByParam* attribute, follow these steps:

1   In the same directory as the previous example, create a new file named VaryByParam.aspx.

2   Add the standard HTML tags, including a *<form>* tag pair with the *runat="server"* attribute, and @ *Page* directive.

3   Within the *<form>* section, add an ASP.NET *Label* control and a *Textbox* control, as well as an *HtmlGenericControl* (a paragraph tag with a *runat="server"* attribute) with a static message.

```
<form runat="server">
    <asp:label id="Label1" runat="server">Enter your name:
    </asp:label>
    <asp:textbox id="Name" runat="server"/>
 <p id="P1" visible="false" runat="server">The text above was
 rendered with an ASP.NET Label Server Control, then the output
 was cached for 30 seconds.</p>
</form>
```

4   Add a *<script>* block to the *<head>* section of the document containing a *Page_Load* event handler. In the event handler, set the *Visible* property of the *Textbox* control to *False*, set the *Visible* property of the *HtmlGenericControl* to *True*, and set the *Text* property of the *Label* control to a greeting that includes the name entered in the *Textbox* control and the current time/date.

```
<head>
    <script runat="server">
        Sub Page_Load()
          If IsPostBack Then
                Name.Visible = False
                P1.Visible = True
                Label1.Text = "Hello, " & Name.Text
                Label1.Text &= ". The Current date and time is " &
                    Now()
          End If
        End Sub
    </script>
</head>
```

5   Add an @ *OutputCache* directive to the page, specifying the duration as 30 seconds and the parameter to vary by as the name of the *TextBox* control.

```
<%@ OutputCache Duration="30" VaryByParam="Name" %>
```

6   Save and browse the page. The initial output should look like the following figure.

Type a name in the text box, and then press the Enter key to submit the page. The result should look like the following figure.

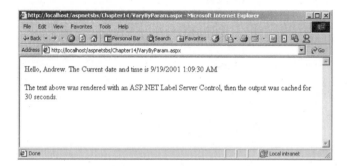

If you click the browser's Refresh button (and click Retry or OK to repost the form), the page will refresh from the cache. If you click Back and enter a different name, you will get a fresh version of the page. Try entering different names, refreshing, and then going back and entering the same names as earlier requests. You should see that all requests with the same name are cached for 30 seconds.

Using Response.Cache

In addition to using the @ *OutputCache* directive, you can also enable output caching for a page using the methods of the *HttpCachePolicy* class, which is exposed by the *Response.Cache* property.

The code required to perform the same output caching as shown in the OutputCache.aspx example is shown in the following listing.

ResponseCache.aspx

```
<%@ Page Language="VB" %>
<html>
<head>
```

```
<script runat="server">
   Sub Page_Load()
      Label1.Text = Now()
      Response.Cache.SetExpires(DateTime.Now.AddSeconds(10))
      Response.Cache.SetCacheability(HttpCacheability.Public)
   End Sub
</script>
</head>
<body>
   <asp:Label id="Label1" runat="server"/>
   <p>The text above was rendered with an ASP.NET Label Server
      Control, Then the output was cached for 10 seconds using the
      Response.Cache methods.</p>
</body>
</html>
```

This code is equivalent to an *@ OutputCache* directive with a duration of *10* and a location of *Any* (or no location attribute). To set the cache location to client, you would use the *HttpCacheability.Private* enumeration member instead of *HttpCacheability.Public*. To turn off caching entirely, you would use *HttpCacheability.NoCache*.

In addition to the *SetExpires* and *SetCacheability* methods shown in listing ResponseCache.aspx, you can also use the *SetNoServerCaching* method in combination with the code from ResponseCache.aspx to provide the equivalent of an *@ OutputCache* directive with a duration of *10* and a location of *Downstream*.

Caching Arbitrary Data

Like the *Application* and *Session* ASP intrinsic objects, the ASP.NET Cache engine offers a simple, straightforward means of saving arbitrary data to the cache and accessing that data through key/value pairs. The following code shows how to add a simple text value to the cache and retrieve it:

```
Cache("myFoo") = "foo"
Response.Write(Cache("myFoo"))
```

An important difference is that unlike the *Application* and *Session* collections, which can be accessed by either key or numeric index, cache items can only be accessed by their key.

You can use this technique to store more than just strings, too. For example, the code in the following listing, CacheAuthors.aspx, checks the cache to see if a dataset already exists. If not, it calls a method that creates a dataset containing data from the Authors table of the Pubs sample SQL Server database, and then it saves that dataset to the cache before setting the *DataSource* property of an ASP.NET *DataGrid* control to the default view of the first table in the dataset (0).

CacheAuthors.aspx

```vb
<%@ Page Language="vb" %>
<%@ Import Namespace="System.Data" %>
<%@ Import Namespace="System.Data.SqlClient" %>
<html>
<head>
<script language="vb" runat="server">
    Sub Page_Load()
        Dim DS As DataSet = Cache("myDS")
        If Not DS Is Nothing Then
            Msg.Text = "Dataset retrieved from cache"
        Else
            DS = GetData()
            Cache("myDS") = DS
            Msg.Text = "Dataset retrieved from database"
        End If
        MyGrid.DataSource = DS.Tables(0).DefaultView
        MyGrid.DataBind()
    End Sub
    Function GetData() As DataSet
        Dim myDS As New DataSet()
        Dim ConnStr As String
        ConnStr = "server=(local)\NetSDK;"
        ConnStr &= "database=pubs;Trusted_Connection=yes"
        Dim SQLSelect As String
        SQLSelect = "SELECT au_id, au_lname, au_fname, "
        SQLSelect &= "zip FROM Authors WHERE zip = '94609'"
        Dim mySqlConn As New SqlConnection(ConnStr)
        Dim mySqlDA As New SqlDataAdapter(SQLSelect, ConnStr)
        mySqlDA.Fill(myDS)
        Return myDS
    End Function
</script>
</head>
<body>
    <form runat="server">
        <asp:label id="title" text="DataSet Caching Example"
```

```
            font-name="Verdana" font-size="18" runat="server"/>
        <asp:datagrid id="MyGrid" bordercolor="black"
            borderwidth="2" cellpadding="3" runat="server">
            <headerstyle backcolor="silver" font-bold="true"/>
            <itemstyle backcolor="black" forecolor="white"/>
            <alternatingitemstyle backcolor="white" forecolor="black"/>
        </asp:datagrid>
        <asp:label id="Msg" font-style="italic" runat="server"/>
    </form>
</body>
</html>
```

The output of the page on first execution is shown in the following figure.

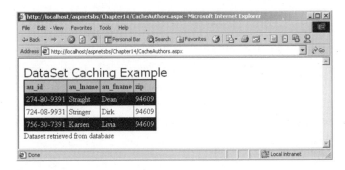

The output of subsequent requests is shown in the following figure.

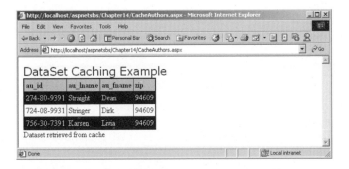

note

To use a trusted connection to connect to SQL Server as shown in the preceding listing, you will need to either enable Windows authentication and impersonation or set up the ASPNET worker process account as a SQL Server login, as described in Chapter 11.

Using the Cache APIs

The question that comes to mind is, "How do I remove the dataset from the cache?" There are a couple of answers to this question, one simple and one more complex. Let's leave the more complex answer for the next section. The simple answer is that you can remove an item from the cache programmatically by calling the *Remove* method of the *Cache* class and passing it the key of the item to be removed. For example, you could add an ASP.NET button to the preceding example, and add the following line to the *Click* event handler for the button:

```
Cache.Remove("myDS")
```

This would clear the dataset from the cache and force the page to be rendered again using fresh data. (Note that since the *Page_Load* event fires before the *Click* event for the button, you may need to click the button twice before the datagrid and the label are updated.)

Understanding Expiration and Scavenging

The more complex answer to the question of how to remove items from the cache is that ASP.NET will actually do it for you. The complex part is that if you want to control *how* ASP.NET decides which items to remove from the cache, and when it does so, you need to provide ASP.NET with that information when you add an item to the cache.

You can do so by using the *Add* or *Insert* methods of the *Cache* class. Both let you pass parameters that tell ASP.NET when and/or on what basis to expire your cached content, as well as the priority your cached content should have when ASP.NET scavenges the cache for items that can be removed to free memory.

ASP.NET determines the order in which items are scavenged from the cache based on their priority. Over time, if an item is not accessed, ASP.NET will reduce its priority periodically. When its priority reaches a predetermined point, it may be scavenged. You can set the priority of an item by passing one of the values of the *CacheItemPriority* enumeration when calling the *Add* or *Insert* method. You can also set the rate at which an item decays by passing one a value of the *CacheItemPriorityDecay* enumeration to *Add* or *Insert*.

The following code is an example of the *Insert* method:

```
Cache.Insert("myDS", myDS, Nothing, DateTime.Now.AddMinutes(2), _
    TimeSpan.Zero, CacheItemPriority.High, _
    CacheItemPriorityDecay.Slow, Nothing)
```

This inserts a dataset into the cache with the key *"myDS"*, passes *Nothing* as the *CacheDependency* parameter, sets the expiration for two minutes from the time when the item is added to the cache, sets the *SlidingExpiration* parameter to

TimeSpan.Zero (no sliding expiration), sets the cache priority for the item to *High*, sets the priority decay for the item to *Slow*, and sets the callback function for the item to *Nothing* (no callback function).

> ## note
>
> The *Add* and *Insert* methods of the *Cache* class provide essentially the same functionality, with two differences. The first difference is that all parameters of the *Add* method are required, so even if you are not using a particular parameter, you must still pass a placeholder parameter. The *Insert* method is overloaded, which makes this method easier to use when you want to pass only some of the possible parameters.
>
> The second difference is that the *Add* method returns an object that represents the item just added to the cache, while the *Insert* method doesn't return a value.

You can also call the *Insert* method passing just the *Key (String)* and *Item (Object)* parameters, passing the *Key*, *Item*, and *CacheDependency* parameters, or passing the *Key*, *Item*, *CacheDependency*, *AbsoluteExpiration (DateTime)*, *SlidingExpiration*, and *(TimeSpan)* parameters.

Understanding File and Key Dependencies

Another important parameter that can be passed to either the *Add* or *Insert* method is the *CacheDependency* parameter, which takes an instance of the *CacheDependency* class as its value. The *CacheDependency* class allows you to create a dependency for a cached item on one or more files or directories (file dependency), or on one or more other cache items (key dependency). The constructor for the *CacheDependency* class has the following three forms:

```
' Monitor a file or directory for changes
Dim myDependency As CacheDependency
myDependency = New CacheDependency("myFileorDirName")


' Monitor an array of file names and/or paths for changes
Dim myDependency As CacheDependency
myDependency = New CacheDependency(myFileorDirArray)


' Monitor an array of file names and/or paths, and an
' array of keys for changes
Dim myDependency As CacheDependency
myDependency = New CacheDependency(myFileorDirArray, myKeyArray)
```

Note that in order to set up a key dependency without any file dependencies, you must create an array of keys (even if there is only one key) and pass *Nothing* (or *null* in C#) as the first argument to the constructor, passing the array of keys as the second.

```
Dim Keys(0) As String
Keys(0) = "myKeyName"
myDependency = New CacheDependency(Nothing, Keys)
```

Once the instance of *CacheDependency* has been created, it can be passed as a parameter to the *Add* or *Insert* method of the *Cache* class.

```
Cache.Insert("myDS", myDS, myDependency)
```

Invalidating the Cache Automatically on Data Change

One of the biggest challenges in using caching in your application is how to get the most out of it, even when you're dealing with data that either is frequently updated or must always be fresh. Although setting absolute and/or sliding expiration times for a cached item may reduce the likelihood of a user getting stale data, it's still possible.

What you need is a way to notify the ASP.NET cache when a table has been updated, in order to remove an item from the cache. Fortunately, the *CacheDependency* class and the SQL Server Web Assistant make this easy.

To force a cached copy of the *Authors* query seen in the CacheAuthors.apsx example to be expired whenever the data in the Authors table is modified, follow these steps. Because this example uses the SQL Server Web Assistant, which does not ship with MSDE, it requires a full SQL Server installation.

First create a trigger on the Authors table that uses the SQL Server Web Assistant to write a new HTML file when the data in the table changes.

1 Open SQL Server Enterprise Manager and select the *Tables* node of the Pubs database. (This should be the Pubs database in your SQL Server instance, rather than the NetSDK MSDE instance you've used for other examples.)

2 Right-click the authors table in the table list and select All Tasks, Manage Triggers.

3 Make sure that the *<new>* item is showing in the Name drop-down list. Add the following text to the trigger, replacing *filepath* with the path to the directory where you have saved the examples for this chapter and the file name authors.htm, and click OK.

```
CREATE TRIGGER WriteFile ON [dbo].[authors]
FOR INSERT, UPDATE, DELETE
AS
EXEC sp_makewebtask filepath, 'SELECT * FROM authors'
```

Now you need to follow these steps to create the page that will use the cache:

1   Start by opening the CacheAuthors.aspx example file created earlier in this chapter and saving a copy as AuthorsTrigger.aspx.

2   Replace the line that reads *Cache("myDS")=DS* with the following code, which adds a file dependency on the file created by the SQL Web Assistant:

```
Cache.Insert("myDS", DS, New _
    CacheDependency(Server.MapPath("authors.htm")))
```

3   Modify the connection string in the file to point to the SQL Server instance where you created the trigger.

4   Save and browse the file. The result should look like the following figure.

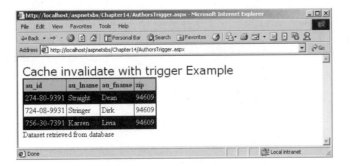

If you click the Refresh button on the browser, the data will be served from the cache and the output will look like the following figure.

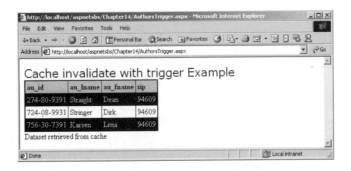

Finally to make sure this works, open the Authors table in SQL Enterprise Manager (right-click the Authors table and select Open Table, Return all rows) and change one of the values in a row in the table that matches the query criteria for CacheAuthors.aspx (zip=9469). (Move the cursor off the row being updated to make sure the update occurs.) Now refresh the browser. The output should look like the first figure.

Chapter 14 Quick Reference

To	Do This
Cache page or user control output	Add the @ *OutputCache* directive to the page or user control, or use the methods exposed by *Response.Cache*.
Vary the cache based on user input	Add the *VaryByParam, VaryByHeader,* or *VaryByControl* attributes to the @ *OutputCache* directive.
Cache arbitrary data	Insert items into the cache using either the simple syntax *Cache("myKey") = myItem* or by calling the *Add* or *Insert* methods of the *Cache* class.
Expire a cache item when another item changes	Insert the item to be expired with a key dependency on the other cache item.

15

Deploying an ASP.NET Application

In this chapter, you will learn about

✔ *The runtime structure of ASP.NET Web applications*

✔ *Storing application-specific configuration settings for easy deployment*

✔ *Steps to set up a target IIS application*

✔ *Methods for copying content, Web Forms pages, Web services, and assemblies*

✔ *Deployment options in Visual Studio .NET*

Deploying applications has been a long-standing bane of many a classic ASP developer's existence, and for good reason. While it was easy enough to deploy or replace static content and the ASP files themselves, other portions of the applications, such as components and application-specific configuration settings, required greater effort to deploy and often necessitated a shutdown of the application to replace.

Deployment is another one of the areas where the improvements in ASP.NET truly shine. ASP.NET eliminates many of the deployment shortcomings in classic ASP, making it possible for the first time to deploy an ASP.NET application simply by copying all of the necessary files to the IIS application directory where the application will be deployed.

This chapter will discuss the steps for deploying ASP.NET Web applications, both manually and through Visual Studio .NET.

Understanding the Structure of ASP.NET Applications

Although you learned about the structure of ASP.NET Web applications in Chapter 5, it is worthwhile to review this information. Understanding the structure of an ASP.NET application will make the deployment process smoother, and can help prevent unexpected errors and problems in your deployed applications.

Each ASP.NET application needs to have a corresponding IIS application root to function properly. The application root provides the boundary for the application. The physical file system directory that maps to the application root is the location where the root Web.config file for the application, as well as the application's bin directory (which contains all managed assemblies related to the application) and the Global.asax file (if you choose to use one), are deployed. If the IIS directory that is the root of the application is not configured as an application root, certain configuration settings may fail, and the assemblies located in the bin directory (if present) will not be loaded.

To determine if a directory in IIS has been configured as an application, complete the following steps:

1   Open the Internet Services Manager by clicking Start, Programs, Administrative Tools, Internet Services Manager.

2   Navigate to the directory whose configuration you want to check by expanding the Web site containing it and expanding other nodes as necessary. If the directory is configured as an application root, it will show an icon of a black globe in a gray box. If the directory is not configured as an application, it will either show a folder icon (for content that resides directly within the path of the parent application root) or a folder icon with a small globe (for content that resides elsewhere in the file system). The following figure shows examples of these icons.

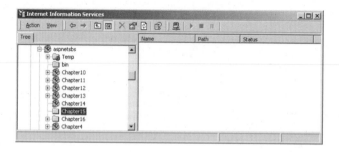

3 If the directory is not configured as an application, you can create an application root at this level. Right-click the directory, select Properties, and then click the Create button on the Directory tab (or Virtual Directory tab) of the Properties dialog. The Properties dialog for the Chapter15 directory is shown here.

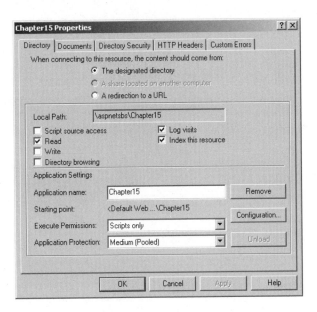

4 Click OK to update the directory with the new setting. The directory should now show the icon for an application root, as shown here.

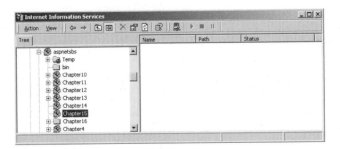

As you can see in these figures, IIS application roots can be nested one beneath the other. However, each application root defines its own application boundary. One advantage of this is that it allows you to partition your application as necessary. For example, you can provide customized configuration settings or use different versions of a private assembly with different parts of your application. The most important thing to remember, however, is that the application root is where the bin directory and Global.asax and Web.config files should be located.

15

Deploying Apps

Distinguishing Between Physical Path and URL

An important distinction to make when discussing deployment is between the physical path of an application (that is, the application's location within the file system of its server) and the URL of the application. This distinction becomes important when discussing the array of different tools available for deployment, some of which (like the DOS XCOPY command) use file or network paths, and some of which (like FTP and WebDAV) use URLs.

There is only a single file path for a given application root in IIS. However, there may be more than one directory in IIS that maps to a single physical directory in the file system. This allows you to set up URLs for both public and private access to a given application, with different IIS settings for each. If more than one IIS application root points to the same physical directory in the file system, each IIS application root will have its own IIS-specific settings. It is important to note, however, that if the physical directory contains ASP.NET-specific configuration and start-up files (Web.config and Global.asax), the settings in these files will be shared by both IIS applications.

One important caveat to this sharing is that when a subfolder containing a Web.config file and/or Global.asax file is defined as an application root in one of the IIS applications, it's not configured as an application root in the second IIS application. In the first case, which is illustrated by the following figure, requests to this subfolder will use the Global.asax file for start-up code.

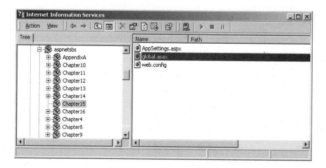

In the second case, illustrated by the following figure, the Global.asax file contained within this subfolder will be ignored.

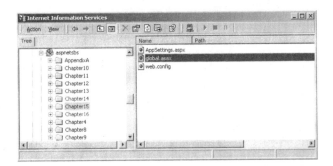

You should also note that there are certain settings in the Web.config file that are only applicable at the application root level. For example, if the Web.config file contained in the Chapter15 folder illustrated in the preceding figure contains an *<authentication>* section, a configuration error will result because this section can only be defined at the machine (Machine.config) or application root level.

The URL for a specific application root in IIS is a product of the domain name (if any) associated with the IP address that is assigned to the IIS Web site, plus the folder hierarchy between the IIS Web site and the application root. Thus, in the previous figure, where the aspnetsbs application root resides under the default Web site, the URL to reach the Chapter15 directory would be either *http://localhost/aspnetsbs/Chapter15/* or *http://servername/aspnetsbs/Chapter15/*.

This works because requests for *localhost* or *servername* (where *servername* represents the name of the Web server) are automatically directed to the default Web site. If you wanted to make the content of the Chapter15 application root available on the Internet, you'd need to create a new IIS Web site, assign a publicly available IP address on the machine to the Web site, and then create (or have a DNS provider create) a DNS entry that maps your chosen domain name (say, *www.aspnetsbs.com*) to that IP address. Then you would create a new application root under the new Web site that maps to the Chapter15 directory in the file system. Then you could access this application from the Internet using the URL *http://www.aspnetsbs.com/Chapter15/*.

Note that if you have directory browsing disabled (the default), you will need to set a default document on the documents tab of the Properties dialog for the directory, in case the user does not enter a document name. The name of the default document should match the name of a page that exists in the directory. This will allow access to content using a URL that does not contain a document name, such as the preceding URLs. Otherwise, the name of the desired file must be appended, or an error will occur.

Storing Application-Specific Configuration Settings

One of the challenges with deploying most non-trivial Web applications in classic ASP is figuring out where to store application-specific configuration information. In classic ASP, there were a number of approaches, including using custom keys in the system registry, storing configuration information in a back-end database, reading configuration settings from a custom configuration file, and building settings into components. Each approach has its own set of drawbacks that make it less than ideal.

For example, storing configuration information in the system registry makes that information relatively secure (particularly if proper registry security procedures are followed). However, adding that information to the registry or modifying it from a remote machine may be difficult, if not impossible, due to permission settings designed to protect the registry from remote tampering. Additionally, accessing settings within the registry can be expensive from a performance standpoint.

Neither storing configuration information in a back-end database nor in custom configuration files provides easily repeatable procedures for multiple applications. The database solution requires that changes to the Web application and the configuration database be synchronized so that users always get the correct information. The custom configuration file solution requires building logic into pages or components to parse and cache the application settings, while periodically checking to see if settings have been modified and loading the new settings if they have.

To simplify this situation, ASP.NET provides a special section of the Web.config and Machine.config files called appSettings, which allows you to store application-specific configuration settings as a set of key/value pairs.

```
<appSettings>
    <add key="myConfigKey" value="myConfigValue" />
</appSettings>
```

When your application starts up, ASP.NET caches the values of the appSettings section in a string collection called *ConfigurationSettings.AppSettings*. These settings can be accessed by passing the desired key to this collection, as shown here:

```
Label1.Text = ConfigurationSettings.AppSettings("myConfigKey")
```

In addition to automatically loading and caching these values for you at application start-up, ASP.NET monitors the Web.config file(s) for changes and dynamically reloads the appSettings if changes are detected.

important

While appSettings provides a storage location for application-specific configuration settings that is almost ideal in its ease of use and performance, it should be noted that since the values are stored as plain text in a file in the Web space, there is some security risk associated with this approach.

If a vulnerability in the Web server allowed access to the Web.config file, any sensitive information stored in appSettings could be compromised. For this reason, it is important to avoid storing sensitive information, such as usernames, passwords, or credit card or account numbers, in the appSettings section of Web.config. For items of medium sensitivity, one solution would be to add the items to the appSettings of the Machine.config file, which is not located within the Web space, making it harder to compromise. Keep in mind, however, that the appSettings stored in Machine.config are available to every application on the server, unless they are locked down using the *<location>* tag. (See Chapter 7 for more information on locking down configuration settings.)

Deploying a Web Application Manually

If you're developing ASP.NET applications against the .NET Framework without the benefit of Visual Studio .NET, most (if not all) of your deployment work will be manual. The great news is that ASP.NET applications are simple to deploy.

Setting Up the Target Deployment Directory

In order to successfully deploy an ASP.NET application, the first thing you need is a target directory on the server that will host the application. This directory must be set up in IIS as an application root if you want to use the automatic loading of assemblies in the bin subdirectory or use a Global.asax file, and if you want to have a root Web.config file for the application. (Certain configuration sections cannot be set below the application level, and they will cause errors if used in a Web.config file that resides in a subdirectory.)

Copying Files to the Target Directory

Once you've set up the target directory in IIS (mapped to a physical folder on the host machine), you're ready to copy all the necessary files to the target directory.

This can be done using any number of commonly available tools, from the XCOPYcommand to WebDAV. You can even drag and drop files to and from a network share using Windows Explorer.

If you're using code-behind in your Web Forms pages and/or user controls, you'll need to decide whether or not to deploy the code-behind class files containing your source code to the target server. If you're using the *Src* attribute of the @ *Page* or @ *Control* directive to have ASP.NET dynamically compile your code-behind classes, you will have to deploy the class files or the application will not function. If you want to avoid deploying the code-behind class files, you can use the *Inherits* attribute of the @ *Page* or @ *Control* directive instead of the *Src* attribute. Recall from Chapter 9 that using the *Inherits* attribute requires you to manually compile your code-behind classes and put the resulting assemblies in the application's bin subdirectory.

Deploying Content

Deploying static content (such as HTML pages and images), Web Forms pages, user controls, and code-behind classes is as simple as copying them from the development application directory to the deployment target directory. For example, you would use the following command to deploy content from a local directory C:\inetpub\wwwroot\myDevApp to a remote directory for which a mapped drive, X:, has been created:

```
xcopy c:\inetpub\wwwroot\ASPNetApp1 x:\ /E /K /O
```

The parameters passed to XCOPY are as follows:

- *■* */E* specifies that all subdirectories are to be copied, whether empty or not.
- *■* */K* specifies that file and directory attributes on the destination should be set to match the source.
- *■* */O* specifies that ownership and ACL information should be copied to the destination. This is useful when using domain accounts to set ACLs.

You can find out about all of the command-line parameters available with XCOPY by executing XCOPY /?.

Deploying Assemblies

One of the areas of great improvement in deployment is .NET managed assemblies over COM components. With classic ASP applications that used custom COM components, not only did you need to copy the component file to the machine on which the application was being deployed, but you also needed to register that component in the system registry, which was difficult to do remotely.

Additionally, registering a component made it available to any application on the server, which is not allowed in a shared server environment.

Because .NET assemblies are self-describing and assemblies are private to an application by default, you can simply copy an assembly to the bin subdirectory of an application and it will be available for use by the application automatically. Private assemblies do not need to be registered to be used, and they are available only to the application in whose bin directory they reside.

Global Assemblies

The exception to the rule of XCOPY deployment applies to assemblies that you want to make available to more than one application on the server without having multiple copies of the assembly (one for each application). These assemblies need to be installed in the GAC. Remember that assemblies installed in the GAC must be strongly named. This can be done by using the al.exe command-line tool. Once you have a strongly named assembly, there are several ways to install it into the GAC.

- **Windows Installer 2.0**   This is the preferred method for installing assemblies into the GAC because it performs reference counting and provides transactional installation, neither of which are available with the other options. See the Windows Installer documentation for more information on packaging and installing applications with Windows Installer 2.0.
- **gacutil.exe**   This command-line utility lets you add assemblies to the GAC, remove assemblies from the GAC, and list the contents of the GAC.
- **Windows Explorer**   The .NET Framework installs a shell extension that lets you simply drag and drop strongly named assemblies into the GAC from any Windows folder. The GAC is located at %WinDir%\assembly.

Deployment and Assembly Versioning

One nifty thing about global assemblies that compensates for the additional overhead of installing and removing them from the GAC is that they can contain versioning information. This allows two or more versions of the same assembly to be executed side-by-side, and it allows client applications to request the version of an assembly they want to use, or to accept the latest revision of an assembly.

Updating Assemblies

In addition to the problems of registering COM components, IIS locked any COM component as soon as it was called. Because of this, replacing or updating a COM component often required stopping the IIS Web service, unregistering the old component, copying over the new component, registering the new component, and restarting the Web service. For many applications, this meant an unacceptable amount of downtime.

With private assemblies, this is no longer a problem because of the way ASP.NET loads assemblies. Unlike IIS under classic ASP, which loaded a component into memory and locked it on disk until the Web application (or IIS) was shut down, ASP.NET first makes a shadow copy of each assembly file and then loads and locks the shadow file instead of the original. ASP.NET then monitors the original files for changes. If changes are detected, ASP.NET fulfills any existing requests with the current copy of the assembly, and then it loads the new assembly and fulfills new requests using the updated assembly, discarding the old assembly. This allows you to easily update any private assembly used by your application without needing to shut down the Web server, even temporarily.

Setting IIS Permissions for Subdirectories

Once you've copied your content and assemblies to the target directory, it's a good idea to double-check the IIS permissions on any subdirectories in the application. Fortunately, ASP.NET actually takes care of one of the most important checks for you. It automatically removes all permissions on the bin subdirectory of the application, effectively preventing the contents of the directory from being listed, read, downloaded, or executed.

Now, preventing IIS from executing the assemblies on behalf of clients might sound like a *bad* thing, but it's not. In fact, when a request comes in for a resource that ASP.NET handles, such as an .aspx, .ascx, or .asmx file, IIS simply hands the request over to ASP.NET, which processes the request from there. Since ASP.NET alone is responsible for loading assemblies, preventing IIS from attempting to execute assemblies is a *good* thing.

If you have subdirectories that contain static content, such as images, you should ensure that the only permission allowed on these subdirectories is *Read*.

Most importantly, if you need to allow users to upload content to your Web application, it is absolutely essential that you set up a separate subdirectory for this purpose, and set only the *Write* permission. *Read* must not be allowed on this subdirectory, nor should the *Execute* permissions be set to anything other than *None*. Failure to follow these guidelines could allow an attacker to upload and execute hostile code in your application.

You can view and modify the IIS permissions for any directory by right-clicking the directory name in Internet Services Manager and selecting Properties. The permissions are set on the Directory (or Virtual Directory) tab, which is shown in the following figure.

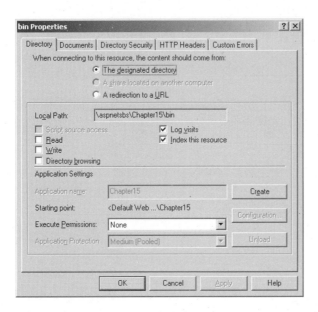

Deployment Options in Visual Studio .NET

If you are developing Web applications with Visual Studio .NET, it is still possible to manually deploy your applications using XCOPY, WebDAV, etc. However, you will probably find that it is more efficient to take advantage of one of the built-in deployment features available in the Visual Studio .NET IDE. These include the *copy project* command, which provides a fast and simple method for copying a project from one machine to another or from one directory to another on the same machine, and the Setup and Deployment Projects type, which provides much more fine-grained control over how your application is deployed.

Using Copy Project to Deploy a Web Application

The *copy project* command, which is accessed by clicking Project, Copy Project, allows you to copy just the files needed to run an application (only the .aspx files and related assemblies, plus any static content; code-behind class files are not copied), all of the files in the project, or all of the files in the source project folder, whether they are a part of the project or not.

You can copy files either to a URL using the FrontPage server extensions, or to a file share. The Copy Project dialog is shown in the following figure.

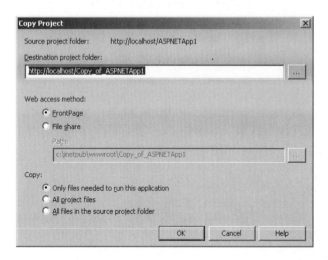

Using Copy Project is simple and straightforward, but it offers only limited control over which project files are copied and how they're copied.

Using a Web Setup Project to Deploy a Web Application

Another method that Visual Studio .NET offers for deploying Web applications is the Web Setup Project, which is one of the templates available in the Setup and Deployment Projects project type. The following figure shows the Web Setup project selected in the Add New Project dialog box.

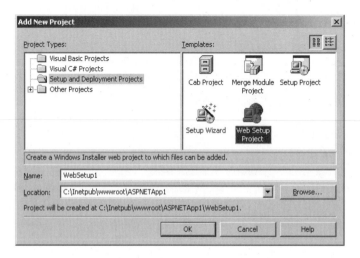

A Web Setup project allows you to specify a variety of options about how the application will be deployed, ranging from which files to include to the name of the deployed application, and the location of the deployed files. When built, the Web Setup project creates a Windows Installer .msi file that can be copied to the target machine and executed to deploy the application.

You can use the following steps to use a Web Setup project to deploy a Web application.

1   Open an existing Web application solution in Visual Studio .NET.

2   Right-click the solution name in the Solution Explorer window, and select Add, New Project. The Add New Project dialog will appear. (See the figure on page 456.)

3   Select the Setup and Deployment Projects type, select the Web Setup Project template, and then click OK to accept the default project name. The File System editor for the Web Setup project will appear.

4   In the Properties window, modify the ProductName property to match the name of the Web application project you opened in step 1.

5   Right-click the Web Application Folder node in the left pane of the File System editor, and click Add, Project Output. The Add Project Output Group dialog will appear, as shown in the following figure.

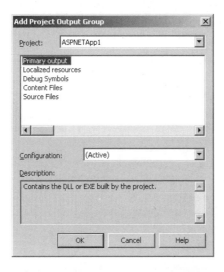

6   Select both the Primary output and Content Files items from the list. Use the Ctrl key to select multiple items. Then click OK.

7   Select the Web Application Folder node in the File System editor. Then locate the VirtualDirectory entry in the Properties window and change it to the name of a target directory on the deployment target. This directory does not need to exist; it will be created.

8   Also in the Properties window, set the DefaultDocument property to the name of the default document for the Web application opened in step 1.

9   Build the solution by clicking Build, Build Solution.

10   Locate the set-up package created by the Web Setup project. It should be located in the Debug or Release subdirectory of the directory containing the Web Setup project. Copy the file to the target server and execute it.

11   Browse the newly deployed application using the URL *http://machinename/ vdirname/*, where *machinename* is the name of the machine where you installed the set-up package and *vdirname* is the name that you specified for the Virtual-Directory property in step 7. If the deployment worked correctly, you should see the default page for the Web application.

In addition to providing fine-grained control over the files and outputs included in the installation package, this method also allows you to automatically install shared assemblies in the GAC. It also allows you to uninstall a Web application with a single command, either by right-clicking the installation package and selecting Uninstall or by locating the application's entry in the Windows Add/ Remove Programs applet, which can be accessed from the Control Panel.

Chapter 15 Quick Reference

To	Do This
Verify that a directory in IIS is an application root	Navigate to the directory in Internet Services Manager and look at the icon for the directory. If the directory is not an application root, you can make it one by right-clicking the directory, selecting Properties, and clicking Create on the Directory tab.
Store application-specific configuration settings	Add an appSettings section to your Web.config or Machine.config file, with an *<add>* tag for each item to be added to the appSettings.
Deploy content and private assemblies	Set up the target directory in IIS on the machine to be deployed to. Then use XCOPY, WebDAV, Windows Explorer, or another means to copy the files and folders of the application to the target directory.
Create an installation package with fine-grained control of installation items and uninstall ability	Add a Web Setup project to the solution for the Web application to be packaged, and set its properties and outputs as desired.

CHAPTER

16

Tracing and Debugging ASP.NET Applications

Debugging

In this chapter, you will learn about

✔ *Tracing*

✔ *Debugging*

✔ *Using the .NET Framework SDK debugger*

This book has covered a wide variety of topics related to ASP.NET development. Hopefully, you'll be able to avoid too many problems while developing your ASP.NET Web applications. Inevitably, however, there will be times when your code doesn't do what you expect it to, or you'll run into errors or problems that prevent your application from working. This final chapter will look at what to do when that happens. It's not intended to make you an expert debugger, but rather to give you an overview of the tools available for debugging in ASP.NET.

To say that classic ASP did not offer developers much support for debugging their applications would be a colossal understatement. Despite being a very simple and productive development environment, classic ASP left a lot to be desired in terms of debugging and error messages.

For example, in classic ASP there was no convenient way to access the state of the current HTTP request (apart from writing code in each application to access and log, or write to the page, the contents of the *Request.Headers* collection) or of the other collections, such as the *QueryString* or *Forms* collections. ASP.NET addresses this through a new feature called *tracing*, which is discussed in the first part of this chapter.

Additionally, classic ASP error messages were often cryptic at best. If you were lucky, they told you the line of the ASP page on which the error occurred. Unfortunately, this information could be misleading. The error might have occurred in a function called by that page, but you wouldn't know that from the error message. ASP.NET provides much richer error reporting than classic ASP, including a stack trace of the functions that led up to an error condition, making it much easier to locate the root cause of the error.

The .NET Framework SDK ships with its own debugger, so developers who are not using Visual Studio .NET can attach it to the process of their ASP.NET application and step through their code to find and fix problems. This improved error reporting and the SDK debugger are discussed in the second half of this chapter.

Tracing

As mentioned, one weakness of classic ASP was the lack of an easy way to get information about the current request. Apart from creating reusable include files to write out the contents of the various collections of the request object, there was no simple method of making this information available. ASP.NET provides a solution in the form of tracing, which provides a substantial amount of information about requests that have been executed, either at the page level or the application level, as well as a way to get your own custom debug information without exposing it to the users of your application.

Enabling Page-Level Trace Output

The simplest way to access trace information is through the *Trace* attribute of the @ *Page* directive. By adding the *Trace* attribute to any .aspx page, you can instruct ASP.NET to append the trace output for that page to the rendered content of the page. A portion of the trace output is shown in the following figure.

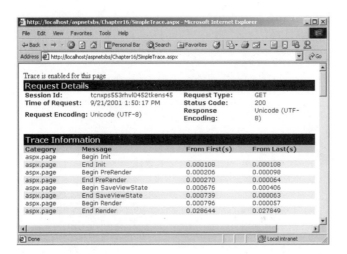

The trace output includes such information as the contents of the cookies, forms, and querystring collections. Therefore, page-level tracing using the *Trace* attribute of the @ *Page* directive should be restricted to nonproduction systems because the output is visible to any client requesting that page. Although it is possible to use one of the configuration options detailed in the next section to configure ASP.NET to provide page-level trace output only for requests from the local system, it is probably best to stick to application-level tracing on publicly available applications.

Enabling Application-Level Trace Output

In addition to providing trace output at the page level, ASP.NET can be configured to log trace output for a specified number of requests for later review. The primary advantages of this approach are that it hides trace output from users of the page, allowing its use on production or customer-facing systems, and that it allows tracing to be enabled for an entire site at once.

Application-level tracing is enabled by adding the *<trace>* section to the Web.config file for the application and setting its attributes to the desired values. The following listing shows a *<trace>* section that enables application-level tracing and tells ASP.NET to log the last 40 requests. (Logged requests must be cleared manually when the request limit has been reached.) The attributes for the *<trace>* section are detailed in Chapter 7.

Web.config Containing a <trace> Section

```
<configuration>
    <system.web>
        <trace enabled="true"
            traceMode="SortByCategory"
            requestLimit="40"
            pageOutput="false"
            localOnly="true"/>
    </system.web>
</configuration>
```

To allow access to the logged trace output, ASP.NET provides an *HttpHandler* that is mapped to a special URL called *trace.axd*. Appending *trace.axd* to the base URL for the application will display the list of currently available traces, as shown in the following figure. Clicking the View Details link for a particular trace displays its output. Clicking the clear current trace link clears all current entries from the trace log and allows more requests to be logged.

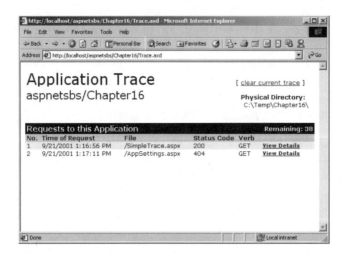

Writing to the Trace Output

At one time or another, most developers who have ever tried debugging a classic ASP application have resorted to using *Response.Write* to output the value of variables to the page, or for placing flags within their code to determine where the code is breaking by seeing how much of the page gets executed before execution is halted. While this was (and still is) a very useful technique for debugging, it is only useful for development machines that are not accessible by users. And many of the aforementioned developers have gotten calls from their supervisors when they forgot to take the *Response.Write* statements out before migrating a page to a production server.

important

The page level setting for trace functionality will override the setting in Web.config. So even if you have tracing enabled in Web.config, setting the *trace* attribute of the @ *Page* directive to *False* will still disable tracing for that page. Likewise, even if tracing is disabled at the application level in Web.config, setting the page-level *trace* attribute to *True* will still enable tracing for that page. For this reason, if you use page-level tracing, you should always double-check your pages before publishing them to a public server to ensure that the *trace* attribute for each page has been removed or set to *False*.

ASP.NET's trace functionality solves this problem by allowing developers to write to the trace output, instead of writing to the page output. Assuming that page-level trace output has not been enabled, this prevents end-users from seeing the trace statements written by the developer.

important

Enabling tracing for a page or for an application does carry some performance overhead. Even though the ASP.NET trace functionality makes it possible to leave tracing enabled without trace output being viewed by end-users, when performance is important, it is a good idea to disable tracing for an application at both the page and application level.

The trace output is exposed to developers via the *TraceContext* class, which is available from the *Page.Trace* property (which can be accessed within a page simply by *Trace*, since the *Page* is assumed). There are two methods for writing to the trace output, *Trace.Write* and *Trace.Warn*.

Determining If Tracing Is Enabled

To keep developers from wasting time attempting to write to the trace output when tracing is not enabled, the *TraceContext* class exposes a boolean property called *IsEnabled*, which contains the current status of tracing for the page.

This is especially helpful if you are performing expensive processing or database lookups as a part of your trace logging.

Using Trace.Write

The *Trace.Write* method of the *TraceContext* class is overloaded, and it can be called in one of the following three ways:

```
Trace.Write(message)
Trace.Write(category, message)
Trace.Write(category, message, errorInfo)
```

message is a string containing the message to be written to the trace output. *category* is a string containing a description of the message (variable, statement, or whatever the developer desires as a category). And *errorInfo* is an exception object, which allows exceptions to be logged to the trace output. The *category* and *errorInfo* parameters allow developers to set up sophisticated application-wide tracing by defining specific categories of logged information and using them consistently across an application.

The following listing shows the code for a page that tests if tracing is enabled for the page, and then writes a simple message to the trace output.

TraceWrite.aspx

```
<%@ Page Language="VB" Trace="true" %>
<html>
<head>
   <script runat="server">
      Sub Page_Load()
         If Trace.IsEnabled = True
           Label1.Text = "Writing 'Hello from Page!' to Trace Log..."
         End If
         Trace.Write("Hello from Page!")
      End Sub
   </script>
</head>
<body>
   <asp:label id="Label1" runat="server"/>
</body>
</html>
```

The following figure shows the output of this page.

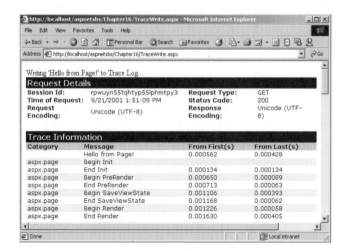

Using Trace.Warn

Another method offered by the *TraceContext* class for writing to the trace output is *Trace.Warn*. The primary difference between the two methods is that output written with *Trace.Warn* appears in the trace output as red text, making it ideal for highlighting important entries such as exceptions.

Understanding the Trace Output

The trace output for a page contains a great deal of information. The following table lists the sections of the trace output and describes the information contained in each.

Trace Output Sections	
Section	**Description**
Request Details	Displays request-specific information such as session ID, request type, request status code, and encoding.
Trace Information	Displays messages relating to stages of page processing, as well as execution times for these stages.
Control Tree	Displays a tree representation of all controls on the page, including *LiteralControls* for static HTML text within the source file. Also displays the render size and *ViewState* size of each control.

(continued)

Trace Output Sections (continued)	
Section	**Description**
Cookies Collection	Displays the name, content, and size of all cookies sent as part of the request.
Headers Collection	Displays a list of all HTTP headers sent as a part of the request.
Form Collection	Displays a list of the names and values of all form fields sent as part of a *POST* request.
Querystring Collection	Displays a list of the names and values of all querystring values sent as part of a *GET* request.
Server Variables	Displays a list of the server variables for the request.

Debugging

In an ideal world, all programmers would be sufficiently skilled and attentive to detail as to write bug-free code. Unfortunately, we do not live in an ideal world. As such, debugging, or tracking down the source of errors and erroneous results in your programs, is an important task that all developers need to perform before they allow end-users to use their applications. This section will discuss some techniques for reducing the number of bugs in your code up-front, as well as the tools and techniques in ASP.NET and the .NET platform for debugging applications.

Understanding Bug Categories

There are three broad categories of bugs, with differing characteristics and differing levels of difficulty.

- **Syntax errors**   These errors occur when code breaks the rules of the language you're using, such as writing a VB *Sub* statement without a closing *End Sub*, or forgetting a closing curly brace (}) in C#. These errors are the easiest to locate. The language compiler or IDE will alert you to them and will not allow you to compile your program until they are corrected.

- **Semantic errors**   These errors occur in code that is correct according to the rules of the compiler, but that causes unexpected problems such as crashes or hanging on execution. A good example is code that executes in a loop but never exits the loop, either because the loop depends on a variable whose value was expected to be something different than it actually was or because the programmer forgot to increment the loop counter. These bugs are harder to detect and are one type of run-time error.

- **Logic errors**   These errors are similar to semantic errors in that they are run-time errors. That is, they occur while the program is running. But unlike semantic errors, they do not cause the application to crash or hang. Instead, logic errors result in unexpected values or output. This can be due to something as simple as a mistyped variable name that happens to match another declared variable in the program (an argument for descriptive variable names rather than simple ones, for example). This type of error can be extremely difficult to track down and eliminate, particularly since in complex programs it may be difficult (if not impossible) to reproduce a logic error reported by a user.

Preventing Bugs

Before we even get into the discussion of how to debug the various errors you're apt to run into in your applications, let's take some time to look at strategies for preventing bugs in the first place. Preventing bugs is a much more efficient and much less expensive way to produce bug-free software.

The following list contains a few strategies that will help. This is not a comprehensive list by any means, but applying these strategies consistently will help you spend less time debugging code and more time enjoying the rewards of having written it.

- **Write readable code**   Choose (or develop) and make consistent use of naming and coding standards. It's not that important which standard you use, such as Hungarian notation (txtFirstName) vs. Pascal Casing (FirstName), as long as you use one. You should also strive for consistency in comments and encourage liberal commenting of code. Anything that makes code more readable and easier to understand will help eliminate bugs from the get-go.

- **Create effective test plans**   The only effective way to eliminate logic errors is to test every path of your application with every possible data value (or representative range of data) that could be entered by a user. This is difficult to manage without effective planning. Test plans should be created at the same time as the application is being designed, and they should be updated as the application design is modified. To be effective, the test plans need to describe how to test each piece of functionality in the application. Test plans and other design documents can also help highlight design problems before they are implemented, preventing a wide array of bugs.

- **Use a rich IDE**   You don't necessarily need to use Visual Studio .NET to develop your Web applications since ASP.NET does not require it, but you should consider developing in an IDE that provides syntax checking as you type. If you develop with Notepad, it is too easy to amass a number of syntax errors that go unnoticed until you try to run the page. Then you get to spend the next half-hour or more eliminating the errors, one at a time, until you finally get the code to run. This is not an efficient way to write code.

■ **Get another pair of eyes**   Whether you're working on a team or building an application on your own, it is important to have someone else review your code (and test it, if possible). Developers are simply too close to their own code to catch every bug before testing, and sometimes even after. A review by a different pair of eyes can help a lot.

Compiling Web Forms Pages in Debug Mode

As mentioned in the introduction to this chapter, ASP.NET provides a great deal of information to developers when a bug or error halts execution of an application by throwing an exception. Some of this information, such as the stack trace, is available regardless of the mode that the code was compiled in. The following figure shows the output of a page compiled in release mode that divides by zero in code to force an exception to be thrown.

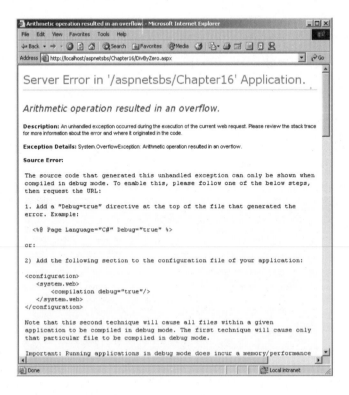

Other information is only available if the page or application is compiled in debug mode, which makes debug information available to the runtime, which can then provide additional information such as the line of code on which an error occurred. Using the SDK debugger to step through your code also requires that the code be compiled in debug mode.

To indicate that a page should be compiled in debug mode, add the *Debug* attribute to the @ *Page* directive and set its value to *True*. To indicate that all pages in an application should be compiled in debug mode, edit the compilation section of Web.config (or add it if it doesn't exist), adding the *debug* attribute with a value of *true*.

```
<configuration>
   <system.web>
      <compilation debug="true"/>
   </system.web>
</configuration>
```

Setting the *debug* attribute of the page shown in the previous figure to *true* results in the output shown in the following figure.

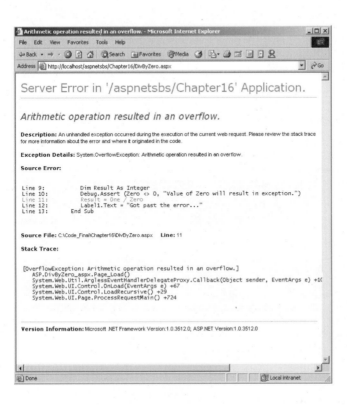

Understanding ASP.NET Error Messages

Anyone who's seen the infamous ASP 015 error probably realizes just what a dramatic improvement the information in the previous figure represents. ASP.NET will provide descriptive information for both semantic and syntax errors, including the type of exception thrown (which allows you to provide effective and specific exception handling when you cannot completely prevent the exception) and the stack trace for the current request. As mentioned previously, you can also write to the trace output, and any trace statements that occur before execution is halted by an exception will be shown in the trace output.

Invoking the Runtime Debugger

While the error information provided by ASP.NET at runtime can be useful in locating and eliminating syntax errors, most semantic errors and logic errors require a *debugger*. This tool uses the source code for a program and an executable compiled with debug symbols to let a developer step through his code line by line, set breakpoints, and examine the state or values of variables during program execution. You can also use the *Assert* method of the *Debug* class (part of the *System.Diagnostics* namespace) to test for certain conditions in your code and write messages to the output window of the debugger when the assertions fail.

The .NET Framework SDK comes with its own debugger, which provides rich debugging functionality for ASP.NET applications. The debugger is installed in the *drivename*\Program Files\Microsoft.NET\FrameworkSDK\GuiDebug folder and is named DbgCLR.exe. You can execute the runtime debugger by double-clicking this file in Windows Explorer or by entering the path and file name in the Run dialog (Start, Run). The following figure shows the runtime debugger at start-up.

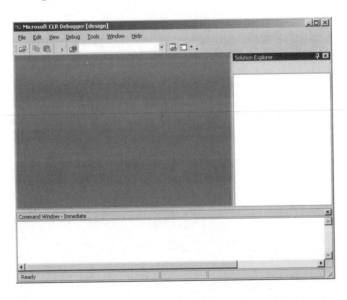

Opening a Source File

In order to debug a Web Forms page, you need to load the source for the page into the debugger. To do so, click File, Open, File and browse to the source file for the page. Remember that to debug the page, it must be compiled in debug mode, either by inserting the *Debug* attribute in the @ *Page* directive or by enabling debugging in Web.config.

Attaching Processes

Once you've loaded the source file for the page, you'll want to call up the page in a browser and attach the debugger to the process of the browser window that is requesting the page. But first, you'll need to attach to the ASP.NET worker process to allow the debugger to break the execution of the code.

To attach the ASP.NET worker process and the process for your page, follow these steps:

1   Open the page to be debugged in a browser.

2   Click Tools, Debug Processes. The Processes window will appear, as shown in the following figure.

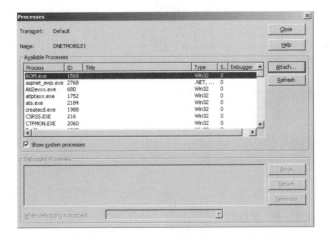

3   Select the aspnet_wp.exe process (on systems with the Beta 2 ASP.NET Premium Edition installed, this will be aspnet_ewp.exe) and click Attach.

4   Locate the process of the browser that is requesting the page (the Title column can help you locate the correct process), select it, and click Attach.

5   Click Close to close the Processes dialog.

Setting Breakpoints

Once you've loaded the source for a page and attached the necessary processes, you can step through your code by setting a breakpoint prior to the line of code on which the error occurs (if known) or on the first line of executable code. Breakpoints halt execution of your code and allow you to check the value of local variables and step through your code.

To set a breakpoint, click on the left border of the editor window next to the desired line of code. Alternatively, you can click Debug, New Breakpoint or press Ctrl+B to open the New Breakpoint dialog. This allows you to specify additional information about the breakpoint, such as conditions under which the break should occur or the number of times the breakpoint is effective. The following figure shows the example page DivByZero.aspx in the debugger with a breakpoint set at the first line of the *Page_Load* event handler. When the browser window containing the program is refreshed, the debugger will halt execution of the program, allowing local variables to be examined in the locals window and allowing the code to be stepped through using the commands in the Debug menu.

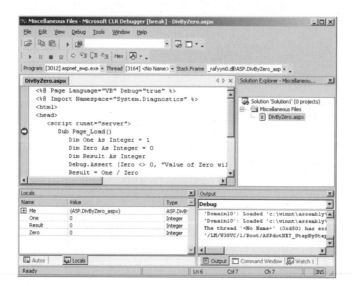

Using Debug.Assert

As mentioned, you can add *Debug.Assert* messages to your code to test certain conditions. The *Assert* method is overloaded and takes the following forms:

```
Debug.Assert(condition)
Debug.Assert(condition, shortmessage)
Debug.Assert(condition, shortmessage, longmessage)
```

condition is an expression that evaluates to true or false, *shortmessage* is a string containing a brief message to display when *condition* returns false, and *longmessage* is a string containing a detailed message to display when *condition* returns false. The following figure shows the runtime debugger after stepping past an *Assert* statement. Notice that the Output window is displaying the short message defined by the *Assert* statement.

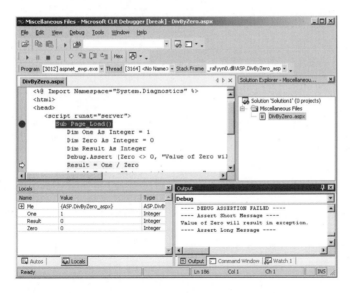

In order to call the *Debug* class without explicitly including the namespace, you need to import the *System.Diagnostics* namespace using the @ *Import* directive, as shown in the preceding figure.

Chapter 16 Quick Reference

To	Do This
Enable page-level tracing	Add the *Trace* attribute to the @ *Page* directive and set its value to *true*.
Enable application-level tracing	Add the *<trace>* configuration section to Web.config with the desired attributes. At a minimum, the *enabled* attribute is required and should be set to *true*.
Write to the trace output	Call either the *Trace.Write* or *Trace.Warn* method, passing the appropriate arguments.
View detailed error information, or prepare for using the runtime debugger	Compile your page or pages in debug mode by either adding the *Debug* attribute to the @ *Page* directive with a value of *true* or adding the *<compilation>* section to the Web.config file and setting its *debug* attribute to *true*.
Invoke the runtime debugger	Locate the file DbgCLR.exe and execute it.
Debug a page using the runtime debugger	Ensure that the page is set to compile in debug mode. Load the source code for the page into the debugger, load the page in a browser, and then attach the ASP.NET worker process and the process of the browser requesting the page. Set breakpoints as desired and reload the page in the browser. Step through the code using the commands in the Debug menu.

A

Migrating from ASP to ASP.NET

Migrating classic ASP code to ASP.NET will be a relatively painless process in many cases, particularly if good programming practices were followed in writing the code, such as separating the code into procedures wherever possible. Because of the changes to both the ASP.NET object model and the Visual Basic language, which is used in ASP.NET in place of Visual Basic Scripting Edition, it is likely that you will have to make some changes to most (if not all) of your classic ASP pages to make them run in ASP.NET. This appendix will look at some of the issues you're likely to run into in this migration process, show you an example of migrating a page that accesses data using ADO, and discuss some programming practices that you can use in your ongoing classic ASP development to make the migration process easier.

Migration Overview

Almost all of the issues you'll encounter in migrating your classic ASP applications to ASP.NET will fall into two categories: page structure changes and language changes. The next two sections will discuss the types of changes in each of these categories, and how you'll need to update your code to work with them.

Page Structure Changes

The page structure changes from classic ASP to ASP.NET can be further broken down into two areas: changes in the structure of code blocks and changes to the syntax of page directives.

Code Blocks

As discussed in Chapter 9, there are significant changes between how code could be structured in classic ASP and how it can be structured in ASP.NET. These changes, which are designed to make your code more readable and maintainable, are likely to be the most common issue in migration.

In classic ASP, server-side code could be written in either code render blocks, indicated by the syntax <% %>, or code declaration blocks, indicated by the <script runat="server"></script> syntax. Either syntax could be used anywhere in the page and could contain either statements or procedures.

One problem is that it could be difficult to tell which code would execute when, leading to unnecessary bugs. Another problem is that it was easy to write spaghetti code, with render blocks all over a page, mixing procedures and raw statements. This made the code difficult to read and to maintain. Excessive mixing of HTML and render blocks also tended to negatively affect page performance.

In ASP.NET, the purposes of render blocks and code declaration blocks have been narrowed considerably. Render blocks in ASP.NET can contain only executable statements, not procedures, while code declaration blocks can contain only global variable declarations and/or procedures.

Another significant difference is that in classic ASP, multiple <script runat="server"> code declaration blocks could be used on a page, and each one could use a different language through the *language* attribute, which could be set to VBScript or JScript. ASP.NET only supports a single language per page, which is Visual Basic .NET by default.

Top-to-Bottom vs. Event-Driven Programming

Classic ASP pages using render blocks always executed from top to bottom, with code in <% %> render blocks being executed and output to the response stream as it was encountered by the ASP interpreter.

ASP.NET code is compiled into an instance of the *Page* class, and execution is event-based. Rather than placing start-up code in the first render block in a page, start-up code in ASP.NET is placed in the *Page_Load* event handler, which is fired when the instance of the *Page* class that represents the page is loaded into memory. Likewise, a *Page_UnLoad* event is fired just before the page is removed from memory and can be used to run any clean-up code that is necessary.

Page Directives

In classic ASP, the primary directive used in pages was the @ *Language* directive, which specified the language to be used for render blocks. Other less commonly used directives included @ *Codepage*, @ *EnableSessionState*, @ *LCID*, and @ *Transaction*.

In ASP.NET, these directives are attributes of the @ *Page* directive, which should appear at the top of each ASP.NET Web Form page. See Chapter 9 for a full discussion of the @ *Page* directive and its attributes.

One new attribute of the @ *Page* directive that is important to discuss in this context is the *AspCompat* attribute. By default, ASP.NET runs as a multi-threaded apartment (MTA) process. This means that components that run as single-threaded apartment (STA) components, such as those written in Visual Basic 6, are not compatible with ASP.NET. This includes the ADO components, which are installed to run as STA components by default. (You can modify this by running a batch file that changes the registry settings for ADO, but that is beyond the scope of this discussion.) Setting the *AspCompat* attribute to *true* forces ASP.NET to run in STA mode, making it possible to use STA components in ASP.NET pages.

important

Setting AspCompat to true should be considered a short-term solution in migrating from ASP to ASP.NET, because this setting can have a significant negative impact on the performance of your application. For best performance, you should rewrite components written in earlier versions of Visual Basic using Visual Basic .NET, and you should migrate existing ADO code to use ADO.NET.

Language Changes

In addition to changes to the structure of pages in ASP.NET, there are some significant changes to the Visual Basic language that will likely require modifications to your code. These include the following:

- *Set* and *Let* are no longer needed or supported. Object references can be set by simple assignment.

  ```
  Object1 = Object2
  ```

- Parens are now required for calling *Sub* procedures as well as *Function* procedures (including methods that do not have parameters).

  ```
  Response.Write("Hello, World!")
  ```

- The *Variant* data type does not exist in Visual Basic .NET. The replacement is *Object*.

- Default properties are no longer supported. All properties must be called explicitly.

  ```
  MyString = TextBox1.Text
  ```

■ Property declaration syntax has changed. Instead of *Property Set*, *Property Get*, and *Property Let*, Visual Basic .NET uses the following syntax (keep in mind that *value* is a special keyword that contains the value submitted to the *Set* portion of the *property* statement).

```
Public Property MyProperty As String
   Get
      MyProperty = MyInternalVariable
   End Get
   Set
      MyInternalVariable = value
   End Set
End Property
```

■ The default for passing parameters to procedures has changed from *ByRef* to *ByVal*. To pass values by reference, you must explicitly add the *ByRef* keyword (reference parameters allow you to change their value in the procedure to which they're passed and retrieve their value outside the procedure).

```
Sub MySub(ByRef MyValue As String)
   MyValue = "Hello!"
End Sub
```

Migrating a Data Access Page to ASP.NET

To demonstrate some of these changes and show you how to deal with them, let's walk through the process of migrating a classic ASP page that accesses data in a SQL Server database through ADO and writes it to the page as an HTML table. First you'll go through the process of making the page work in ASP.NET, while still using ADO for data access and using the same logic for writing the data as an HTML table. Then you'll modify that code to access the data through ADO.NET and use an ASP.NET DataGrid to automatically render the data as a table. The following listing shows the classic ASP page that you'll start with.

GetAuthors.asp

```
<%@ Language=VBScript %>
<html>
<head>
<%
Dim objConn
Dim objCmd
Dim objRS
Dim strConn
```

```
strConn = "PROVIDER=SQLOLEDB;INITIAL CATALOG=PUBS;"_
   &"SERVER=(local)\NetSDK;uid=sa;pwd=;"
Set objConn = Server.CreateObject("ADODB.Connection")
Set objCmd = Server.CreateObject("ADODB.Command")
Set objRS = Server.CreateObject("ADODB.Recordset")

objCmd.CommandText = "SELECT * FROM Authors"
objConn.Open strConn
Set objCmd.ActiveConnection = objConn
Set objRS = objCmd.Execute

Sub FormatTable

    Dim objField

    If Not objRS.EOF Then
       Response.Write "<table border=2 cellspacing=0>"
       Do While Not objRS.EOF
           Response.Write "<tr>"
           For Each objField In objRS.Fields
               Response.Write "<td>" & objField & "</td>"
           Next
           Response.Write "</tr>"
           objRS.MoveNext
       Loop
       Response.Write "</table>"
    Else
       Response.Write "No Records!"
    End If

End Sub
Sub CleanUp()
   objConn.Close
   Set objConn = Nothing
   Set objCmd = Nothing
   Set objRS = Nothing
End Sub
%>
</head>
<body>
```

```
<%
FormatTable()
CleanUp()
%>

</body>
</html>
```

The following figure shows the output of this page.

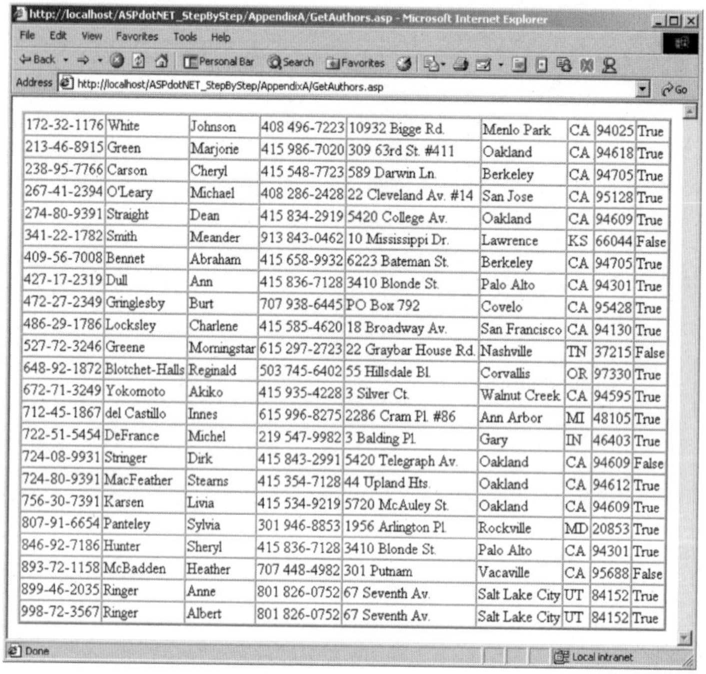

172-32-1176	White	Johnson	408 496-7223	10932 Bigge Rd.	Menlo Park	CA	94025	True
213-46-8915	Green	Marjorie	415 986-7020	309 63rd St. #411	Oakland	CA	94618	True
238-95-7766	Carson	Cheryl	415 548-7723	589 Darwin Ln.	Berkeley	CA	94705	True
267-41-2394	O'Leary	Michael	408 286-2428	22 Cleveland Av. #14	San Jose	CA	95128	True
274-80-9391	Straight	Dean	415 834-2919	5420 College Av.	Oakland	CA	94609	True
341-22-1782	Smith	Meander	913 843-0462	10 Mississippi Dr.	Lawrence	KS	66044	False
409-56-7008	Bennet	Abraham	415 658-9932	6223 Bateman St.	Berkeley	CA	94705	True
427-17-2319	Dull	Ann	415 836-7128	3410 Blonde St.	Palo Alto	CA	94301	True
472-27-2349	Gringlesby	Burt	707 938-6445	PO Box 792	Covelo	CA	95428	True
486-29-1786	Locksley	Charlene	415 585-4620	18 Broadway Av.	San Francisco	CA	94130	True
527-72-3246	Greene	Morningstar	615 297-2723	22 Graybar House Rd.	Nashville	TN	37215	False
648-92-1872	Blotchet-Halls	Reginald	503 745-6402	55 Hillsdale Bl.	Corvallis	OR	97330	True
672-71-3249	Yokomoto	Akiko	415 935-4228	3 Silver Ct.	Walnut Creek	CA	94595	True
712-45-1867	del Castillo	Innes	615 996-8275	2286 Cram Pl. #86	Ann Arbor	MI	48105	True
722-51-5454	DeFrance	Michel	219 547-9982	3 Balding Pl.	Gary	IN	46403	True
724-08-9931	Stringer	Dirk	415 843-2991	5420 Telegraph Av.	Oakland	CA	94609	False
724-80-9391	MacFeather	Stearns	415 354-7128	44 Upland Hts.	Oakland	CA	94612	True
756-30-7391	Karsen	Livia	415 534-9219	5720 McAuley St.	Oakland	CA	94609	True
807-91-6654	Panteley	Sylvia	301 946-8853	1956 Arlington Pl.	Rockville	MD	20853	True
846-92-7186	Hunter	Sheryl	415 836-7128	3410 Blonde St.	Palo Alto	CA	94301	True
893-72-1158	McBadden	Heather	707 448-4982	301 Putnam	Vacaville	CA	95688	False
899-46-2035	Ringer	Anne	801 826-0752	67 Seventh Av.	Salt Lake City	UT	84152	True
998-72-3567	Ringer	Albert	801 826-0752	67 Seventh Av.	Salt Lake City	UT	84152	True

The page in the previous listing accesses the Authors table of the Pubs SQL Server sample database (in this case in the NetSDK MSDE instance installed with the .NET Framework SDK samples), calls a render function to write the data to the page as an HTML table, and then calls a clean-up function to close the connection to the database and set the object references to *Nothing* to ensure that the COM subsystem knows these objects can be destroyed.

> **important**
>
> One thing this sample code has in common with much of the sample code you will encounter (and, unfortunately, some production code) is its use of the *sa* SQL Server login account with a blank password. (This is the default for SQL Server 6.5 and 7.0 installs. You must explicitly choose a blank password in order to use a blank *sa* password in SQL Server 2000.) In practice, the *sa* account should always be given a strong password because this account has full administrative rights on the SQL Server machine. This includes the ability to run operating system commands through a special extended stored procedure. In a production application, never use the *sa* account for accessing data from a page.
>
> If you cannot use a trusted connection to SQL Server, you should set up one or more special user accounts for each Web application with the absolute minimum rights necessary to allow access to that application's data. This will reduce the risk of overbroad rights, resulting in data being compromised.
>
> Another security issue in the sample is the placing of user ID and password information directly in the page. In practice, connection string information should be stored somewhere more secure. In order of increasing security, options include storing it as an *appSetting* in Web.config, storing it as an *appSetting* in Machine.config (not appropriate in a shared server environment), and hard-coding it as a private member of a compiled component.

Short-Term Migration

In the short term, your goal may be to simply move your pages over to ASP.NET while still using most of the existing logic in the page. Keeping in mind that this choice has performance implications, it may allow you to make your migration easier by letting you do it in stages. Making the code in the previous listing work as an ASP.NET page is largely a matter of modifying it to comply with the rules for ASP.NET code.

The first thing you should do is save a copy of the page to be migrated with a .aspx extension and try to run it. Although it's unlikely that pages of any complexity will run unaltered, you might be surprised at what will run. More importantly, when you attempt to run the page and it fails, ASP.NET will give you information about why it failed and which line caused the failure. (Remember from Chapter 16 that in order to get the most error information, pages should be set to compile in debug mode. You can do this either by setting the *debug* attribute of the @ *Page* directive or by turning on debug mode in Web.config.) The following figure shows the page that results from attempting to run GetAuthors.asp as an ASP.NET page.

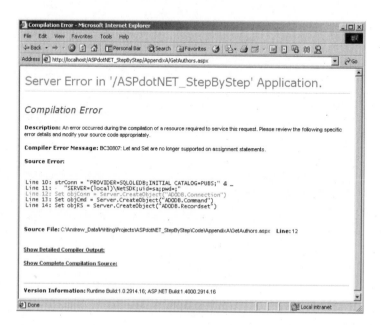

As you can see in the preceding figure, you get immediate feedback that the *Set* statements need to be removed from your code. Thanks to the improvement in error information in ASP.NET, you can simply change a page's extension to .aspx, attempt to run it, correct the error that is flagged, attempt to run it again, correct the next error to be flagged, and so on until the page runs without errors.

This example will take a more structured approach and correct all of the structural and language incompatibilities before attempting to rerun the code.

1   If you haven't already, save the code in in the listing that starts on page 480 as GetAuthors.asp (changing the user ID and password to one that is set up on your machine). Once you have that running, save a copy as GetAuthors.aspx.

2   Starting from the top of the page, modify the @ *Language* directive to @ *Page* to use Visual Basic as the language, and add the *AspCompat* attribute so that you can use the ADO components in STA mode:

```
<%@ Page Language="VB" AspCompat="True" %>
```

3   While the code that creates and instantiates the ADO objects will run in a render block without modification in ASP.NET, the *FormatTable* and *CleanUp* procedures will not. They need to be moved into a *<script>* block. Since leaving the ADO code in a render block will not allow you to control when it executes, move it into a *<script>* block as well and run it in the *Page_UnLoad* event handler. Move the clean-up code to the *Page_Load* handler. (You no longer need the *Set obj = Nothing* statements because ASP.NET takes care of this clean-up for you.) Note that you have also removed the *Set* statements from the code and added parens to the call to *objConn.Open*.

```
<head>
<script runat="server">
    Dim objConn
    Dim objCmd
    Dim objRS
    Sub Page_Load()
        Dim strConn

        strConn = "PROVIDER=SQLOLEDB;INITIAL CATALOG=PUBS;"_
            &"SERVER=(local)\NetSDK;uid=sa;pwd=;"
        objConn = Server.CreateObject("ADODB.Connection")
        objCmd = Server.CreateObject("ADODB.Command")
        objRS = Server.CreateObject("ADODB.Recordset")

        objCmd.CommandText = "SELECT * FROM Authors"
        objConn.Open(strConn)
        objCmd.ActiveConnection = objConn
        objRS = objCmd.Execute
    End Sub
    Sub FormatTable

        Dim objField

        If Not objRS.EOF Then
            Response.Write("<table border=2 cellspacing=0>")
            Do While Not objRS.EOF
                Response.Write("<tr>")
                For Each objField In objRS.Fields
                    Response.Write("<td>" & objField.Value & "</td>")
                Next
```

```
                    Response.Write("</tr>")
                    objRS.MoveNext
                Loop
                Response.Write("</table>")
            Else
                Response.Write("No Records!")
            End If
        End Sub
        Sub Page_Unload()
            objConn.Close
        End Sub
    </script>
    </head>
```

4   Save the page and browse it. The output should be the same as in the figure on page 482.

Long-Term Migration

Techniques such as using *AspCompat* to allow use of STA components in ASP.NET can help you get pages up and running in ASP.NET more quickly. But in the long run, it's best to fully migrate your code to take advantage of the features offered by ASP.NET and ADO.NET. The following listing shows the changes necessary to get the equivalent functionality of GetAuthors.asp using ADO.NET, and using an ASP.NET *DataGrid* to display the data rather than writing your own rendering code.

GetAuthors2.aspx

```
<%@ Page Language="VB" %>
<%@ Import Namespace="System.Data" %>
<%@ Import Namespace="System.Data.SqlClient" %>
<html>
<head>
<script runat="server">
    Sub Page_Load()
        Dim myDS As New DataSet()
        Dim ConnStr As String
        ConnStr = "server=(local)\NetSDK;database=pubs;"
        ConnStr &= Trusted_Connection=yes"
        Dim SQLSelect As String
        SQLSelect = "SELECT * FROM Authors"
```

```
            Dim mySqlConn As New SqlConnection(ConnStr)
            Dim mySqlDA As New SqlDataAdapter(SQLSelect, ConnStr)

            mySqlDA.Fill(myDS)
            MyGrid.DataSource = myDS.Tables(0).DefaultView
            DataBind()
        End Sub
    </script>
    </head>
    <body>
        <form runat="server">
            <asp:label id="title" text="ASP to ASP.NET Migration: Step 2"
            font-size="18" runat="server"/>
            <asp:datagrid
                id="MyGrid"
                autogeneratecolumns="true"
                border="2"
                cellpadding="0"
                runat="server"/>
        </form>
    </body>
    </html>
```

---

note

To use a trusted connection to connect to SQL Server as shown in the preceding listing, you will need to either enable Windows authentication and impersonation or set up the ASPNET worker process account as a SQL Server login, as described in Chapter 11.

The code in the preceding listing offers better performance because it does not rely on *AspCompat* to run. It takes advantage of ADO.NET instead of using ADO through COM Interop, which carries some performance overhead. The code could be made even more efficient by using an ADO.NET DataReader to access the data. The code in the preceding listing also provides greater flexibility for modifying the look of the rendered table. Now you can modify this by adding attributes to the *DataGrid* tag. Using an ASP.NET *DataGrid* also provides built-in support for paging, editing, and filtering. See Chapter 11 for more information on these features.

Best Practices for Preparing for ASP.NET

As you can see from this appendix, migrating from classic ASP to ASP.NET does not need to be terribly painful. However, a lot depends on how your classic ASP code is written in the first place. Code that is written with a great deal of intermingled HTML and render blocks will be more difficult to migrate, as will code that does not follow good coding practices. The following are several coding practices you can put in place in your ongoing classic ASP development to make migrating it to ASP.NET easier:

- For procedures that take parameters, use *ByVal* or *ByRef* to explicitly state which type of parameter is desired. This will prevent code that relies on the default assumption of *ByRef* in classic ASP from breaking when migrated to ASP.NET.

- Write all procedures in *<script>* code declaration blocks, rather than in render blocks.

- Use render blocks sparingly, particularly when intermingled with HTML tags.

- Do not rely on default properties. Instead, explicitly name properties such as *objRS.Value*.

- Do not use multiple languages in server-side *<script>* blocks. Choose the language you're most comfortable with and use it exclusively on a per-page basis.

Additional Code Listings

Chapter 4

Animals.vb

```vb
Imports System
Imports System.IO

Namespace Animals

Public Class Animal
    Overridable Public Sub Eat()
        Console.WriteLine("Yum!")
    End Sub
    Overridable Public Sub Sleep()
        Console.WriteLine("Zzzzz...")
    End Sub
End Class

Public Class Cat
    Inherits Animal
    Overrides Public Sub Eat()
        Console.WriteLine("Yum, Yum...Meow, Meow!")
    End Sub
End Class
```

```
Public Class Dog
    Inherits Animal
    Overrides Public Sub Sleep()
        Console.WriteLine("Zzzzzz...woofwoofwoofwoof...zzzzzz!")
    End Sub
End Class

End Namespace
```

UseAnimals.vb

```
Imports Animals

Public Class UseAnimals
    Public Shared Sub Main()
        Dim MyCat As New Cat
        Dim MyDog As New Dog

        MyCat.Eat
        MyCat.Sleep
        MyDog.Eat
        MyDog.Sleep
    End Sub
End Class
```

Chapter 11

BoundColumn_Sort.aspx

```
<%@ Page Language="VB" %>
<%@ Import Namespace="System.Data" %>
<html>
    <script runat="server">
    Dim SortExpression As String

    Function CreateDataSource() As ICollection
        Dim dt As New DataTable()
        Dim dr As DataRow

        dt.Columns.Add(New DataColumn("IntegerValue", GetType(Int32)))
        dt.Columns.Add(New DataColumn("StringValue", GetType(String)))
        dt.Columns.Add(New DataColumn("CurrencyValue", GetType(Double)))
```

```vb
        Dim i As Integer
        For i = 0 To 8
            dr = dt.NewRow()

            dr(0) = i
            dr(1) = "Item " + i.ToString()
            dr(2) = 1.23 * Rnd * (i + 1)

            dt.Rows.Add(dr)
        Next i

        Dim dv As New DataView(dt)
        dv.Sort = SortExpression
        Return dv
    End Function
    Sub Page_Load(sender As Object, e As EventArgs)
        If Not IsPostBack Then
            ' need to load this data only once
            If SortExpression = "" Then
                SortExpression = "IntegerValue"
            End If
            ItemsGrid.DataSource = CreateDataSource()
            ItemsGrid.DataBind()
        End If
    End Sub
    Sub Sort_Grid(sender As Object, e As DataGridSortCommandEventArgs)
        SortExpression = e.SortExpression.ToString()
        ItemsGrid.DataSource = CreateDataSource()
        ItemsGrid.DataBind()
    End Sub
    </script>
<body>

    <form runat=server>

        <h3><font face="Verdana">BoundColumn Example</font></h3>

        <b>Product List</b>

        <asp:DataGrid id="ItemsGrid"
            BorderColor="black"
```

```
              BorderWidth="1"
              CellPadding="3"
              AllowSorting="true"
              OnSortCommand="Sort_Grid"
              AutoGenerateColumns="false"
              runat="server">

         <HeaderStyle BackColor="#00aaaa">
         </HeaderStyle>

         <Columns>

            <asp:BoundColumn
                 HeaderText="Number"
                 SortExpression="IntegerValue"
                 DataField="IntegerValue">
            </asp:BoundColumn>

            <asp:BoundColumn
                 HeaderText="Description"
                 SortExpression="StringValue"
                 DataField="StringValue">
            </asp:BoundColumn>

            <asp:BoundColumn
                 HeaderText="Price"
                 SortExpression="CurrencyValue"
                 DataField="CurrencyValue"
                 DataFormatString="{0:c}">
            </asp:BoundColumn>

         </Columns>

      </asp:DataGrid>

   </form>

</body>
</html>
```

Chapter 12

LoginControl.cs

```csharp
using System;
using System.Web;
using System.Web.UI;
using System.Collections;
using System.Collections.Specialized;
using System.Web.UI.WebControls;

namespace ASPNETSBS {

    public class LoginControl_CS : Control, IPostBackDataHandler,
        IPostBackEventHandler {

        private string _UserName = "";
        private string _Password = "";

        public string UserName {
            get {
                return _UserName;
            }
            set {
                _UserName = value;
            }
        }

        public string Password {
            get {
                return _Password;
            }
            set {
                _Password = value;
            }
        }

        public event EventHandler AuthSuccess;
        public event EventHandler AuthFailure;
```

```
protected virtual void OnAuthSuccess(EventArgs e){
   if (AuthSuccess != null)
      AuthSuccess(this,e);
}

protected virtual void OnAuthFailure(EventArgs e){
   if (AuthFailure != null)
      AuthFailure(this,e);
}

public bool LoadPostData(String postDataKey,
   NameValueCollection values) {
   string newValues = values[postDataKey];

   string newUserName = "";
   string newPassword = "";

   int Index = newValues.IndexOf(',');

   // get the UserName
   newUserName = (newValues.Substring(0, Index));
   // get the Password
   newPassword = (newValues.Substring(Index + 1,
      newValues.Length - Index -1));

   if((newUserName != UserName) ||
      (newPassword != _Password)) {
      _UserName = newUserName;
      _Password = newPassword;
      return true;
   } else {
      return false;
   }
}

public void RaisePostDataChangedEvent() {
   // Respond to changes in posted data
}
```

```
public void RaisePostBackEvent(String eventArgument) {
    if (eventArgument == null) {
        return;
    }
    if (this._UserName == "SomeUser" &&
        this._Password == "password") {
        OnAuthSuccess(EventArgs.Empty);
    }
    else {
        OnAuthFailure(EventArgs.Empty);
    }
}


protected override void Render(HtmlTextWriter output) {
 output.Write("<h3>User Name: <input name=" +
    this.UniqueID + " id = UserNameKey" + " type=text value=" +
    this.UserName + "> </h3>");
 output.Write("<h3>Password: <input name=" + this.UniqueID +
        " id = Password" + " type=password > </h3>");
 output.Write("<input type=button " +
        "value=Submit OnClick=\"jscript:" +
        Page.GetPostBackEventReference(this) + "\">    ");
 output.WriteLine("");
 output.WriteLine("<br>");
 output.WriteLine("<br>");
    }
 }
}
```

LoginControl_Client_CS.aspx

```
<%@ Page Language="vb" %>
<%@ Register TagPrefix="ASPNETSBS" Namespace="ASPNETSBS"
    Assembly="LoginControl_CS" %>
<html>
    <head>
    <script runat="server">
        Sub Auth_Success(Source As Object, e As EventArgs)
            Message.Text = "Authenticated!"
        End Sub
```

```
            Sub Auth_Failure(Source As Object, e As EventArgs)
                Message.Text = "Authentication Failed!"
            End Sub
        </script>
        </head>
        <body>
            <h3><font face="Verdana" color="black">
            Login Control</font>
            </h3>
            <form runat=server>
                <ASPNETSBS:LoginControl_CS id="Login"
                    OnAuthSuccess="Auth_Success"
                    OnAuthFailure="Auth_Failure"
                    runat=server/>
                <asp:label id="Message" Font-Bold="True" ForeColor="Red"
                    runat="server"/>
            </form>
        </body>
    </html>
```

Afterword

When I was first exposed to ASP+, which would become ASP.NET, I was immediately reminded of the '80s song by a band called Timbuk 3. The refrain was "The future's so bright, I gotta wear shades." In the 18 months since then, I think the future of Web development, and ASP.NET's place in it, has only grown brighter.

In many ways, ASP.NET and the .NET Framework have opened up new possibilities to developers who have existed solely in the world of Notepad and scripting languages. In some development circles, ASP developers have been treated as second-class citizens—no more. Whether you use a text editor or a rich IDE like Visual Studio .NET, the .NET Framework and ASP.NET offer you the power of fully compiled languages and object-oriented programming.

As with any big step forward, there are costs associated with the move to this new platform. The learning curve for some of the technologies used in ASP.NET may be a little steeper than with classic ASP; but the reward for this learning is greater power, greater productivity, and substantially better applications.

I hope that this book helps developers get up to speed with this great new technology. I also hope that you, the reader, will help me by letting me know whether I have met that goal. I welcome all reader feedback at *feedback@aspnetsbs.com*.

G. Andrew Duthie

Index

A

`<a>` element, 252
Abandon method, 105
access control, 186
access permissions, 20, 87
accounts, 182
ACLs (Access Control Lists), 200
ActiveX Data Objects. *See* ADO
`<add>` element, 135, 152, 154, 163
Add New Item dialog box, 24–25
AddAt method, 362
Added row state, 326
Address connection string key, 303
ADO (ActiveX Data Objects), 5, 61
ADO.NET, 297–298
    creating connections to databases in, 301–305
    data-binding, 331, 333
        DataBound controls in, 334–349
        simple, 332
    datasets in, 317
        data columns, 318–322
        data rows, 318–322
        data tables, 318, 322
        using DataAdapters, 317
        using DataViews, 329–330
        XML data, 318
    reading data with commands in, 308–317
    reading data with data readers in, 330–331
    updating data with commands in, 308–317
    XML in, 301
AdRotator control, 282–284
alias attribute, 163
AllKeys property, 99

`<allow>` element, 146
`<allow>` tag, 201–202
allowOverride attribute, 123
AlternatingItemTemplate, 347
APL programming language, 14
Application Center 2000, 10–11
Application collection, 99–100
application design, 170–185
application flags, 101
Application Name connection string key, 303
application root, 82–86, 446–447
application state, 98–100
    limitations of, 102
    and scalability, 107–108
    storing information in, 101
    synchronizing access to, 100
    using, 101
Application.Lock() method, 100, 108
Application.Unlock() method, 100
Application_BeginRequest event, 91
Application_EndRequest event, 91
Application_OnEnd event, 91
Application_OnStart event, 91
appRequestQueueLimit attribute, 128
`<appSettings>` element, 165, 450
arbitrary data, 437–439
.ascx files, 34
.asmx files, 34
`<asp:label>` tags, 238
ASP.NET
    architecture
        familiar features, 14
        new features, 14–16
    configuration, 117–119

ASP.NET, *continued*
  development tools, 17–27
  error messages, 472
  file types, 34–35
  migrating from classic ASP, 477
    best practices in, 488
    changes in language, 479–480
    changes in page structures, 477–478
    changes to syntax of page directives,
      478–479
    data access page, 480–482
    long-term, 486–487
    short-term, 483–486
  project types, 31
    Web applications, 32–33
    XML Web Services, 33–34
  server control state, 114
  server controls, 213, 236–237
ASP.NET Mobile controls, 295
ASP.NET pages
  adding controls to, 25–26
    custom server controls, 239–240
    HTML controls, 237
    user controls, 232–236
    Web controls, 237–238
  browsing, 27
  code locations, 89–90
  compiling in debug mode, 470–471
  creating, 86
  debugging, 473–475
  elements, 211
  event handling in, 240
    Application_OnEnd event, 91–92
    Application_OnStart event, 91–92
    control events, 243–244
    page errors, 244
    page events, 242–243
  HTML codes for, 18
  importing namespaces into, 92
  lifetime, 213–214
  names, 21

ASP.NET pages, *continued*
  page language for, 88–89
  processing stages, 241
  runtime structure, 245–246
  saving, 27
  writing codes in, 228–229
  See also Web Forms
AspCompat attribute, 215, 479
.aspx files, 18, 34
  code locations, 89–90
  creating, 86–90
  page language for, 88–89
assemblies, 5, 359
  deploying, 452–454
  global, 453
  installing, 453
  updating, 453
  versioning of, 453
<assemblies> element, 134
assembly attribute, 135, 223
@ Assembly directive, 224
AssemblyVersionAttribute attribute, 359
AttachDBFilename connection string key, 303
attributes, 403
auditing, 186–187
AuthenticateFailure event, 372
AuthenticateSuccess event, 372
authentication, 191
  Passport, 194–195
  Windows-based, 192–194
<authentication> element, 140–144
Authentication Methods dialog, 193–194
<authentication> tag, 192
authorization, 199
  NTFS ACLs (Access Control Lists), 200
  URL-based, 200–202
<authorization> element, 145–147
auto-complete, 22
autoEventWireup attribute, 136, 216
autogenerated documentation, 39
auto-hide, 38

B

base classes, 354–355
basic authentication, 192
batch attribute, 130
batchTimeout attribute, 131
binding to controls, 333
BizTalk Mapper, 10
BizTalk Orchestrator, 10
BizTalk Server 2000, 10
blank passwords, 178–181
block-level variables, 58
<body> element, 253
Boolean data type, 53
boxing, 55
breakpoints, 474
<browsersCaps> element, 163–165
Browse permissions, 87
browsers, 27
    configuring, 94
brute force attacks, 180
buffer attribute, 136, 216
BufferResponse property, 404
bugs, 468
    categories of, 468–469
    preventing, 469–470
Build Errors, 44
Build menu, 47
building, 27
<button> element, 252
buttons, 45
Byte data type, 53

C

C# programming language, 13, 36
    data types, 53–54
    declaring variables in, 60
    namespaces in, 59
cache APIs, 440–444
Cache class, 440
Cache property, 227

CacheDependency class, 441–442
CacheDuration property, 404
CacheItemPriority enumeration, 440
CacheItemPriorityDecay enumeration, 440
caching, 15, 428
    arbitrary data, 437–439
    cache APIs, 440–444
    expiration, 440–441
    file dependency in, 441–442
    invalidating on data change in, 442–444
    key dependency in, 441–442
    multiple versions of output, 434–436
    output, 226, 428
    scavenging in, 440–441
    and session state, 107
    user controls, 432–434
    using Response.Cache property in, 436–437
    Web Forms pages, 431–432
Calendar control, 284–287
<case> element, 165
Case Else statement, 65–66
certificates, 188–191
CGI (Common Gateway Interface), 87
Char data type, 53
character encoding, 126
child configuration files, 123
child elements, 132
class library, 5–6
Class View window, 41
classes, 5–6
    as code containers, 74
    for custom server controls, 354
    derived, 6, 73
    inheritance in, 73–76
    listing of, 41
    parent, 73
ClassName attribute, 216
<clear> element, 134, 153, 155
Clear method, 99
ClearChildViewState method, 227
client Console applications, 422–424

clientConnectedCheck attribute, 156
clientScriptsLocation attribute, 162
client-side <script>blocks, 212
client-side cookies, 113
<clientTarget> element, 163
ClientTarget attribute, 216
ClientValidation Function property, 290
CLS (Common Language Specification), 5
    support to data types, 54
COBOL programming language, 14
code declaration blocks, 212, 229–230
code-access security, 150, 204
code-behind, 33
    in Web Forms, 247–249
Codebehind attribute, 216
CodePage attribute, 216
codes
    blocks, 477–478
    code-behind modules, 33
    containers for, 74
    location options, 89–90
    modules, 27, 52
    parameters, 62–64
    render blocks, 230
    reusing, 33
    server-side, 212
    writing in Web Forms, 228–229
columns, 318–322
COM components, 92–93
comAuthenticationLevel attribute, 157
comImpersonationLevel attribute, 157
Command mode, 37
Command window, 37
commands, 37
Comment tasks, 44
Commerce Server 2000, 8–9
Common Gateway Interface (CGI), 87
common language runtime
    debugger, 472
    support to data types, 54
    in Web Services, 400

Common Language Specification. See CLS
CompareValidator control, 289, 293
Compilation configuration option, 94
<compilation> element, 129–134
<compiler> element, 133
compilerOptions attribute, 133, 216
compilers, 5
    warning levels, 134
<compilers> element, 132
configuration elements
    <appSettings>, 165
    <authentication>, 140–144
    <authorization>, 145–147
    <browsersCaps>, 163–165
    <clientTarget>, 163
    <compilation>, 129–134
    <customErrors>, 138–140
    <globalization>, 125–126
    <httpHandlers>, 152–153
    <httpModules>, 154–155
    <httpRuntime>, 127–129
    <identity>, 144
    <machineKey>, 147
    <pages>, 135–137
    <processModel>, 155–161
    <securityPolicy>, 148–149
    <sessionState>, 150–151
    <trace>, 124–125
    <trust>, 149–150
    <webControls>, 162
    See also elements
configuration files, 117–119
    child, 123
    editing, 120–121
configuration settings
    locking down, 122–123
    overriding, 122
    storing, 450–451
<configuration> tag, 123
configurations, 15, 93
ConfigurationSettings.AppSettings, 450

Connection Lifetime connection string key, 303
Connection Reset connection string key, 303
connection string keys, 303–304
Connection Timeout connection string key, 303
connectionString attribute, 151
Console applications, 422–424
constants, 61
ContentType attribute, 217
Control class, 228
@ Control directive, 221–222
control events, 243–244
control tree, 245–246
controls, 384–390
    adding to pages
        declaratively, 259–260
        programmatically, 260–262
        with Visual Studio .NET, 263
    applying styles to, 264–265
    manipulating, 246
    templated, 384–390
    types of, 251
        ASP.NET Mobile controls, 295
        HTML controls, 251–258
        Internet Explorer Web controls, 295
        specialty controls, 281–295
        Web controls, 258–260
Controls collection, 227
ControlToCompare property, 289
ControlToValidate property, 288
cookie authentication, 195–199
cookieless attribute, 151
cookieless sessions, 109, 112
cookies
    client-side, 113
    persistent, 113–114
    reliance of session state on, 103
Copy Project command, 455–456
Count property, 99, 104
counter variables, 101
cpuMask attribute, 158
CreateChildControls method, 352, 383

creating
    application root, 82–86
    ASP.NET pages, 23–25
    .ASPX pages, 86–90
    client Console applications, 422–424
    client Web Forms pages, 421
    custom server controls, 352–362
    Global.asax files, 90–93
    subdirectories, 86
    user controls, 231–232
    virtual directories, 19–20
    Web applications, 23
        with .NET Framework SDK, 82–94
        with Notepad, 18–21
        with Visual Studio .NET, 81–82
    Web Forms, 23–25
    Web Services, 400–415
    Web.config files, 93
<credentials> element, 143
credit card numbers, 114
.cs files, 35
CSS (Cascading Style Sheets), 40
culture attribute, 126, 217
Current data, 325
Current Language connection string key, 303
custom accounts, 182
custom server controls, 213
    adding functionalities to, 363
        methods, 365–367
        properties, 363–364
    adding to pages, 239–240, 360
        declaratively, 360–362
        programmatically, 360–362
    classes, 354
    compiling, 356–357
    creating, 352–362
        through composition, 383–390
    events in, 367–369
    extending, 390–393
    inheriting from base class, 354–355
    namespaces, 353

custom server controls, *continued*
    registering, 359
    rendering output from, 355–356
    templated, 384–390
    See also server controls
<customErrors> element, 138–140
CustomValidator control, 290

D

data encryption, 114
data forgery, 169
Data Source connection string key, 303
data types, 53–54, 409
    reference types, 54–55
    sizes of, 53–54
    value types, 54–55
DataAdapters, 317
database accounts, 182
Database connection string key, 303
databases
    connection strings, 101
    creating connections to, 301–305
    reading data with commands in, 308–317
    updating data with commands in, 308–317
DataBind method, 331
DataBinder.Eval method in, 333
data-binding, 331
    binding to controls, 333
    DataBinder.Eval method, 333
    DataBound controls in, 334–349
    simple, 332
DataBinding event, 369
DataBound controls, 294, 334–349
DataGrid control, 295, 334–343
DataList control, 295, 334, 344–347
datareaders, 299, 330–331
DataRows, 322–324
DataSet class, 300–301
datasets, 101, 107, 300–301
    accessing values in, 322–324

datasets, *continued*
    in ADO.NET, 317
    columns, 318–322
    relationships in, 322
    rows, 318–322
    tables, 318–322
    typed, 326–329
    updating, 324–326
    using DataAdapters in, 317
    using DataViews in, 329–330
    XML data, 318
DataSource property, 331
DataTable class, 300, 322–324
DataView class, 329–330
Date data type, 53
DCOM, 157
DDoS (Distributed Denial of Service), 169
debug attribute, 131
Debug menu, 47
debug symbols, 219
Debug toolbar, 46
Debug.Assert messages, 475
debugger, 472
debugging, 37, 46, 468–475
Decimal data type, 53
decryptionKey attribute, 147
Default data, 325
default page, 21
defaultLanguage attribute, 131
defaultRedirect attribute, 138
Deleted row state, 326
delimiters, 39
<deny> tag, 201–202
derived classes, 6, 73
Description attribute, 217
Description property, 404
design patterns, 73
Design view, 44
Designer/Source Editor window, 40
Detached row state, 326
development tools, 17–27

dialog boxes
    Add New Item, 24–25
    New Project, 23
    Options, 48
dictionary attacks, 180
digest authentication, 192
Dim keyword, 59
directives, 211
    @ Assembly, 224
    @ Control, 221–222
    @ Implements, 223
    @ Import, 222
    @ Output Cache, 429–430
    @ OutputCache, 224–226
    @ Page, 215–221
    @ Register, 223–224
directories, 88
    subdirectories, 86
    virtual, 88
disco.exe options, 416
discovery documents, 412, 416
    advertising Web Services through, 412
    disco.exe options, 416
    locating Web Services with, 416
Display property, 288
DisplayMode property, 291
Dispose method, 370
Distributed Denial of Service (DDoS), 169
<div> element, 253
Do... loops, 69
Document Outline window, 44
document relative URLs, 127
Domain Controller, 192
domains, 416
DOS (Denial of Service), 169
Double data type, 53
DropDownList control, 239, 333
Duration attribute, 225, 429
Dynamic Help window, 39

E

Edit menu, 46
EditItemTemplate, 347
Eiffel programming language, 14
elements
    <a>, 252
    <add>, 135, 143, 152, 154, 163
    <allow>, 146
    <appSettings>, 165, 450
    <assemblies>, 134
    <authentication>, 140–144
    <authorization>, 145–147
    <body>, 253
    <browsersCaps>, 163–165
    <button>, 252
    <case>, 165
    <clear>, 134, 153, 155
    <clientTarget>, 163
    <compiler>, 133
    <compilers>, 132
    <customErrors>, 138–140
    <div>, 253
    <error>, 139
    <filter>, 165
    <font>, 253
    <form>, 252
    <forms>, 141
    <httpHandlers>, 152–153
    <httpModules>, 154–155
    <identity>, 144
    <img>, 252
    <input type="button">, 252
    <input type="checkbox">, 252
    <input type="file">, 252
    <input type="hidden">, 253
    <input type="image">, 253
    <input type="password">, 253
    <input type="radio">, 253

elements, *continued*
    <input type="reset">, 252
    <input type="submit">, 252
    <input type="text">, 253
    <machineKey>, 147
    <pages>, 135–137
    <passport>, 144
    <processModel>, 155–161
    <remove>, 135, 155
    <result>, 164
    <securityPolicy>, 148–149
    <select>, 253
    <sessionState>, 150–151
    <span>, 253
    <table>, 253
    <td>, 253
    <textarea>, 253
    <th>, 253
    <tr>, 253
    <trust>, 149–150
    <trustLevel>, 149
    <use>, 164
    <user>, 143
    <webControls>, 162
Else statement, 65
e-mails, sending, 265–275
enable attribute, 158
Enable Logging checkbox, 187
EnableClientScript property, 288
enabled attribute, 124
Enabled property, 289
EnableSession property, 404
enableSessionState attribute, 137, 217
enableViewState attribute, 137, 217
enableViewStateMac attribute, 138, 217
encapsulation, 74
encryption, 114, 143
Enlist connection string key, 303
enterprise servers, 7
envelopes, 400
<error> element, 139

error handling, 70–71
    structured, 72–73
    unstructured, 71–72
ErrorMessage property, 289
ErrorPage attribute, 218
errors, 70–72
    logic, 70, 469
    runtime, 70
    semantic, 468
    syntax, 70, 468
event handlers, 91–92, 212
    in ASP.NET pages, 240
    in Web Forms, 240
EventName event, 368
events, 367
    creating, 368
    handling, 368
    inherited, 369
    overriding, 369
exception handling, 71
exceptions, 72
Exchange 2000 Server, 8
Execute permissions, 87
ExecuteReader method, 330
executionTimeout attribute, 128
Exit Sub statement, 72
explicit attribute, 131, 218
<%#expression%> syntax, 332
expressions, 52–53
extension attribute, 133

F

FAT file system, 170
febug attribute, 217
file dependency, 441–442
file extensions, 34–35
File menu, 46
file system directories, 20
file systems, 170
File Transfer Protocol (FTP), 184
fileEncoding attribute, 126

<filter> element, 165
FindControl method, 227
firewalls, 34
flow control, 64
    error handling, 70–71
    If statements, 65
    looping statements, 67
    Select Case statement, 65–66
folders
    InetPub, 20
    WWWRoot, 20
<font> element, 253
FontInfo class, 265
FooterTemplate, 347
For Each... loops, 68
For... loops, 67–68
ForeColor property, 289
<form> element, 252
Formatting toolbar, 46
<forms> element, 141
Forms-based authentication, 195–199
Friend keyword, 59
FTP (File Transfer Protocol), 184
fully qualified URLs, 127
Function procedures, 64

G

GAC (Global Application Cache), 359
gacutil.exe, 453
Get method, 99
GET request, 225
GetKey method, 99
Global Application Cache (GAC), 359
global assemblies, 453
Global.asax files, 35
    creating, 90–93
    creating components in, 92–93
    creating object instances with, 100
    event handlers in, 91–92
    importing namespaces in, 92
<globalization> element, 125–126

H

hard drives, 102
Haskell programming language, 14
HeaderTemplate, 347
HeaderText property, 291
HelloWorld Web Service
    creating, 404–408
    primitive data types in, 409
Help menu, 47
hisecweb.inf template, 177, 180
Host Integration Server 2000, 9
HTML (Hypertext Markup Language), 33
    controls, 251–258
    editor, 38
    elements, 251–255
HTML comments, 211
HTML controls, 237, 251–258
    examples, 255–258
    See also server controls
    See also Web controls
HTML editor, 38
<html> element, 39
HTML elements, 252
    <a>, 252
    <body>, 253
    <button>, 252
    <div>, 253
    <font>, 253
    <form>, 252
    <imag>, 252
    <input type="button">, 252
    <input type="checkbox">, 252
    <input type="file">, 252
    <input type="hidden">, 253
    <input type="image">, 253
    <input type="password">, 253
    <input type="radio">, 253
    <input type="reset">, 252
    <input type="submit">, 252
    <input type="text">, 253

HTML elements, *continued*
    <select>, 253
    <span>, 253
    <table>, 253
    <td>, 253
    <textarea>, 253
    <th>, 253
    <tr>, 253
    See also elements
HtmlAnchor control, 252
HtmlButton control, 252
HtmlControl class, 254
HtmlForm control, 252
HtmlGenericControl control, 253
HtmlImage control, 252
HtmlInputButton control, 237, 252
HtmlInputCheckBox control, 252
HtmlInputFile control, 252
HtmlInputHidden control, 253
HtmlInputImage control, 253
HtmlInputRadioButton control, 253
HtmlInputText control, 253
HtmlSelect control, 253
HtmlTable control, 253
HtmlTableCell control, 253
HtmlTableRow control, 253
HtmlTextArea control, 253
HTTP (Hypertext Transfer Protocol), 34–184
    and application state, 97
    default port for, 184
    headers, 225
    verb types, 202
HttpApplicationState class, 98
HTTPBrowserCapabilities class, 94
<httpHandlers> element, 152–153
HttpHandlers configuration option, 94
<httpModules> element, 154–155
HttpModules configuration option, 94
<httpRuntime> element, 127–129
HttpServerUtility class, 227
HttpSessionState class, 104

I

IDE (Integrated Development Environment), 17–18
    multilanguage, 37
<identity> element, 144
<identity> tag, 203
idleTimeout attribute, 158
If statements, 65
IIS (Internet Information Services), 17
    authentication methods, 193–194
    creating virtual directories in, 19–20
IL (Intermediate Language), 5
<img> element, 252
Immediate mode, 37
impersonate attribute, 145
impersonation, 145, 203
@ Implements directive, 223
@ Import directive, 222, 360
INamingContainer interface, 384
include files, 236
InetPub folder, 20
inheritance, 6, 73
    across languages, 76
    in .NET Framework, 76–77
    using, 74–76
inherited events, 369
Inherits attribute, 218, 452
Init event, 369
Initial Catalog connection string key, 303
Initialize method, 370
InitialValue property, 290
in-process session state, 109
<input type="button"> element, 252
<input type="checkbox"> element, 252
<input type="file"> element, 252
<input type="hidden"> element, 253
<input type="image"> element, 253
<input type="password"> element, 253
<input type="radio"> element, 253
<input type="reset"> element, 252

<input type="submit"> element, 252
<input type="text"> element, 253
instances, 100
    references to, 101, 107
Integer data type, 54, 56
Integrated Security connection string key, 304
Integrated Windows (NTLM) authentication, 192
IntelliSense tasks, 44, 46
interfaces, 223
Intermediate Language (IL), 5
Internet, 167
Internet Explorer Web controls, 295
Internet Protocol (IP), 21
Internet Security and Acceleration Server 2000, 10
IO threads, 159
IP (Internet Protocol), 21
IPostBackDataHandler interface, 372
IPostBackEventHandler interface, 372
IsPostBack property, 227
IsValid property, 289
ItemTemplate, 345–347

J

JScript, 35
JScript .NET, 13

K

key attribute, 166
key dependency, 441–442
Keys property, 104

L

language attribute, 133, 218
language tools, 11–14
languages, 11–14, 35–36
LCID attribute, 218
level attribute, 150

lifetime, 56–57, 213–214
LiteralControl server control class, 245
Load event, 369
Load method, 370
LoadPostData method, 370
LoadViewState method, 370
local hosts, 21
local level variables, 58
localOnly attribute, 124
Location attribute, 225, 429
<location> tag, 122–123, 204
Lock method, 100
logging, 186–187
logic errors, 70, 469
login control, 372–380
loginUrl attribute, 141
logLevel attribute, 159
Long data type, 54
loopback address, 21
looping statements, 67
    Do... loops, 69
    For Each... loops, 68
    For... loops, 67–68
    While... End While loops, 70

M

MAC (Machine Authentication Check), 138
machine name, 21
Machine.config file, 117–118
    See also Web.config files
<machineKey> element, 147
mailing lists, 51
managed codes, 5
manifests, 5
master configuration file, 117, 121
match attribute, 165
Max Pool Size connection string key, 304
MaximumValue property, 290
maxIoThreads attribute, 159
maxRequestLength attribute, 128
maxWorkerThreads attribute, 159

MD5 hash algorithm, 148
Me.UniqueID property, 373
memory, 102
memoryLimit attribute, 159
menus, 46
MessageName property, 404
metadata, 5
Metadata attributes, 402–403
methods, 73
Microsoft .NET, 3–4
    language and language tools, 11–14
    .NET Enterprise Servers, 7–11
    .NET Framework, 4–6
Microsoft Developer Network (MSDN), 51
Microsoft Intermediate Language (MSIL), 5
Microsoft Management Console (MMC),
    173–175
Microsoft Passport, 414
Microsoft Product Security Notification service,
    186
Microsoft Technet, 170
Microsoft Transaction Server (MTS), 172
Min Pool Size connection string key, 304
minFreeThreads attribute, 128
MinimumValue property, 290
minLocalRequestFreeThreads attribute, 129
ML programming language, 14
MMC (Microsoft Management Console),
    173–175
mode attribute, 139, 141, 151
Modified row state, 326
module-level variables, 58
modules, 52
    compiling, 27
MSDE, 178–181, 315
MSDN (Microsoft Developer Network), 51
MSIL (Microsoft Intermediate Language), 5
MTA (multi-threaded apartment, 479
MTS (Microsoft Transaction Server), 172
multilanguage IDE (Integrated Development En-
    vironment), 37
multi-threaded apartment (MTA), 479

N

name attribute, 141, 149, 154, 224
Namespace attribute, 223
namespace-level variables, 58
namespaces, 6, 59
    containers for, 74
    for custom server cotrols, 353
    importing, 222
        in Global.asax files, 92
    name, 359
    in XML, 238
Net connection string key, 304
.NET Data Provider, 298
.NET Enterprise Servers, 7
    Application Center 2000, 10–11
    BizTalk Server 2000, 10
    Commerce Server 2000, 8–9
    Exchange Server 2000, 8
    Host Integration Server 2000, 9
    Internet Security and Acceleration Server
        2000, 10
    SQL Server 2000, 7–8
    See also servers
.NET Framework, 4
    class library, 5–6
    common language runtime), 4–5
    inheritance in, 76–77
    working with mulitple languages in, 36
.NET Framework SDK (Software Development
    Kit)
    creating Web applications with, 82–94
    data types, 53–54
    installing, 18
.NET managed assemblies, 5
Network Address connection string key, 303
Network Library connection string key, 304
Network Security Hotfix Checker, 186
New Project dialog box, 23
newsgroups, 51
Notepad, 11
    creating ASP.NET applications in, 18–21

O

Oberon programming language, 14
Object data type, 54
<object> tag, 93
object-oriented programming, 73–74
objects, 73
   encapsulating, 74
   instances, 100
OLE DB .NET Data Provider, 298
OleDbAdapter class, 299, 317
OleDbCommand class, 299, 313–314
OleDbConnection class, 299, 305
OleDbDataReader class, 299, 330
On Error statement, 71–72
OnEnd event handler, 91–92
OnStart event handler, 91–92
operating systems, 170–171
Operator property, 289
Option Explicit statement, 60, 71
Option Strict statement, 60, 71
Options dialog box, 48
Original data, 325
originUrl attribute, 150
out-of-process session state, 109–110
output caching, 226, 428
Output window, 44
@ OutputCache directive, 224–226, 429–430

P

Packet Size connection string key, 304
Page class, 6, 227–228
@ Page directive, 215–221
   AspCompat attribute, 479
   Trace attribute, 462–463
page errors, 244
page events, 242–243
page name, 21
Page_Error event handler, 244
pageBaseType attribute, 136
pageOutput attribute, 125

<pages> element, 135–137
parameters, 62–64
parent class, 73
Pascal casing, 300
Pascal programming language, 14
Passport authentication, 194–195
<passport> element, 144
password attribute, 144–145, 161
Password connection string key, 304
passwordFormat attribute, 143
passwords, 416
   blank, 178–181
   storing, 181–182
   weak, 178–181
patching, 185
path attribute, 123, 142, 153
Perl programming language, 14
permissions, 454–455
Persist Security Info connection string key, 304
persistent cookies, 113–114
physical memory, 102
pingFrequency attribute, 159
pingTimeout attribute, 160
PlaceHolder control, 262
policyFile attribute, 149
polymorphism, 73
Pooling connection string key, 304
ports, 184–185
POST request, 225
postbacks, 213, 239, 371–372
PreRender event, 369
PreRender method, 370
private assemblies, 359
Private keyword, 60
procedure-level variables, 58
procedures, 61
   Function procedures, 64
   Sub procedures, 62–64
<processModel> element, 155–161
programming languages, 11–14, 35–36
Project menu, 47

properties, 73
Properties window, 42
Proposed data, 325
Protected keyword, 60
protection attribute, 142
proxies, 416
proxy classes, 418–421
Public keyword, 59
PWS (Personal Web Services), 170
Python programming language, 14

Q

Query menu, 47
querystring keys, 225

R

RaisePostBackEvent method, 368, 370
RaisePostDataChangedEvent method, 370
RangeValidator control, 290
RCW (Runtime Callable Wrapper), 357
Read permissions, 87
ReadXml method, 318
redirect attribute, 139
redirectUrl attribute, 144
reference types, 54–55
Regional Options setting, 126
@ Register directive, 223–224, 239–240, 360
registration wizards, 275–281
RegularExpressionValidator control, 290, 293–294
relative URLs, 127
<remove> element, 135, 155
RemoveAll method, 99
RemoveAt method, 105
<% %> render blocks, 212, 230
Render method, 352, 370
RenderChildren method,, 352
Repeater control, 295, 334, 347–349
requestEncoding attribute, 126
requestLimit attribute, 125, 160

requestQueueLimit attribute, 160
RequiredFieldValidator control, 290–293
Response.Cache property, 436–437
Response.Write statements, 464–465
responseDeadlockInterval attribute, 160
responseEncoding attribute, 126, 218
responseRestartDeadlockInterval attribute, 160
restartQueueLimit attribute, 161
<result> element, 164
roles, 201–202
roles attribute, 146–147
root configuration file, 117
root relative URLs, 127
rows, 318–322
    multiple versions of data in, 325
Run Scripts permissions, 87
runtime, 245–246
runtime (common language runtime), 4–5
Runtime Callable Wrapper (RCW), 357
runtime errors, 70

S

sample applications, 182–183
SaveViewState method, 370
saving
    ASP.NET pages, 27
    Web Forms, 27
scalability, 107–108
scavenging, 440–441
schemas, 38
Scheme programming language, 14
scope, 58
<script> code declaration blocks, 212, 229–230
scripts, 87
security, 16
    access control, 186
    auditing, 186–187
    code-access, 150, 204
    importance of, 168
    logging, 186–187
    online resources, 170, 204

security, *continued*
    passwords, 178–182
    patching, 185
    and sample applications, 182–183
    server set-up and application design, 170–185
    SSL (Secure Socket Layer) protocol, 188–191
    threats, 169
    validation, 183
Security Configuration and Analysis tool, 176–178
Security configuration option, 94
Security Templates tool, 174–176
<securityPolicy> element, 148–149
<securityPolicy> tag, 204
Select Case statement, 65–66
<select> element, 253
SelectedItemTemplate, 347
semantic errors, 468
SeparatorTemplate, 347
Server connection string key, 303
server control state, 114
server controls, 15
    adding, 25–26
    adding functionalities to, 363
        methods, 365–367
        properties, 363–364
    adding to pages, 239–240, 360
        declaratively, 259–260, 360–362
        programmatically, 260–262, 360–362
        with Visual Studio .NET, 263
    applying styles to, 264–265
    classes, 354
    compiling, 356–357
    creating, 352–362
    custom, 239–240
    events in, 367–369
    extending, 390–393
    namespaces, 353
    registering, 359
    rendering output from, 355–356
    types of, 251
        ASP.NET Mobile controls, 295

server controls, *continued*
        HTML controls, 251–258
        Internet Explorer Web controls, 295
        specialty controls, 281–295
        Web controls, 258–260
    using, 236–237
Server Explorer window, 41
ServerChange event, 254
ServerClick event, 254
serverErrorMessageFile attribute, 161
servers, 34
    access control, 186
    accounts in, 182
    auditing, 186–187
    certificates, 188–191
    logging, 186–187
    online resources, 170
    operating systems, 170–171
    passwords, 178–182
    ports, 184–185
    purpose of, 171
    sample applications in, 182–183
    security threats to, 169
    services, 172–173
    setting up, 170–185
    validation in, 183
    variables, 164
    See also Web servers
server-side codes, 212
server-side comments, 212
ServerValidate property, 290
session state, 102–104
    enabling, 105–106
    limitations of, 107
    recommendations for, 106–107
    settings, 94
    storing, 108
        in-process, 109
        out-of-process, 109–110
        in SQL Server, 111
        using cookieless sessions, 112
Session_OnEnd event, 91

Session_OnStart event, 91
SessionID property, 104
<sessionState> element, 150–151
Set method, 99
SetCacheability method, 437
SetExpires method, 437
SetNoServerCaching method, 437
SGML (Structured Generalized Markup Language), 119
SHA1 hash algorithm, 148
shared application flags, 101
shared assemblies, 359
shopping carts, 103
Short data type, 54
ShowMessageBox property, 291
ShowSummary property, 291
shutdownTimeout attribute, 161
Single data type, 54
single-threaded apartment (STA), 479
single-user applications, 167
Site Server 3.0 Commerce Edition, 8
<sitename> Properties dialog box, 187
Smalltalk programming language, 14
SMTP (Simple Mail Transport Protocol), 184, 265
SOAP (Simple Object Access Protocol), 34
    envelopes, 400
    and Web Services, 399
Solution Explorer window, 40
Source Code Control status, 40
source codes, 22, 33
source files, 473
<span> element, 253
specialty controls
    Adrotator, 282–284
    Calendar, 284–287
    data-bound, 294
    Validation, 288–294
    Xml, 288

SQL Server
    Enterprise Manager utility, 180
    password security in, 178–181
    storing session state in, 111
SQL Server .NET Data Provider, 298, 300
    classes, 298–299
SQL Server 2000, 7–8
SqlCommand class, 299, 308–312
SqlConnection class, 299, 303–304
    creating connections to databases with, 301–302
sqlConnectionString attribute, 151
SqlDataAdapter class, 299, 317
SqlDataReader class, 299, 330–331
Src attribute, 218, 223–224
SSL (Secure Socket Layer), 188–191
STA (single-threaded apartment), 479
stack trace, 470
Standard toolbar, 45
state management, 16
    application state, 98–102
    and scalability, 107–108
    session state, 102–107
StateBag class, 381
static HTML tags, 211
statusCode attribute, 140
stored procedures, 314–317
strict attribute, 132, 219
String data type, 54
strings, 165
    filtering of, 164
    mapping of, 164
structured exception handling, 72–73
Structured Generalized Markup Language (SGML), 119
Sub procedures, 62–64
subdirectories, 86
    configuration settings, 122
subfolders, 86

syntax coloring, 22
syntax errors, 70, 468
System.Globalization.CultureInfo class, 126
<system.web> tag, 123
System.Web.UI namespace, 352

T

Tabbed Documents, 38
<table> element, 253
Table menu, 47
tables, 318–322
TagName attribute, 223, 239
TagPrefix attribute, 223, 239
Task List window, 44
TCP/IP (Transmission Control Protocol/Internet Protocol), 184
<td> element, 253
Technet, 170
tempDirectory attribute, 132
templated controls, 384–390
Text Editor toolbar, 46
text editors, 21–22
<textarea> element, 253
TextBox control, 239
<th> element, 253
third-party languages, 14
threads, 128
timeout attribute, 142, 151, 161
Timeout property, 104
toolbars, 45
    Debugging, 46
    Formatting, 46
    Standard, 45
    Text Editor, 46
Toolbox, 43
Tools menu, 47
ToString method, 99, 105
<tr> element, 253
Trace attribute, 219, 462–463
Trace configuration option, 94

<trace> element, 124–125
Trace.Warn method, 467
Trace.Write method, 466
TraceContext class, 465
traceMode attribute, 125, 219
tracing, 94
    enabling, 220, 465–468
    Response.Write statements in, 464–465
    trace output
        application-level, 463–465
        page-level, 462–463
        sections of, 467
        writing to, 464–467
Transaction attribute, 219
TransactionOption property, 404
Triple-DES (3DES) encryption, 148
Trojan virus, 169
<trust> element, 149–150
<trust> tag, 204
Trusted Connection connection string key, 304
trusted connections, 306
<trustLevel> element, 149
Try... Catch... Finally exception handling, 72–73
type attribute, 134, 153, 155, 164
typed datasets, 326–329

U

UDDI (Universal Description, Discovery, and Integration), 413
    locating Web Services with, 417
uiCulture attribute, 126
unboxing, 55
Unchanged row state, 326
UNIX workstations, 34
UnLoad event, 369
Unlock method, 100
unstructured error handling, 71–72
URL-based authorization), 200–202
URLs (Uniform Resource Locators)
    formatting, 112

URLs (Uniform Resource Locators), *continued*
    fully qualifed, 127
    vs. physical path, 448–450
    relative, 127
<use> element, 164
useFullyQualifiedRedirectUrl attribute, 129
user controls, 212, 231
    adding to pages
        declaratively, 232–234
        programmatically, 234–236
    caching, 432–434
    creating, 231–232
    vs. include files, 236
    loading, 226
    registering, 223
<user> element, 143
User ID connection string key, 304
User property, 227
User tasks, 44
userAgent attribute, 163
userControlBaseType attribute, 137
User-Defined data type, 54
userName attribute, 145, 162
usernames, 417
users
    authenticating, 191
    authorizing, 201–202
users attribute, 146
user-specific settings, 106

V

Validate property, 289
validation, 183
validation attribute, 148
Validation controls, 288
    CompareValidator, 293–294
    RequiredFieldValidator, 291–293
    shared members, 288
    types of, 289–291
    validating with

Validation controls, *continued*
        by comparison, 293–294
        required fields, 291–293
    See also controls
ValidationExpression property, 290
validationKey attribute, 148
ValidationSummary control, 291
value attribute, 166
value types, 54–55
ValueToCompare property, 289
var attribute, 164
variables, 53
    accessibility, 59
    data types, 53–54
    declaring, 56
    lifetime of, 56–57
    local, 58
    naming, 56–57
    scope, 58
        block-level, 58
        module-level, 58
        namespace-level, 58
        procedure-level, 58
    visibility of, 58
VaryByControl attribute, 226, 429
VaryByCustom attribute, 225, 430
VaryByHeader attribute, 225, 430
VaryByParam attribute, 225, 430, 434–436
.vb files, 34
VBScript, 35
verbs attribute, 146–147, 153
View menu, 46
ViewState method, 137, 380–382
ViewState property, 227
virtual directories, 88
    access permissions for, 20
    creating, 19–20
    default page for, 21
    names of, 21
virtual memory, 102
visibility, 58

Visual Basic .NET, 12–13, 35–36
  namespaces in, 59
  procedures, 61
    Function procedures, 64
    Sub procedures, 62–64
Visual C++, 13
Visual Studio .NET, 12
  adding server controls to pages with, 263
  advantages of, 22
  creating Web applications with, 23, 81–82
  customization in, 48
  deploying Web applications with, 455–458
  enabling session state in, 106
  HTML editor in, 38
  IDE (Integrated Development Environment)
    enhancements to, 37–38
    menus, 46–47
    new features, 38–39
    options, 48
    toolbars, 45–46
    windows, 39–45
  Toolbox, 43

W

warningLevel attribute, 134, 219
weak passwords, 178–181
Web applications, 32–33
  adding new pages to, 23–25
  application root, 82–86, 446–447
  configuration settings, 121, 450–451
  creating, 23
    with .NET Framework SDK, 82–94
    with Notepad, 18–21
    with Visual Studio .NET, 81–82
  debugging, 468–475
  deploying manually, 451–455
    copying files to target directory, 451
    deploying assemblies, 452–454
    deploying content, 452

Web applications, *continued*
    setting IIS permissions for subdirectories,
      454–455
  deploying with Visual Studio .NET, 455–458
    using Copy Project command, 455–456
    using Web Setup Project, 456–458
  physical path, 448–450
  tracing, 462–468
  URLs (Uniform Resource Locators), 448–450
  See also ASP.NET pages
  See also Web Forms
  See also Web Services
Web controls, 237–238
  examples, 265
    registration wizards, 275–281
    sending mail, 265–275
  types of, 258–260
  See also HTML controls
  See also server controls
Web farms, 102–103
Web Forms, 15, 32–33
  adding controls to, 25–26
    custom server controls, 239–240, 360–362
    HTML controls, 237
    user controls, 232–236
    Web controls, 237–238
  browsing, 27
  caching, 431–432
  client, 421
  code-behind in, 247–249
  compiling in debug mode, 470–471
  creating, 23–25
  debugging, 473–475
  elements, 211
  event handling in, 240
    control events, 243–244
    page errors, 244
    page events, 242–243
  example of, 209–211
  lifetime, 213–214

Web Forms, *continued*
processing stages, 241
runtime structure, 245–246
saving, 27
writing codes in, 228–229
See also ASP.NET pages
See also Web applications
Web gardening, 161
Web Server Certificate Wizard, 188–189
Web servers
access control, 186
accounts in, 182
auditing, 186–187
certificates, 188–191
online resources, 170
operating systems, 170–171
passwords, 178–182
ports, 184–185
purpose of, 171
sample applications in, 182–183
security threats to, 169
services, 172–173
setting up, 170–185
validation in, 183
See also servers
Web Services, 15, 33–34
accessing data in, 409–411
additional needs for, 400
advertising, 411
through discovery documents, 412
through UDDI (Universal Description, Discovery, and Integration), 413
creating, 400–415
declaring, 400
examples, 404–408
locating, 415
with discovery documents, 416
with UDDI (Universal Description, Discovery, and Integration), 417
overview, 398–399

Web Services, *continued*
primitive data types in, 409
securing, 413–415
and SOAP (Simple Object Access Protocol), 399
using, 415
Web Forms client for, 421
See also Web applications
Web Setup Project, 456–458
Web sites
default home directory, 88
security threats to, 169
virtual directories of, 20
Web.config files, 35
basic structure of, 119
creating, 93
<trace section>, 463–465
See also Machine.config file
<webControls> element, 162
webGarden attribute, 161
<WebService()> attribute
exposing methods with, 403
properties, 404
specifying XML namespaces with, 402
WebService class, 401
inheriting from, 402
While... End While loops, 70
Window menu, 47
windows, 39
Class View, 41
Designer/Source, 40
Document Outline, 44
Output, 44
Properties, 42
Server Explorer, 41
Solution Explorer, 40
Task List, 44
Windows .NET Server, 6
Windows 2000, 170
Windows Event Log, 186

Windows Explorer, 453
Windows installer, 39, 453
Windows NT, 170
Windows operating systems, 4
Windows servers, 34
Windows Update site, 185
Windows-based authentication, 192–194
worker threads, 159
Workstation ID connection string key, 304
workstations, 170
Write permissions, 87
WriteXml method, 318
WSDL (Web Service Description Language), 412, 418
wsdl.exe utility, 419–420
WWWRoot folder, 20

X

XCOPY command, 452
XML (Extensible Markup Language), 38–40
   in ADO.NET, 301
   and Machine.config file, 117
   namespaces, 402

XML, *continued*
   and Web.config files, 119
Xml control, 288
XML data, 318
XML editor, 38
.xml files, 38
XML Web Services, 33–34
   accessing data in, 409–411
   advertising, 411
      through discovery documents, 412
      through UDDI (Universal Description, Discovery, and Integration), 413
   locating, 415
      with discovery documents, 416
      with UDDI (Universal Description, Discovery, and Integration), 417
   overview, 398–399
   securing, 413–415
   using, 415
xp_cmdshell, 178
.xsd files, 38
XSL Transform document, 288

About the Author

G. Andrew Duthie is the founder and Principal of Graymad Enterprises, Inc., providing training and consulting in Microsoft Web development technologies. Andrew has been developing multitier Web applications since the introduction of Active Server Pages. He wrote about developing scalable n-tier applications in *Microsoft Visual InterDev 6.0 Developer's Workshop*, also from Microsoft Press.

Andrew is a frequent speaker at events, including Software Development, the Dev-Connections family of conferences, Microsoft DeveloperDays, and most recently, VSLive!

In addition to his writing, consulting, training, and speaking, Andrew enjoys playing music, smoking fine cigars, and most recently, playing Dead or Alive 3 tag-team matches with his wife, Jennifer, on their new XBOX.

You can reach Andrew by e-mail at *andrew@graymad.com*.

Hammer

Most of the hand tools used today have changed little since the Middle Ages, the only major improvement being the use of steel instead of iron for cutting edges. The most common hand tools include saws, planes, and chisels, and such miscellaneous tools as hammers and screwdrivers, which are used in conjunction with fasteners. A hammer is a hand tool consisting of a shaft with a metal head at right angles to it, used mainly for driving in nails and beating metal.

At Microsoft Press, we use tools to illustrate our books for software developers and IT professionals. Tools are an elegant symbol of human inventiveness, and a powerful metaphor for how people can extend their capabilities, precision, and reach. From basic calipers and pliers to digital micrometers and lasers, our stylized illustrations of tools give each book a visual identity and each book series a personality. With tools and knowledge, there are no limits to creativity and innovation. Our tag line says it all: The tools you need to put technology to work.

* *Microsoft Encarta® Reference Library 2002.* © 1993–2001 Microsoft Corporation. All rights reserved.

The manuscript for this book was prepared, galleyed, and composed using Adobe FrameMaker 6. Pages were composed by *TIPS* Technical Publishing, Inc., with text in Sabon and display type in Syntax. Composed pages were delivered to the printer as electronic prepress files.

Cover Designer:	Patricia Bradbury
Interior Graphic Designer:	James D. Kramer
Principal Compositor:	Lorraine B. Elder
Copy Editor:	Sean Medlock
Principal Proofreader:	Juanita Covert
Indexer:	Ariel Tupelano

Get a **Free**
e-mail newsletter, updates,
special offers, links to related books,
and more when you
register on line!

Register your Microsoft Press® title on our Web site and you'll get
a FREE subscription to our e-mail newsletter, *Microsoft Press
Book Connections.* You'll find out about newly released and upcoming
books and learning tools, online events, software downloads, special
offers and coupons for Microsoft Press customers, and information
about major Microsoft® product releases. You can also read useful
additional information about all the titles we publish, such as detailed book descriptions, tables of contents and indexes, sample
chapters, links to related books and book series, author biographies,
and reviews by other customers.

Registration is easy. Just visit this Web page and fill in your information:

http://www.microsoft.com/mspress/register

Microsoft®

- -